BERNIE

BERNIE

THE BIOGRAPHY OF BERNIE ECCLESTONE

SUSAN WATKINS
FOREWORD BY SIR FRANK WILLIAMS

Haynes Publishing

First published in hardback in December 2010
First published in paperback in November 2011

A catalogue record for this book is available from the British Library

ISBN 978 0 85733 131 1

Library of Congress catalog card no 2011927862

Published by Haynes Publishing,
Sparkford, Yeovil, Somerset BA22 7JJ, UK
Tel: 01963 442030 Fax: 01963 440001
Int.tel: +44 1963 442030 Int.fax: +44 1963 440001
E-mail: sales@haynes.co.uk
Website: www.haynes.co.uk

Haynes North America Inc.,
861 Lawrence Drive, Newbury Park, California 91320, USA

Printed and bound in the USA by Odcombe Press LP,
1299 Bridgestone Parkway, LaVergne, TN 37086

Cover photograph credits: sutton-images.com (front),
Getty Images (rear)

CONTENTS

Dedication

To those who can't sit still.

FOREWORD

BY SIR FRANK WILLIAMS

When you have known someone for more than forty years it is not always easy to accurately remember every tiny detail of the relationship. My memories of the early years of my friendship with Bernie are a collection of images, the order of which is now a little jumbled. These glimpses of the past illustrate much about the man. I met him first in an Italian restaurant in Knightsbridge. It was 1969 and I was with my driver Piers Courage and his wife Sally. Bernie came with Jochen Rindt – whom he was managing – and Jochen's wife Nina. We were young and ambitious. A year later both Piers and Jochen were dead. I have a haunting memory of Bernie at Monza in 1970, running to the Parabolica curve after Jochen went missing and we heard there had been an accident. He adored Jochen and was devastated by the loss of his friend.

Bernie was always a racer through and through and I remember realising just how passionate he was about the sport when we met up a few months later in Colombia, in a series of pretty obscure Formula 2 races that were held at the time. You had to be keen to travel all the way to South America in those days. I learned that he was an intensely practical man when we were flying home in a Douglas DC-8 from Miami to London. I marvelled at the fact that without any fuss he got down on the floor between the seats, with a blanket and a pillow, and went to sleep. He never moved for eight hours.

Fairly soon after that he acquired the Brabham Formula 1 team from Ron Tauranac, and he began to take the first steps in building a World Championship-winning team. This was a great success for him; in the period from 1972 to 1988 he won twenty-two Grands Prix and two Drivers' World Championships, in 1981 and 1983, both with Nelson Piquet, so beginning the process of developing the financial potential that he had seen in the sport. At the time there was no cohesion between the teams. The race promoters would take advantage of us and give all the money to the big teams, such as Lotus and Ferrari. The small guys fought for the scraps. Bernie got us all to work together and he stopped that. Everyone was given a fair share of the money, which made it easier for us all to keep our businesses going.

Yet we were always competing, and on many different levels. Bernie was always up for a challenge. I remember one year in Argentina he and I found ourselves with our cars side by side a long way back on the grid. It was not a great place to be but, as everyone was getting ready for the start, he said: 'I'll give you a fiver if you can beat me to the front of the grid', and we both set off. He ran up one side of the grid and I ran up the other. I do not remember who won, but it was a perfect example of Bernie the competitor.

Much has been said of Bernie the businessman. There are many self-made men around these days, but he was one of the originals. He is still going strong and over the years he has made a fortune. He helped many others, including myself, to be far better off than we might ever have imagined we could be. We have not always agreed on everything about Formula 1, but I am very aware that he has always done what he believes is best for the sport. He thinks a great deal before he acts and has always been very determined when he believes that he is right. I have often been in awe of his foresight and astuteness. He has turned Formula 1 into a global sport that rivals the Olympic Games and the World Cup, which is extraordinary given where we started out. He has a rather tough image, but he is a great deal more fun than people imagine. He gets a twinkle in his eye and you know that something is going to happen.

There is another side to him that very few people ever see.

When I had my road accident in 1986, Nelson Piquet rang Bernie from the scene and he immediately sent a chartered jet out to Marseille, with Professor Sid Watkins on board. The same day he chartered a second plane for my wife and Patrick Head. He has never let me pay him back for either. After that he would come to visit me in hospital in London every Sunday evening when I was recovering. He would sit with me for half an hour and chat, even if he had just flown home from a Grand Prix. That is another side of Bernie. He is a man with a big heart, a loyal friend, and a doting father.

I am proud to have known him all these years and it is both an honour and a pleasure to be asked to introduce the story of his extraordinary life.

Frank Williams

INTRODUCTION

In 1976, six weeks after sustaining major facial burns – and with the edges of his skin graft still bleeding – Niki Lauda donned a helmet to race in the Italian Grand Prix at Monza. Niki's accident had occurred during the German Grand Prix at the Nürburgring, in a place he later called 'barbecue corner'. James Hunt, the media's golden idol, took the chequered flag in Germany, the ninth race of the season, and thereafter the underdog started to gnaw at Niki's heels. When Niki Lauda entered the race at Monza, he was fighting to retain his title; and he needed to overcome the fear that had begun to torment him. On the day, Niki came fourth while James ended up in a sand trap. Next, at Mosport Park near Toronto, James Hunt drove his McLaren to a clear victory; he was stoked up with rage, having been told that a win earlier in the season at Brands Hatch had been disqualified over a debatable infringement of the rules, which meant that Niki's finish in the British race was elevated from second to first. But in Canada Niki only managed a meagre eighth due to a problem with his Ferrari's rear suspension. At Watkins Glen, in New York State, they crossed the finish line with James in first place and Niki in third. Going into the final race of the 1976 Grand Prix season, at Mount Fuji circuit in Japan, Niki and James were only one point apart in their duel to secure the World Championship.

On race day in Japan the circuit was besieged with torrential rain, meaning the showdown would be ankle-deep in water. The start was delayed because many drivers refused to race in such appalling conditions. But eventually, after much taunting from the crowd, the drivers came out to take their places on the starting grid. James Hunt made a superb start, splashing to the front of the pack, with a great geyser of spray fanning skyward from the back of his car as he drove/sailed onward, blurring the vision of those trailing behind. After two laps Niki decided that it was too dangerous to continue; he drove into the pit lane and retired. It was a decision as courageous as any ever taken in Grand Prix racing, for it yielded to James the World Championship. In his book *To Hell and Back*, Niki later wrote of the conditions on that day at Japan's circuit of 'streams', he had felt 'as helpless as a paper boat'. When he stepped from the cockpit and removed his helmet, the damaged tissue from the burns to his face had prevented him from blinking his eyes against the pouring rain.

By the end of the race James was so confused he was unaware that he had become the new Formula 1 World Champion until, back in the pits, a McLaren mechanic pulled the number 11 from the side of James's car, ripped it in two and paraded a jagged number 1 before him.

These events inspired Bernie Ecclestone to launch two major initiatives. First, he realised that the drama just enacted could lead to the development of a visually cohesive entertainment and, with it, a worldwide television audience. Second, as a result of Niki Lauda's accident coupled with a string of deaths, he began a crusade for safety. During the Grand Prix at Silverstone in 2004 – watched by 400 million television viewers – Jarno Trulli stepped out of his car, unaided, after a barrel-rolling accident without impact in which the g-forces in the car were recorded at 40g overall. That same year, at Indianapolis, Ralf Schumacher had a puncture at 200mph and slammed backwards into a wall, with the car sustaining 109g; he suffered only mild concussion and minor damage to two spinal vertebrae. In Montreal the previous week, Felipe Massa had a frontal accident at close to 100mph with a peak of 116g; he walked away with a painful elbow. In 2009 Felipe would owe his life to his new Formula 1 helmet. Struck by a spring detached from Barrichello's car, travelling at 200mph, Massa suffered a compound depressed fracture of the skull – but a year later returned to the grid in fighting form. A spectacular accident resulting in a less serious injury occurred in 2008 when Robert Kubica's car struck the wall in Montreal and barrel-rolled across the track, finally smashing into the concrete barrier on the opposite side. He was mildly concussed – but more upset with his doctor's advice: to forego the next race, Indianapolis. And we won't soon forget the terrifying aspect of Mark Webber's recent accident in Valencia, where his car – launched by a collision – landed upside down, rolled across the tarmac, then somehow turned around, regained its wheels and slammed into the barrier. He was unhurt and, in fact, sufficiently annoyed to throw his very expensive steering wheel out of the cockpit before stepping out himself.

The cultivation of Formula 1 into a global television entertainment and the remarkable developments in safety were attained through a series of pragmatic appointments and the manipulation of the structure of the world governing body of motorsport, the FIA. The whole of motor racing – everywhere – has benefited. Bernie's changes have also meant that the sport has produced massive earnings, and many of its participants have become extremely wealthy. Bernie, himself, has become a multi-billionaire.

The changes that Bernie has brought about in Formula 1 have also cast him upon the world stage as a leading figure. He befriends kings and heads of state and, occasionally, keeps prime ministers waiting. As he flits about the paddock on any Grand Prix weekend he will be photographed hundreds of times, a throng will hover at his side begging an opinion, a word, an interview – only two or three will be granted – before he returns to his travelling office, 'the Kremlin', a dark grey motorhome luxuriously equipped with satellite television and advanced communications systems so that he is in continuous contact with all and any events that might influence his operations. Outside the Kremlin dealers line up awaiting their turn to negotiate. And then at some point in the day – every day – around the globe people by the score will be writing about him.

The extraordinary conditions of Bernie's life have not been achieved without his ruthless pursuit of ambition. 'I've hurt people,' he said to me in 2001, reflecting on his life.

I first met Bernie on a Saturday, in 1981, in the paddock at the Montreal Grand Prix. I had arrived in Montreal the previous night, having been sent there to interview Professor Sid Watkins, whom the American press had been hailing as 'the world's leading neurosurgeon'. My editor wanted to know why such an eminent figure was fooling around with racing cars and: 'What *is* Formula 1 anyway?' I should say that the publication I worked for was located in Naples, Florida, where concepts of outdoor entertainment never embrace anything that is fast and makes a noise. Sid had visited Naples to give a lecture – much more the Neopolitans' sort of pastime – on international healthcare systems. He was featured in the local press and evening news programmes, my magazine had a snippet, but after he became national news they wanted more. Sid had granted the interview to my colleague, whom he had befriended, but when at the last minute she was unable to go to Canada, I was sent – protesting – in her place. On the Friday night, over dinner, Sid and I had a planning session discussing where I should position myself at the circuit and potential interviews that might contribute to the article; Bernie wasn't mentioned.

Until the next morning, as we were walking around the paddock, Sid noticed Bernie in the distance and pulled me along for an introduction: 'Now *here's* someone you *really* ought to meet. He *is* Formula 1,' said Sid. Bernie, clad in jeans with knife-sharp creases, white shirt and pink-lensed glasses beneath a mop of Ringo Starr hair, smirked as he put out his hand. His other hand was flopped over the shoulder of a young man with dark curls and dark, laughing eyes: 'And *here's* the next world champion, Nelson Piquet,' Sid added. This precipitated mutual grins like a trio of knowing rascals, giving me the impression that I had been left on the outside of their strictly insiders' story. I felt uncomfortable. Which is why I can't remember the rest of the conversation, only that I was glad when we had moved on. I regained my composure with a dose of superior smugness: 'I mean, really, didn't all these people have something better to do with their weekends?' I thought.

Since then I have attended every Montreal Grand Prix and countless others, save one or two when I was in the throes of this book. In the early days, it was a means of being with my husband, Sid, whom I married a few years after the interview. Also, five of our six children have worked for Formula 1 teams or as medical support; then a grand prix became an excuse to tag along and admire them. And there were all those family holidays couched around Spa or Hockenheim or Silverstone; Montreal was for reunions with North American friends, Budapest was usually for the two of us, as were Monaco, Monza and Imola; Malaysia was for recovery after Australia and the twenty-three-hour journey that took us there. For Sid the races were his workplace, first and foremost; it was in the hotels and restaurants that he came home to us.

Our extended family has included racing drivers: Innes Ireland, Stirling Moss, Frank Gardner, Jackie Stewart, James Hunt, Jody Scheckter, Ayrton Senna, John Watson, Michael Schumacher; race officials: Dean Delamont, Derek Ongaro, Robert Langford, Jean-Jacques Isserman; team principals: Ron Dennis, Ken and Bob Tyrrell and their families; and Karl Heinz Zimmerman. And Bernie. Bernie has always been there in the background, moving to the foreground when we needed him. Sid needed his help when Frank Williams was injured, and when it was necessary to delay practice or a race on the grounds of safety. For me, Bernie has been the support I have sought for charities and, beyond that, he has given me the impression that I can depend upon him – no matter what.

In 2001 I had just finished a book on Mary Queen of Scots and the experience had left me feeling drained. I'm not the kind that goes daintily into such projects; I wallow. My dreams – set in the sixteenth century – were of menacing court proceedings, clammy dungeons and beheadings. These would be interrupted with a moan or a scream, followed by a whisky poured by Sid. Sleep was becoming something I dreaded, as were the feelings of self-doubt that crept in about four in the morning. Then I had a reprieve: I woke up and thought of Bernie. I wanted to write his biography. Right there. Right then. It suddenly seemed so obvious: what I needed was a change, and here, after books on Jane Austen, Elizabeth I and Mary, was a complete transformation staring me in the face. I didn't know why I hadn't thought of him before. Well, actually I did know. I was standing so close I couldn't see him, not as a book. He had become the walls of my Formula 1 world, part of our extended family, a loyal friend. Now, when I again needed my friend, he was there, in the foreground, as always. But could I objectively write Bernie's story? No, that was not possible. The best I could hope for was some sort of balance; and then I reasoned that this was a story that could only be written from the inside out, like in Montreal that Saturday, nearly thirty years ago. Except, that I now felt I was on the inside.

With regard to that Montreal weekend, I never did write the article. When I got home on Monday I couldn't write a word, not during all of the following week nor the week after. Eventually I had to reimburse the publisher for the airfare. You see those two days at the circuit were beyond anything in my experience, or comprehension. Oh, I have always been able to cobble something together to fill up a space. But just then I was too stunned. So it remained an obligation undischarged. This book – I hope – settles that obligation, because Bernie's story is also the story of Formula 1, which is partly Sid's story too. At least I think it explains why they were *both* fooling around with racing cars.

Which is not to say that getting this book into print has been all smooth sailing. There have been unexpected – and hugely disappointing – halts in publication. First, in 2005, when my contract with Bernie meant the biography could not be published without his permission; although he'd already agreed every chapter, he asked for a delay. Second, in 2007, when it was explained that his 'service agreement' with his business associates gave a third party indirect power over the book; the third party wanted an indefinite postponement.

Bernie generously reimbursed me for six years' work, travel expenses, research assistants' fees, my agent's fees and the advance from my then publisher, which had to be repaid. In exchange, he or an entity he wished to nominate or his estate was to receive fifty per cent of my future advances, royalties and any other profits from the sale of the book. He has since withdrawn his financial claim as the book – originally written as an authorised biography – has now been designated 'unauthorised'.

The upside has been the adventure of exploring Bernie's life. A favourite piece of research fleshed out the Warren Street years in the fifties and early sixties. Bernie could recollect very little from this period, so it took some digging, which resulted in a rather delightful afternoon in 2004 spent 'down the pub', interviewing a group of his former colleagues. Sadly, many of these individuals – like several of his friends from Bexleyheath and motor racing – have, in the interim, passed on, a fact that became all too evident when I was writing the acknowledgements. Interviews also provided the means of re-establishing friendships made during all those years on the road with the 'circus'. When I was unable to go to races, interviews were conducted by Sid, no doubt trying the patience of our friends with the long list of questions I'd tucked into his suitcase. But I must say, overall – for both of us – it has been a joy.

Three years on and endless updates later we're about to go to print. There has been another wobbly moment, actually a wobbly two months, but Bernie has at last said: 'please publish the book'. Amen.

PART I

CHAPTER 1

'TITCH'

The Bermuda Triangle of Suffolk – popularly known as 'the Saints' – is that part of north-east Suffolk in which Bernie's birthplace, St Peter, South Elmham, is located. The area is called 'the Saints' because virtually every village within the confines of some fifteen miles by seven is named after a saint: St Cross, St Margaret, All Saints cum St Nicholas, St James, St Michael, St Lawrence, St Andrew, St John and St Peter. The villages are connected by a maze of single-track roads bounded by miles of open pastures and farmland. The locals joke that during the War they had seen an American serviceman drive into 'the Saints' and he has not yet found his way out! Such is the intricacy of this remote but beautiful area of Suffolk. And, of course, most of the villages boast a splendid church. The Church of St Peter's, built during the thirteenth century and surrounded by ancient headstones, is only two doors down from Hawk House where, on 28 October 1930, Bertha Sophia Ecclestone gave birth to a son – Bernard Charles.

Hawk House belonged to Bernie's grandmother, Rosina ('Rose') Westley, and takes its name, according to the present inhabitants, from an association with the nearby moat-enclosed St Peter's Hall. The Hall dates from around 1280 and was extended in the sixteenth century utilising stone and other architectural plunder from Flixton Priory following its dissolution in the 1520s. Yet, it seems the extension, though lavish, was not large enough to accommodate all of the numerous guests to St Peter's Hall, so the excess were lodged – along with their falcons – at Hawk House. Hence the name of Bernie's first home. Another version of the story suggests that a building existed on the present site of Hawk House since the time of Flixton Priory, established in 1258, and that it was used by nuns for their hunting pleasure as well as for vermin control. Throughout the nineteenth century it was variously known as an inn and a pub, becoming a private residence at the beginning of the twentieth century.

Whatever its history, the house in which Bernie spent his early years certainly dates from around the time of the Hall's extension in the sixteenth century, with a pitched, tiled roof and the long dimensions so typical of Suffolk. Inside, the rooms are snug, with thick walls and the heat from two fireplaces. The house is set beside a ditch-lined road that borders open farmland, and makes up a straggle of about half-a-dozen homes that comprise the village – more like a hamlet – of St Peter. A trickle of a river, the Brett, flows through one end of St Peter and is crossed by the derelict remains of a bridge. All the architectural distinction of the village belongs to St Peter's Hall and, more immediately, to the Church.

It was in St Peter's Church that Bertha Westley, twenty-two, and dressed 'all in violet' had married Sidney William Ecclestone, twenty-four, on 17 December 1927. Three years later, Bernie was christened in the small square church with its flint and rubble walls. Friesian cows grazed on a meadow in front of the church, and across the road a horse-drawn reaper cut the corn, which was then stooked in the fields. St Peter's church is small, holding only about sixty parishioners, but the Ecclestones rarely joined the congregation. Weddings and christenings apart, the family were not regular churchgoers, and Bernie's attitude to religion remains non-existent: 'I don't have any beliefs,' he will readily admit. But despite that, when he was recently asked 'if he could send a small donation' to help pay for repairs to the roof of St Peter's Church, Bernie gave them £20,000 – the entire cost of the work. 'They were so happy,' he says, smiling.

Bertha may have given birth in Hawk House by the light of a paraffin lamp, as Bernie distinctly recalls that his grandmother's house lacked electricity, 'and I remember that there was a pump in the kitchen... and an outdoor toilet'. When Bernie was old enough to walk, his mother allowed him to totter about in the large field at the back of the house, where there was a barn that intrigued him. His life at 'the Hawk' was thus far idyllic, the family's concerns as pastoral as the scenery. But when Bernie was about two years old, his mother began to suspect that her then only child had a vision problem. Indeed, Bertha soon became so distressed that she packed her young son on to the back of her push-bike and cycled fifteen miles to have him examined by an eye specialist in Norwich. Bertha's suspicions were proved right: Bernie was diagnosed with congenital atrophia, the lining of his right eye was underdeveloped causing, in that eye, near blindness. 'I couldn't see out of one eye, that's all,' says Bernie, 'not enough to recognise things'. For much of his life, Bernie would be under the care of consultants at Moorfields Eye Hospital in London. Otherwise, the visual defect has affected his daily life – and his overall attitude to life – 'not at all', he now says.

It was in Bertha's nature to make important decisions regarding the family, and then to act upon them. Years later, when Britain was at war with Germany, she refused to allow her children to be evacuated. By then she also had a daughter, Marian, eight years younger than Bernie and his only sibling. Marian recalls her mother's determination to keep the Ecclestone family unit intact: 'We are a family and if anything is going to happen to us, it will be as a family, not with the children away.' Marian, who died in 2005, described her mother as 'a lovely person, she never had a bad word to say about anybody. She was firm, but really kind... but, you couldn't get away with anything.' Bertha also managed the family's finances. Her husband, Sidney, would take work wherever he could find it, then hand his earnings over to Bertha. 'There wasn't a lot of money,' said Marian. 'We were never on the poverty line, she always managed, and there was always that bit there.'

Bertha came from a family of six children, four sisters and

two brothers. She was born in Dover, where her father, George Henry, had worked as a keeper at Dover Castle before taking up a job at the department store, Waring & Gillow, 'in London's Tottenham Court Road'. The new job meant a move for the Westley family, to the suburban town of Enfield. The Waring & Gillow connection gave Rose Westley a slightly haughty air (though George later became a foreman packer), and she was disappointed when her daughter chose to marry Sidney Ecclestone, 'whose family were in printing'. Sidney's father, Robert Henry Ecclestone, made his living as a compositor, setting type for printing. He and his wife, Flora, had four sons and two daughters with Sidney's birth occurring in the middle of their brood. Around 1910 the family moved from Tonbridge to Bungay in Suffolk, where the printing firm, Clays (later the Chaucer Press), was undergoing phenomenal expansion providing jobs aplenty for willing compositors. Indeed the printing firm grew to such an extent that it eventually boasted three-quarters of the worldwide sales of the Bible and, more recently, the *Harry Potter* adventures.

Back in 1913, fingering into line passages of Bible scripture may have produced a spiritual awakening in Bernie's grandfather, or at least a change in denomination along with a pair of permanently black thumbs. For on 2 February of that year he had all six of his children christened at St Mary's, Bungay; Sidney was then eight years old. Bungay was to play yet another role in the Ecclestone family history, for it was there, just three miles north of St Peter, that Sidney and Bertha met. After their marriage the couple lived in Bungay, when Sidney chose to fish for his livelihood rather than follow his father into printing. He is described on the marriage record and also on Bernie's birth certificate as simply 'a fisherman'.

By the time Bernie was born, three years later, the couple had moved in with Rose Westley – possibly because Rose was, by then, separated from her husband and so had room for all of them at Hawk House, or perhaps because Sidney had taken a job on a steam trawler sailing out of Lowestoft, one of the largest ports in East England. Sidney's fishing boat was away for three-week trips, hauling in nets full of herring and mackerel. It was a hard life, and no doubt it eased his mind to know that his wife and young son were in comfortable surroundings, under the protective wing of Rose Westley. While away at sea, Sidney also managed to attend to his own comfort and privacy, hanging curtains around the bunk where he slept. Marian described her father as 'extremely shy – an extremely private person'. He was also fastidious, later instructing Bernie to follow his example, by polishing his shoes – without fail – every day 'as soon as he got home'. Bernie did likewise until he could afford 'to have someone come in and clean my shoes' as well as press his suits for him. Private, fastidious – these were to become hallmarks of Bernie's character. His father also told him: 'Don't waste money, but always buy the best you can afford' – which Bernie took to heart.

In 1928 Sidney Ecclestone had made maritime history (and future entertainment for his children) when, on the night of 30 December, his trawler *Elnet*, battered by a violent gale, went aground on Lowestoft North Beach. The lifeboat *Agnes-Cross* responded to the ship's whistle for assistance, making several attempts to approach the trawler, but was swept aside by mountainous waves. Eventually, the crew of eleven were hoisted ashore by the coastguard's new life-saving apparatus, the breeches-buoy, which had been attached to the foundering vessel by the use of a rocket. All of the crew suffered from the effects of immersion, but happily were 'brought round' in the coastguard's watchtower. Sidney, it seems, was never to forget that nightmare. But he was undaunted enough – and ambitious enough – to apply for his Master Mariner's Certificate; he wanted to become the captain of his own ship. Interestingly, it was a visual difficulty that tripped him up. He was colour-blind, unable to distinguish red from green, which was enough to fail him. Sidney Ecclestone's career as a fisherman was to last only about seven years, ending in 1934, but he never lost his love of fishing. In the Seventies Bernie would acquire a great park with a lake in it, and he would stock the lake with carp – 'real fighters' – so that his dad, at leisure, could resume fishing.

With Sidney away fishing, the household at Hawk House naturally became matriarchal, with Rose Westley maintaining the upper hand. Bernie grew to adore his grandmother, affectionately recalling that she 'was immaculate with her hair back in a bun'. Even today, those who have been closest to Bernie are quick to mention his love for his grandmother. 'She was a very nice person,' he adds. 'Disciplined; I'm disciplined myself.' Indeed, fastidious, private and disciplined – in spades.

When Bernie was four years old the Ecclestones moved to the nearby village of Wissett where on 12 June 1935 he attended his first school. The Victorian schoolhouse had been built to accommodate fifty children, though there were only sixteen when he began there; 'eight' according to Bernie's recollection, and it consisted of 'one classroom'. The young boy walked to school on most school days but sometimes he rode the short distance by horsepower, 'on the milk cart'. Perhaps Sidney Ecclestone, who had now taken up farm work, had arranged for his son to join the milk round, as a treat to amuse the boy. With half of Suffolk turned to arable land, there was little difficulty for Sidney to get work, and the appeal of becoming master of his own household may also have swayed his decision. For Bertha, living away from Rose Westley now gave her the freedom to assume the role of chief nurturer – and disciplinarian. Bernie recalls that his mother 'was good at bringing up kids... she knew what was right and wrong'.

The two years that the Ecclestones lived in Wissett (1934–6) coincided with the increasing threat emanating from Europe. In 1933 Adolf Hitler had become Chancellor of the German Reich and immediately set his country to work building arms, making Germany, by 1936, a leading military power intent upon seizing control of Europe. However, 1936 also brought choice diversion in the much-publicised dalliance of the new King Edward VIII with American – not yet divorced – Wallis Simpson. By the end of the year Mrs Simpson would obtain her divorce and Edward would abdicate, choosing life with 'the woman I love' over the throne. This royal scandal was the talk of every household in the country including the Ecclestones of Wissett. At Bernie's school royal activities were dutifully acknowledged, with the children being given a holiday in November 1935 on the Duke of Gloucester's wedding day, and in January 1936 for the funeral of George V. These were the events that really stirred Wissett, as did the whooping cough epidemic that kept Bernie and two other children absent from school; and heavy rains that flooded roads. The roads were principally occupied by farm machinery and people on bicycles riding half-a-dozen miles to purchase what could not be grown locally or from the eclectic selection of items in the village post office. If a car drove through Wissett, people stared, then confidently identified its manufacturer – usually incorrectly – while picking up the scent of petrol over the universally acknowledged 'good old-fashioned farm smell' of manure.

Bernie remembers little of his early years at school, apart from the highlight of riding on the milk cart and playing in the school ground with 'a couple of boys' who enjoyed the company of the small child who had 'worn glasses from a very young age'. Bernie looks vague when he says this, then impatient with the blur of time, unable to offer any more details except that 'the school had only one teacher and there was a separate entrance for girls and boys'. Details are not often conveyed by shy children, as Bernie certainly was. 'I don't like to think about the past,' he says. 'I prefer the future.'

But there must have been a guiding light at the school, for in December 1935 a host of local dignitaries were feted at the school's Christmas party, and at the end of the year the inspectors of Wissett School reported that 'due care and attention has been given in teaching. The children are interested and consequently happy', although Bernie says, 'I didn't have a very good education'. But happy or otherwise, change was afoot and would soon encroach upon the bucolic atmosphere of rural north-east Suffolk, and envelop all Britain.

On 14 September 1936 Bernie spent his last day at Wissett School: the Ecclestones were moving to Dartford in Kent, on the periphery of London. Not yet six, Bernie made the move ahead of his parents, to get settled into his new school. At first he stayed with his mother's sister, Auntie May, who was already living in Dartford, and had told Rose Westley about its opportunities. Then Bernie's determined grandmother urged Sidney Ecclestone to seek work in this bustling quasi-medieval, quasi-industrial town. Sidney's Suffolk farm work may well have included driving one of the steam engines used to thresh grain and stack straw. Driving a steam engine may have given him the confidence to exchange work on the farm for work driving a crane at Seagers engineering works and foundry in Dartford.

At first the Ecclestones moved into an apartment in a late Georgian, red-brick townhouse on busy East Hill leading to the High Street. But after only a few months the family moved up the hill to a bungalow in Priory Close, amid acres of white-washed stucco – now mostly pebble-dashed – one- and two-storey houses built during the Thirties. Bernie may have walked past the scant remains of the fourteenth century Dominican nunnery on his way to school. But during the coming years Priory Close, with its ordered streets and tidy gardens, would become an increasingly dangerous place to raise a family, and Bernie would soon walk to school carrying a gas mask.

Back in Suffolk, farmland was steadily being bulldozed and paved to create airfields. Bernie, had he remained there, would have watched this process as an interesting – even exciting – progression towards war. In Dartford, war just happened. Indeed, it had been talked about, but as something in the distance, as yet intangible. Then it was expected. Then it came in a rush. Adjustment – for everyone – had to be immediate.

Never again would Bernie know the snug, secure embrace of Suffolk. Never again would he return – even out of curiosity. Suffolk would be wrenched out of him, becoming, for Bernie, a foreign land.

Bernie's sister Marian was born in September 1938, the same month Britain's Prime Minister, Neville Chamberlain, signed the Munich Agreement, virtually abandoning Czechoslovakia to the Germans. By May the following year

Germany and Italy had formed a firm military alliance, and the illusion of 'peace in our time' completely dissolved four months later when the German military machine struck Poland; France and Great Britain responded by declaring war on Germany. Having a new baby in the family was probably a welcome distraction for the Ecclestones, while they, along with the rest of England, waited for the *Luftwaffe* to attack. Air strikes became the new kind of warfare – there would now be no distinguishing between the soldier and the civilian, between the adult and the child. What is Bernie's most vivid memory of the war years? 'BOMBS!'

In the late spring of 1940 Germany unleashed its offensive, initially making daylight raids against air bases, but it was the nightly blitz that was soon to terrorise London and its surroundings. Dartford was located within the area known as 'bomb alley' and consequently suffered many casualties. For a little while, Bernie recalls that the Ecclestones 'lived in an air-raid shelter in the garden – an Anderson shelter'. They also had 'a sort of air-raid shelter in the house' – a Morrison shelter, a steel table-like affair with open sides under which one could sleep or a family could crouch for protection. In the morning Bernie would collect exploded fragments, 'all the bits and pieces from the night before', and, more disturbingly, 'the shells and things'. Marian, who was to become the mother of two sons and a daughter, respected her mother's desire to keep the Ecclestone children at home regardless of the hazard. 'It was not an easy option,' said Marian, 'especially where we lived. At the end of our garden in Priory Close was the mainline railway, and two or three stations up from where we were was the Woolwich arsenal where the munitions were stored – not the easiest of places to live.' At night a red glow – cast by bomb-ignited fires – settled over the sky.

Bernie remembers that the bombing made his schooling 'disrupted, the teachers and the kids sometimes didn't turn up, things like that; it was pretty chaotic'. When they did turn up the only subject that Bernie looked forward to – and excelled in, then, – was maths. At the age of 'twelve or thirteen', Bernie put his mathematical prowess to work in his first entrepreneurial enterprise – selling cakes to his schoolmates; what Bernie calls his first venture in 'wheeling and dealing'. 'Early in the morning I went to the shop near the train station, bought all the cakes that they had just baked – they were on ration, but the guy was quite friendly – and I put them into a suitcase, took them to school and sold them in the break period.' But he was never tempted to eat the cakes himself; 'that was profit', and therefore sacred.

School then was West Central Secondary School, but Bernie had probably first become a paid employee while still at Dartford Primary School, when he delivered newspapers on two separate rounds. He got up at about five o'clock in the morning, 'went to the paper shop, got the papers and did one round, then went back and got another lot, did another round'. He also earned money picking fruit and potatoes. With many farm workers away fighting in the war, the harvest was necessarily gathered by the remaining men, women and – children. Schools often organised outings to farms so that students could help feed the nation by filling the labour shortage, but Bernie is quick to point out that he was never a part of any harvesting activities arranged by his school; he picked strictly to earn money. Even this was not without hazard. He recalls one particular day in 1944 when picking potatoes at a farm in Kent, a V1 'doodlebug' flying overhead appeared to turn away from its course for London and came down towards the field, seemingly aimed at him. 'I ran like hell,' he says. Fortunately, 'it didn't cause any serious damage, but it sure helped to get the potatoes up!' Out of the harvest season, fourteen-year-old Bernie Ecclestone switched to selling fountain pens – which he bought in bulk and later sold for a profit in Petticoat Lane market in London's East End. 'Yeah,' laughs Bernie, 'I was doing a market study for the pen company!'

Over sixty years on, Bernie appears to relish that first swagger; during the war years he had effaced all traces of rural Suffolk. As a child of nearly six arriving in Dartford, his relatives had come to think of him as a shy boy. By the time he became a teenager he was still shy, but had learned not to show it. Humour was the device he used to conceal discomfort. He was then, as now, ready with jokes by the truckload. Today he can still ease every situation with laughter. His shyness also appears to evaporate when he is buying and selling; then he exudes steely confidence. A confidence that took root in his early teenage years when he decided how he would live the rest of his life: on his own terms; avoiding dependence; self-determinate; as an entrepreneur.

Even at this stage the degree of Bernie's self-reliance – useful though it may have been during wartime – had set him apart from others, including his family. His parents were certainly not entrepreneurial in character. Sidney Ecclestone continued to hand over his wages to Bertha so that she could manage the needs of their small family whose members she kept presentable with 'one outfit for best, one in the wash and one to wear'. Towards the end of the war the Ecclestones moved to their last home in Dartford, 'a terrace house with a parlour' on nearby Marcet Road, where at the end of the war an effigy of Hitler was hung from a lamppost. At Marcet Road, just as at Priory Close and elsewhere, Sidney and Bertha were contented to provide a modest but 'meticulous' home, warmth in the winter and simple fare. When asked what motivated him to earn money at such an early age, Bernie's answer is simple: 'I needed to buy things' such as his Sea Scout's uniform. Not the Scouts, mind you, but the Sea Scouts, even though he now lived several hours from the sea. He wasn't a member for long, however. More interesting is the fact that he joined in the first place. Bernie isn't interested in exploring why, but it appears to have been a sign of respect for his father's adventures; and, perhaps, a farewell nod to the past.

Bernie's parents, like most of their generation, tended not to be outwardly affectionate, but there was a great deal of love and support within the family. There were also regular visits with grandmother Westley who had moved to a house near the Ecclestones. Rose Westley took considerable pride in her appearance, which, of course, met with Bernie's approval: 'Gran would always be immaculate, even at ninety,' by which time he had arranged for her care in a nursing home. She always thanked him when he visited, but never failed to mention: 'The trouble with this place is that there are too many old people!' He admired her competence in raising her children, for the most part on her own, adding: 'I have very good memories... she died at age ninety-four or ninety-five.' Then Bernie looks reflective. 'I don't get upset externally. Internally, I... [mumbling, almost whispering] get emotional... you're upset when these things happen.'

Bertha's sister May and her husband Godfrey were also included occasionally in the Ecclestone's family gatherings. At some point during the early Forties a fifth member of the Ecclestone household arrived – 'Skipper' (the sea again), their pet spaniel. On a fine autumn day the family would make an excursion to the countryside to 'scrump' (pilfer) windfalls – apples and sweet chestnuts – from Kent. The whole family enjoyed it, like a refreshing breeze blowing away the war and the ever-present clamour of Dartford's new industries, and the trains, laden with ammunition, thundering along the bottom of their garden. So on clear, cool autumn days the Ecclestones escaped. The Suffolk that they had known was flat, worked land, whereas north-east Kent was all green rolling hills, but it would suffice because it was wide open and quiet with only the occasional but welcome sound of distant farm machinery. It soothed like a happy memory, and it made them light-hearted – Bernie almost as much as the others, though he preferred to fill his time earning money.

One autumn day Bernie took his young sister to pick blackberries, also taking along his mother's watch, so that they could be certain of returning home at a particular time. Bertha had been fretting about the children being out of doors after dark. Some hours later Bernie and Marian returned with a container full of berries, but without the watch – it had been lost. Bernie didn't offer to replace it; the watch was not on his list of things he 'needed to buy'; it was gone and never talked about. But in years to come he would shower his mother with gifts even though she was not one to ask for – or expect – anything. It was his way of expressing love. Something else that Bernie and Marian shared was the unpleasant task – particularly for the fastidious adolescent – of following the milk wagon, collecting horse manure for Bertha Ecclestone's garden.

In addition to money-making Bernie developed an early fascination with the cinema. This was not so unique when there was a good deal of quality film drama available, which also provided escapism from the war. But then the teenager added the wanton luxury of a projector to his list of must-haves. With his newly acquired film projector Bernie would often hang up a sheet, said Marian, 'for a picture show' in the hall of their bungalow. Bernie called his sister 'Giggy Woo', and when she was older, just 'Woo', though due to the eight-year difference in their ages, they were never really playmates. But there were always 'older guys about, and I used to tag along with them,' said Marian. The 'older guys' had become her brother's band of protectors. During the early teenage years when most boys begin to gain height, Bernie says, 'I just didn't get any bigger'; his schoolmates 'often' called him 'Titch'. When collecting cash during the cake-selling enterprise, he had realised that he was vulnerable to attack from the school's bullies, and quickly took evasive action by gathering around himself a gang of friends for protection.

With shoes on, Bernie stands 'five feet six inches' tall; five feet three inches without, or thereabouts, and is perfectly proportioned. He was a handsome young man, and in keeping with fashion pomaded his brown hair into a sleek 'Pompadour' worn straight back off the forehead. In photographs from this period his blue eyes look rascally, as if he's about to crack a joke, or play a prank. Bernie reflects: 'I was just trying to look cool,' meaning 'good, not too bad'. But he was cool to the point of numbness when it came to daring pranks. Fear was never part of his make-up – as long as he was in control. Protecting his cake money had just been smart. Amusing, quick-witted and with pockets full of cash, it was always easy to attract friends. Marian recalled that her brother's friends 'treated me unmercifully, as they do little sisters'. Perhaps to make amends, Bernie often gave Marian his pocket change. When he had saved enough of his earnings to buy Marian a doll, he took her by trolley bus to the toy shop so that she could choose the one she wanted – 'probably the most expensive,' laughed Marian. Later he bought her a wooden scooter, which she smashed to splinters on the first test run. Bernie still 'loves giving presents, and yet he doesn't like receiving presents, it embarrasses him'.

Bertha enjoyed recounting the story of her son's cake-selling business, and it seems that she was equally impressed with his stint at trading in bicycles – not motorcycles but bicycles – or rather, bicycle. When he was about sixteen, he bought a second hand push-bike. He took it apart; put it together again and sold it – 'for a profit'.

While Bernie was making money, school held little attraction for him. 'School was just somewhere to go,' he says, although he admits to enjoying physics and chemistry, and he went on to attend Woolwich Polytechnic Boys' School, a few stops by train from Dartford. But more than anything he wanted to be out in the world wheeling and dealing, not confined to a classroom. So at the age of fifteen he finished with classrooms and schoolwork. His parents were not happy with their son's decision, which left them in something of a dilemma. Marian clearly remembered their reaction: 'They thought that if they opposed him, he's going to do it anyway, so they might as well give him their blessing, which they did.' Sidney Ecclestone did voice his opposition while delivering his blessing, and then offered a compromise: 'My father insisted that I did something with chemistry.' says Bernie. 'So I went and worked at the gasworks in Dartford, in a laboratory.'

The disparate elements of Bernie's early years – the rural start in an all-female household, the 'one-room' schoolhouse, the 'disruptions' of the war years – did not hinder his ambitions. The sight-impaired, undersized teenager was about to soar into the world of business. Yes, he dutifully respected his father's wishes, and for two years punched a clock at the gasworks laboratory. But from the moment he donned his white coat, the lab assistant's job was eclipsed by the demands of his other money-gathering ventures. 'He could sell snow to the Eskimos,' said Marian, reflecting on her brother's early talent for business. 'It's just the way he's always been.'

So, what or who inspired the entrepreneurial skill that Bernie immediately strapped into overdrive? Was there a role model, perhaps someone at school who got him started or that he wanted to emulate, then exceed? 'No,' says Bernie, 'it was just there.'

'Just, there?'

'Yeah,' says Bernie.

'It's a good argument for reincarnation.'

No response.

'Or a sonic boom.' And that was about to sound over Britain's post-war marketplace.

CHAPTER 2

METALLIC BLUE

A fundamental element for success that Bernie possessed, along with his innate entrepreneurial skill, was a nose for timing. During the post-war years commerce became increasingly unfettered – and flourished, at least for anyone with products to sell. Rationing had left shops with only a paltry selection of goods, and there were years of shortages still to come. Yet ordinary working people, especially those who had been employed in factories instead of the services (often working double shifts, earning well), were eager customers. Individuals swift to react to the scent of profit – any profit – found a ready market. Bernie spotted his opportunity in the sale of motorcycles. 'I raced bikes [motorbikes] early on,' he explains, so he mixed with people who wanted to buy motorcycles and who could name a dozen other determined customers. From the post-war years through to the early Fifties, motorcycles were in everyday use as a principal means of transportation, although this would change towards the end of the decade when cars started to become more affordable. Bernie's most pressing task was to procure the goods to sell. Having achieved that, profit – for the budding Svengali of sales – was a certainty.

The head chemist at the gasworks' laboratory, a Mr Richardson, was bedevilled – or so he must have felt in moments when it became unclear whether his assistant, young Ecclestone, was working for him or if, in fact, he had become the unpaid employee of the assistant! Officially, Bernie was being paid to analyse the gases supplied to industrial and domestic premises, 'to make sure the gas would do its job'.

He liked the work, not for his contribution to the efficacy of gas, but for the use of the company's telephone; another axiom of the successful entrepreneur – *use other people's money.* Bernie was now concentrating his efforts on buying privately owned motorcycles and selling them on. He would scan the classified advertisements in all the local newspapers, select his prospects and then begin negotiations giving out the laboratory telephone number as his point of contact. The telephone was, and still is, his *modus operandi* though in this instance the cost of the instrument was defrayed to his employer. Business was brisk, keeping Mr Richardson on his toes answering endless telephone enquiries. Fortunately, the head chemist was good-natured, and even entered into the game by canvassing for trade: 'I've got one for a BSA!' He'd shout to Bernie across the laboratory. And Bernie would waste no time in finding a BSA motorcycle for Mr Richardson's buyer. His mark-up for procuring the goods 'was as much as possible'. So on he went, buying more motorcycles and selling them, buying and selling – ring, ring, ring.

The chemist's assistant understood his wares from the ground up, for he had competed in motorcycle races since he was sixteen. He entered hill-climbs and motorcycle scrambles riding cross-country through the woods of Kent. Bernie's first motorcycle circuit race was on a grass track at Brands Hatch. His future associations with this famous Kent circuit would become manifold, but even in the late Forties Bernie and Brands got off to an interesting start. In particular he remembers an Easter meeting there, 'crashing on Good Friday, ending up in hospital in Fawkham' (near the circuit). He had suffered a concussion, but by the following day 'recovered consciousness and raced on the Sunday'. Not wearing a crash helmet meant that his limp, concussed form would be stretchered off to hospital more than once, and he was often covered in bruises though, remarkably, he never fractured any limbs. Sidney and Bertha Ecclestone may have succumbed to a certain amount of hand-wringing at this point, but whatever their private anxieties, Bernie received their unstinting support.

When Bernie first began competing in motorcycle scrambles Sidney would ride to the race on a motorcycle of his own, with Bernie in the sidecar and the actual motorbike to be raced in tow. Later, Sidney would help his son load a recently acquired van with the motorcycle and other paraphernalia then off to the track they would go; an adventure for both. Father and son proudly posed for a photograph taken in front of the van, with the racing bike, already stowed aboard, viewed in the background. Bernie's sister Marian was also something of a racing enthusiast and enjoyed recalling hill-climbs: 'They used to start off up quite steep hills… they had to have three runs and at the end of the day whoever went up the quickest was the winner.' When Bernie returned from racing, Bertha Ecclestone would clean the mud from her son's motorcycle, leaving it gleaming. The bike would then be as immaculate as his black racing leathers (cost £3 or £4) which, following the multiple smashes, always needed Bertha's attention. Bertha probably also cleaned her husband's motorcycle, his principal means of transport. After the war, Sidney found evening work on the tote payout at the local dog track, and the motorcycle was the most convenient means of getting there. He later added a sidecar and would take Bertha on outings; 'sometimes' he collected Marian from school. To own a motorcycle at this time carried a certain amount of status; having a sidecar as well conferred an added measure of importance. So it is not surprising that the motorcycle was never allowed to stand out in the rain, but kept under cover when not in use, in the small garage at the end of their garden.

It seems that only Sidney was allowed to ride this motorcycle. When Bernie became interested in motorcycles he first 'had to buy one [a Velocette] and then learn how to ride it'. And he rode with confidence, the visual difficulty caused by his limited eyesight was 'not a problem, it was more difficult in cars than bikes'. Having learned to ride, he didn't trouble himself with obtaining a licence to operate the vehicle, though he did manage to get a licence to drive a motor car, and the Dartford police were most obliging: 'When I got nicked for speeding on a bike they endorsed my car licence,' he recalls. Racing officials were equally accommodating: when Bernie turned up for scrambles and hill-climbs he was never discomforted by having to produce a motorcycle licence.

It was some time in the late Forties that Jack Surtees visited Bernie at the Ecclestone's Marcet Road bungalow. Jack had brought along his fourteen-year-old son John and the pair found Bernie near the kitchen at the back of the house tinkering over his newest acquisition – a racing Excelsior Manxman motorcycle. For Bernie, not yet eighteen, the bike was his pride and joy. While he sometimes has difficulty recalling details from the past, he can rattle off 'racing Excelsior Manxman – and be sure you get the word "racing" in there' – like he'd just bought it. Bertha Ecclestone, a scrupulous housekeeper, must have understood her son's attachment to the machine, which is why she allowed him to work on it in such close proximity to her kitchen. Cleanliness, a faultless presentation, taking care of one's possessions: these were the doctrines engrained in Bernie by both his parents.

Before the war Jack Surtees had been British motorcycle and sidecar champion. After the war, and after serious injuries resulting from an accident, he continued to race, though at a less demanding level. At the same time, he opened a motorcycle business in Forest Hill, south London, which is where he met and soon became impressed with the young motorcycle trader – Bernard Ecclestone. John Surtees remembers 'my father coming home and talking about the deals they'd heard Bernard had done and how he used to go along and mesmerise people by putting whole groups of things together and making them offers before they really realised what they'd done'. Bernie recalls that his dealings with Jack Surtees worked 'both ways', the pair totting-up multiple sales in 'Triumphs, Vincents, Matchlesses'. Jack Surtees also dealt in cars, having dabbled in the motor trade before the war. 'He knew everybody in the business,' says Bernie, a useful source of contacts for the enterprising young Ecclestone who now also bought and sold cars alongside the flourishing motorcycle trade; the cars changed hands on 'a sale-or-return basis'.

Jack Surtees's son, John, next saw Bernie in 1950 at the then recently tarmacked Brands Hatch circuit where they were both competing. Bernie rode a Manx Norton to which he had fitted a JAP engine, John was on a Vincent Grey Flash. 'The bike he rode was worth more money than the bike I rode [which cost £12 without the engine] when we started in 1950,' says John, 'but it still wasn't a sort of grand prix type bike.' Neither John, wearing his father's baggy racing leathers, nor Bernie finished the race, but John Surtees would soon overcome the disappointment of his first attempt on a paved circuit by winning seven motorcycle world championships, and in 1964 would triumph on four wheels, becoming Formula 1 World Champion.

During the 1950s motorcycle races at Brands attracted thousands of spectators – exhilarating stuff for the riders, including Bernie, who was now a seasoned rider and holder of the motorcycle lap record. 'Dad and Bernard used to go bike racing at Brands Hatch when it was a grass track,' recalled Marian. 'Laurel wreaths used to be laid out by the tower at the finish line… Motorbikes were a very dominant factor in his life.' Bernie was so proud of his motorcycling that he later commissioned a portrait of himself – astride a Triumph Tiger 70. His enthusiasm for the sport continued decades into the future. Even today, he cannot resist watching motorcycle races on television. He also took part in a twenty-five-mile bicycle race at Headcorn in Kent, but this was only a novelty. It was racing two-wheeled vehicles – with powerful engines – that captivated him.

With so much motorcycle activity – selling, riding and racing – the time had come, in 1948, for Bernie to make a move from the gasworks' laboratory – where he was being paid '£5 per week'. He started working at Harcourt Motor Cycles in Bexleyheath, just a few miles down the road from Dartford. The proprietor, Les Cocker, then in his forties, had a relaxed manner and let Bernie, still in his teens, 'run things. I saw it as an opportunity,' says Bernie, 'to buy and sell bloody motorbikes!' And he did just that – at every opportunity, and wherever an opportunity could be created. 'It was good with

Les, I was doing a lot of deals.' Indeed, Bernie became so adroit at spotting business opportunities that it took little more than a glance at the neat, well-maintained Compton & Fuller car showroom, just across the street from Harcourt's, for Bernie to yearn for expansion. After just eighteen months at Harcourt's, Bernie had undoubtedly realised that the commercial district of Bexleyheath, around the two businesses, attracted a considerable volume of passers-by – the kind of circumstance to quicken his pulse.

The showroom Bernie had spotted was the property of Fred Compton and his partner Derek Fuller, their surnames emblazoned in large white letters above the entrance. They had begun the business in 1946 taking over a building that had housed one of the oldest garages in Kent; it was old enough to include a few horse mangers. The cars they sold were second-hand, 'bought from lock-up garages and sold for four times the price,' says Fred Compton. Bernie has a more realistic recollection: 'more like double the price, really'. Not too flashy or energetic, Compton & Fuller gave the impression of providing a service rather than turning a profit, and Fred, affectionately known as 'the Major' for his military bearing and well-groomed moustache, brought the correct degree of class to the proceedings (Fred had actually served as a Lieutenant in the Home Guard). Bernie, dressed in a smart suit, and Italian knitted tie – a style he now began to favour – made his initial approach, asking Fred if he could lease space on the forecourt to sell motorcycles. At first Fred didn't take the young man seriously, and declined. But Bernie didn't accept rejection and kept persisting: 'I'll give you a percentage of the profit and you don't have to do anything.' Fred eventually gave in; after all he had nothing to lose. As part of the bargain Fred tossed in a small, neglected store on the premises for Bernie to use as an office. Bernie promptly cleaned out the store, painted it and in the effort nearly collapsed from inhaling paint fumes.

'Right from the word "go" Bernie was a goer,' says Fred. 'More and more motorbikes sold, more and more and more.' Motorbike sales quickly outpaced car sales and inevitably the sedate car showroom was transformed into a slick motorcycle dealership with young Ecclestone at the ready, greeting every customer as an acknowledged motorcycle worshipper, the instant – if not before – they stepped through the door. Within three years the surnames displayed over the entrance in large white letters read 'Compton & Ecclestone'. Derek Fuller, having for some considerable time 'wondered what he was doing there', had been bought out. With Derek gone, Bernie had a mezzanine built with two luxurious offices, one for himself and one for Fred, each with their own secretary. At the age of twenty-one Bernie was now earning serious money. 'I was earning good,' says Bernie, 'never in trouble financially, I didn't worry about money.' In fact, he was earning enough to pay Charles and John Cooper for the construction of a racing car. 'I stopped racing bikes and started racing cars,' says Bernie, his voice emphatic, underlining a significant fact. '*I wanted to race.*' It was not obvious at the time, but the history of Bernie Ecclestone and the history of motor racing had now begun to merge.

A renewed infatuation with things mechanical was a curious by-product of the war. Yes, the international devastation brought about by machines resulted in agony for many, but also wonder. There was glory too, for the thousands of young men some of whom, with as little as three weeks training, mastered the skies while causing widespread destruction below as they defended their countries. Machines and daring – speed, control, power – became reality rather than just figments of the imagination or terms of speech. By the end of the war, all of these were in demand from the general public. Demand, however, was not limited to a fascination with the potential of machines. It also came pent-up, existing from a hiatus in most motor racing activities since the outbreak of hostilities, and a yearning for normality – if such a term can be used in association with motor racing. Following the war the clamour to resume racing was such that France held a race meeting in the Bois de Boulogne, in Paris, on 9 September 1945, not yet four months after VE Day. The first race was called the *Coupe Robert Benoist* in honour of the driver who had won four of the five Grands Prix held in 1927. Benoist had been active in the French Resistance, but was captured and executed in Buchenwald concentration camp. The following races on that day were entitled the *Coupe de la liberation* and the *Coupe des prisonniers*. The cars that were driven – Bugatti, Talbot, Delahaye, Alfa Romeo, Maserati – were about a different kind of glorious past, and about an exclusivity that was now thoroughly over.

The resurgence in the manufacture of motorcycles after the war made fast machines more easily available, and in 1946, in Britain, racing cars also came within reach of more buyers, with the reconfiguration of engine and chassis at a reasonable price: a 500cc 'four-wheeled motorcycle' produced by the factory of Charles Cooper and his son John. New racing circuits were also opening up. Former RAF airfields across the country – including Silverstone, Thruxton and Snetterton – joined the likes of Crystal Palace, Donington Park (used as a supply depot) and Brands Hatch as venues for all types of race meeting.

The concept of motor racing for all had, in fact, begun in the 1930s as the cherished aim of a few Bristol enthusiasts. The idea gained impetus during the war years with the laying down of rules for a low-cost, single-seater formula. The rules, which had been generated by a correspondence in *Motor Sport* magazine, went as follows: Cars were to have a cubic capacity of no more than 500cc; weigh no less than 500lb; carry one gallon of fuel; and 'a body [was desirable]'. Motorcycle engines matched the required capacity and thus were transplanted into the new class of racing car.

During the Fifties British motor racing entered a new – and arguably its most exciting – era that was to resonate in technologies and financial spheres as yet undreamed of. Attention to the sport would become global. But first a tug-of-war between the past and the present had to be played out.

Grand Prix motor racing, begun in France in 1906, was generally regarded as a pastime of the wealthy. Terms from horse racing, another recreation of the well-to-do, were carried over to motor racing, such as the 'paddock' (where cars are prepared before a race) and the use of 'stewards' (officials who enforce the sporting regulations and take decisions over protests between competitors). Rewards in money were modest, though silver trophies – a cup or perhaps a napkin ring – graciously bestowed by the local monarch or member of the nobility were not considered trifling. But the real prize, of course, was to drive fast, handling with skill a powerful racing car.

The best drivers were from Germany, Italy and France. Whereas Britain's motorcyclists and motorcycles were among the world's best, in Grand Prix racing British manufacturers had not yet attained international prestige; Bentley, however, must be mentioned for their wins at Le Mans from 1927 to 1930. Early in the century, motorsport had become a matter of national pride, with national colours: green for Britain, blue for France, red for Italy and silver for Germany. On the Continent, in the Thirties, it became associated with power. Hitler purposely chose motorsport to demonstrate German technology and the superior ability of German manufacturing; sleek, silver Mercedes and the Auto Union cars – designed by Dr Ferdinand Porsche – were both financed by the Nazi Party. British driver Richard Seaman, who had enjoyed success in both Delage and ERA cars, won the 1938 Grand Prix held at the Nürburgring, but in a Mercedes, and he was living in Germany at that time.

After the war the Italians and French again entered motorsport and, in 1954, the Germans rejoined the racing scene – a scene that each of the three countries intended to dominate. But by 1950 the first rear-engined car, the admittedly unimpressive-looking (the colloquialism 'rinky-dink' comes to mind) Cooper-JAP driven by Harry Schell, made its appearance at the Grand Prix of Monaco, bringing with its humble frame a new dynamism that would soon feature in the annals of motor racing history; an appreciable share of the sport's power and prestige would now originate in Britain. A contributing factor to this success was the 500cc racing formula.

John Surtees – who in 1960 would take the chequered flag at Goodwood in a Ken Tyrrell Cooper Formula Junior and go on to purchase his own Formula 2 Cooper – describes the works factory of Charles and John Cooper as 'little more than a blacksmith's shop'. Bernie disagrees: 'It was actually much more than that.' The 'more' was a combination of resourcefulness and determination that set them to work welding together bits of junk metal – including discarded Anderson shelters – to create, initially, low-cost 500cc single-seater cars. Mike Lawrence, in his book *Cooper*, describes the procedure: '… in essence they took the front suspension from two Fiats, separated them by a box-section ladder frame, added telescopic dampers, popped in a JAP Speedway engine, made by Prestwick [later Norton engines were used], behind the driver, and clothed the result with a simple aluminium body.' Actually, the idea for the car belonged to Charles and John along with John's friend, Eric Brandon, but most of the work was undertaken by Michael 'Ginger' Devlin who would go on to build the first Mini Cooper, launched in 1961, and run the highly successful works Mini racing team.

In 1949, nineteen of the forty entries for the 500cc race at the British Grand Prix meeting had been Coopers. The following year Coopers won every important race in Britain and, in the lightweight category, on the Continent too including Stirling Moss's win in the support race at the Monaco Grand Prix. All of Europe – chortle though they may have done – was now starting to take notice of this 'rough and tumble' level of racing. The Fédération Internationale de l'Automobile (FIA), the world governing body for motorsport, announced that from 1950 the 500cc class would become known as Formula 3, the first international class of racing founded in Britain. The rules for the new international formula were much the same, though the weight was reduced, and a minimum ground clearance of four inches was now required. The Cooper was challenged by manufacturers from the Continent who built their own versions of the car, and in Britain by smaller outfits such as Kieft and JBS. But for the time being Charles and John supported by the rest of their team at the small Surbiton factory in Surrey continued to dominate. A new epic had begun. 'Charles and John were real racers,' says Bernie; it is not merely an acknowledgement, but rather the highest of compliments.

In 1951, Alan Brown – a friend of Bernie's – and Eric Brandon won both main British Formula 3 Championships driving an Ecurie Richmond Cooper. Perhaps more significantly, Formula 3 meant that British drivers, in increasing numbers, could now afford to race on the Continent. The 500cc class was responsible for widening the opportunity for more people to become involved in motor racing – so much so that it took several heats and a final to accommodate them all. Also, with low running costs plus starting money, plus prize money, plus trade bonuses, the sport now offered a reasonable standard of living, and drivers not put off by the demands of tight scheduling and often little sleep, could now take it up as a profession. During the Fifties the British professionals included Stirling Moss, Mike Hawthorn, Jim Russell, Tony Brooks and Roy Salvadori. During the next ten years the Cooper factory would continue to unsettle its competitors in Formula 3, before moving on to develop larger engined cars for the Formula 2 category, most notably the Cooper-Bristol and Cooper-Climax, finishing up with two World Championship wins.

Other British teams – Frazer Nash, Connaught, BRM, Vanwall, Lotus – were now inspired to go international. Vanwall won three Grands Prix in 1957 with Stirling Moss coming second in the World Championship. The Cooper cars responded with a vengeance. In 1958 Vanwall won the inaugural Constructors' Championship, but the Cooper-Climax, driven by Stirling Moss for private entrant Rob Walker, won the Argentine Grand Prix and, in Monaco, Maurice Trintignant won in Walker's car. In 1959 it was Cooper's turn to take the Constructors' Championship and, again, in 1960. The Coopers' success was aided by pragmatism and by keeping a hawk eye on the competition: 'They're doing that, why don't we do this?' The alterations would be considerable, but it was the Cooper blueprint that paved the way for further development by Lotus, Brabham and others, and they all evolved from that original scrapyard amalgamation.

The Coopers' Surbiton factory became, for Bernie, a school. He was already an established master at selling motorcycles, and was becoming increasingly adept in the sale of cars. But when it came to motor racing, he needed extensive lessons. Bernie's method of study was observation, or more exactly – osmosis – for he absorbed motor racing into every bodily cell, categorised it and stored it, until the amassed data could be applied in future strategies. His teachers during this phase of his motor racing career were Charles Cooper, 'a good practical engineer', and in particular Charles's son John. Charles Cooper was an irascible creature who blustered about the Surbiton factory, barking at his mechanics when they huddled about the workshop's only heat source, an old and inefficient coke boiler. 'Hey you blokes, stop standing round the fire!' he would yell. Over-zealous scrimping also caused him to covet like rare pearls the odd washer or bolt that had fallen on to the floor. 'They cost me tuppence each!' he would announce to everyone within shouting range while clutching in his fist the treasured object.

But beneath the crust there existed a warm heart. John Cooper was his father's exact opposite, all kindness and high spirits, and he delighted in sharing jokes. They were like 'good cop, bad cop' said senior mechanic Michael Devlin, which is how and why the factory managed to function, and what bound them together 'was a love for cars and motor racing'. Bernie says that he 'had a great respect and admiration' for John Cooper, as he also had for two other men – Colin Chapman and Enzo Ferrari. But it was John's principal characteristic – 'enthusiasm' – that Bernie respected. Here was a man who totally enjoyed his life's work – motor racing. Unlike Charles, 'John didn't worry all that much about money,' says Bernie. But what 'they both wanted [was] to build race cars and go and race.' Racing was everything to them.

The process of obtaining a racing car from the Coopers' factory was literally a hands-on experience – or what former racing driver and team owner John Coombs calls 'an absolute comedy act'. Tim Parnell, the son of British racing champion Reg Parnell, explains further: 'You had to build your own car.' Tim, a former racing driver and team manager, was well indoctrinated in the procedure: having bought the car, or rather the possibility of a car, from Charles and John, 'the best way to get the right parts on it was to virtually live at Coopers,' he continues. 'And you had to be there early, first thing in the morning and perhaps last thing at night otherwise people used to pinch the parts off your car.' When shock absorbers and newly chromed wishbones arrived at the Surbiton factory, 'it was absolute rush-hour to grab the part you needed'. Bernie agrees: 'A chaotic, chaotic place, but I liked to see the cars.'

Roy Golding, who began work as an engineer at the Cooper factory in 1948, remembers this arrangement as a benefit to prospective Cooper owners who were 'a bit short on the money side, so it was agreed that they did so much work and paid so much for the car'. Roy also remembers Bernie coming into the factory: 'He looked like a solicitor's clerk, a thin, pale youth... and his hair was combed back... not the right style for a racing driver.' Bernie supplied a Norton engine for the Cooper Mark V chassis and quietly beavered away installing it. When not assembling the car Bernie was seen standing about the garage – watching everything that occurred, listening and learning: 'I went there to see what was going on,' he admits, in fact, to totally ingest it. Bernie chose metallic blue as the colour for his racing car, with red wheels and red upholstery. 'Metallic blue, was my colour in those days,' he says, 'I really liked the colour... everything was metallic blue.'

He remembers in 1951 driving 'one of the best, new, modernist American Fords' to Silverstone, towing his Cooper on a trailer. He had gone there to drive in the Formula 3 support race; the main event was the British Grand Prix, won by José Froilán González from Argentina driving a 4½-litre Ferrari – a car that Bernie would eventually acquire to add to his extraordinary private collection. The car had a special significance – it was Ferrari's first Grand Prix winner. In 1999

John Surtees drove the Ferrari at Monza in celebration of the team's 500th Grand Prix victory.

The night before the race at Silverstone Bernie slept in his Ford – 'alone', adding 'I was still a virgin in those days', although he was by now in love with Ivy Bamford, a buxom young woman with light brown hair. He claims to have maintained his celibate state until their wedding night on 5 September 1952. Before her marriage Ivy, four years older than her twenty-one-year-old husband, had been a telephonist, an occupation well suited to one described as 'charming', having a 'bubbly personality', traits that would certainly have appealed to Bernie. 'I was a young virgin,' he adds again, 'and I suppose, you know, going into a new field' – carnal knowledge – with a novice's trepidation. He can't remember where they met. 'No idea, not the slightest idea, but not in a pub, I didn't drink,' he says. Ivy shared – at least she never objected to – Bernie's fascination with motorsport.

In addition to buying 'one of the first' Cooper-Nortons, Bernie also 'drove it for the factory', and he raced in a Cooper-Bristol, a Cooper MkV fitted with a JAP engine and a Cooper-Jaguar, enjoying reasonable success. He confesses that his eyesight gave him a few moments of concern: 'I couldn't see on certain corners.' Still, the press were enthusiastic over his performance. At Brands Hatch in April 1951, the newcomer Ecclestone was 'amazing'; at Goodwood, in May, he 'drove brilliantly'; and the same month back at Brands there was a 'lightning getaway' and an 'effortless win'. New Zealander Peter Ashcroft, a former racing driver, was often heard relaying the story of one particular 500cc race in which he was on pole position and Bernie was a couple of rows behind. Just before the flag dropped for the start of the race, Bernie called out to Peter, saying: 'When you're in front just make sure you're out of the way because I'm coming through!' At Thruxton in 1953, he started 'coming through' even before the start, inching ahead his Cooper-Bristol to squeeze into a slot on the row in front, cheekily grinning over his own cunning – which, however, failed to bring him victory, or even any points.

By the end of 1951 Bernie had chalked-up six heat wins, plus a win, a second place, a third place and a tenth place in various finals. At Brands Hatch in 1952 he would achieve one more overall victory, before venturing to the Continent in May of the following year to test his ability on the challenging Nürburgring in Germany – the circuit that had been Hitler's pet project. At the 'Ring Bernie drove a Kieft 500 with a Norton engine, competing against his friends George Wicken and David Walker; no results were recorded. Back in Britain, in the 'inching ahead' race at Thruxton in Hampshire on 3 August, he spun off. Bernie's final race of 1953 was at Crystal Palace on 19 September, finishing fifth behind the new works Cooper-Alta driven by Stirling Moss.

Brian Whitehouse, then the teenage son of Bernie's friend from Bexleyheath, racing driver Bill Whitehouse, remembers the privilege of being asked to transport the Cooper-Bristol to the circuit: 'I'm racing at Crystal Palace,' said Bernie, 'and I need you to drive the car there for me, and bring it home… will you do it?' Young Whitehouse, of course, couldn't agree quickly enough and promptly turned up with the Cooper-Bristol. After the race Brian was able to drive it back to Bexleyheath. Payment for this service was not forthcoming but, for Brian, to be allowed to drive the car was reward enough: 'Just to get into a racing car, to drive that – was like Formula 1 driving!'

Fred Compton also has fond memories of Bernie racing at Crystal Palace. Together they had bought a Cooper-Jaguar, in which Bernie took the chequered flag. 'He won! He actually won!' Fred recalls, his voice still bright with the unexpected good fortune. Other friends of Bernie's only recollect the smash-ups. 'He was a great shunter,' says Roy Salvadori, and another former racing driver, John Young, chuckles while replaying a scene or two in his mind: 'Prangs! Ol' Bernard, he was always having prangs!'

Brian Whitehouse also laughs, remembering the collisions, and in particular a prank played by his father Bill Whitehouse on shunt-prone Bernie. Several laps into a race at Brands Hatch there occurred a spectacular multi-car accident involving Bernie. Bill Whitehouse, who had also been competing, saw debris scattered about and Bernie slumped over the steering wheel of his wrecked car. Bill then stopped his own vehicle and ran to his friend shouting: 'Bernard, you all right?' To which a dazed Bernie mumbled something that sounded affirmative. 'Good, now stay still because you've killed someone in the crowds and they'll kill you.' Of course, nothing so distressing had happened, but according to the story, Bernie remained motionless, corpse-like until the perceived threat had passed. More serious was the mishap that had occurred on 28 September 1951 when, to quote a report in the local press, 'André Loens' rear wheel collapses, slides into Ecclestone, who goes through fence into spectators – youth suffers fractured thigh.' The youth, it seems, was an eight-year-old boy.

The next month Bernie again raced at Brands Hatch, coming fourth in the first heat, then retiring in the final. During the series of races at Brands that day – 26 October – four spectators were injured and there was one fatal accident. Bernie was not responsible for these incidents, but he always reacted to tragedy. 'Not at the time, but later,' he admits. 'Even if the people weren't a friend, not that close. That's the way it was, people got killed.' Whether or not the carnage was getting to be too much for Bernie, his involvement in motorsport, after putting in a full season in 1951, clearly became sporadic, suggesting perhaps that he was uncertain about his performance as a racing driver. There were, after all, those 'certain corners' that he was unable to see. But Bernie also has another, more straightforward, reason: 'I couldn't see much future in it, and I was running my business for Christ's sake. There were eight of us top guys including Moss, Collins and Schell [American racing driver Harry Schell]. I got £100 per year from Shell; we all got £100.' To Bernie, £100 was, by then, meagre pickings.

Brian Whitehouse says that Bernie told him he was going to quit driving in races because, simply: 'I can't afford it' – meaning he could not afford the time that racing demanded. Motorsport was the natural habitat for Bernie's fiercely competitive character. But then, he also craved measurable success that, on his particular balance beam, meant money. Lots of it. Eventually he would discover ways of combining business and motor racing that were ultra-successful, and thus self-validating. But at this point, the only reliable engine propelling him forward was buying and selling – motorcycles, cars, anything he could get his hands on. Immediately. Because Bernie was a young man in a hurry – in a hurry to get ahead at an ever-increasing pace. Nothing would be permitted to distract him – not even his wedding. 'Bernard took only half an hour off to get married,' says Fred Compton, who with his wife Jean had stood as witnesses to the marriage performed at the register office in Dartford. It was half an hour that nearly didn't happen. 'I met her [Ivy] at the register office. I didn't want to go to a church,' says Bernie. 'She was with her mother and somebody else, all crying. It was very disturbing. I said, "let's forget it, come back another day".' That seemed to cheer the two women up and the marriage went ahead. But, as soon as the nuptials were completed, 'Bernard turned around and marched off', adds Fred Compton.

'Haven't you forgotten something Mr Ecclestone?' said the lady registrar.

'What?'

'Your bride!'

Fred, Jean, Bernie's parents, his sister Marian and Ivy's mother merely looked on. It had been an emotional day, he needed to wind down with a quick refresher – wheeling and dealing. Without that, no day was complete. He had to keep moving on financially, forward, all of the time, trading and dealing. One of the most successful dealers in the motorcycle trade was on his way to surpassing himself dealing in the world – a sometimes murky world – of second-hand car sales.

CHAPTER 3

THE WHIPPET

Throughout the 1950s, the Cooper racing car was the common denominator that joined together a fraternity of car dealers who were also racing drivers. Certainly dealer/drivers Roy Salvadori, John Coombs, John Young and Alan Brown had first met feisty fellow dealer Bernie Ecclestone at the round of circuits – Brands Hatch, Crystal Palace, Thruxton, Silverstone and so on – where they were each competing, with playful rivalry bordering on a dare with death, in a Cooper. The fraternity also included a senior member, the experienced amateur racer Bill Whitehouse, and the fun-loving Cliff Davis. While Bernie may have begrudged weekends away from his operations in Bexleyheath, he took up the slack by talking business and doing business at the circuits with other members of the fraternity. His focus there tended to be on the sale of cars rather than motorcycles, and the unique camaraderie formed at the race track provided a further boost to trade.

Meanwhile, back in Bexleyheath, business at the motorcycle showroom of Compton & Ecclestone was expanding at what Fred Compton describes as 'a frantic pace'. A congenial family man who liked to make time for golf as well as business, Fred was finding Bernie's scale of turnover overwhelming. 'Come on Fred, keep up with me,' Bernie would prod, and Fred would answer, wearily, 'Coming Bernie.' Inevitably, a certain amount of stress began to seep into the partnership. Yet, away from business they remained friends with Fred and Jean often joining Bernie and Ivy for dinners, house parties and even picnics; and Bernie and Ivy would sometimes babysit for the Comptons' three children. But the pace of work – Bernie's pace – was making Fred ill. Eventually, Bernie became aware of his partner's suffering and encouraged him to 'go home to bed'. Bernie later visited Fred at his home and suggested an extended convalescence involving a change of scenery: 'Go off to the South of France, take as long as you like.'

Fred was apprehensive, but at the same time could not envisage the partnership continuing. 'I had a feeling that if I went away I'd lose my business,' he recalls, 'so I asked Bernard if he would like to buy me out.' Quick as a flash Bernie made a counter offer: 'Well, actually Fred, I was thinking – how would you like to buy the business from me?' 'So like Bernard,' Compton reflects with humour. Bernie, of course, bought Fred's interest in the partnership: 'Fifty per cent transferred on a handshake' in 1955. Fred reverted to his preferred business, the selling of cars, and soon opened new premises in Beckenham, South London, specialising in Hillmans. To this day, Fred Compton maintains: 'Bernard was very fair.' With an instinct always attuned to expansion, Bernie also bought Harcourt Motor Cycles from his former employer, Les Cocker. At Harcourt he reached out to an even wider market by featuring for sale motorcycles with sidecars. Bexleyheath was now well and truly becoming Bernie's turf, and the harvest of money – 'plenty', with obsessive cultivation – was continuously produced. 'I can't put a number on it. But I was earning good because I was always wheeling and dealing,' says Bernie.

The trappings of wealth were not flaunted by Bernie, but they were nonetheless agreeable. The year before his marriage to Ivy Bamford he had bought a house in Bexleyheath's Pickford Close. It was a fairly ordinary semi-detached home, built in the 1930s in a quiet cul-de-sac. However, Bernie soon transformed the property with new paintwork, bathrooms and an entirely new kitchen. What we consider common practice today was, in the early Fifties, extravagant nonsense. Within a few years he gave the house to his parents and moved into an upmarket home on Danson Road described as 'one of the nicest roads' in the Bexley area. Unlike her husband, 'Ivy was not ambitious and not interested in money,' says Bernie, and she was content to let him mastermind the home refurbishments. At Danson Road he again indulged in his practice of clearing out and replacing anew, enhancing the home's Art Deco character. Then in 1956 the couple moved to a grand five-bedroomed, mock Tudor home on Parkwood Road in the village of Bexley; the house was modestly named 'Barn Cottage'. Bernie, just twenty-six, had bought the house from Peter Wardman, said to be 'a very brash car dealer'. A team of interior designers were employed to create a cottagey Tudor ideal, with an 'English Rose' kitchen, oak beams galore and solid New England colonial furniture specially imported from Boston. All electrical leads were concealed as were pipes and plumbing fittings – creating occasional nightmares for workers called in to make a repair. But the presentation was, as usual, flawless. With the Tudorisation complete, Bernie then added a room on stilts to accommodate his snooker table. To achieve this 'out-of-character' addition, it had been necessary to charm a recalcitrant female neighbour out of her objections.

The road cars owned by Bernie followed a similar upwardly mobile pattern. Before his marriage he drove a Morgan three-wheeler. When he married Ivy he was driving an Austin-Healey – occasionally racing around Bexleyheath plying the power of his sports car against the motorcycles driven by young Brian Whitehouse and a group of his friends – according to Brian. 'Not true,' says Bernie. The Austin-Healey, though much admired, was traded for a silver-coloured, 'gull-wing' Mercedes 300SL, with perhaps a few vehicles in between, but not long after the move to Barn Cottage, Bernie was well remembered around Bexley driving his 'gull-wing'. One morning, according to several accounts, he had driven from Barn Cottage at considerable speed, lost control of the vehicle on a congested Bexley street and rammed it into the front of a double-decker bus, where it became embedded. The bus suffered a broken axle, and Bernie came away with a painful arm.

Racing driver Bill Whitehouse also owned a 300SL that was identical to Bernie's, a fact that was well-known in the community. So when Bernie overheard onlookers commenting: 'That's Whitehouse's car, it's his car, that's Whitehouse's,' he instantly conceived a neat payback for Bill's earlier Brands Hatch prank. 'Definitely,' shouted Bernie above the rest. 'That's Bill Whitehouse's car, mad he is... he drives too fast!' Having thus unloaded the blame while evening the score, he returned home to nurse the arm, which he said had been 'killing him'. Later that day when Bill Whitehouse learned that his gull-wing Mercedes had somehow crashed into a bus he rushed to the garage where he had left the car and was much relieved – though perplexed – to find it still intact. With the joke repaid, Bernie retrieved his damaged Mercedes and sent it on to Germany for reassembly. When the car was – by all appearances – restored to perfection, he deftly sold it to his friend John Young.

Bill Whitehouse was more amused than offended by the prank and the forty-something six-foot three-inch racing driver/dealer and the twenty-six-year-old, five-foot three-ish ex-racing driver/dealer remained close friends. Besides business and racing they shared an interest – bordering on an addiction – in gambling. 'See two flies crawling up a wall and Bernie would bet on them,' says John Coombs. Monopoly, gin rummy, dog racing, there was always a wager and Bernie's brain, clickety-click was always calculating the odds. One evening when Bill was returning home from his garage with the day's takings in a bank bag tucked under his arm, Bernie caught up with him and suggested that they gamble the night away. 'How much are you going to gamble for?' said Bill. 'Well, that'll do!' answered Bernie snatching the bag full of money. Many a long night was spent gambling at the Whitehouses in Wilmington near Dartford, or gathered round the small roulette table that was carted around from drawing room to drawing room.

Another eager participant at the tables was Sidney Young, who owned a shop specialising in televisions and other electrical goods just down the road from Compton &

Ecclestone. In fact, the favoured game with Mr Young was 'pitch and toss', which involved two half-crown coins placed on the finger, one tails up, one heads up. The bet was usually £5. The coins would then be tossed, with the winner's coins being those that turned up heads. The gambling would continue for hours on end, with the total in winnings often amounting to hundreds of pounds. Sometimes Sidney Young, with his wife Violet, and the Ecclestones would fly down to Nice for a few days of 'chemin de fer' and roulette in the Casino. They liked to stay at the Royal Hotel overlooking the Promenade des Anglais. Britain, at the time, enforced severe restrictions on the amount of currency that could be taken out of the country, which would have left the gamblers short of betting funds, so an 'arrangement' was set up days before their departure for Nice. The arrangement was known as 'Peter and Paul', working under a respectable title – the Riviera Vacation Service. A letter from the company would be received confirming the date and time of arrival. Upon the couples' arrival in Nice, 'Peter' would meet them and hand over as much cash as they required. When they returned to England that sum plus a commission would then be paid to 'Paul'.

Years later rumours among the Young family suggested that Bernie fell out with Sidney over a dispute involving £5 in a game of pitch and toss. Sidney's son, Alan Young, disregards this tittle-tattle: 'I am loyal to Bernard because if my parents had not known him, my father would not have enjoyed the last nine years of his life. He would not have gone to Nice and he would not have done the things Bernie encouraged him to do.' Bernie too was appreciative of the friendship. For the Youngs' twenty-fifth wedding anniversary Bernie gave them a silver fruit bowl, and years later, when Violet Young celebrated her seventieth birthday, Bernie telephoned with his congratulations.

Get-togethers with other couples always included Ivy. Bernie would take her to all the motor racing dinners and dances held at London's grand hotels such as the Grosvenor House, Park Lane, and the Dorchester and also to Crockfords, one of the city's most exclusive casinos. The couple enjoyed variety shows at the Palladium and the big-band music of Ted Heath. Outside London, Bernie and Ivy frequented the Beaverwood Club in Chislehurst, Kent, where the cuisine was reputedly 'better than average' though, perhaps more importantly, the club offered gambling that went on until four o'clock in the morning. During Bexleyheath social gatherings, Bernie's sense of humour, for the most part light-hearted, could occasionally become a little trying. One friend remembers a particular dinner party during which he politely offered round a bowl of nuts. When he came to Bernie, 'he'd go "bang" and knock the nuts right up in the air, then walk away saying, "what on earth have you done that for?" Sometimes Bernard would drive you mad, drive you mad.' But, always generous, Bernie liked to buy gifts for Ivy, including expensive shoes with stiletto heels – the latest fashion.

In 1955 the couple celebrated the birth of their daughter, Deborah Ann, born at Bexley Maternity Hospital. Bernie was elated, buying Debbie, as she became known, armfuls of toys and the biggest and best pram that Bexleyheath had to offer. Her room was decorated like a fairy-tale with many of the furnishings inscribed with her name. When Debbie was old enough to walk Bernie had a playhouse made for her in the garden at Barn Cottage, complete with furniture, miniature kitchen equipment, and even a chimney sprouting from the tiled roof. He also encouraged Debbie, when still very young, to share his enthusiasm for motorsport, while showing her off, beautifully dressed, around the paddock at Brands Hatch. Bernie, throughout his life would take an interest in children, his own and others, and still delights in their company.

Barn Cottage, however, was not a haven of perpetual joy. Ivy had to contend with a husband whose need for success was unrelenting, who worked six days a week and longer, and who could not tolerate imperfection. During Deborah's christening party Ivy accidentally broke one of their rather special cocktail glasses and, terrified that Bernie would discover the breakage, she swiftly hid the fragments. At the first opportunity she bought a replacement. When she dropped a pot, marking the vitreous enamel sink in the 'English Rose' kitchen, she telephoned friends pleading for support against Bernie's rage.

'I like to see things done properly,' says Bernie. 'If that's being a perfectionist, then I'm a perfectionist. If things aren't being done properly I put them right. As you grow older you get more mellow. But it's frustrating if you can't do anything about it. It's still upsetting when things could be done and people aren't bothered. I think that's what upsets me more, the fact that things could be done better and people don't bother about it.' He pauses for a moment, then adds: 'I strive to get things better, but if somebody can prove me wrong I don't battle against the odds. I mean I can sit in a meeting and voice my opinion, and if people can prove I'm wrong, I normally say: "I was joking, [laughs] I was just testing you". I'm happy to change.'

Commenting on Bernie's mood swings, a motor racing associate says: 'He's a split personality. Sometimes he can be so nice, so polite, so kind and then when he gets upset you don't realise what's hit you.' But Deborah, recalling her childhood and the Ecclestone family life, remembers only her father's kindness: 'he had no nasty temper.' Christmas festivities, however, always put him out of sorts: 'He hated Christmas and would be in a bad mood because he couldn't go to work and because everything was closed.'

In August 1956 Bernie acquired Hill's Garage, a Mercedes agency about a quarter of a mile from Compton & Ecclestone. He was now ready to throw himself headlong into the sale of automobiles. So much so that nineteen months later he bought another car company, James Spencer Ltd, from owner Jimmy Spencer. Hill's Garage then became James Spencer (Bexleyheath) Ltd. Jimmy Spencer, described as 'a live wire' was made a director of the company, but appears to have fallen out with Bernie, after which Sidney Ecclestone, Bernie's father, was given the directorship. While keeping the name 'James Spencer' over the entrance, Bernie virtually reconstructed the garage showroom premises. All the surfaces became sparkling white, even inside the garage itself where doors were fitted with washable handplates. An elegant spiral staircase ('Bernie always liked fancy stairs,' recalls Sidney Young's son Alan) graced the showroom with his glass-enclosed office above, looking down over his new domain. The showroom, featuring Austins and MGs – Bernie was the distributor for Kent – and a variety of second-hand cars, was the talk of Bexleyheath.

Bernie usually kept to his office, shackled to the telephone, buying cars – countless cars – on description. He never consulted a dealers' handbook on market values as all the figures he needed were stored in his brain. When the cars arrived, if they resembled the descriptions given over the telephone he bought them. Sometimes, of course, they came with a few quirks. Alan Young remembers buying a red Ford Corsair from Bernie. While driving the car from the showroom a pedal fell off. When he complained, he was consoled with, 'don't worry, you'll be all right, now away you go', and was sent round to the garage where it was screwed back on.

While Bernie tended to stay upstairs in his office, Sidney Ecclestone was downstairs greeting customers and, between customers, keeping the white showroom spotless. Bernie's friends were fond of Sidney and liked to joke with him: 'See that Sid, see that bit of dirt over there – oh dear, you'd better get rid of that or there'll be trouble!' Bernie's friends called Sidney 'Eyes' – Bernie's eyes. With his down-to-earth working man's attitude towards life, Sidney Ecclestone was thought to be a little in awe of his son. He enjoyed 'ordinary chat' without broadcasting information, and was thus suited to 'keeping an eye on the cars and on the people – finding out what they were up to'. Later Bernie employed the eyes of Les Underwood, 'his right-hand man'. Les, recalls dealer/driver John Young, 'looked around and made sure everything was OK', then he would take up his station beneath a canopy at the foot of the stairs, occasionally signalling to the 'master' when a deal looked imminent. Bernie responded by descending the stairs.

Les Underwood was 'occasionally' joined in his surveillance by Jack 'Spot' Comer's men who were seen lingering about

Bernie's showroom. 'The king of the underworld', Jack Spot was one of the most powerful criminals in 1950s Britain. He came from a gang called the 'Yiddishers' in London's East End and began his career opposing Sir Oswald Mosley's Blackshirts in the famous battle of Cable Street on 4 October 1936. Thereafter he added gambling rackets and robbery to his repertoire. Interestingly, the son of Oswald Mosley – Max – would later come to play a major role in Bernie's life. Today, a few of Bexleyheath's residents still speak with a kind of reverence in whispered tones, recalling the sombre, overcoated figures at the James Spencer showroom, like sentries on watch. The situation was not completely dissimilar to his schooldays when Bernie felt the need to gather bigger boys round him to protect his cake money. Now his money – and assets – had grown to the point that Bernie sometimes needed to hire professional protection.

For the members of the dealer/driver fraternity and anyone seriously interested in buying or selling cars, the hot-bed of business was Warren Street just off London's Tottenham Court Road. It was the trade market for cars, like Covent Garden was for fruit or Hatton Gardens for diamonds. Surrounding streets such as Fitzroy Street and Great Portland Street made up the Warren Street complex. 'Several of the traders were pre-war, Brooklands [racing circuit] people,' says former racing driver Roy Salvadori, who himself bought cars at Warren Street; Roy's brother, 'Ozzi', worked there 'five days a week selling quality cars with mileage below 10,000, if possible,' Roy recalls. 'Most of the traders started small, but many of them became involved in the biggest franchises in London.' Every day a minimum of 100 cars were sold in Warren Street and then 're-traded' in locations around the country; a den of fast deals, it was not for the faint-hearted. John Young remembers that 'you had to be pretty hairy-chested' to wheel and deal in Warren Street. This was the place where all the 'naughtiness and niceness' of trading in cars existed, a sort of open-air used-car market where people in the motor trade could 'go and park and start doing business with each other'. So that he could toughen up on trading skills, John Young had to endure a course of Warren Street boot camp before being allowed to join the family business, Rose & Young, an established Mercedes dealership in Streatham, south London.

It was also the natural habitat for the shadiest of the shady – 'lots of men in big coats,' says John. Men such as racketeer Stanley Setty who had traded in stolen cars until he trod too heavily on the toes of his competitors. In 1950 Setty's body was thrown – in bullet-riddled chunks – from a private aeroplane flying over Essex and the English Channel. Brian Donald Hume, a training pilot, confessed to the murder, but not until 1958. 'Donald Hume was a nutcase, I always remember Donald Hume,' says former Warren Street trader Les Lilly, adding: 'He was a dog of all dogs, he was the scum of the earth.' Setty, on the other hand, 'was a very nice man, and his cheques were good, he wasn't a rogue.' Les has his own view on why Hume killed Setty: 'Because he couldn't con him out of money.' Fred Compton says 'you just learned who to avoid', adding there were also 'legit dealers with small showrooms'. He remembers haggling over a purchase with one such dealer when three 'heavies' entered the office, shoved the dealer up against a wall, and then stuffed a wad of paper into his mouth. 'You put that through again and you'll never leave here!' They threatened, and then left. The wad of paper was a writ. It seems the thugs, or whomever they represented, owed the dealer money. 'You just didn't talk to the bad chaps,' says Fred. 'There were one or two scumbags,' adds Les Lilly, agreeing that 'there were people you wouldn't talk to. Ever heard of an organisation called the Mafioso? It was like that, everybody knew who was who. But I will tell you something, some of the straightest people you could deal with were in Warren Street. There were a few people there you could lay your life down for – definitely, absolutely.'

Bernie's introduction to Warren Street was through a friend from Dartford, Derek Wheeler who, Roy says, 'had worked in a petrol station, but was soon attracted to the hustle and bustle of Warren Street.' An ebullient, energetic individual, Derek convinced Les Lilly to take him on as 'co-director'. He mixed with ease among other traders, he was well-liked, and if you needed someone to vouch for you, Derek Wheeler was a good choice. 'Derek knew everybody,' says Les, with whom he sold cars that were 'not top of the range, the middle – Mercedes, BMW – that sort of thing'. To buy cars on Warren Street you had to be 'known', another dealer had to vouch for you, or as Les Lilly says 'you had to get into bed with someone who was known enough, someone who could guarantee your cheque. We were pretty shrewd operators, too shrewd for anybody that thought they could get away with giving us a dud cheque... if you weren't trusted you would have to bring cash; no bankers' orders, it's gotta be cash. There was a lot of what you call counterfeiting... you had to be trusted, you had to be known. When Bernie first came into Warren Street people were worried about him, he wasn't known. But then he was able to say "look, ask Derek Wheeler or Les Lilly to guarantee my cheque and you'll find that it will be all right", and that's what we used to do... and soon he was choosing who he dealt with and he became known enough to be known as Bernard Ecclestone.'

After that, Bernie was 'in' – he would have his share of the 100-a-day used cars and sell them on for a nice profit. Les Lilly liked him. 'He was confident, yes confident – not to the point of being brash, but he was an old head on young shoulders. I had no doubts about him at all. I always thought he would be a fella who would go somewhere.' For those who wanted to get ahead but lacked the financial wherewithal, there was an additional – and apparently accepted – method of advancement. Another former dealer explains: 'Sometimes if you didn't have much money, you bought the car on a cheque or your word, sold it on, and then you were covered for the earlier debt. Everything was well, providing you didn't bounce a cheque. There was the odd occasion when a villain got amongst us.'

So Bernie's second-hand car business grew from getting 'known' and having his 'cheques vouched for', to walking up and down Warren Street with confidence, talking and dealing like – or better than – the other 'shrewd operators'.

Compton & Ecclestone, Hill's Garage and James Spencer Ltd were the inevitable rewards for conquering this riveting hub of Britain's second-hand car sales. The conquest was aided by the powerful force of his determination coupled with the street knowledge he had learned in Dartford. It was about 'being sharp and feeling sharp, it's thinking on your feet,' says Les Lilly, 'that was the foundation. If you've done business and been successful in Warren Street, how you deal with people in the future becomes easier; wherever you go after that – it's easy.'

Bernie became so successful, and 'known', at Warren Street that he was given a nickname, 'the whippet' – sleek, slim and fast, very, very fast, to the point of being daunting. Even 'the hard-bitten dealers were terrified of Bernard,' recalls John Young, who physically cringes at the mention of Warren Street, then smiles remembering the times he had been outsmarted by his friend. 'If I bought a car from Bernie I always paid more than I should have done,' John says. 'If I sold him a car I always got less than I should have done.' At some point John sold Bernie a Bentley that Bernie sold on to a racing driver. The car, after a lapse of some months, came back into Bernie's possession and he then sold the Bentley back to John Young. But then within the fraternity cars would often 'go around in circles' from one member to another. Roy Salvadori, who owned an Alfa Romeo dealership in Cobham, Surrey, remembers Bernie coming into the showroom, and after a few minutes' chit-chat saying:

'Well, what are you doing here Roy?'

'We sell cars.'

'All those cars for sale?'

'You bloody well know they are, what's going on Bernard?'

'All those cars Salv, you want to sell them I suppose?'

'Yes!'

'I'll give you £52,000 for the lot.'

Roy was tempted, and tried to do a rapid calculation while Bernie feigned impatience: 'Well, if you don't sell cars…'

'Of course, you know I'm selling cars,' responded Roy, somewhat distracted with mental arithmetic. Bernie got more impatient: 'Do you want a cheque?' For an instant, Roy thought that perhaps Bernie had at last slipped up, but then experience took over and he realised that Bernie had probably arrived at the showroom about ten minutes earlier, and before entering had glanced through the window and 'got it all figured out'. *Pressure applied while the other party is speedily reckoning* is one of Bernie's favourite techniques, or as an associate who knew them both put it: 'Roy Salvadori could walk into a showroom and put a value on every car, but Bernie could walk into the same showroom and give you the total'. Roy then decided to keep his Alfas, and later, with pencil and paper in hand, determined that had he done the deal, 'I would have been 1,500 quid adrift.'

In a selling position, however, Bernie had all the time in the world. John Coombs, who bought a few cars from Bernie, remembers the strategy of the waiting game: 'Bernie would never say what he wanted for an article,' just 'what would you offer?' Whatever was offered, Bernie would of course consider the figure absurd. The matter would then be forgotten for six months or even two years, until at a seemingly opportune moment negotiations resumed.

'Bernie, that car, have you still got it?'

'Yes, have you come to your senses, you want to give a good price now?'

'Well, what do you want for it now?'

'The price has gone up…'

But the type of deal Bernie preferred above all others was a part-exchange, known in the trade as a 'chop'. He avoided parting with money by 'unloading something he'd got and changed it round that way'. That is, he exchanged a slow-selling car for one that might be more attractive to buyers. To chop successfully, however, it was necessary to be ultra shrewd at valuing cars: paying too much for the part-exchange meant losing money and until the part-exchange was sold there was no profit. To Bernie, 'who knew everything there was to know about negotiating', it was child's play. He even took a chop on Barn Cottage – complete with its Boston, Massachusetts, furniture. In exchange he received a house on Bexley's Parkhill Road, which he soon refurbished – house and garden – and sold to a Mike Chapman. Mike would prove to be the ultimate customer for, along with the house, Bernie sold him a car to fit in the garage, and then proceeded to sell him Jennings. Once a Twenties-era department store, with toys displayed alongside draper's goods, Bernie had acquired the property some months earlier and transformed it into a commodious space. Under Mike Chapman, Jennings was reborn as Mike's Bargain Bazaar.

Several of Britain's racing drivers and car dealers along with others involved in motors and in motorsport looked forward with anticipation to Cliff Davis's 'men only' Christmas parties. A racing driver, Davis had raced a Maserati against Bernie's Cooper at Thruxton in August 1953; both failed to finish. Away from the circuit Cliff Davis 'drank like a fish and enjoyed life' in the company of other racing drivers, among them David Blakely who was murdered, in 1955, by Ruth Ellis; she was later hanged for the crime. Cliff Davis was also a dealer with a showroom in Shepherds Bush where he specialised in American big-finned, big-engined cars; his attitude to entertaining was big too. Extraordinary cabarets featured in his Christmas parties with female entertainers stripping down to dance on tabletops, though one – swathed in snakes – kept to her outerwear. Racing driver Graham Hill was a regular at these frolics. Emboldened with alcohol he liked to join the entertainers performing his 'famous striptease act', but upon mounting a table, it gave way – to either his weight or exertions – and he completed the routine by gingerly picking shards of wine glass from his leg.

Bernie was also a regular and, says Tim Parnell, 'would turn up looking like the big chief.' In fact, he was usually wearing dark glasses, no matter what the hour, and affected Italian casualness in dress with his suit jacket draped over his shoulders like a cape. Always, according to Tim, 'he was seated at the head table.' Bernie says that he 'never went to Cliff Davis's parties', then adds: 'It was different in the Cliff Davis days, everything different, Salvadori and those people, they were a different breed... These things don't happen today. Nothing is like it was, people move on – good or bad – there have just been big changes. If I went back to those days now, I don't know how I'd find it. I'd probably find it boring. There's been some progress since then, and you change as things change.'

With fewer weekends devoted to motor racing, Bernie decided to take up flying; the need to be propelled by machines was, it seems, omnipresent. Bernie was a natural in control of a joystick and after only a few lessons at Rochester in Kent handled the training captain's aircraft with ease. John Young remembers joining captain and student for one of the more advanced lessons. It began steadily enough, but then Bernie, behind the controls, decided to show off and threw the plane into a series of loop-the-loops, and other daredevil contortions. Upon landing John was effusive in his expressions of joy considering his green and shattered condition. Bernie, unmoved, calmly drove his friend back to London at breakneck speed. Eventually Bernie took his pilot's licence exam, but failed – not due to technique, but to eyesight. 'I never got a pilot's licence because I couldn't see, which was a prerequisite,' says Bernie. The aviation licensing authorities were more scrupulous than those who then governed the licensing of racing drivers. In any event Bernie would soon employ pilots to operate his aircraft for him. In 1961 he decided to purchase a six-seater aeroplane from the General Electric Company and took fellow dealer Ray Morris along for a test flight at Biggin Hill, also in Kent. The drive to the airport in Bernie's Sunbeam Rapier was enough to make Ray 'feel sick' but then on the plane Bernie instructed the pilot to 'put it through its paces'. Ray was finished: 'I would have been better off dead.'

Back on the ground a new diversion and money-making opportunity beckoned: 'Blood and Thunder', or stock-car racing, the madcap brand of motorsport recently imported from America. In hotrods clad as street cars, drivers banged their way around speedway ovals with a conscious 'disregard for other people's property', says Bernie who raced at West Ham and Catford near London, and at a track in Essex. He usually drove Fords, with the aim of having a clear run, but inevitably the racing became a contact sport with 'other car dealers getting a bit rough' and 'trying to push him' and each other off the track; racing drivers Graham Hill and Jim Russell were among them. Stirling Moss would also have a go at 'stox' before the sport gave way in the Sixties to monster specials and carnival gimmicks. But before that Bernie, together with racing driver Dave Walker, experimented with stock-car promotion at Neath, in South Wales, where Dave had bought waste land and turned it into a track. Unfortunately, they 'used local people for the gate' who, having gathered in all the takings, suddenly vanished. It was better to be tucked behind the steering wheel of a Ford dodging souped-up V8s; and Bernie did, on occasion, emerge unscathed. The Youngs, father and son, both enjoyed the breathtaking spectacle and carnage of stock-car racing, but they were confounded when a blue Ford, driven in the race by Bernie, came away from the mayhem looking 'immaculate' and polished, and absolutely James Spencer showroom perfect.

On Wednesday nights, if he wasn't at the Crayford dog track, Bernie enjoyed the company of family and friends watching the whacks and cracks of the sport that still encourages fisticuffs – ice hockey. The matches took place on the ice rink at Streatham High Street in South London. Bernie's sister Marian was sometimes there, along with Sidney Ecclestone, John Young, Bill and Brian Whitehouse and another dealer-driver, 'Pop' Lewis-Evans and his racing driver son, Stuart, whose physique was amost identical to Bernie's; a reason, perhaps, for the bond that existed between them. 'Pop' Lewis-Evans, who owned a Vauxhall garage in Bexleyheath, had raced Cooper 500s with notable success as had his son, who with five seasons in Formula 3 was ready to expand his expertise by driving in Formula 1 races.

Bernie took on a managerial role assisting his fun-loving but unassuming friend with the negotiation of contracts and starting money: 'I used to look after things for him that he didn't do,' says Bernie, 'like contracts, he wasn't up to that.' Margaret Leckie, then Stuart's wife, finds Bernie's statement 'misleading', adding, 'Stuart previously had years of 500cc racing both in the UK and all over the Continent arranging his own starting money, transport and sponsorship with companies such as Shell, Dunlop, Lodge plugs etc.' What isn't in dispute is the fact that by 1956 Stuart Lewis-Evans was considered 'a rare talent' on the circuit, one whom Bernie – a man with an acute phobia of praise-giving – describes as 'a very good driver'; it doesn't get much better than that.

From August 1956 into the early months of 1957 Lewis-Evans drove Connaughts with success, including a second place at Brands Hatch and fourth at Monaco. He then signed with Ferrari to drive sports cars, finishing fifth overall at Le Mans. Ferrari had also held out the promise of a Grand Prix drive and in July at the French Grand Prix at Rouen, Stuart turned up expecting that promise to be fulfilled. He was disappointed. But not for long. As fate would have it, the Vanwall team was lacking not one but two drivers: Tony Brooks was recovering from injuries and Stirling Moss had been sent home with a severe sinus infection. Roy Salvadori was selected to drive one of the cars and, after an informal arrangement with Enzo Ferrari, it was agreed that Stuart Lewis-Evans would drive the spare car. Engine failure put both cars out of the race but the following month at Pescara Lewis-Evans finished fifth, and at Monza he put the Vanwall on pole. In 1958 he would go on to make a crucial contribution to Vanwall's success in securing the first Formula 1 Manufacturers' (later Constructors') World Championship. Bernie went to all of Stuart's races and, at the request of the team's owner, Tony Vandervell, organised the team's start money (for appearing on the grid) at each race; Vandervell had come to appreciate Bernie's expertise in negotiations. But otherwise Bernie kept himself to himself, standing at the back of the pit, quiet, but watching. 'You couldn't possibly have been less obtrusive than Bernie,' says Tony Brooks, 'but he never missed a thing that was going on... really soaking it all up.'

Winning the Constructors' championship was half of the Holy Grail for team owners; the other half was having in their stable a World Champion driver. These were, and are, the principles that justify their never-ending quest for financial backing. But regardless of championship status, motor racing has always been a gamble and in 1957 it swallowed another victim – the Connaught works team (Connaught Engineering). In 1955 at the Syracuse Grand Prix in Sicily Connaught had, with driver Tony Brooks, become the first British car to win a Formula 1 Grand Prix for thirty-two years. Yet, after seven seasons this well-respected team had folded, and during a three-day auction of Connaught's assets, on 17–19 September, Bernie bought two Formula 1 cars. He paid £1,950 and £2,100 for the two B-series cars, one of which, with a radical wedge-shaped body, was the so-called 'toothpaste tube'.

Bernie made no secret of the fact that his intention in buying the cars was to sell them on, and a profitable market at the time existed in New Zealand. So during the winter of 1957–8, Bernie put his cars on show by entering them in the Tasman series. At Ardmore in New Zealand, one of the Connaughts was driven by Roy Salvadori and the other by Stuart Lewis-Evans. Roy finished the race in a valiant fifth place having been dogged throughout with an engine misfire, while Stuart's Connaught was eliminated due to loss of oil pressure. The victor on the day was Jack Brabham driving a 2-litre Cooper-Climax. Roy returned to Britain but Stuart stayed on to compete in another event – unsuccessfully – and to carry out Bernie's instructions to sell the cars. Buyers were not hungry for these apparently fallible Connaughts, so Stuart was thrilled when he managed to negotiate an exchange: the cars for a stamp collection. Stuart could hardly contain himself when he telephoned Bernie with the wonderful news. But as soon as he was told about the nice 'foreign gentleman offering a stamp collection' the deal was 'scotched', and Stuart Lewis-Evans and the cars were summoned back home to England. Fed up with the performance of his Connaughts 'B.C. Ecclestone' himself attempted to qualify one of the cars for the Monaco Grand Prix of 18 May 1958. He had intended to give the drive to Paul Emery, but at the last moment changed his mind, saying: 'Get out of the way, I'll try.' Even so, the Connaught failed to qualify. What is more, that night Bernie sustained a savage blow from the roulette table at the casino where he promptly lost 'my start money for the cars!' There were more motor racing tears shed at the British Grand Prix where both Ivor Bueb and Jack Fairman qualified for the race although neither finished. Still, the Connaught experience wasn't entirely disappointing for Bernie; the cars eventually achieved a few respectable race results while along the way he had a bit of fun before achieving his earlier objective – selling them on.

The year of 1958 has been described as 'a golden year' for British racing cars. Of the year's ten championship events eight were won by British drivers, the other two went to Ferrari. But the season was also steeped in tragedy with the loss of Peter Collins, Luigi Musso, and – particularly distressing for Bernie – Stuart Lewis-Evans. At the Moroccan Grand Prix in Casablanca on 19 October, the race order after forty laps was Moss, Hawthorn, Hill, Bonnier and Lewis-Evans. Then, suddenly with only twenty-five minutes remaining in the race, Stuart crashed his Vanwall on the back leg of the circuit, sending torrents of black smoke skyward. He was alive but massively burned. Roy Salvadori who had also been driving in the race remembers: 'It was something so horrid it's not true [his overalls had caught fire and he ran away from the car]. If only he had rolled in the sand'. Stuart was flown back to England – via Paris – in an aeroplane chartered by Vanwall entrant Tony Vandervell; Bernie was with him.

In England, Stuart was admitted to the Queen Victoria Hospital in East Grinstead, Sussex, made famous by plastic surgeon Sir Archibald McIndoe and his burned fighter-pilot patients, the 'Guinea Pigs'. But even the best medical and surgical expertise was not enough to save him. On 25 October 1958 Stuart Lewis-Evans, only twenty-eight years old, died. He left a widow, Margaret, and two children. Bernie, who would turn twenty-eight five days later, was stunned with grief; all his Bexleyheath friends still remark on the extent of his sadness. 'Stuart was sent back in the plane too early,' says Bernie, reflecting on the tragedy. One can only imagine what 'Pop' Lewis-Evans suffered who, 'ever the gentleman, in his Rolls-Royce' continued to attend every Silverstone Grand Prix until his own death a few years ago. For Margaret and her children the tragedy was compounded by the news that there would be no financial compensation for their loss: 'When Stuart died we were told that the contract with Vanwall was unsigned as Ferrari had not officially released him. He was only insured by Ferrari for driving their own cars. I found, as Stirling Moss discovered several years later when he had his bad crash, you fall between two stools and end up with no insurance cover at all.'

For Bernie, the loss of Stuart came hard upon the pain of losing his old friend 'Big Bill' Whitehouse, who the previous year had died from injuries suffered during a race at Rheims in France; he had been driving a streamlined Cooper. Bill's son, Brian Whitehouse, then a novice at wheeling and dealing in cars, was left with the business. Bernie gave him tuition in 'learning the trade', as Brian remembered: 'Bernard was the man, I mean, I used to pick up the phone and he would value anything I wanted… you see there had never been a learning curve with Bernard, he was right there, knew it all, knew all the numbers. Wonderful to me he was. If you were to sum up Bernard, he's somebody I could always go to if I had a problem or if I ever needed anything.' Brian Whitehouse became a multi-millionaire, owning several showrooms that made up one of the largest dealerships in Britain.

While all the members of the driver/dealer fraternity agree that 'Bernie's as good as his word' and 'straight', Roy Salvadori, commenting on Bernie deals, adds: 'As sure as eggs are eggs you suddenly wind up realising it was a deal you shouldn't have done!'

CHAPTER 4

CARS FOR STARZ

*W*ork is salvation. This is a banner slogan that Bernie has expropriated from the Salvation Army and made his own. Just as he had coaxed young Brian Whitehouse out of the doldrums with a hefty dose of wheeling and dealing, Bernie soothed his own aches with a continuous application of the same faithful remedy. When his sales technique became – even for Bernie – inordinately aggressive, turnover was being hurled at emotional discomfort. 'When Stuart died I was pretty upset,' says Bernie. 'I just went off the scene [motor racing] and cracked away at business – anything to do with cars.' But he would never actually address the cause of his pain nor would he ask for help; Bernie keeps his personal troubles to himself. Though in recent years he has been known to air his woes over the telephone to a close friend, it is only a brief respite. He soon immerses himself in work again, ultra-tenacious, and eventually his cheerfulness returns. As the Sixties approached, shifting cars in volume not only lifted his spirits but was also prudent – the demand for motorcycles was showing hints of decline.

The producers of motorcycles in Britain had failed to notice the tell-tale signs when Japanese engineers began turning up to observe the Isle of Man Tourist Trophy, a tough road race and a thorough testing ground. British managers then became neglectful when they should have been fine-tuning their business practices, and their neglect contributed to industrial unrest and massive strikes. This at a time when British racing cars were on the ascendant and road cars were becoming more plentiful. In 1957 Prime Minister Harold

Macmillan had declared to the nation, 'most of our people have never had it so good', and with new-found wealth car ownership in the Sixties would double to twelve million vehicles. Motorcycles, not surprisingly, were going out of fashion. Conditions were crying out for sharp new leaders to answer the challenges facing the motorcycle manufacturing industry, and forward they came like bees buzzing around the irresistible post-war honey pot. But, of course, the buzz didn't come from British manufacturers, those glory days had been allowed to slip away. First on the scene was Honda, followed by Suzuki, Yamaha and Kawasaki.

The turning point occurred in the mid-Sixties, but back in September 1959, Bernie knew – with unerring intuition – that while the market still appeared to be strong it was time to sell his Compton & Ecclestone motorcycle business. Interestingly, he held a redemption on the lease, meaning that if a future owner got into financial difficulties and could not fulfil his or her obligation, Compton & Ecclestone would revert to Bernie. Enter car dealers Victor White, Harold O'Connor and John Croker. Harold, 'a good North Country dealer, one of the chaps' on Warren Street and, to a lesser extent, Victor, were friends of Bernie's. Together they had been involved in 'two or three all-night sessions buying, selling and swapping twenty to thirty cars with hooligans up north'. The deals were 'complex' says Bernie, but not 'shady' – Bernie is sensitive about his business reputation.

When he decided to sell Compton & Ecclestone, Victor and Harold introduced him to John Croker. A businessman who believed in diversification, Croker dealt in washing machines imported from Italy as well as cars and owned a hire-purchase company. But then his financial acumen apparently dissolved, for only two months after acquiring the business from Bernie, the lease on Compton & Ecclestone was resold to their mutual friends Victor White and Harold O'Connor. The latter, described as a 'mug punter', is not favourably remembered in Bexleyheath, being blamed – rightly or wrongly – for 'making a bit of a mess-up' of the business. According to Bernie, Victor was the partner 'who didn't do much'. Either way, the result was the same: Compton & Ecclestone landed once more in Bernie's hands. Finally, in 1961, Bernie leased the premises to Ray Morris, who dispensed with the motorcycles and used the showroom for selling cars; Compton & Ecclestone had now come full circle.

Harcourt Motor Cycles, where Bernie had specialised in motorcycles with sidecars, was acquired by car dealer Bobby Rowe. Bobby also raced motorcycles, and at the end of 1959 asked Bernie to sponsor him for the coming racing season. Bernie provided a Norton on which, Bobby says, 'we'd done quite well'. Bernie also negotiated the starting money together with money from the Shell Oil Company totalling £200, which, in Bobby's estimation, was 'a fortune'. In addition, Bernie negotiated the terms at Brands Hatch and at such circuits as Silverstone, Aintree, Thruxton, Snetterton and Crystal Palace, plus circuits in Ireland and north-west England. It was like renewing the raptures of first love; motorcycling would always tug on Bernie's heart. Thrilling, fast and piquant with the unexpected – the perfect potion. Add the chess-play of negotiations along with a potential for gain and the allure package is complete. Before Bobby Rowe, Bernie's Norton was 'given a good ride' by Laurence Flury during the 1959 season. 'We ran factory Nortons,' Bernie points out, 'and we had a guy called Steve Lancefield who was the best tuner there was.'

While in his mid-twenties Flury had become friends with fatherly Sidney ('Pop') Ecclestone at Seagers in Dartford, the engineering works/foundry where they had both been employed. Flury spent his weekends racing motorcycles around Brands Hatch, Crystal Palace, Oulton Park and elsewhere, but he needed sponsorship to continue. So Sidney played matchmaker between aspiring motorcyclist and cash-load by introducing Flury to his son. Bernie provided the Norton, paid all expenses and made certain that his new protégé was properly kitted out with a smart set of black racing leathers – which he wears to this day at vintage events. The arrangement suited both in that they 'got on all right', and Flury recognised in Bernie 'an efficient sort of person who knew what he wanted and went about getting it'. Bernie attended most of Flury's races and on display today amongst his vehicle collection housed at Biggin Hill in Kent – 'the best collection of front-engine F1 cars from the Fifties,' says Bernie – is a motorcycle that Laurence Flury once rode to victory.

With the motorcycle industry heading for a slump, Bernie had naturally been wise to get out, but he could still steal a few hours of pleasure trackside; sponsoring a Lawrence Flury or a Bobby Rowe was a good excuse. But if the circuit resembled a farmyard deep in slurry, the mood would be squelched by the threat to Bernie's well-polished Italian moccasins. This was the condition of a circuit where Bobby had mounted the Norton, regardless of heavy rain, and was about to race. Perched on tiptoes in an attempt to rise above muck, Bernie could no longer bear it: 'I'm going,' he said, and left without a backward glance. Bobby won the race. He also won the Newcomer's Award at the Isle of Man in 1960, and offered to put the trophy in the showroom window of James Spencer Limited. Bernie was touched, but felt that it properly belonged to the rider: 'No, no, you keep it.'

One night, a few years later, Bobby Rowe was passing James Spencer Limited and was dumbfounded by what he saw. The showpiece of Bexleyheath had, earlier that evening, burned to ashes. Firemen were still dousing down a few lingering flames within the blackened shell of the showroom, but all was lost – cars, showroom, spiral staircase – everything. Nevertheless by ten o'clock the next morning, 'and don't think I'm exaggerating', Bobby was even more amazed to find that all the burnt-out cars and the rubble had been cleared away. The site of James Spencer Limited was as clean as a remote island beach upon which a cabin-like office had been set up, telephone lines installed and functioning, and Bernie was – as ever – back in business. What Bobby Rowe is still unable to fathom is the extent of Bernie's determination – which is boundless. *I will not be stopped no matter what* is a policy that he implements, without hesitation, whenever necessary. The cause of the fire was unknown, but the building had been insured. Soon a new garage showroom was shimmering with fresh white paint enhancing its sleek – almost shrugging – contemporary style, 'standing free like a palace' in comparison to the area's typical Thirties shopfronts.

Having by now been in the car-selling business for more than ten years, Bernie knew that he would be ignoring a ready market if he didn't offer finance for his customers 'on site at the showroom'. Accordingly, in March 1961 he formed a hire-purchase company called Arvin Securities based at James Spencer (Bexleyheath) Limited. Bernie's friends were amused by the name of the company thinking he had chosen it as a play on 'Alvin' of the novelty 'Singing Chipmunks' fame. Always the prankster, Alvin spoiled the cartoon group's little ditties by singing his part either out of tune or too late. It is perhaps more amusing that the address given to James Spencer (Bexleyheath) Limited was Arvin House. In 1968 Bernie set up a similar company, Arvin Credit Facilities. Roy Salvadori remembers Bernie's hire-purchase company: 'I was involved with a hire purchase company so I knew all about it and I must say he had all the things set out correctly, all the searches, all the things you have to do when you take a client on HP... I mean you'd go in there and there was nothing that he couldn't tie up'. Ask Bernie about Arvin and he can't resist teasing: 'We stole the cars, clocked them, changed the numbers and sold them on using our own finance company.' On a more serious note he admits that 'some people said that I clocked cars. But what actually happened was I lent a car to another dealer to sell and he couldn't sell it. So the car was returned, clocked. Someone reported it to the Weights and Measures people, who then sent their inspector to have a look. I told him that we were busy clocking cars all the time and that if we stopped we'd be putting people out of work. He was not amused. Anyway, we went to court and proved that another dealer had borrowed the car and pleaded that when it came back it had been clocked, so we got off. Clocking in those days was a criminal offence.' It was also commonplace. More money could be made on cars that were clocked and indeed the practice was not limited to second-hand car dealers; many car owners disengaged the drive to the odometer and ran their cars, sometimes for years, without registering a single mile.

For some time Bernie had been toying with the prospect of acquiring a large dealership, the Strood Motor Company, near Rochester in Kent, which he finally bought in 1963. His burning ambition for success, measured by the accumulation of money, could be similarly assessed in large tangible assets – providing not only a sense of achievement and with it self-worth, but also power. Bernie's friend Bob Lobell recalls: 'Ever since the first minute I knew Bernie, in the Sixties, he had money, and he was in charge and in command, and everybody knew it.' The company – 'the distributorship of British Leyland cars for all of Kent,' Bernie points out – was certainly sizeable, but it was also lumbering in its practice, 'an old sort of Dickensian-run company' little changed since the Twenties; he knew that he could improve it. Here was the kind of project that Bernie liked to ponder at bedtime like a soothing lullaby. In his mind he husked the business of dead wood, revealing a streamlined, efficiently run organisation. Come morning, he applied himself to making the vision real; a mini industrial revolution was about to begin. Thirty-three years old but looking much younger, Bernie, the new jockey-sized, jacket-caped owner of the revered Strood Motor Company, turned up for his first official get-acquainted tour. While he was being conducted from department to department, Bernie avoided pleasantries and kept instead to a pertinent assessment of the chattels, including the workforce.

'What are they doing here?'

'They're part of an apprenticeship arrangement. We have to do that.'

'Well, what are *they* doing here?' He was pointing to a couple of young men playing darts.

'Same programme, we have to have them. We have to have so many, the government insists.'

'Well, I don't want them here any more. I want them out by the end of the month.'

'Oh, you can't do that!'

'Well, that's what I want done, and by the end of the month.' Bernie then gave his guide, the soon-to-be former managing director, a look that indicated the matter was forever closed. In another room an old man wearing greasy, paint-splattered overalls was painting a sign on the side of a van.

'How many jobs does he get?' asked Bernie.

'Well, he doesn't do a lot, just one now and again.'

'When did he get the last one?'

'Oh, well, ages ago.'

'We don't need all this, we need to get rid of it.'

It was 'like a dynamic whirlwind had gone through the place,' recalls car dealer Ray Morris, who had been with Bernie during the tour. 'He turned it round so quickly and made some money and then he sold it about a year later.'

As in his twenties, Bernie in his thirties had not lost his passion for gambling. But now the stakes were higher, and Bernie could afford to take a sizeable loss. At Crockfords, the opulent casino in London's Mayfair, Bernie rubbed shoulders with a galaxy of celebrities, multi-millionaires and heads of state. Among the glitterati was film director Otto Preminger with whom Bernie had struck up a gambling-related acquaintance. With films under his belt such as *River of No Return* (1954) with Marilyn Monroe, *The Man with the Golden Arm* (1956) with Frank Sinatra and *Anatomy of a Murder* (1959) with James Stewart, Preminger could afford to lose £40,000 during one particular session at the roulette table. The owner of James Spencer, Arvin and the Strood Motor Company lost a comparatively modest '£4,000', according to fellow Bexleyheath dealer, Ray Morris, who had been with him. Bob Lobell also remembers gambling with Bernie at Crockfords. Bernie had just lost 'a fairly significant amount of money at "Chemy" [chemin de fer], and I was at the Blackjack table playing for ones and twos, and he came over and said: "How are you doing?" I said, "I'm up £100", and I was over the moon. He said: "Come over here, sit down", and he won back his money. So in gratitude he sent me home in a big Daimler limousine. At the time I was living off the Kings Road so it was the biggest car there and it ticked my friends off [that] I went home in style. It was three o'clock in the morning and he got his money back, but losing is not a word in Bernie's book.'

Bernie at this time became somewhat enamoured with show-business figures and their bank accounts. He had become friendly with agents Eve Taylor and her partner Maurice Press. Bernie got to know 'a lot of people' through Eve including singer and television star Val Doonican; singer/actor Adam Faith, who often accompanied Bernie on gambling sojourns to the South of France, and remained a close friend until Adam's death in March 2003; and the Beatles. Mimicking the Beatles' shaggy locks, Bernie's slicked-back hair-do now lost its lacquer, becoming increasingly tousled, as it still is. The hedonistic lifestyle of the 'Swinging Sixties' suited Bernie's freedom-loving nature. While he was not interested in drugs or drink, he did like flirting with the so-called 'fast set' that zoomed through relationships, money, cars; and then there was the enchantment of the new rhythm and beat. London, Bernie's pleasure ground, swayed – and Bernie swayed with it. With his newly earned wealth he could buy fun, as much as he wanted, and it was all readily available. His taste was for gambling until all hours, cars, and mixing with celebrities.

Eve Taylor and Maurice Press also introduced Bernie to statuesque singer Sandie Shaw, winner of the 1967 Eurovision Song Contest with perhaps her best-remembered hit, *Puppet on a String*; they became friends and Bernie kept in touch with her for several years. Lulu, the teenage chart-topper from Glasgow, star of the 1967 film *To Sir With Love* and whose career later spanned television, theatre and concerts around the world, 'probably' bought one his 'posh cars' during the course of her acquaintance with Bernie. The method of acquiring one of these vehicles from James Spencer Limited was pure Ian Fleming, and confirms what Bernie readily admits: 'I like all the James Bond films.' Upstairs in the rebuilt showroom there was 'a high-tech control panel set into a large desk behind which Bernie sat,' recalls former Lotus Team Manager Peter Warr. 'From his control centre he could press a button to highlight a particular car as if it were on show.' Mostly what the general public saw were just ordinary vehicles, nothing fancy. But when a wealthy buyer was looking for something 'special', Bernie touched that button and – *voilà!* – a mirrored wall of the showroom folded concertina-like to reveal the 'special' reserve. 'Amazing cars,' says Peter: Lamborghinis, Rolls-Royces, Ferraris, Maseratis. The visual presentation – so intrinsically important to Bernie – was being given full rein. The teenager who had bought a projector to show films to his family was again staging shows, but now his participation had considerably broadened.

What was the make of the car that he sold to Lulu? Bernie 'can't remember'. More memorable is her performance in a Grand Prix fund-raising gala at London's Albert Hall when mid-song she had the spotlight – *à la* James Spencer – turned on Bernie, obliging him to sing a few lines. Back on the showroom floor Bernie's James Bond-style gadgets resulted in mounting sales. With his gambling winnings Adam Faith bought from Bernie a blue Rolls-Royce; cabaret singer Pearly Gates was another customer. But it was when Bernie was occasionally seen lunching with *Goldfinger* songstress Shirley Bassey that James Spencer Limited gained a reputation as the venue that attracted some of the best-known names in show business.

At night the show business stars peppered the plush and gilded Crockfords as fortunes were gambled away by the hour and, across roulette tables, men exchanged smiles with persuasive diamond-laden women dressed in full-length gowns or Mary Quant mini skirts. Here too, the scene was reflected in a wall of mirrors, in this instance etched with a smoke effect that could have been plucked from one of the then novel James Bond films, or perhaps the borrowing was the other way around. The atmosphere oozed intrigue, but not for Ivy Ecclestone. For some time she and Bernie had been living separate lives and their marriage ultimately ended in divorce. 'Why does anyone split up?' Bernie asks now. 'It was just one of those things, we grew apart.' The couple have long since ceased to be in contact, but Bernie still maintains that Ivy 'was a very nice person'. Ivy preferred quiet pursuits, looking after their daughter, home and shopping – those were her interests; the antithesis of Bernie's. He was not conventional. She was. They had become ill-suited. Some of their friends and neighbours from Bexleyheath hold the view that Bernie's 'love of the high life' drove the couple apart, or that like his former partner, Fred Compton, Ivy 'just couldn't keep up'. Ivy later married another car dealer.

In 1968, Bernie moved to a home in Chislehurst, a leafy London suburb of upper middle-class mock-Tudor houses laid out in neat developments nudging an occasional Georgian mansion of historical interest. Even the shops had been designed to fit with the village-like ambiance and the overall effect was, and is, pleasing – apart from the unplanned-for glut of traffic. Bernie was already familiar with the area, having sold a home there to Sidney Young, formerly of Bexleyheath, which he then resold to his friend Dave Walker. The house he chose for himself was one of the multitude of three-bedroom mock-Tudors, and as usual he found it necessary to clear out the house's interior and start again with a blank canvas, adding all-new fittings. When the interior alterations were under way he focused his attention on the garden at the front of the house, for which he designed a waterfall. Lorry-loads of boulders were brought to the garden and dumped – to be arranged later – as the backbone of the waterfall, by a ginger-haired gardener and by Bernie. The results of their efforts were mixed: sometimes the water gently cascaded over the boulders, at other times it seeped up from beneath the lawn, flooding the garden. Bernie became well-practised at 'mopping up'.

Back in the office, Bernie continued to talk numbers – ever-increasing numbers – down the telephone lines. The cars were still moving like fury, and the hire-purchase business was proving a healthy sideline. But, feeling the bruises of divorce, he needed to do more. He had enjoyed playing with makeovers in the domestic property market, appreciating gains that were generally tax-free. Commercial property however was a more exacting game, the province of accountants and lawyers formulating complex tax strategies in an attempt to realise profit margins that were, at least, variable. At first he went solo, not yet appreciating the advantage – and protection – that might be had in hiring opinions. Later on his accountants and lawyers would become legion. Over the next twenty years his investments in property would amount in the 'tens of millions', says Bernie, realising gains that would elevate him to the strata of the super-wealthy. Even during the 1960s when profits from 'car trading made the most substantial' contribution to Bernie's overall wealth, profits made from trading in property, of all types, were coming a close second.

But then, he was an old hand at property ventures. In 1950, at the age of twenty, he had bought and sold industrial premises in Greenwich, south-east London. During the Sixties, in addition to his commercial interests in Bexleyheath, he acquired land in Erith, Kent, where he had commercial buildings constructed for leasing to small businesses. In 1971 he had Pentbridge Properties Limited set up to formally encompass his British property dealings and, in 1989, Pentbridge Services. 'Look anywhere in London and you'll see on this corner, on that corner a building that Bernie owns,' says a fellow property dealer and friend of Bernie's. His eventual transactions in land and buildings outside the UK would belong to another bulging catalogue.

As part of the Erith development, in 1969 Bernie opened one of his better-known enterprises, Mid-Week Car Auctions, complete with 'a nice little restaurant' and closed-circuit television – a security device then considered avant-garde. With surveillance in place and tasty food on offer (prepared by the girlfriend of a bodyshop owner) along with a selection of cars, some of them 'exotic' (including many of his own vehicles), Bernie was open for business. The lights went on, the crowds shuffled in and the first showroom beauty, 'an Italian number', hit the auction block. When the professional auctioneer said 'What am I bid for this?' the response was stone-cold silence. There were no takers, not even any bidders. The customers in Erith that evening were apparently shy.

Bernie, however, was quick with an antidote. He understood how to warm them up, sell cheap – *the loss-leader, use only in an emergency.* And it would take an emergency for Bernie, who always flinches against attention, to willingly stand up in front of a crowd. But then this was a selling situation and he was the master sorcerer about to conjure up 'I'll take it' from the dry mouths of the onlookers.

In an instant he swept aside the auctioneer and was up at the podium. 'Now then, who's gonna give £1,000 for it?' Bernie demanded through the microphone. Then, as if obeying a command, someone put up his hand, and then another, a third, a fourth person and they were off in a commotion of hands being raised, fingers pointing towards the ceiling, heads wagging. 'This is good,' thought Bernie, and from then on 'the whole place sparked up and went'. It was fun and it was fast, but it was not enough to keep him attached to the auction room when a quick turn around was on offer. In the summer of 1970 the Erith auction premises were leased to David Wickens, founder and chairman of British Car Auctions; he ran the Erith auction for two years before moving down to Tunbridge Wells. Wickens would later try to buy Brands Hatch racing circuit but the deal didn't go through. Bernie had also made a failed attempt to purchase Brands Hatch, back when it was still a grass track – pre-1950 – and when Bernie was still in his teens. David Wickens, says Bernie, was 'big in property deals'. Bernie is correct. One such property, twelve acres in Hampshire, was purchased for £800 and sold for £9.5 million. On the business side, Wickens' auction business, with a turnover of £14 billion, was sold to a public company for a reported £720 million.

Away from work Bernie's social life continued to revolve around gambling, mostly at Crockfords and other well-to-do establishments, but on Wednesday nights he sought a leisure activity that tended to draw more of the blue-collared – greyhound racing. After the death of Stuart Lewis-Evans his attendance at the ice hockey matches in Streatham became infrequent. The Crayford Greyhound Stadium now predominated on his Wednesday nights though, occasionally, he favoured the dog track at Charlton, south-east London. 'Bernie used to enjoy his night out at the dogs to relax,' says his friend and bookmaker, Tony Morris. 'Gambling is in his make-up.' During evenings at home Bernie could be found huddled at the kitchen table playing gin rummy for high stakes. A frequent house guest at Chislehurst was a lanky, solemn-faced Austrian racing driver – and gin rummy addict – Jochen Rindt. Bernie had introduced him to the card game and to the excitement of playing for a wager. Then he helped Jochen to increase his earnings. Jochen was to become one of Bernie's closest friends. Jochen would also become a kind of Rosetta Stone, unlocking Bernie's future – Formula 1 Grand Prix motor racing. Now it would all start to come together, to make sense: his education at the Cooper factory, lessons learned as a racing driver, as the entrant of the Connaughts, as the manager of Stuart Lewis-Evans, the years of wheeling and dealing, his tough negotiating skills, gambling, and even the glamour of show business, but moreover, tenacity – these are the elements that would shape the future of Formula 1 and therein Bernie's career, a career that he had been preparing for – inadvertently – all along.

CHAPTER 5

RINDTSTONE

I t is former dealer/driver Roy Salvadori who takes the credit for playing an 'instrumental' role in getting Bernie back into motor racing. In the summer of 1964 Roy had invited Bernie to 'help out in the pits' during a sports car race held at Brands Hatch. Roy was driving a Cooper-Maserati in which he had finished the race in third place, with some criticism from Bernie, who 'didn't think we were tackling our racing in the right way'. Bernie then suggested that he should enter a sports car for Roy in races in 1965. But by then Salvadori had made up his mind to retire and was not interested in taking up Bernie's proposal. More than four decades later, Roy still wonders 'whether I missed out on one of the best opportunities of my racing career!'

Roy Salvadori's retirement at the end of 1964 was to a certain extent hastened by his decision to become racing manager for the Cooper team. He was also appointed a director of the Cooper Car Company. When Charles Cooper died in October 1964 his son, John, had suffered the loss both personally and on a business level. Charles had always been the practical one, counting the pennies and scrutinising every detail of the company's operations. Unlike his father, John's main interest was racing, so much so that it soon became evident that Cooper Cars was at risk of falling into financial difficulties. On advice from Roy Salvadori, John sold the company to the Chipstead Group of Companies in April 1965. The deal gave John 'something over £200,000' along with the freedom to become wholly involved in motor racing.

The Cooper team's number one driver in 1965 was New Zealander Bruce McLaren, and the number two – with a three-year contract – was Jochen Rindt. The previous year Jochen had had a taste of Formula 1 when he drove a Brabham racing car in the Austrian Grand Prix for privateer Rob Walker, a much-loved, languid character and an aristocrat of a bygone age who on his passport put his occupation as 'gentleman'. Rob was a good amateur racer who, on the insistence of his wife, handed the wheel to other drivers to drive his cars for him and, later, during the 1980s, he took up reporting on races for an American magazine; Rob died of pneumonia, aged 84, in 2002. But it was in Formula 2 that Jochen shot – like a bolt of lightning – to the attention of British racing fans by winning the London Trophy at Crystal Palace, beating Graham Hill and the amazingly prolific Scot, Jimmy Clark, who was thought by many to be the fastest man in the business. It was then not unusual for drivers to drive in more than one type of race and in more than one type of racing car. In 1965 Jochen further demonstrated his skill – and versatility – when he drove a Ferrari to victory with American Masten Gregory at Le Mans, the twenty-four-hour race often referred to as 'Le Grand Prix d'Endurance'. And it was dangerous not only for the drivers in the race but also for those who watched it; ten years earlier eighty-three spectators had been killed when, as a result a collision, a car was launched into the stands.

In October 1965 Bernie again managed to take time off from work to help out in the pits. But this time it wasn't just a day out for a dose of motor racing at nearby Brands Hatch. This time Bernie set aside more than a week to join Roy Salvadori and John Cooper in Mexico. For Bernie this was a gross dereliction of duty regarding the ever-present opportunities for wheeling and dealing back home, a clear measure of his fondness for Roy and John. They met up in Acapulco to laze in the sun and slurp tall drinks, along with other teams, while their cars were being trucked to Mexico City from New York State's Watkins Glen, the previous Grand Prix. Tim Parnell, who was there as manager of his father's team, Reg Parnell Racing, recalls 'we were all falling about at this wonderful hotel on the beach, diving into the pools, frolicking and playing pranks on each other… that's how it was in those days, a lot of camaraderie and wonderful times'. And it was in Acapulco that Roy introduced Bernie to the twenty-three-year-old, chain-smoking Jochen Rindt. Despite the twelve-year age gap, Bernie and Jochen became, says Tim, 'very pally'.

Born in Mainz, Germany, in 1942, Jochen had been raised by his maternal grandparents in Austria in the provincial town of Graz. Both his parents had been killed in an Allied bombing raid on Hamburg, a tragedy that may have caused Jochen to feel that he was entitled to a larger share of life. Perceived shortcomings made him moody, though money wasn't among them, for he had inherited wealth along with a flattened nose – his most distinctive feature – suggesting that he belonged in a boxing ring, and he readily admitted to 'always fighting', getting into scrapes while still at school. When he wasn't frowning he laughed, easily drifting into humour and many warmed to his acknowledged charisma. Bernie thinks that 'Jochen was a special person, like Senna'. Following their initial meeting in Acapulco Bernie and Jochen soon became 'very good friends, really very good friends… Jochen was all right, we had lots of laughs, and he liked to play gin rummy – we used to play all the time.'

During the race weekend in Mexico City Bernie's unstoppable determination came to the rescue – temporarily – when the Cooper team was beset by radiator problems while trying out the cars. Roy Salvadori enjoys recounting the story: 'We had trouble with our radiators. Bernie said "I'll get those done", so we got him into a car with a couple of the Cooper radiators (he spoke not a word of Spanish of course) and let him loose in Mexico City. And he's gone. Where's he gone? Half an hour later, an hour, two hours, six, seven hours later he came back with two mechanics and two shiny radiators which had been extended because the cars were overheating, and he got the mechanics to return with him just in case they were required to do any further modifications. I said "what did that cost?" "Don't worry," he said, "it's all organised."

He had given them a couple of tickets to the race. That was the first sponsorship we ever really had! How did he talk them into it, they didn't speak a word of English, how did he do it? In the end you give him any job because you know something will happen.'

Nevertheless, the Mexican Grand Prix proved to be a disappointment for Jochen. His Cooper-Climax was scuppered due to a lost wheel-suspension bolt and he was forced to retire from the race.

The 1966 Grand Prix season was considerably better. Driving the more powerful but unwieldy Cooper-Maserati, Jochen managed to finish in a close second place behind a Ferrari driven by John Surtees in the Belgian Grand Prix at Spa-Francorchamps – the circuit that separated 'the men from the boys'. Jochen again took second place in the US Grand Prix at Watkins Glen and came third in the German Grand Prix at the Nürburgring. He now merited a personal mechanic, nineteen-year-old Ron Dennis, drafted in from Thomson & Taylor, part of the Chipstead Group. Ron, who was then 'just starting an engineering apprenticeship', would go on to achieve motor racing greatness as supremo of the mighty McLaren empire and a figure of immense power in Formula 1. 'There were some very dominant characters in grand prix racing then,' recalls Ron. 'In our particular team we had Jochen Rindt whose car I was responsible for, he was a very dominant character. Roy Salvadori, the team manager, was a very dominant individual, and a lot of other people like Colin Chapman and Ken Tyrrell, all of these great names, and, of course, they were the ones that had the presence and the sense of characters – and Bernie, but he was playing a peripheral role in that period. I basically saw him as a friend and guiding light of Jochen Rindt... I first came into contact with Bernie – I remember it quite well – when he was playing backgammon with Jochen.' John Surtees also recalls Bernie's relationship with Jochen, adding: 'Bernie was pushing Jochen, behind the scenes, all the way through.'

Bruce McLaren had parted from Coopers at the end of the previous season to develop his own team. He was replaced, in 1966, by American Richie Ginther who drove in the first two Grands Prix, Monaco and Belgium, then mid-season the mega-talented Surtees joined the Cooper team following an acrimonious split from Ferrari. While the arrival of John Surtees may have taken some of the gloss off Jochen's achievements in Formula 1, he still continued to collect points and finished the season third in the World Championship behind Australian Jack Brabham and Surtees. By now Bernie had become a near fixture with Coopers, frequently playing hookey from his Bexleyheath showroom to travel with the team. Motor racing was in his blood, the sound of engines, the thrill, the gamble with money, with human life, playing the odds and trying to win, always trying to win. This was the world he gravitated towards, it was something that he needed, and he had begun to accept that fact. Hereafter, his schedule would always include travelling the world in connection with motor racing.

While John Surtees was still with Ferrari he had – in a blaze of red – led the throng around the tight street circuit of Monte Carlo. This is Grand Prix motor racing's heartland, and for a few days each year, since the race was inaugurated in 1929, Grand Prix cars are allowed to tear along the petticoats of architectural dainties – the mansions and hotels reminiscent of ballgowns from the belle époque – flouncing the circuit. The cars also roar alongside the majestic azure harbour, chock-full of ocean-transversing yachts and condominium-sized private liners, all overlooked by the cliff-top Grimaldi Palace, seemingly spun from pink sugar. Monaco is also a tax haven where the glamorous, overtly wealthy – including many racing drivers – cluster and inevitably grate upon the sensibilities of the more staid *Monégasques*. During the Grand Prix festivities the juxtaposition of Old World manners, glitz and piercing engine noise is intoxicating.

Small wonder director John Frankenheimer decided that the Monaco Grand Prix provided the correct mixture for setting the stage – and the opening scenes – of his 1966 film, *Grand Prix*. Frankenheimer's film, starring James Garner and Yves Montand, contains race footage of thirteen Grand Prix drivers, including Jochen Rindt. American racing driver Phil Hill acted in the film and lookalikes resembled Jackie Stewart and Jimmy Clark. Jochen, along with Graham Hill, Jo Bonnier, Juan Manuel Fangio, Bruce McLaren and Richie Ginther, all had speaking parts. Tim Parnell also 'helped do the film' and 'it was a great time with John Frankenheimer'. While it was 'an education to see the making of a major film, quite amazing', there were 'boring times as well with all the reshooting and the different angles and things, but it was good and it earned Jochen quite a bit of money.' John Surtees remembers that 'Bernie was always there in the background advising Jochen', so he would have encouraged his friend to obtain hefty compensation for his contribution to the production. Beyond this, Bernie was intrigued by the complexity of filming dramatic, though plausible, spectacles such as a BRM careening into the harbour and multi-car pile-ups, and he was most impressed with the final product, which even now he occasionally watches on video.

Eleven years later Bernie offered advice to director Sydney Pollack on the making of *Bobby Deerfield*, the story of an international racing driver played by Al Pacino. In May 1997, Hollywood again haunted Monaco, and Bernie, in the form of actor/director Sylvester Stallone who was eager to make a film based on Formula 1. Hunky 'Sly', displaying an acutely sunburned face, was seen chatting up drivers and Formula 1 kingpins in the gilded, multi-chandeliered entrance hall of Monte Carlo's Hotel de Paris, and soaking up the atmosphere in the circuit's harbour-side pits where, during the race, team mechanics put their souls on the line. Four months later, Bernie signed 'a bit of paper', as a comfort measure for the film's investors, which purportedly allowed the project to go ahead. In return, Bernie required script approval to ensure that Formula 1 was not negatively portrayed. This presented an impasse that could not be resolved.

'There were so many different producers and people involved, the whole project wasn't up to scratch,' says Bernie. Sylvester Stallone was furious and threatened to sue, but when his rancour had cooled he thought better of it and decided, instead, to tailor his script to CART (Championship Auto Racing Teams), the American Indycar series. His film, entitled *Driven,* was released in April 2001 and, like the 1966 film *Grand Prix,* its characters more than hint at real Formula 1 figures, in this instance driver Michael Schumacher, team owner Sir Frank Williams and the pious Ayrton Senna. The crash scenes are breathtaking and well depicted and much of the film is entertaining. But unlike *Grand Prix* the race scenes are too improbable for motor racing purists. However, Stallone did acquire a useful measure of insight while hanging about Bernie and Formula 1 circuits which he then converted into the sub-thesis of his film: great success and wealth in motor racing bring a deluge of hangers-on and, according to Bernie, people who are 'always trying to get at you' as well as an emotional and personal cost – a threadbare theme but still a reality that many racing champions, and Bernie, have had to accommodate. Today, Bernie 'can't understand why anyone would bother to make a film on Formula 1... it's just too risky, too complex.' A documentary, yes, or the races shown on the big screen, but a full-length drama with actors, special effects and a music score? He remains to be convinced. Actually, he'd enjoy being convinced, just as long as the film maintained the integrity of the sport – and 'would it make money?'

The 1967 Grand Prix season turned out to be comparatively lacklustre for Jochen. Of the ten grands prix in which he drove, he managed only to haul the Cooper-Maserati into fourth place at Spa-Francorchamps and again at Monza in Italy. The rest of his Formula 1 results were a chronicle of mechanical woes. He was painfully aware of the Cooper's shortcomings – in this instance justified; the small outfit that had so brilliantly developed the rear-engined racing car, and with it changed motor racing history, was faltering. Going into the season they had not won a race since 1962. However, Jochen – along with the rest of the Cooper team – was soon to receive a big surprise.

The season opened with the South African Grand Prix at Kyalami in Johannesburg, and the British car to beat was now the Lotus 49-Cosworth. Jochen was joined by a new number two driver, Mexican Pedro Rodriguez, who replaced John Surtees after he left to join the Honda team. Jochen 'didn't take to Pedro on the first meeting,' recalls Roy Salvadori, 'and his feelings became increasingly difficult during practice when Pedro's car out-performed his. We tried our damnedest to cure the problems with Jochen's car, but all Jochen wanted to do was to get hold of Rodriguez's car.' It was not Roy's policy to switch cars from one driver to the other, 'which made Jochen very disgruntled'. To give the cars a good run before the race and – it was hoped – to resolve the problems with Jochen's engine, Bernie and the others searched around for a quiet bit of land. What they found was an abandoned gold mine on the top of a hill with a suitable road around it. But when they got the cars up there the whole place – the mine, their makeshift circuit, the barren surroundings – 'well, it was like a deserted town that you see in one of the westerns,' says Roy, continuing the story: 'We were up there all night, and I shall never forget Bernie then organised some tea and organised a table and we've got Jochen churning round and churning round, and somebody's giving him pit signals until we can get rid of the mist. Jochen would do maybe ten laps and then it would get better, and then it would get worse, and although the car had a slight stutter, we couldn't do much with it. But all the time Jochen kept getting out of the car, hopping mad, telling us what was going on and telling the mechanics while Bernie and I kept playing gin rummy. So, he was getting more and more furious. "Well," I said, "there's nothing we can do, we're not mechanics you know, that's the way it goes".'

Jochen remained ill-tempered going into the race. But his car performed very well, at least during the first thirty laps, which found Jochen and Pedro in third and fourth place in the eighty-lap race. But then Jochen, 'who was so very hard on cars at this stage in his career', came out with a faulty gearbox and tyres so badly worn that he would not have been able to complete the race with even the best possible engine. To make matters worse, the less experienced Pedro continued to drive steadily, lap after lap, on an increasingly depopulated circuit. Drivers were retiring left and right, and eventually – to everyone's astonishment, particularly Jochen's – Pedro brought the Cooper-Maserati home to victory!

During the return flight to Britain Jochen continued to smoulder. His frown – weighty as bronze – was ignored by Bernie and Roy as they busily totted up dollar bets in an almost continuous game of gin rummy. 'That's the way it went, we were just killing time,' says Roy. Then Jochen decided that he wanted to play. 'That's it, you go and have Bernie over,' encouraged Roy, offering Jochen his hand. 'So he played Bernie, and he kept losing until in the end he gave up.' Pedro Rodriguez, who had been watching all this with the brisk fascination of an absolute newcomer, was now bursting to have a try: 'I'd like to play, I'd like to play!' 'Well, OK,' Roy told him. 'You play Bernie.' So, Rodriguez played Bernie, and he wasn't doing too badly. Roy takes up the story: 'Rodriguez asks me "What have I got?", showing me his hand, and I saw the best hand you've ever seen! I told him "It's a hand to bet on if you really want to bet". So he was a few dollars up, and Jochen, he couldn't wait, he was fighting to play Rodriguez. Bernie looked at me and shrugged his shoulders. We gave up and moved out, and the two of them got together. They certainly didn't like each other I can tell you. Of course, Rodriguez's luck continued and he slaughtered Jochen, and Jochen was furious.' Jochen was in such a foul mood that when the aircraft stopped in Nairobi, he left and didn't return to the group even though he had a ticket through to London.

'Jochen was so bad-tempered!' says Roy, his voice for an instant raised a few decibels. 'But he and Bernie got on extremely well, they were a good pair, pulling each other along. You see Jochen had no sense of humour when he first started. In the end he was as sharp as Bernie.'

By the time the team headed to Monte Carlo for the Monaco Grand Prix, Roy Salvadori and Jochen had called a truce over the matter of switching cars and were once more on relatively friendly – some would call it cold war – terms. Together with Bernie they had decided that it would be expedient to charter a large boat to be anchored in the harbour near the circuit's pits. Bernie offered to arrange this, making sure that the boat had three master cabins. This was supposed to have been done, but when the three arrived at the boat Bernie quickly leapt aboard ahead of the rest and immediately secured a master cabin – the only master cabin – for himself, leaving Roy and Jochen to bunk in the crew's quarters. But when the sea became choppy and the boat began to heave, Bernie got fed up. 'I'm not having this,' he said. 'I've got a reserve on a suite at the Metropole, so I'm off.' Roy and Jochen objected, reminding Bernie that he was in for a third of the cost. 'I'll pay, I'll pay, and I'll get something out of it, don't you worry. I'll be back in half an hour.' Promptly half an hour later Bernie returned, and the captain took several deeply upholstered chairs and a couple of tables off the boat and set them up on the quay. Bernie ordered the captain to serve tea – the usual prelude to gin rummy – which then commenced and went on, almost without interruption, for three days. Bernie never again set foot on the boat: 'It was all right for gambling, but not for sleeping.' But, he did indeed 'get something out of it'.

Despite the occasional fun Jochen had had with the Cooper team, and the sometimes promising results – more often disappointing – he knew that when his three-year contract was up at the end of 1967 that it was time for a change, and Bernie was ready to change with him. His advice to his friend during the past seasons had now turned firmly managerial and, whatever the future held, they would make that journey together. For the 1968 Grand Prix season, that future was with the Brabham Racing Organisation.

Of course, the Cooper team had tried to hold on to Jochen for the 1968 season, but he and Bernie wanted a retainer of £25,000. John Cooper had baulked at the idea of paying a driver so much money and was supported by the Chipstead Group. Roy Salvadori had 'tried to get John Cooper to agree to paying the extra, because Jochen attracted sponsors, but he wouldn't agree'. That was the end of it. Except, as a parting salvo to the team Jochen had 'deliberately booted [his engine] as hard as possible so that it would blow up spectacularly and could never be used again'. This had happened at Watkins Glen, the penultimate race of the season. To be fair, Jochen knew that the engine was in terminal decline; he was just hastening the process. He didn't bother to turn up for the last race, Mexico City. So he wasn't around when Roy, Bernie, Pedro Rodriguez and Tim Parnell went out for a night of jai alai. Bernie was fascinated by this fast-moving game, a Basque form of pelota in which the opponents, using long scoop-like implements attached to one arm, catch and return a ball by hurling it against a wall at terrifying speed. Pedro, having sensed Bernie's enthusiasm, was explaining the finer points of the game when Bernie noticed 'tennis balls' being thrown among the crowd. 'What the hell are those chaps doing?' he asked. 'They use the balls to place a bet' – the magic word, and Bernie was off in his own game of savage ball-hurling.

Like Jochen, Roy too resigned from Cooper at the end of the 1967 season. Roy had been uncomfortable with the introduction of two new directors at Cooper, which had led to increasing 'dissension'. As 1968 approached, Roy felt that it was time to move on. He became an Alfa Romeo distributor, having bought Thomson & Taylor (Brooklands) Limited from the Chipstead Group, and acquired a BMW dealership. In 1971 he sold these to a public company, William Jacks Ltd, and three years later fulfilled his 'long ambition of going to live in Monaco'. The Cooper team, during 1968, lost much of its sponsorship and the cars became so uncompetitive that by the end of the season the team withdrew from racing.

Bernie spent several Christmases with Roy and his wife Sue at their home in Surrey and, later, in Spain or in the south of France. Roy liked to play chef, turning out superb dinners. Dealer/driver John Coombs was frequently included in the party. Roy, John Coombs, John Cooper (who died in 2001), dealer/driver John Young, car dealer Brian Whitehouse, bookmaker Tony Morris and a few others are Bernie's golden friends, the group from the 1950s and 1960s to whom

'Bernard' is just one of the gang, forever the light-hearted, Cooper 500-loving, Bexleyheath wheeler-dealer with a touch of the 'salt-of-the-earth' Suffolk, amusing, sometimes outrageous and, above all, loyal. Jochen, after their three years together, was becoming such a friend. Bernie affectionately nicknamed him 'the Kraut' and in return was called 'Bernie' by Jochen. Bernie had often used this shortened version of the name by which he had been christened. Now 'Bernard' all but disappeared, along with much of his previous life.

Jochen was a regular at Bernie's Chislehurst home – where he was so *at home* that he never bothered to knock. Upon arrival he just walked right in, dropped his duffle bag on the floor of the entrance hall and headed for the kitchen to indulge in an all night gin rummy session. 'They were like two small kids,' said Bernie's then girlfriend, Tuana Tan, 'always joking away and playing gin rummy.'

Another member of the Chislehurst clan was Oddjob, Bernie's English bulldog named after the butler/assassin character in the James Bond film, *Goldfinger*. The animal was hard to ignore for the preponderance of wind it produced, which did not trouble Jochen who was fond of the beast and often volunteered to take it for walks.

In 1967 Jochen had married beautiful Finnish model Nina Lincoln (daughter of racing driver Curt Richard Lincoln), who says of her husband that 'he was very straightforward, no bullshit, but very human, the Austrian public loved him.' He was also 'very ambitious'. Nina wanted her husband to take her to nightclubs where they could mix with couples their own age. Bernie, then thirty-nine, 'seemed so old'. But Jochen insisted on spending every available moment with his friend: 'I always learn so much from Bernie.' In 1968 Jochen and Nina celebrated the birth of their daughter, Natascha. A talented child, Natascha grew up to become an accomplished skier and pilot, eventually joining the four pilots who operated Bernie's fleet of Learjets. She went on to fly the FIA Learjet during Max Mosley's presidency.

The Rindt family lived in Switzerland, and Nina remembers an incident when, together with Bernie and Deborah, Bernie's then teenage daughter, they were flying from Geneva to Monte Carlo for the Grand Prix. During the flight, Deborah and Nina were startled out of their wits by a 'cracking sound'. 'My God, we'll hit the mountain!' screamed Nina, who was hysterical because Jochen and Bernie were fooling around… and to make things worse the pilot, who had recently broken his leg in a speedboat accident, was hobbling around with his leg in plaster. In any event, there were no further disturbances and the group landed safely at Nice airport. Of these trips to Monaco, Deborah particularly remembers being driven around the circuit by Jochen in a road car. He was then being widely heralded as 'one of the fastest drivers in the world', and Deborah adored his attention and endless mischief-making. 'I suppose you would call it hero worship,' she fondly remembers.

While Jochen's previous experience in Formula 1 had not brought him the championship that he so longed for, in Formula 2 the winner's place on the podium was indisputably his, and he won it while driving a Brabham for Roy Winkelmann Racing. So when Denny Hulme left the Brabham Formula 1 team to drive for McLaren, Jochen quite naturally filled the vacancy. The Brabham cars, with Australian-made Repco engines, had been most effective in 1966 and 1967, taking Jack Brabham and Denny Hulme to their respective World Championships. It seemed, therefore, that in 1968 the Rindt-Repco-Brabham combination should have been unstoppable, and Jochen's own, well-deserved World Championship a certainty. But just as he had been surprised in 1967, he was in for an even bigger surprise, or rather heart-wrenching disappointment, in 1968.

This time it was not a matter of driving the car too hard, throwing it around from lock to lock shearing rubber off the tyres. The problem was now twofold, and beyond his control: Brabham was using Repco's new, experimental, four-valves-per-cylinder engine, which could not compare with the power of the Cosworth. In addition the Cosworth was no longer exclusive to Lotus and that made the sport more competitive, sending McLaren and Tyrrell (Matra) snapping at the front of the grid. Those with other engines had to put in the drive of their lives just to qualify – and be happy with that. The second problem was put down to 'quality control', bits just kept breaking, or worse, falling off – unheard of for Brabham. Still, the potential was evident – poignantly evident as it turned out – when Jochen was second fastest in practice for the Dutch Grand Prix at Zandvoort and when he put his car on pole position for the French Grand Prix at Rouen. He retired from both races, though he did scrape two third places, in South Africa and Germany. But these were only crumbs of that ultimate and still elusive victory breeding anguish in the soul of the supremely talented German/Austrian. Jochen walked away from the 1968 Grand Prix season with a gut full of might-have-beens, and with Bernie playing with numbers and contracts with possible new teams; somehow or other between the two of them they would yet embrace the World Championship, and substantially increase their wealth while they were about it.

Colin Chapman could pick up the scent of Jochen's discontent a mile away. He was always on the prowl for talent – fast and hungry – and his cold blue eyes had fixed on Jochen. Money dripped from Chapman's lips in ever-increasing numbers and Jochen liked the sound of the figures and could taste a fat future in which he would become World Champion – once, perhaps twice – before retiring to capitalise on his name and engage in the many businesses that he had talked over with Bernie. As Rindtstone, Jochen and Bernie were already conjoined, not just in friendship but in an enterprise dealing in aeroplanes and aeroplane parts. They had also talked about a joint venture in the manufacture of sports clothing and other businesses. The opportunities were boundless, requiring only a little dreaming and conversation; application was automatic. But their most immediate concern was the opportunity for Jochen to become World Champion. He only had to step into the cockpit of Chapman's Lotus-Cosworth.

Fine, except that even in the face of Colin Chapman's delectable promises Jochen was still nagged by feelings of loyalty to the Brabham Racing Organisation. He admired Jack Brabham for his professionalism, for the fact that he raced in his own cars and for the relaxed, amiable atmosphere he generated trackside under stress and back in the factory. The 1968 season had certainly been frustrating for Jochen, but for all that he had endured his frustration in welcoming, friendly surroundings. This too counted with Jochen who had come to regard Brabhams as a kind of surrogate family, and he absolutely trusted Jack Brabham, who was also a superb mechanic and engineer. Anyway, 'we had an agreement at that time,' says Jack. 'We shook hands and were going to fix up the contract and all the terms were agreed.' But then 'Rindt was tackled by Colin Chapman who offered him another £10,000 or something. Rindt came back to me and said, "look, I've been offered this money for next year", so I said, "take it, don't mess around".' Jochen had even offered to stay on at Brabham for half of what Chapman was prepared to pay. But the team could not meet even that figure, they simply could not afford to keep him. Bernie too had been fond of Brabhams. 'We used to see a lot of him at the factory,' recalls Jack, 'and he did a very good job managing Jochen. Bernie was always there in the background. I never really had a problem with Bernie at all. He does what he says he'll do, and, you know, he often says "no", and if he says "no" he means "no", and if he says "yes", he means "yes". He's been that sort of person all the time. I've found him to be straight all the time... you don't have to write anything down, if he shakes hands on it, it's a deal, it's fixed.'

Of course Bernie had encouraged every syllable of the money talk. But when all the final figures were before them he – uncharacteristically – held back. In his view Jochen, and Jochen alone had to decide whether or not to take the drive with Lotus. Bernie was sensitive to Jochen's qualms, redoubled by another factor – fear. His friend and contemporary, Jackie Stewart, had refused to drive for Lotus because he considered the cars unsafe. Eight months earlier Jimmy Clark, driving a Lotus, had been killed in a Formula 2 race, though perhaps the cause of his crash had been 'a small piece of debris picked up in the race', which punctured a rear tyre sending his car slithering sideways to wrap around a tree. There were immediate flutterings within the motor racing community about the supposed flimsiness of Lotus-built cars. 'The amount of drivers who had accidents through Colin's design and build were just too numerous to mention,' says John Coombs. 'I lost three wheels and the chassis broke in my days at Lotus… Chapman's idea was to build them so that if the car didn't break it was too heavy, and if it broke, well then… so of course a lot of people got hurt and very badly injured.'

But Jochen eventually put his reservations aside and made up his mind to go for the largest offer – Chapman's – and for what he perceived to be the fastest available car – Lotus. Furthermore, Colin would make Jochen equal number one to team-mate Graham Hill who, following the death of Jimmy Clark, had carried forth the Lotus standard, becoming World Champion. 'I'm sure Chapman regretted the day he met Ecclestone,' says Roy Salvadori, 'because when Rindt went to Lotus, Ecclestone agreed the contract, and the usual contract when Graham Hill was there – as I understood it – was very restrictive. But those restrictions didn't exist once Bernie had been through it!' Reflecting on Jochen's decision to sign with Lotus, Bernie says: 'I told Jochen that the Lotus was not as safe as the Brabham, but could win the World Championship.'

Aerodynamic wings, mounted on absurdly high struts, had developed in Formula 1 in the second half of 1968 and became a dominant theme in the early races of 1969. The purpose of these structures was to enhance aerodynamic downforce, allowing the cars to corner at greater speeds; they were to become Jochen's *bête noire*. At Kyalami in South Africa, the opening race of 1969, Jochen was forced to retire with a broken fuel pump. But for the Spanish Grand Prix he took pole position – aided by a widened and higher rear wing – on the frighteningly fast street circuit of Montjuich Park in Barcelona. During the actual race Jochen held the lead while on the ninth lap team-mate Graham Hill crashed into a guardrail. He was unhurt. The wing of his Lotus had deformed under stress, sending him into an uncontrollable slide. Upon examining his car Graham realised that the same physics would undoubtedly impact on Jochen's car and he immediately made an attempt to warn him, but it was too late. Devoid of downforce, as the result of a collapsed rear wing, Jochen spun into the wreckage of Graham's car and was flipped topsy-turvy before landing; here was exacting proof that the rear wing, as then used on the Lotus, was a disaster. Concussed and bleeding profusely from a broken nose, Rindt was taken to a local hospital. Bernie went with him.

Fortunately, Jochen's head injury was not as serious as it initially appeared and he recovered quickly, bucked-up by rage. No longer would he quietly play the role of Chapman's expendable laboratory rat. Jochen needed to yell. So that Colin might hear he used, as a megaphone, an 'open letter' addressed to all European motoring journalists: '... F1 racing is meant to be a serious business and not a hot rod show. Wings are dangerous, first to the drivers, second to the spectators.' It was now Colin Chapman's turn to fume, and the two would not speak to each other except through Bernie or through Chapman's friend – and eventual biographer – Gérard ('Jabby') Crombac, a well-respected motor racing journalist and also a former racing driver, mechanic and team manager. Bernie laughs at their behaviour: 'We had three adjoining rooms from which to telephone each other so we didn't have to meet!'

Due to his injuries Jochen had to miss the Monaco Grand Prix, but he now had the satisfaction of knowing that the spindly wings were hereafter banned by a decree from the motor racing authorities. Encouraged by the success of his 'open letter', Jochen now wrote directly to Colin outlining 'the whole situation' – the car's fragility: '... your cars are so quick that we would still be competitive with a few extra pounds used to make the weakest parts stronger... I can only drive a car in which I have some confidence and I feel the point of no confidence is quite near.'

During this season Bernie and Jochen also managed to fit in a few leisure hours mixing with Sixties icons. Frank

Williams recalls: 'I'd see Bernie around because he was looking after Jochen, and by 1969 I was doing Formula 1 with Piers [Courage], so I'd see Bernie at a track or dinner, because Piers and Jochen were both attracted to each other and their lifestyles were similar, pretty glamorous. Bernie was always around there as well, as was a well-known sort of socialite and fashion man called Justin de Villeneuve, who was Twiggy's boyfriend. I was very much on the outskirts of all this. But I think that was the earliest I came across Bernie more than once.'

Jochen was back behind the wheel for the Dutch Grand Prix, though he again retired with mechanical trouble, and at Clermont-Ferrand for the French race he was plagued with double vision, a delayed side effect or the aftermath of his concussion. But at Silverstone, Jochen was back in championship form and snatched pole position from Jackie Stewart. During the race Rindt and Stewart battled it out like shuttlecocks, tossing the lead from one to the other until lap sixty-two, when Jochen's rear wing end-plate worked loose and began to destroy a tyre. Jackie signalled to him, indicating there was a problem, to which Jochen responded by hurtling into the pits. Following a hasty repair he returned to the circuit in second place only to run low on fuel. After another unplanned pit stop he finished – exasperated – in fourth place; Colin Chapman was set to receive the full blast of Jochen's temper. Nina Rindt recalls hearing Jochen and Colin 'arguing all the time, arguing, arguing and arguing, and nothing else. Colin thought of his business and not the driver.'

In the Italian Grand Prix at Monza, Jochen and Jackie Stewart again fought for the lead, which in the end went to Jackie, along with the World Championship. In the race Jochen took second place followed by a third-place finish in the Canadian Grand Prix. But at Watkins Glen his world-class potential was, at long last, realised when he won the US Grand Prix. Jochen's smile was as broad as the Paul Revere punchbowl trophy that he held aloft from the podium. Standing next to him was his close friend, second-placed

Piers Courage who had been driving a Brabham. So the day should have been perfect, but it was not; the celebrations were marred by the crash of Graham Hill, who sustained serious leg injuries. From this point onward Graham's career gradually faded though he still held on to his old enthusiasm, and enjoyed a few rousing successes before it all came to an end in 1975 with his death in a plane crash.

As Jochen contemplated the 1970 racing season his distrust of Colin Chapman was approaching paranoia. Jack Brabham made overtures to woo him back to his old friends, and Jochen was tempted. Furthermore, knowing that Colin would outbid all comers, Bernie made an effort to facilitate the reunion by urging Goodyear – who funded much of the Brabham budget – to enhance the Brabham package. (Bernie would later become the Goodyear motorsport distributor for Europe through his company International Racing Tyre Service; he intended to displace Firestone, making Goodyear the only tyre in Formula 1.) But Colin would not be manoeuvred out of the running and reacted by padding his lure with the addition of a Formula 2 team to be called Jochen Rindt Racing – run by Bernie. Jochen capitulated, having first toyed with every other reasonable alternative, including a drive with the recently formed March team headed by barrister and racing driver Max Mosley, driver Alan Rees and designer Robin Herd. They were an extraordinary trio, but Jochen lacked confidence in the team and their talks foundered. Meanwhile, Robin Herd's talents, in particular, had attracted the notice of both Jochen and Bernie and they set about entertaining him with a lavish dinner in London, over which they sketched out a proposal for a Rindt/Ecclestone/Herd venture in a Formula 1 team. But it came to nothing, and Colin was flaunting a car with a radical new design, the Lotus 72. If Chapman had intended to overwhelm he succeeded: Jochen stayed with the Lotus stable. In the end Bernie had 'recommended' that Jochen take up Colin's offer, but not before he had thoroughly explored the alternatives and – at the very least – attempted to make them competitive. That said, 'Jochen made up his own mind,' says Nina. 'He was influenced by no one.'

While Chapman was keeping an eye on Jochen, Bernie was digesting the Colin Chapman method of operating a motor racing business, taking what he needed and discarding the rest. Colin was the second of the three individuals (Cooper, Chapman, Ferrari) whom Bernie claims he 'most admired'. Think of these men as professors helping Bernie, by now a post-graduate in motor racing, further refine and distinguish his approach to his speciality; Colin would influence Bernie's life in ways that would be far-reaching, though intermittent. John Hogan, who is a friend of Bernie's and has been involved in Formula 1 since the early 1970s, says: 'There are three people who are responsible for Formula 1 being what it is today. Bernie Ecclestone, Colin Chapman and Enzo Ferrari, simple as that. The three most significant people in Formula 1, ever. Colin was this genius designer [and engineer], there's no other word for it. Almost every significant technical breakthrough since Formula 1 was invented came from Colin Chapman's head... he would have been unbelievable in a war if you had to push the boundaries to get things done, he would have been stunning.' Indeed, boundary-stretching is where Colin preferred to operate. He even asked former Lotus engineer Peter Wright to design a flying saucer, although it didn't progress beyond the draft paper. Colin himself had kept to more down-to-earth projects. Back in the Fifties, adds Hogan, 'one of the reasons Vanwall [the team for which Stuart Lewis-Evans had raced] was so successful was because the car was designed by Colin Chapman and Frank Costin [the aerodynamicist]. Chapman was seen then as actually being the driver of the car with Stirling Moss and Tony Brooks, he was that good.'

At the time, Bernie persuaded Tony Vandervell, the team's owner, 'to make Chapman the designer, because if he kept driving the car he would only kill himself, and that would have been a real waste'. Peter Warr, then the Lotus team manager, adds that Colin, like John Cooper, 'was fired with such enthusiasm', something that Bernie would have identified with, and also that 'Colin was a fantastic motivator of people', which Bernie would try to emulate. More significant was the fact that Colin had begun to appreciate – and then to exploit – the potential for business attached to motorsport; Bernie was all attention.

In 1968, in response to teams' escalating costs, the world governing body had allowed sponsors' names to be displayed on cars. The rule was specific: a sponsor's logo could be no more than twelve inches square. Within days of the rule being laid down a Lotus appeared in the Tasman series entered as Gold Leaf Team Lotus with the original green and yellow livery over-painted red and gold, and John Player's logo occupying the mandatory square foot. As motor racing author Mike Lawrence explains: 'Colin Chapman had read his rulebook, found his loophole and had driven a coach and horses through it'. The era of the motorised billboard had arrived. Here indeed was fertile territory for study and in years to come Bernie would take this notion and roll it out like a great blanket encompassing every aspect of Formula 1 and beyond. In 1969 he was content to play with Jochen's new Bell Star racing helmet and place the words 'This Space To Let' on either side.

A Colin Chapman trait that Bernie particularly 'admired' was the fact that 'he was a risk-taker'; he would gamble everything, even the company finances, for motor racing. 'They were very much two of a kind,' says the then Lotus mechanic Michael ('Herbie') Blash, who eventually became a close friend of Bernie's. 'Colin was a very ruthless guy, very, very ruthless, and I think Bernie learned quite a lot from the ruthless side, because Bernie can be very ruthless, but he does it with a smile, and that's where Bernie's very clever, a typical car salesman. He can have people over and they walk away very happy in the fact that they've been screwed, and I think that – if anything – he would have learned from Colin.' And Bernie, in return, was becoming an influential member of the Lotus organisation, so much so that he had attempted to get Jackie Stewart to drive for Chapman: 'It was going to be a kind of super-team, Jochen and Jackie,' recalls Herbie, 'but then I don't think Jochen was so keen.' Neither was Jackie keen. Mechanic Bob Dance, who had spent ten years with Colin Chapman, describes him as a man 'totally focused on winning who would do whatever he had to do to win – best drivers, fastest cars, leading the team from the front. He believed in a small team and tight control... he was his own man.' These were all characteristics that Bernie shared, or would share. In turn Colin was developing considerable respect for Bernie, but their relationship was about to be tested, almost beyond forbearance.

For Jochen and Bernie the 1970 Formula 1 racing season began with the conviction that the World Championship would soon be theirs. In South Africa, however, Jochen again retired with engine trouble. It was becoming monotonous – and a tad galling as Jack Brabham was the victor. More disappointment ensued when, during practice for the Spanish Grand Prix, a part of the car's disc brakes sheared away throwing Jochen into a sudden spin. When equilibrium returned, he stomped back to the pits and reportedly shouted at Chapman saying that he was never 'going to get into that bloody car again'. But Colin knew when it was time to soothe, and with gentle words and an arm sympathetically draped around Jochen's shoulder he coaxed him back into the Lotus though, as it happened, the car became undriveable during the race and was withdrawn after the tenth lap.

They then headed for the next Grand Prix, in Monaco, where – after positioning eighth on the grid, in the previous year's car – Jochen saw his chances for a place on the podium as middling, and for much of the eighty-lap race he dawdled along – or so it seemed – in sixth or seventh place. But then, as if suddenly confident that the Lotus would hold up to the full force of his ability, Jochen burst ahead gaining more and more speed while throwing the car about in his old Salvadori-objecting style. He set a new lap record and no doubt singed the streets of Monte Carlo as he squeezed the pressure on and squeezed the pressure on, shortening the distance between himself and race leader Jack Brabham. At the start of the last lap Jack was in the lead with 1.5 seconds in hand, but Jochen continued to close the gap by hurling his car into straight after straight, all the while under-braking until Jack made a critical mistake and slammed into a barrier of straw bales. Jochen slipped past and won the race. It was one of the most outstanding drives of his career, for a few critical moments he had seemingly entered a territory beyond physical entitlement, where there is a force that cradles every move in pure perfection.

At Spa-Francorchamps Pedro Rodriguez again niggled Jochen by winning the Grand Prix for BRM against all odds. But this was the only interruption to a streak of first-place triumphs that followed the reintroduction of a much-modified Lotus 72 and was to extend to the next four races; the championship was in his sights. Victory, however, would be hollow, overshadowed by grief for his friend Piers Courage who died after his de Tomaso-Ford, run by Frank Williams, crashed in flames during the Dutch Grand Prix on 21 June. Bruce McLaren had been killed in testing at Goodwood less than three weeks earlier. On the podium at Zandvoort, Jochen looked wooden as he went through the motions of receiving the trophy. He would never again feel the same desperate enthusiasm for motor racing. Instead, he now yearned for property deals, the sports clothing and other Rindtstone ventures to be explored in retirement and the further development of his racing car exhibtion in Vienna, the Jochen Rindt Show. It was even rumoured that Jochen had wagered Nina $20,000 that he would retire at the end of the season, just two races away. If there was any hunger for winning left in him, it was reserved for the first World Championship Austrian Grand Prix at the Osterreichring, not far from Graz, his home town, where he had been such a handful as a boy. But it was not to be. He was holding fourth place when the engine of his Lotus failed leaving the cheering crowds disappointed, and Jochen further disgusted.

The last race of the European season was the Italian Grand Prix at Monza, and on the day before the race, Saturday 5 September, Jochen went out on to the circuit for the usual qualifying session. What was unusual was 'the absence of a rear wing,' says team manager Peter Warr. Colin Chapman had had the car stripped of its rear wing, now a much more secure structure, in an attempt to gather additional straight-line speed, and in this Jochen, who disliked wings anyway, had concurred. Furthermore, 'there were different compounds of left and right tyre'. Braking hard into the Parabolica, the fast final curve before the pit straight, Jochen's Lotus 72 'began to shimmy from left to right, hit the Armco supported by a post and became wrapped around it'. Jochen had refused to wear a crotch strap so the collapsed frame of the car pulled him down into the cockpit. His foot was amputated when the front of the car was torn off as the nose cone jammed under the barrier, and his throat was gashed on the harness buckle, severing his jugular vein. He died within fifteen to thirty seconds of the accident.

Bernie immediately ran to the scene but, unable to help his friend, he walked away 'devastated', carrying Jochen's helmet under his arm. 'They put Jochen in a Volkswagen van,' says Bernie, 'and were banging on his chest. 'The van went first to the wrong hospital, and then on to another.' The Italian authorities did not declare him dead until his body had been taken to the second hospital where Colin, Nina and Bernie stood in the corridor, dazed with shock, listening to the words confirming Jochen's death. Bernie remembers that 'the doctor then said to me that Jochen's eyes were unusual in that they were so close together'. Peter Warr recalls: 'Bernie was dreadfully, genuinely, humanitarianly upset.' Later, Nina recalled, 'Bernie was angry about how it was all handled.'

Jochen Rindt became Formula 1's first, and so far only, posthumous World Champion. Italian law required that Colin Chapman be charged with homicide, of which he was eventually cleared. Bernie, as a final kindness to his friend, helped Nina set up a trust for Natascha, becoming one of its trustees to make certain that Jochen's daughter would always be properly looked after.

In the Formula 2 season of 1970 Jochen had won eight of seventeen races. During the race at Brands Hatch Bernie 'would come out and talk to people and then he would go into race control and talk to the staff,' mused Royal Automobile Club official Neil Eason Gibson, who had been on hand at the race. Here as elsewhere it had been noticed that Bernie took his partnership in Jochen Rindt Racing Ltd very seriously, just as he had taken every aspect of Jochen's Formula 1 racing career very seriously. He had ingested the whole, from inside out, and began to wonder at its potential. In the process – for better or worse – Bernie became forever committed to the 'fast, exciting' sport; 'I love it,' he admitted. Yes, Bernie felt remorse for Jochen's death – 'it shouldn't have happened, such a waste of life' – and for a moment he questioned his own judgement: 'What am I doing here?' But it was only a momentary doubt for he would not allow himself to be overcome by anguish. Instead he would leave the wound untreated, tamping down despair with work. The wound would fester and in weeks to come make him physically ill, but just then he would not think about it. Better to contemplate a wider picture of Formula 1 motor racing, an image he visualised intuitively. This time Bernie would not turn away. Not now, not ever.

CHAPTER 6

TEAM BERNIE

Towards the end of the Sixties Bernie made a decision that would set the pattern for the rest of his life: he decided to buy a Formula 1 team. Which team was not yet entirely clear, and Jochen's death had left him disorientated, angry and frustrated, because Jochen had been so much a part of the plan. Now Bernie's plans were fluttering in mid-air like a bird unable to find a place to settle. In his thinking he always gravitated towards Formula 1, the single-seaters: motor racing was part of his fibre as much as any vital organ. So the emotional debris would – one way or another – be tidied away. Bernie would have his team, and Formula 1 would be central to his existence. That was absolutely certain.

Back in May 1970, Jochen had introduced Bernie to Ron Tauranac, chief designer and owner of Motor Racing Developments Limited, the company that owned the Brabham Racing Organisation. The purpose of the introduction and subsequent meeting was to explore the possibility of forming a partnership. Although discussions along the same vein with Robin Herd had proved fruitless, Bernie and Jochen had continued to hope that by some means or other they would yet become partners in a Formula 1 team, with Jochen, of course, as the number one driver. The fact that such an arrangement might involve the dear old Brabham team was all the better.

Australian Jack Brabham (now Sir Jack), having raced successfully in Australia, came to England in 1955 to drive for Cooper, where he also contributed to the development of their history-making rear-engined design. In 1959, at the age of thirty-three, he won his first World Championship, and he won it again in 1960, which made him aspire to set up his own racing team and car production company. This he did in 1961 after inviting his friend, fellow Australian Ron Tauranac, a talented designer who had already built – even raced – his own cars, to come to England to be his partner. They called their company Motor Racing Developments Limited and, like Lotus, March and others, constructed various types of cars, in this instance Formula Junior, then sports cars, Formula 2, Formula 3 and, in 1962, their Formula 1 Brabham made its debut. The following year the team finished third in the Constructors' Championship and in 1964 they continued to collect F1 points while steadily scoring finishes in Formula 2. The team again took third place in the 1965 Constructors' title, but 1966 was the year when all honour and glory were theirs, the year – ever after inscribed in motor racing annals – when Jack Brabham won the World Championship for the third time, becoming the only driver to win the title in a car bearing his own name. With the team also winning the Constructors' Championship, Ron Tauranac was now keen to concentrate his own energies on Formula 1. Previously, he had run the business from the factory floor in New Haw near Weybridge, Surrey, but now Ron attended most of the Grands Prix and in 1967 Denny Hulme took the World Championship for the Brabham team.

In 1968, however, their fortunes changed. This was the time of the disappointing four-cam Repco engine that had annihilated Jochen's expectations of collecting Formula 1 laurels; and in 1969, due to family pressure after a worrying accident, Jack Brabham was persuaded to retire. He sold his shares to Ron Tauranac making him sole owner, but when Jochen moved to Lotus Jack decided to stay on to drive for one last season before returning to Australia at the end of 1970 to run a farm business which he had bought the previous year, and to set up a Ford dealership with Ron's brother, Austin Lewis Tauranac.

Shouldering the company on his own, Ron Tauranac was not a man to make fast and furious decisions, nor did he possess the aggressive temperament often required to succeed in the conflicting world of motor racing. Moreover, it was in his nature to be wholly genuine; indeed many find him painfully precise. Thus, as principal team owner, he became increasingly at odds with a profession that in 1970 was beginning to exercise wily boardroom tactics and pumped-up dreamscape scenarios to obtain sponsorship. The demand for such talents was set to increase, but even at a modest level impossible for Ron; he wanted out. So when Jochen and Bernie met with him in May and proposed a partnership, Ron countered with: 'I'd rather sell out instead. I'll work for you and we'll see how we get on… if it all clicks and goes well, then I'll buy some shares back and we'll go into business together.' Bernie went away to mull it over. Meanwhile, Jochen was killed and everything went quiet until about four months later when Ron was contacted by Bernie. He had decided to buy Ron out 'for the value of the assets'. Ron interpreted Bernie's words as a deal, a completed deal.

'I never tell a lie,' says Ron, 'never told a lie in my life.' He would regard unintentional imprecision as a lie: 'before I write you a report I make certain'. The assets were therefore scrupulously analysed and computed, a task that lasted several months until, at the end of the season, a figure of £130,000 was ascertained. 'That was Ron's valuation,' says Bernie. In expectation of this sum Ron established a trust for his two daughters 'and did a lot of personal things, and I'd made several other commitments which meant it was going to be very difficult to continue on with the company.' All of the appropriate documentation supporting an evaluation of £130,000 had been sent to Bernie. But then 'right at the eleventh hour', Bernie rang up Ron saying, 'I'll give you £100,000 for it.' Ron acquiesced, though he now admits, 'I should have said, "hold on, we have a deal and you've got to stick to your word", but I didn't, I just thought: "I'm in real trouble if this doesn't go through now, I'm committed". So after three or four minutes I said "yes" and that was that… that was the deal. I don't blame Bernie. I mean it's what businessmen do, but I thought we had this deal.' From

Bernie's point of view the negotiation process was ongoing, the figure of £130,000 being an outside number, the place from whence both sides argued toward a comfort zone and – ideally – fixed the deal. The fact that Ron had agreed the sum without a tussle would have caused Bernie to wonder if he'd paid too much.

Some time between the first 'deal' with Bernie and the conclusion of the final agreement, in 1972, John Coombs had approached Ron expressing an interest in buying Motor Racing Developments Limited and was told, 'I'm selling it to Bernie'. 'Don't do that, we'll give you more than Bernie,' John had said. Ron then explained that it was very difficult because of the deal with Bernie, then reconsidered, saying he would 'go back to Bernie and tell him there's somebody else'. Having done so, Ron then contacted John and told him: 'I really can't do anything about this because Bernie has mortgaged his house, he's hocked his wife or girlfriend's jewellery, and he's really got himself to the stage of buying.' John was outraged, or amused: 'He doesn't have to hock anything to buy it, it's pocket money to Bernie!' Roy Salvadori thinks differently: 'In my opinion Bernie didn't have a lot of money when he bought Brabham, but Bernie was so game that all he had would go into a venture, that's the thing, that's why you don't want to fight with Bernie because whatever Bernie's got that's it, he'll fight to the end. I wouldn't want to get so involved, I mean Bernie was always prepared to put whatever he had into an operation. To me a man's got to be cautious, to Bernie it's the opposite way round. If he goes for something, he goes for it full-time. And it's worked.'

To Bernie, business ventures were, and still are, merely another form of gambling – which also usually worked in his favour. The previous year during a session of roulette Roy recalls Bernie 'took over the bank, he was down a few thousand pounds and didn't seem to care and went on and on.' Roy got cold feet. 'I couldn't stand it and left about one o'clock in the morning. The next morning I couldn't wait to ring Bernie and he'd got £12,000 up, that was his way, just took over the bank.' With or without an appreciation of

Bernie's tenacity, Ron Tauranac would not be persuaded to stand down from what he then regarded as a firm agreement, though, like John Coombs, Roy Salvadori feels that 'Bernie made a deal that Tauranac should have turned down. So far as I know, I'm not an expert on this, but I think that Bernie then looked at the stock, churned it out, sold it off and he already had his money back when he paid for it.'

What neither Ron nor John nor Roy realised, even now, is that before Bernie could reach the point where he was prepared to buy Brabhams or any motor racing organisation, Formula 1 or otherwise, he first had to overcome an emotional and physical reaction to the death of Jochen Rindt. About a month after Jochen was killed Bernie came down with severe flu-like symptoms, making him 'very ill'. Bernie was so unwell that 'he thought he was going to die' and, for once, was too ill to leave his bed. A doctor was called to his Chislehurst home and after examining Bernie came to the conclusion that his symptoms had been caused by the 'stress' of his friend's death; post-traumatic stress in the current jargon. Now approaching his fortieth birthday, Bernie needed to be reassured that his suffering was not life-threatening. When he got that assurance, Bernie 'tried to snap out of it', which he eventually managed, but not by talking about his sadness. He 'didn't talk about it very much', although the stress was there for all to see, and for some to comment on. But occasionally something would stir a happy memory, then he would talk about 'the Kraut' and laugh. Bernie's tough offer for the purchase of Motor Racing Developments Limited, the £100,000, was certainly disagreeable to Ron Tauranac; for Bernie it was a sign that he had regained equilibrium.

This period of big expenditure also encompassed personal property. In July 1971 Bernie acquired – with money borrowed from a Guernsey-based company – twenty-six acres of woods and parkland in an area called Farnborough Park, situated near the bustling, demi-metropolis of Bromley in Kent, not far from Chislehurst. At the time of this purchase his pockets were rather over-full with cash. Following the sale of his motorcycle business he had retained £10,000 rightfully belonging to the tax authorities. During the proceedings that followed the judge described Bernie's business 'machinery' as 'altogether extraordinary'. Bernie didn't bother appearing as a witness to fight his corner. He just paid the money.

The Farnborough Park property contained a vast two-acre lake, which Bernie had stocked with carp so that his father, Sidney, and close friends could have the pleasure of fishing there. 'He used to have a bucket of fish [actually 'nutrient pellets'] and threw it in, and the whole lake was alive,' says Roy Salvadori. 'You've never seen anything like it – frightening.' The fish were fed every day from a pier in a natural harbour, which was aerated during the winter to prevent that section of the lake from freezing. Bernie and racing driver Carlos Pace indulged in Formula 1 fishing by using the pellets on hooks for bait, which the fish loved as it was their natural food. Fishing out of season continued without interruption. 'I don't take any notice of that,' said Bernie, 'the fish don't know what the date is.' For the fishermen Bernie set two rules: 'Use barbless hooks and put back the fish that you catch.' Among the lakeside amenities was a summerhouse containing a full-size snooker table and, for the comfort of Bernie's bulldog, a fully air-conditioned kennel. Sadly, one of Bernie's dogs (he then had two bulldogs) attempted a spot of fishing on his own and drowned in the lake.

When in 1984 Sidney Ecclestone, at the age of eighty-one, gave up fishing to attend to the needs of his wife, now crippled with arthritis, Bernie sold his Farnborough acreage, making a profit of some £300,000. Bernie's mother, Bertha, eventually became housebound, amusing herself with books, particularly adventure stories of exotic destinations to which she was now unable to travel in spite of the luxuries her son was eager to provide. Her other recreation was painting china figures, impressing her family with her skill. As in their former homes in Suffolk and Dartford, Bertha was 'still the boss'; Sidney would sometimes take out his hearing aid to indicate that Bertha was monopolising conversation. The couple often talked about Bernie, whose success still amazed them. They liked to boast about his global travels and his ventures into motor racing. 'They were always very, very proud of him,' said Bernie's sister, Marian. Apart from the lake, Bernie showed his love for his parents by moving them to an attractive flat, and then into a cottage near Marian, recently widowed. He also bought them the latest high-tech television, as a replacement for the set he had bought in 1953, so that they could watch the Coronation; and he secured the services of the best surgeon for Bertha Ecclestone's hip operation. These and countless other kindnesses demonstrated a devotion that Bernie was uncomfortable putting into words or embraces.

Five years after acquiring the Farnborough Park parcel of land and lake, Bernie purchased a nearby house called 'Knollwood'. He still favoured the mock-Tudor style, and this version had three double bedroom suites, a library (filled out with faux 'books by the yard'), grand reception rooms, and was surrounded by three acres of formal, manicured gardens. His wardrobe now contained colour-coordinated suits by the yard with trousers – like his jeans – sporting knife-edge creases maintained by Bernie's valet, Ron Cunningham, who by now had also relieved Bernie of the solemn responsibility of daily shoe polishing. For shirts, Bernie went to Frank Foster in London's West End. Frank, who has 'done the Bonds – Roger Moore and Sean Connery' – has been making shirts for Bernie since the days of the early James Bond films in the Sixties, and they are still very good friends. He says that Bernie is 'just an ordinary guy' with 'two other personalities – Bernie the businessman and Bernie avoiding the press. He's always a smart, dapper fellow' though 'not a man of fashion, not flashy, always wears cotton shirts buying two or three at a time, but no monogrammed silk, which he would regard as too American'. Bernie's London tailor, of some thirty years' standing, is Edward Sexton who, with his partner Tommy Nutter, had 'brought style to Savile Row', combining ideas from the hip design Meccas of the Sixties and Seventies – Carnaby Street and Chelsea's Kings Road – with quality, traditional tailoring techniques. Of Bernie's own sartorial preferences, Edward says that 'he always wears dark suits, always solid colours – medium to dark grey;

medium blue to black – his taste is conservative with a twist, up-to-the-minute, with the latest silhouette. He also likes soft construction in a garment, very, very soft, and he knows exactly what suits him in fabric and accessories.' And his shoes – 'Bally, side buckle, size five'.

Gone was the suit jacket slung over his shoulders: Bernie now presented himself to the world as a man of studied precision. Like military men, he uses garments to establish command, and then to communicate the order of play. Nor is he a casual shopper; he buys his suits 'six at a time'. 'If he gives you volume,' says Edward, 'he does a deal, and he doesn't need a calculator, Bernie's the Professor of Street Smarts, but always dignified and fair. Just don't deliver the wrong order.' One evening when Bernie was getting dressed for some – to him – loathsome formal occasion, he slipped into the trousers of a new evening suit, only to discover – with appreciable outrage – that the trousers were enormous. A much larger man's suit had been sent to his home. The unfortunate assistant who had arranged the delivery received an upbraiding that left him so shaken that to this day whenever Bernie has a fitting scheduled at Edward Sexton's the man is always away – sick at home, on an errand, on a break, out of the country – whatever, suddenly elsewhere.

Sidney Ecclestone was overheard to say that 'Bernie thought the way to make money was in motor racing', which was reason enough for him to decide to buy Brabham. Fortunately, the purchase roughly coincided with his decision to give up his second-hand car businesses 'because I didn't want to be a tax collector. VAT had just come in so I closed those down.' Until this point he had referred to motor racing as his 'hobby', and in 1972 he still said he considered running Brabham as a 'hobby', even though he hasn't the nature for pastimes; Bernie's pursuits, like gambling, involve money overlaid with the potential for winning, they are, therefore, serious business. What is significant about the acquisition of the Brabham works is that he now had the opportunity to work – and to make money – at something 'that I love, I just love motor racing'. It was kismet, the auspicious moment when he 'realised the possibility of putting it all together'. Fate is not a word that Bernie is likely to use, he prefers destiny: 'I want to be in charge of my own destiny and not have to rely on someone else.' But he was now about to grab either fate or destiny by the tail and was taking no passengers, awkward for Ron Tauranac who was counting on a major role in Bernie's Brabham future.

Disposal of Bernie's 'other interests' didn't involve the actual sale of James Spencer Limited but rather allowing the company's business to dwindle until it ceased trading in 1978. When the government of Prime Minister Edward Heath introduced VAT in 1973, 'Bernard's idea was that the motor trade would never be any good or be the same, according to Bernie's friend Ray Morris, who was then trading in cars from the former Compton & Ecclestone premises. 'And he was absolutely correct. A system had been devised for the motor trade to pay their tax in a different manner to other people [a percentage of profit] and it's quite prohibitive.' Another fellow trader remembers Bernie's vexation with the government's percentage: 'If I want a partner I'll get one!'

Pentbridge Properties handled Bernie's domestic property, so it was Arvin Securities, the hire-purchase company – now expanded to become involved in commercial properties – that had become the source of funds for the purchase of Brabham. But whether it was called Brabham or Motor Racing Development Limited, the company would, in Bernie's heart, be his team, only his. 'The truth is... I like doing things my way,' he says. He was not interested in participating in a *ménage à trois* by sharing his team with Ron Tauranac, who very decidedly had his own way of doing things, though Bernie initially went through the motions of keeping Ron involved.

When Bernie turned up at the Brabham factory on his first day as its new owner, he went 'straight in and started talking to all the employees,' says Ron Tauranac, who was now the new joint Managing Director. Standing on a wooden box, Bernie 'invited them to sound off and they were all criticising me!' he adds, recalling the scene: 'So there were all these criticisms that he listened to, and then the storeman told him he wanted a bigger store and Bernie told him to order in the bricks to make the bigger store. Now, I was told nothing about this. He was going to extend the store within the factory building… and he never discussed it with me. The first I heard about it was when the storeman came to me to say the bricks had arrived… It was just, I think he'd always been his own man running his own little shop and not part of a big organisation where you have to delegate. I think that was the failure of us not getting on, there was never any communication between us.'

Ron admits that he had continued to regard Brabham as 'my company, my expertise', and he had, after all, been integral in making it a success. But, unlike Bernie, he had not heard the talk around the Formula 1 paddock, the talk of Brabham's recent struggles. Bernie made it his business immediately to address the company's failings, whatever they happened to be. Diplomacy was a luxury, which is not to say that he was unwilling to ask for help, whether it came from the manager's office or from twenty-one-year-old Herbie Blash. Bernie had befriended Herbie, a Lotus mechanic, when Jochen had been driving for Colin Chapman and Bernie was running the Formula 2 team, Jochen Rindt Racing. As Herbie explains, he and Bernie had 'just built up a relationship, and it was at that particular point that Bernie said he was thinking about having his own Formula 1 team and would I help him, so I said "yes".' When Jochen was killed 'Bernie was left to sort everything out'. He asked Herbie to take Jochen's car back to Switzerland and thereafter they had 'kept in contact'. When Bernie later told Herbie of his intention to buy Brabham they started 'talking about what we would do… I checked out the quality of the bits and pieces for him beforehand… and moved in with Bernie on the day that he bought it.' But then Herbie was introduced to Ron Tauranac and, realising that they would never get along, quit within a few hours of their meeting. Ex-Lotus chief mechanic Bob Dance also remembers the change in Brabham's ownership. Meeting in a London hotel, Bernie, with Herbie at his side, explained to

Bob and potential new employee Cary Adams that 'he was taking over Brabham, that he would be paying a competitive rate of pay and that he wasn't changing the name [of the company] to Ecclestone' and so on. Like Herbie, Bob, who had 'had good training at Lotus', knew that he 'couldn't fit in with Ron's way of doing things', and it was generally felt that Bernie would be better than Ron at man management.

Herbie still remembers an incident that had occurred in the pits at Monaco in 1969 when an irritable Colin Chapman had been badgering the Lotus mechanics with a 'whole list of jobs for us to do. We were busy doing this job list and Bernie knew we were never going to get finished so he said "leave it to me" and he talked Colin into going off to the hotel... we liked Bernie, he was making life easier.' Bernie would not always make life easier, but he generally understood when the application of pressure was not to his advantage. Unable to hold on to Herbie, Bernie was anxious to prevent Bob's departure and persuaded him to stay on with the encouragement that Bob could 'give him a ring if there was any problem'. Bernie and Ron Tauranac, adds Bob, 'had differences of outlook. Bernie was particular about his workshop and tried to streamline operations.' Their differences were widely evident, at least to the factory's seventeen employees. Ron 'started getting the cold shoulder', his opinions were regarded as interference and, although it clearly wasn't obvious to the former Brabham owner, the man now in charge – apart from Bernie, of course – was Colin Seeley.

Colin had first made his name racing motorcycles, becoming the British Sidecar Champion in 1962 and again in 1963. He then went on to take third place in the World Championship in 1964 and 1966. But it was before these successes, back in 1954, that he got into the business of selling motorcycles, eventually setting up a factory to develop motorcycles of his own design. Ron, initially shocked at being sidelined, started looking for reasons and concluded that Bernie 'had ambitions, not only to have the car racing but also bike racing all together'. He turned out to be correct which, along with other perceived snubs, made his position at Brabham untenable. 'I was in the office and they were all taking their instructions from someone else [Colin Seeley],' says Ron. 'I tried to work there but it became difficult.' So he decided to set up a drawing board at home to carry on working there, 'out of other people's hair'. Team owner Frank Williams telephoned Ron at his home and asked if he 'could take some time to collect a race engine for him in South Africa'. Always striving to be correct, Ron contacted Bernie to obtain permission, which was granted – even though Ron's absence had been 'construed as my leaving'. His departure was subsequently made official in a letter from the Brabham accountant, Brian Shepherd (later Bernie's personal accountant), asking Ron to 'return company drawings' that were in his home along with the 'company car'. Ron duly 'returned the drawings and got a receipt... dropped the car off and put the key through the letterbox'. He then made arrangements to depart for Australia with his family.

Happily, neither motor racing nor England was through with Ron Tauranac, who made his comeback by forming a new company for the development of production cars. But he did so only after Brabham had ceased to make production cars and – with scrupulous correctness – only after again obtaining permission from Bernie, who simply said, 'yes, go ahead'. Ralt, the name of a company that, many years before, Ron had shared with his brother, Austin Lewis Tauranac, and derived from a combination of their names, was resurrected for Ron's new company. For his contributions to motorsport he eventually received Australia's equivalent of the Order of the British Empire. Now, fit and appearing much younger than his eighty years, Ron Tauranac has only recently retired and returned to Australia.

Herbie Blash, today a well-known and respected figure around the F1 paddock, returned to Brabham as team manager soon after Ron's departure. He has continued to work for and with Bernie for much of his career, and their friendship has remained rock solid.

The choice of Colin Seeley as manager had been easy,

for he and Bernie had come from similar backgrounds and they had both, albeit at different times, worked at Harcourt Motorcycles in Bexleyheath. Bernie had then 'moved across the road', to what was then Compton & Fuller. Colin, likewise, soon left Harcourt, setting up his own motorcycle business in 1954 at a shop in Belvedere, Kent. Five years later, while Bernie was sponsoring Bobby Rowe on the Norton, Colin travelled with Bobby to race in the North West 200 in Northern Ireland, and from there they headed to Brands Hatch where Bobby broke his shoulder in a crash. Colin 'went with Bernie in his Maserati, I'll always remember it, to see Bobby Rowe in hospital. That was 1959.' That was also their most extensive contact thus far. Colin was impressed with the savvy Ecclestone, five years his senior: 'I wasn't really in the same league as Bernie', who 'had a reputation in the area for being pretty astute. He wasn't everybody's favourite person… I think people don't know how to deal with Bernie, he's a special case.'

When the British motorcycle industry went into decline during the Sixties, Colin Seeley bought 'the whole race department from Associated Motorcycles' (manufacturers of AJS and Matchless motorcycles), a long-standing company with 600 employees, when they went in to liquidation. He then closed his retail business and dedicated himself to manufacturing the Seeley G-50 and 7-R racing machines. For the next seven years Colin produced motorcycles for talents such as Derek Minter, John Cooper, Dave Croxford, Barry Sheene and Mike Hailwood – 'any top rider you want to name in the UK was on my bikes, and we won the British Championship twice, and were runners-up a couple of times.' Eventually, Colin employed twenty-seven workers, but by 1971 he was 'over-trading' and 'struggling financially', he recalls, and 'needed somebody to put some money into the business… to come in with me.' It was at this point that Colin bought a Ford Capri from Bernie, they naturally started talking motorcycles and a few days later Bernie gave him a call: the tobacco company, John Player Special (JPS), were looking to sponsor motorcycle racing, and he offered to set up a meeting between the representatives of JPS, Colin and himself in his James Spencer offices. But, says Colin, Bernie wanted 'his cut, and I always remember thinking there won't be much left to do the business with.' As it happened, JPS were 'only interested in sponsoring superbikes', and Colin was 'unable to supply the complete machines', so he recommended they invest in the Norton factory instead.

Nevertheless, the two former employees of Harcourt Motorcycles still had a business future together, for a few months later Bernie, according to Colin, invited him to 'join him buying Motor Racing Developments'. Bernie disagrees: 'I never invited him, he didn't have a dollar.' Roy Salvadori's impression that Bernie, at this time, was becoming overstretched appears to be accurate. The combined cost of the Brabham works and the Farnborough acreage was considerable, nearly £200,000, not that Bernie would lose any sleep over it. Like most ventures it was just another roll of the dice, although in the early Seventies the odds did not appear to be tilted in his favour.

Colin had been open about his financial circumstances: 'I haven't got any money Bernie' although 'I was obviously enthused about the whole thing – Formula 1 and bikes.' And production cars, too, for he was then assured that what was really wanted was a joint managing director (in the weeks before Ron Tauranac left) 'to run the production' of what Ron had estimated to be twenty-five Formula 2 and Formula 3 cars. It was also agreed that Colin Seeley Racing Developments would be re-housed at Manor Road in Erith, Kent, upon construction of a factory on what was the site of Bernie's former car auction enterprise; Bernie would be responsible for the management of Formula 1. Colin accepted this combined proposal and looked forward to a bright future.

To seal the deal, Bernie made a statement in the press announcing MRD's 'major assault' on 'both two and four wheel areas' of development. This was 1972, the year of Brabham's first monocoque production cars called BT38s (actually developed in 1971), for which the company took 'about sixty orders' – now Colin's responsibility. In addition, Colin was still trying to keep his staff busy at the motorcycle works in Belvedere. The dream was rapidly turning into a facsimile of Hell's Kitchen with 'Bernie shouting at me' and people endlessly ringing up hollering 'where's my car, where's my car'. It was 'a hell of a stress'. Colin Seeley was then working an eighteen-hour day, dividing his time between Kent and Surrey as well as making frequent trips (in a van provided by Bernie) to the offices of James Spencer in Bexleyheath to report progress and to receive instructions. In turn Bernie visited the Brabham factory near Weybridge 'once a week, normally on a Thursday,' says Colin, 'he'd come down either in a Roller or some flash car.'

McLaren boss Ron Dennis, who had first met Bernie when he was managing Jochen Rindt, remembers that Bernie's involvement – at least when Colin first arrived at Brabham – was more hands-on: 'The next time I came into contact with Bernie was when he bought Brabham, and I was quite amazed because it was a pretty shambolic place. He'd put a person called Colin Seeley in charge of the business and… I have these vivid pictures of going in on a Saturday to pick up some parts or something, and there was Bernie and Colin Seeley, and they were in sort of jeans and T-shirts and they were cleaning the factory, the two of them, up to their eyes in muck and bullets, moving things around, and this was Bernie sort of saying: "Right, we're going to reorganise this". And, of course, Bernie spent quite a bit of money trying to improve the facilities, but it was always the sort of tin shed down the end of a bumpy drive sort of situation. There were World Championship cars that came out of there. That was what was possible in those days.'

Within two years Colin had overseen the manufacture of more than 100 production cars. For his Herculean efforts, Colin says, he did not receive a salary: 'Motor Racing Developments never paid me any money', although 'some money [Bernie's] went into the company [Colin Seeley Racing Developments]. But nothing like Bernie has put into print.' The figure, in fact, was £4,252. 'I just feel that

I worked two years for absolutely nothing. The companies, in theory, had merged. But what Bernie didn't do, as I understand it, is he never registered as a director of Colin Seeley Racing Developments,' and was therefore, Colin believes, not under obligation to the motorcycle company: 'I was a bit naïve, I just wanted to get on with it and it was, you know, all go, go, go. It's my own fault.' For Bernie's part, he had 'intended' to put more money into Colin's company, but when it became obvious that the venture would not be viable, he cut his losses.

In 1973, following a year of success with Barry Sheene on a Seeley Suzuki, Colin's motorcycle development business went into liquidation, never having moved to the now-completed factory on Manor Road in Erith. Yet, remarkably, that was not the end of Colin's business with Bernie. A few months after Colin's motorcycle development company had folded, he agreed to take on the task of managing a Brabham Formula 1 car. Along with two mechanics working out of his factory in Belvedere, Colin looked after the car driven by Andrea de Adamich, who, in 1973, brought sponsorship money along with a fourth-place finish in Belgium, but the Italian's Brabham days came to an end when he broke his leg badly in a multiple accident at the British Grand Prix; he had driven in five races before being replaced for the remainder of the season by German driver Rolf Stommelen. 'Brabhams were not having a good time in Formula 1 that year,' says Colin. But they did manage to finish fourth in the constructors' cup, helped, in part, by the tireless contribution of Colin Seeley who sometimes worked all night with the help of his two associates.

He remembers one occasion, in particular, in Belgium where he had been working until six o'clock in the morning changing engines. He was exhausted, covered in grease, and on coming out of the garage met Bernie, who immediately shouted: 'Get yourself cleaned up!' Colin says, 'It was like I wasn't always clean. Yes I remember that "get yourself cleaned up", that's all he said, like he's out at the casino enjoying himself and we're up working all night... put me off.' But what really annoyed Colin was Bernie's refusal to help his friend Ernst Weiss, a former Swiss hill-climbing motorcycle champion turned truck driver who had hopes of driving the Brabham team's transport van. The truck driver's own vehicle, in which he had been moving car parts from Europe, broke down somewhere in Kent, and he put in a distress call to Colin, asking for assistance. Colin in turn telephoned Bernie requesting 'the use of a tractor unit' to move the truck driver's defunct trailer. Bernie said 'no', Colin recalls: 'I was so disappointed I resigned.'

A year later Colin, undaunted, again started making motorcycles, 'from scratch', particularly the Seeley Honda-750. He then went on to make 150 Phil Read replica motorcycles and Honda-Britains for Honda UK, but this venture also suffered financial difficulties, finishing in 1982 'due to Honda's failure at distribution'. This time Colin had had enough. He turned his back on manufacturing and applied his energies to the restoration of a Victorian vicarage, making it into a residential home, a project that occupied a couple of years until 1986, when Bernie once more contacted Colin and invited him to rejoin Brabham – now in Chessington. This time around Colin's title would be 'Race Team Coordinator' and his role – 'general busybody'. Bernie wanted him to help 'sort the place out'. The team's racing results were then at a low ebb, as was morale, and, says Colin, 'the atmosphere was really bad'.

'Bernie was not very good at getting rid of people,' continues Colin. 'I was the hiring and firing man. I believe I did a good job that year particularly, I got the team spirit up but they were having problems with the car.' Then, in 1987, Bernie made Colin team manager, replacing Herbie Blash, who now became Brabham's sporting manager. But Colin was unhappy in his new role: 'I probably wasn't the right choice if I'm totally honest. But I didn't get the back-up I thought I needed to do that job properly. I'd done a good job as race team coordinator and dealing with all the nitty-gritty things back in the factory and all the dramas.' Even so, by August 1987 it was Colin's turn to get 'the cold shoulder', and he and Bernie soon called it quits. 'He decided that he didn't need me any more, so that was it.' Bernie has been accused of discarding people when they are no longer useful. What is certain is the fact that the exit door is quickly shown to those who 'take liberties' or 'don't show the proper respect'. Neither Ron Tauranac nor Colin Seeley was guilty of these misdemeanours. Still, the former sidecar champion had 'enjoyed the involvement, despite the work. It was one hell of an experience I have to say!' And leaving Brabham was, he concludes, 'the right decision'.

While Colin's manufacturing efforts and involvement with the Brabham team were behind him, his involvement in motorcycles was far from over. Between 1992 and 1994 he ran the Duckhams-Norton team, winning the championship in 1994. Later he ran the official Honda superbike team among others, squeezing in time to write about his experiences – in two volumes. Along the way he also became involved in 'the political side of motorcycle racing' in the UK. Just as in Formula 1, the sport of motorcycle racing – and its politics – have changed out of all recognition; 'it's very big business,' says Colin. Indeed. Today, aged seventy-four and still very active, he sometimes sees Bernie at motorcycle grands prix, and once or twice they've chatted about how to improve the sport. Bernie's passion for motorcycles remained intense. And he would find a new way to turn the two-wheeled passion into a profitable business.

During the mid-Eighties, Bernie began to manage the television rights of the FIM (Fédération Internationale de Motocyclisme) Road Racing World Championship Grands Prix, inventing 'a modern system to manage the motorcycle world championship and commercialise its rights,' says Carmelo Ezpeleta, chief executive officer and managing director of Dorna Sports; the FIM is the world governing body for motorcycle sport. Bernie then created a company called TWP (Two Wheel Productions) for the management of the television rights, and later joined with Dorna Sports to 'commercialise together' the rights of the motorcycle World Championship. In 1993 Bernie sold TWP to Dorna. Since then he has served as a member of the Permanent Bureau of the FIM Road Racing World Championship Grand Prix.

When Bernie completed the deal on Motor Racing Developments in 1972, the odds on making Brabham a success were against him and he was poised for difficult times. No matter, he could look beyond 1972 and the future was rosy; the best, as they say, was yet to come. But first he would have to persuade or goad his team members to reach – vigorously – for that broader vista.

CHAPTER 7

JUGGLING

In 1973 Bernie decided to stop producing Brabham racing cars for sale because the return on investment was long-term. Holding cars in stock, awaiting payment in full, required too much financial thumb-twiddling. Furthermore, due to a series of almost concurring fiscal body blows, the automobile industry in general, along with the rest of Britain, was locked into a downward spiral. The previous year, more than a million workers had been laid off across Britain as a result of a miners' strike, shutting down much of the country's power supplies and leading to the imposition of a three-day working week. A state of emergency had been declared on 9 February 1972. On 4 August, another state of emergency was proclaimed when 42,000 dockers refused to go to work. Unemployment reached levels not seen since the Thirties. Likewise, in May 1973 British Leyland car plants were hit by striking engineering workers, and a general strike over pay and prices reduced the Vauxhall, Ford and Chrysler plants to a standstill; Rolls-Royce was also affected.

Still more trouble ensued when an oil crisis in the Middle East, brought about by the Yom Kippur War, resulted in a quadrupling of fuel costs. Drivers had to adhere to reduced speed limits as the government tried to save fuel and, when it later abolished the maximum price control on petrol, private motorists bore the increases at the pump. Thanks to the world's dependence on OPEC, the English vocabulary gained the word 'stagflation' – the roller-coaster economics of boom followed by bust in repetitious phases. 'Bust' would arrive in 1975, when the world would be plunged into global recession. The early Seventies was not a time to carry dead weight, particularly in the form of racing cars produced for the commercial market.

When Bernie purchased Brabham the company was not only involved in Formula 1 with its own team, but was also manufacturing a range of Formula 2, Formula 3 and Formula Atlantic single-seaters, plus the odd hill-climb car, amounting to some sixty chassis per year. Adding to this burden was the 'intended' expansion into motorcycles. The company was drowning and, with only a smattering of sponsorship money, the other side of the balance sheet was looking far from robust. Inevitably, Bernie had to reconcile his head with his heart and engage in a programme of radical pruning, selling off what he could and ploughing the proceeds back into Formula 1. Only then could he steer a course – a rickety course – for Grand Prix glory.

Brabham's junior designer, twenty-five-year-old Gordon Murray, one of the company's five designers, knew that Brabham was 'not going anywhere... it was a mess'. The Formula 1 cars were 'dreadful' – bottom of the table in the Constructors' Championship in both 1971 and 1972 – and it was becoming 'too risky to stay'. The company was perceived to be going under, and it was now every man for himself. Gordon had received an offer from an individual entrant to design an endurance sports racing car to contest the Le Mans 24 Hours. He had been given the added inducement that, in his new employment, he would be allowed to 'design a complete car' from scratch and all that pertained to it. He had decided to accept. This is what he explained to Bernie when they first met in his office in 1972. Bernie listened patiently to what Gordon had to say, and then he made a snap decision: 'I'm gonna fire the other four guys and you're it. I want a completely new Formula 1 car – from the ground up – for 1973. I want the whole deal. It's your baby, your car, I don't want to use one part from the old cars. You design what you think will win races in 1973.' He also allowed Gordon to 'moonlight' for the other company, just in case. If Bernie's plans fell apart then at least Gordon would have a cushion. On that basis, Gordon accepted.

Like Colin Chapman, Bernie had a knack for spotting talent. What is more, he was better at discovering nuggets of talent and turning them into gold bullion, or gold dust; the end result was up to Gordon, and depended on whether or not he could survive the metamorphosis – returning World Championship status to Brabham's Formula 1 team. His credentials were good: a diploma in mechanical engineering from Natal Technical College in South Africa, his native country, where he had designed 'from scratch' and built 'from scratch' his own racing car. He had even raced cars for a few years, but knew that his height – 6ft 4in – meant that a future in top-level racing would probably be confined to the drawing board and/or the pit lane. Height is potentially costly in motor racing: the extra weight is contrary to its fundamental ethos of achieving optimum performance, and is unnecessary when a lighter driver could do the job. Today's Formula 1 drivers start at about 5ft 4in and most are well below 6ft tall. Another essential, though unstated, credential for the sole designer at Brabham was physical endurance. Even in those days, it normally required the combined effort of four or five people to design a Formula 1 car. With the addition of his Le Mans commitment, Gordon was, he says, 'working all hours under the sun'. And he still had to go to all the grands prix and run both cars as a race engineer. So it was not surprising that, before the end of that first year on his own, Gordon collapsed. He says: 'My body just stopped, basically. It was like somebody put a big band around my chest and was winding it. That was the beginning with Bernie. It started pretty roughly. But the good news was that the little car [the BT42] went to the first grand prix and led it. It led a couple of grands prix that year, and the following year we were winning races again. And that was very, very good. So, I have to look back and say that the first two good things Bernie did for me was to give me the chance, and to have faith. I promise to this day I have no idea why.'

Bernie had backed a hunch and it had paid off. The mustachioed, guitar-playing Gordon with the lean, intense look and locks of Che Guevara – but not the nature, being a disciple of Bob Dylan – had begun to take on a golden lustre. Bernie just stood back and let him shine. 'He left me completely alone, he never interfered,' says Gordon. Which is how Gordon preferred it – 'being in control'. Bernie understood this. They talked a lot about drivers and strategies but 'Bernie never interfered with the cars, ever, apart from styling and colours, he never interfered with the cars right through our fifteen years together.'

When Bernie decided to make Gordon a kind of one-man band he thought a broader title would be more suitable, so Brabham's new chief designer also became its technical director, with responsibilities, as he says, for: 'All the technical stuff in the team, like running the race team and the spare car and the strategies at the circuit, running the test team, deciding on how many cars we made and how many tests we went to, running the wind tunnel programme and so on.' All this in addition, of course, to designing the cars in the first place. Whereas other teams had a chief engineer and a race engineer for each car, Gordon was ultimately alone, working eighteen hours a day until 1978, when his body was again showing signs of punishment. Just to stay awake, he was, he recalls, 'living on pills. I was so single-minded, I didn't want to delegate, I wanted to control the gearbox, the engine, the strategy and everything else.'

Bernie's hands-off approach meant that he was unaware of just how badly his sole designer needed assistance. When he found out, he insisted that Gordon take on some help, and David North joined the team. 'David became a sort of right-hand man,' says Gordon, 'and eventually the pivotal other designer.'

Gordon was also effectively in day-to-day control of Brabham's budget. Bernie never crowded him with: 'We must cut down.' Never would he say: 'We can't do that.' Gentle Gordon, for his part, would never go to Bernie with a pricey shopping list. It went without saying that Brabham was operating at critical mass, and that additional financial stress could cause meltdown. Instead, he used lateral thinking, imagining and contriving: ways to 'make high-cost items cheaply'. Later, these included an on-site wind tunnel (used to determine a car's aerodynamic forces) on which the best-funded teams might spend £4 million. Gordon spent £160,000. He just got on, designed one and built it – in between races – in about three months. He did the same after coming to the conclusion that what Brabham really needed was to have their own carbon-fibre production unit. This involved an autoclave (an oven for baking components) costing as much as £200,000; Gordon spent £12,000. For the autoclave, Gordon used a ship's boiler. For its cooling system, he scavenged scrapyards for a domestic water-heating tank, an old car radiator and a suitable fan, and – hey presto – one carbon-fibre factory. And it is still working. Brabham began using carbon-fibre composite materials in Formula 1 in 1978, three years before big-budget McLaren started using this material. On a salary of £30,000 until the mid-Eighties, Gordon saved Bernie millions; he metamorphosed into twenty-four-carat gold.

On the factory floor it was a similar grind for Brabham's employees – or they could head for the exit door. Totalling seventeen, 'including the girl who made the tea', they had to do the work of twice or even three times their number. Bernie 'didn't allow time off and didn't take time off himself', but the Brabham workforce made 'a nice small group, we could depend on each other'. 'The more people you've got the more trouble you've got,' was Bernie's maxim. With limited staff it was easier to scrutinise quality. He once 'tore off a piece of bodywork on a customer's car because he didn't like the way it looked,' Gordon remembers, and received a nasty gash in his hand for his trouble. Then he 'stomped on a mechanic's car headlamp when the mechanic was damaging the work bench' – a case of do unto others. When Bernie 'flew off the handle' it was usually due to frustration over a failure to achieve what was, in his view, perfection. Similarly, his view of the 'rightness' of things, or a kind of right to expect a certain decorum, would not allow, for example, a telephone to ring unanswered in a room near the one in which he was trying to conduct a meeting. He would, of necessity, leave the meeting, rip the phone from the wall, and then calmly resume as if nothing out of the ordinary had just occurred.

His moods were something else and could blow in like a thunder-cloud, hovering, portending doom or at least an ear-splitting, spirit-soaking deluge: 'You never knew what frame of mind he was in, never quite sure of things,' says chief mechanic Bob Dance. 'You needed to keep your head down when he was in a bad mood.' On the other hand, warmth as tangible as sunshine was felt when Bernie could see that people were making an extra effort. And they basked in it. Also, Bernie 'always commanded respect, right from the beginning he commanded respect', and everyone received equal treatment; 'a mechanic didn't get any worse treatment than a driver, it was absolutely level.' When, in 1972, Graham Hill popped into the factory with a cheery 'Hello campers', and then unceremoniously slid into the cockpit of his racing car, trying it out for size, there was no question of a corresponding: 'Oh hello old boy, how's tricks?' Instead, he was clouted with a shrill: 'Oy, you, outta my car!'

Of course Bernie could not settle at Brabham until he had given it his customary clean-slate treatment as with his own houses and the Strood Motor Company. He possessed a Shaker's sense of order and cleanliness; emancipation from clutter sent him teetering at heaven's gate. And in 1972 there was heavy work at the New Haw factory, awaiting a sturdy willow broom. The factory was situated beside a canal and consisted of two brick buildings, one on each side of a rutted, gravel path. The building on the left of the path was used for almost everything having to do with Formula 1. The building to the right of the path housed the design office, customer car production, the machine shop, metal-working shop, a section for assembling chassis, and the stores. There was an area at the back where cars and the team's transporter were parked on a concrete patch. Gordon Murray liked his quarters, which had 'foxes living underneath and, from the window, you could see the banking of the old Brooklands circuit.' But it was 'very ramshackle, all the drawing paper used to wrinkle because there was basically no heating. In the winter it was freezing and damp.'

Today, similar structures such as the Cooper factory or the

Tyrrell factory are lovingly remembered, broaching negative comparison with the new, NASA-sized McLaren Technology Centre. But in 1972 Brabham's two parallel buildings demanded considerable to-ing and fro-ing – unnecessary steps that wasted time. Bernie soon reorganised the space to achieve a rational flow, and kept a couple of builders on hand to attend, without delay, to the changes. 'He was very particular about his workshops,' says Bob Dance. The exterior of the buildings was smartened up and he had the interior painted lily white, and always, but always, doors – any doors – were to be kept closed, lending further cohesion to the overall appearance. 'Suddenly, everything just got a lot cleaner,' Dance recalls.

Getting rid of the production race cars gave them much needed space in the workshop, but they eventually needed more. In 1977 Bernie would relocate the Brabham factory from New Haw near Weybridge to a 28,000sq ft building on an industrial estate in Chessington, also in Surrey, some six miles away and that much closer to London. The new space, with high ceilings and an abundance of natural light, was hangar-sized and, in Gordon's opinion, far too large for their needs. But he was wrong, as Gordon now concedes: 'It was full within four years; Bernie could see how Formula 1 was going to expand.'

Bernie's own exterior appearance was kept, as always, 'very pressed in white shirt and dark trousers'. 'Presentation was everything,' says Bob Dance. He soon had the mechanics and pit crew smartly turned-out in new overalls, 'orange bibs and braces with different coloured shirts for each day', and later 'black trousers with lemon-coloured shirts'. Bernie wanted the world to take notice. He was already a convert to what is now called 'power dressing' and the Brabham team was soon made to adopt the same doctrine, looking like winners.

At the circuit, when it came to improving working conditions, Bernie always 'sided with the mechanics'. One day at Brands Hatch, for example, when the paddock became over-congested with onlookers and hangers-on, milling about the cars as the drivers and mechanics struggled to do their work, Bernie raged at the circuit boss: 'You wouldn't have a boxer with all these people in his dressing room!' The crowds were subsequently restricted. Herbie Blash recalls an incident at Watkins Glen: 'There was this really tall six foot six guy sitting on the pit wall', and in Bernie's view cluttering up the place. So, in a moderate tone, he pressed the man to 'come on, move out of the way.' 'Who do you think you are talking to?' came the response. Then Bernie, recalls Herbie, 'I still don't know how... lifted the guy up and threw him over the Armco barrier.'

Bernie improved overall conditions for the teams by reorganising the scrutineering of cars so that each underwent the same technical inspection procedure coordinated from one circuit to the next; he also regularised the timing of practice sessions and started the system of season passes. Back in the Brabham pit area, when Gordon Murray suggested to Bernie that they acquire a specially fitted trolley costing 'a few hundred pounds' to hold the mechanics' equipment, so that they did not need to walk far to obtain whatever happened to be required, Bernie agreed without hesitation. 'He really loved that sort of [precision] stuff,' says Gordon.

Brabham had the first articulated race car transporter, also Bernie's idea. It was created by modifying a Trusthouse Forte mobile training unit with a shiny stainless-steel finish on the outside, white on the inside. It held not only the cars but also the mechanics' tools. Later, in a new trailer, a kitchen was installed by Bob Dance. Stella Murray, Gordon's wife, looked after the team's nourishment at the track. For a four-day race weekend, they each paid her £5 with which she bought enough groceries to provide, as she remembers, 'breakfast, sandwiches at lunchtime; and chili, spaghetti or similar dishes for dinner, all served on orange melamine plates. Bernie kept a briefcase full of money in a cupboard in the transporter, but he didn't pay me any salary.' Stella's love for Gordon is what took her to the circuits, but then team spirit took over. Cooking, first over a gas camp stove and later in Bob's 'beautiful' kitchen, was her way of making a contribution.

Bernie had his own quiet way of acknowledging her effort.

When Stella accidentally fell from the transporter, cutting her face, he rushed her to a nearby medical facility, and held her hand while her torn mouth was stitched back together. The Murrays were frequent guests at Farnborough Park and elsewhere, and there was a particular gift of china plates, which they 'still use'. Bernie often urged Gordon to 'take Stella for a holiday'. This he eventually did, but 'it rained'. Bob Dance's memories naturally tend more towards the practical: 'People criticise Bernie, but his alterations to the organisation of the sport really helped', along with 'making the mechanics' lives easier'. He then adds: 'Brabham, if not the biggest team, was one of the better teams to be with… we didn't waste money but we didn't go short… and we won races.'

McLaren supremo Ron Dennis says that 'Formula 1 is the perfect game for an entrepreneur because he must juggle so many balls in the air.' Which tyres? Which engine? Which pit strategy? Which sponsor? For Brabham, in 1972, the answers were difficult to determine and few changes were made, except that Bernie had the team's cars repainted white – that clean slate again – over their long-standing, somewhat turquoise version of British Racing Green. It was his way of announcing his presence, although it didn't herald any immediate wins. Against heavy point-scorers, such as Ferrari, Lotus, McLaren and Tyrrell, Brabham had no chance. Until, a year later, the cars – thanks to Gordon, and skilled drivers selected by Bernie – started gathering World Championship points. Then the juggler began tossing balls up into the air, catching more than he dropped, and spectators began to assemble to marvel at his coordination.

In 1973 Gordon Murray's 'triangular' creation, the BT42, took to the track with Argentine driver Carlos Reutemann at the wheel. Graham Hill had left to form his own Embassy Hill Racing team, and Carlos had arrived with a pocket-full of Argentine sponsorship money. The team was not yet a match for Tyrrell, for which Jackie Stewart won the championship, but Reutemann pulled off two third places, two fourths and two sixths, finishing seventh in the points table, and causing a general stir around the paddock. The number two driver, Brazilian Wilson Fittipaldi, began the season with the year-old BT37, designed by Ralph Bellamy, before switching to Gordon's BT42 and picking up a fifth place and a sixth. With the addition of points gleaned by Andrea de Adamich and Rolf Stommelen, who replaced him, Brabham ended up fourth in the Constructors' championship, having been ninth the previous years. Bernie's team was on a roll.

In 1974 Gordon unveiled his BT44 design that, partnered with the reliable Ford Cosworth DFV engine, saw Carlos Reutemann secure that cherished victory, in March, in the third round of the championship, the South African Grand Prix. The Brabham team had not won a race since 'Black Jack' Brabham himself had succeeded at the same circuit near Johannesburg four years earlier; and this was the first victory of the Ecclestone era. On the podium, the famously dour but handsome thirty-two-year-old Argentine cracked a squiggle of a smile, while Gordon and Bernie grinned right down to their shoe leather – actually canvas and rubber in the case of Gordon, whose own first win had just occurred in his home country.

There was still more to be cheerful about when Reutemann gave a repeat performance in Austria, and yet again in the last race of the season, at Watkins Glen in the United States, where he had led from pole to chequered flag at the head of a Brabham one–two. Since Wilson Fittipaldi had quit to develop a new team, Copersucar Fittipaldi, Reutemann had been teamed variously with Richard Robarts, Rikki von Opel (the heir to the German automobile fortune) and Teddy Pilette. His latest partner was thirty-year-old Brazilian Carlos Pace, and it was he who came in second at Watkins Glen, having driven the fastest lap of the race. It was now all joy and hallelujah down in New Haw, and the big-budget boys began to twitch. 'One of our very good victories was at Watkins Glen with Carlos Reutemann,' recalls Herbie Blash. 'We had pole position, we had fastest lap, we won the race, and Bernie turned round to me and gave me a bollocking because there were some fingerprints on the car… he always kept the pressure on.' The team clearly had a chance of making it to the top but – lest the dream escape – their concentration of effort was girded with steel, especially when they were winning.

During that season, Reutemann also scored a third place and a sixth, and Pace came fifth at Monza, while again posting the fastest lap. Before the mid-season arrival of Carlos Pace, Reutemann had been the only driver to score three wins but, as it turned out, it was the minor placings that, totted-up, determined the Drivers' title chase. It went to Emerson Fittipaldi, Wilson's more talented younger brother, in the cockpit of a McLaren DFV. Overall, Reutemann was ranked sixth, while Brabham came fifth in the Constructors' title. Adding an extra dash of sparkle, Ulsterman John Watson, driving privately entered Brabhams for John Goldie and Hexagon, had finished in the points by coming sixth at Monaco and fourth in Austria.

Immediately following the Brazilian Grand Prix in January 1974, Bernie, working together with driver Emerson Fittipaldi, had brought Formula 1 to a circuit in Brazil's ersatz capital city, Brasilia. It was a one-off non-championship event, involving just twelve of the twenty-five cars that had raced at Interlagos. The city of Brasilia appeared to have been whisked into position from an MGM back lot, with grand but seemingly pasteboard buildings set out in orderly rows along a grid. There was nothing behind the structures except raw jungle, and no obvious reason for the city to exist. But Bernie and Emerson were going to stage a race here, so there must have been substance enough to lure the consummate entrepreneur to this hinterland. John Hogan, head of racing activities for tobacco company Philip Morris, was there. It was John's job to look at the performance or potential of Formula 1 teams, and then to determine which team, or teams, and drivers should receive the – make or break – sponsorship from his company. His company, owners of the Marlboro cigarette brand with its corresponding red and white F1 livery, was supporting McLaren, a team with one of the largest budgets in the business, and the fledgling Williams team, which had one of the smallest. In Brasilia they joined the other teams, cooling their heels – all week – while awaiting instructions from 'Mr E'.

The teams had undertaken the 600-mile journey from São Paulo to Brasilia on the Monday, and had to stay on in the city until the following Saturday, race day. 'It was like we were the only people in town,' says John, 'and we were in this huge hotel. We played games, we tried everything under the sun' to pass the time, ineffectually. 'Bernie could see that we were bored out of our minds. There was a big lake near the hotel so he said "I wonder if there's a bloody boat on this lake somewhere?", and sure enough he actually hired one for a day and we went out on this fishing boat on the lake – it must have been the size of Lake Geneva. Bernie's a very generous man. He didn't allow us to put our hands in our pockets for anything. I mean it was really embarrassing in the end, not even for a Coca-Cola, for five days.'

Staying in this particular hotel was, according to John, 'only one other guy, not part of our group'. He was Ronnie Biggs, one of the infamous gang members convicted of participating in the Great Train Robbery in 1963, later becoming an equally infamous fugitive from justice. While the Formula 1 team members were sitting about the hotel 'playing all sorts of games', someone shouted out 'Hey Bernie, there's a bloke down in reception wants to see you and his name is Biggs.' Although Bernie says that he has never met Ronnie Biggs, he played along, shouting in return 'What a bastard, he owes me a tenner!'

During the previous year Bernie had grown used to spouting glib answers to questions or statements having to do with the Great Train Robbery. It was a widely held notion – pure mythology borne out of an act of kindness – that he had masterminded the crime in which £2.6 million (in used £1, £5 and £10 bank notes) was stolen from the London to Glasgow night mail train on 8 August 1963. In fact, the actual 'brains' behind the operation had been one Bruce Reynolds, an antique dealer and petty criminal who, according to contemporary accounts, 'liked to live well beyond his means and drove an expensive Aston Martin'.

The heist had begun at 3.30am in rural Buckinghamshire, as the train pulled to a halt at false signals rigged up by the gang. When they realised what was happening, the staff inside the Royal Mail sorting coach offered little resistance, and 120 cumbersome mail sacks were hauled away. But the train driver had been wary and received a severe bludgeoning for his pointed enquiries, thus lowering the deed from any possibility of heroic daredevilry to something unsavoury.

To avoid the risk of escaping in daylight, it was decided that the gang members would lie low at Leatherslade Farm in Oxfordshire, a safe house provided by 'the respectable face' of the group, John Wheater, a public school educated solicitor 'who used his proper appearance' to rent the farm. At their hideway, the other central gang members, including Buster Edwards, Gordon Goody, Charlie Wilson, Jimmy Hussey, Brian Field, Roy 'The Weasel' James and Ronnie Biggs, nonchalantly passed the time by drinking tea and playing Monopoly – with real money – while listening to Tony Bennett's classic hit, *The Good Life*. But their attitude was either lax or arrogant. They would soon 'kiss the good life goodbye' – because they left behind a selection of nice, clear fingerprints on the Monopoly board and pieces.

The evidence found on the Monopoly set at Letherslade Farm remains one of forensic science's more interesting breaks in cracking a case. With these, the police were able to identify some of the gang's criminal record-holders such as brawny Buster Edwards, a small-time thief and fraudster, who led in turn to the identity of the rest. Hussey had actually left a hand-print on the outside of the mail train itself. Roy James was traced after he gave a drink of milk to the farm's cat, leaving his fingerprints all over the bowl. He was also connected with the aforementioned act of kindness which, in turn, via wholesale tittle-tattle, has linked Bernie to the crime ever since.

James's contribution to the notorious robbery had been twofold. First, he posed as a teacher planning a lesson in order to research the workings of the mail train's engines; second, he drove the Land Rover getaway car. James was particularly suited to the latter task because at that time, apart from his criminal activities (he had six previous convictions for stealing and receiving), he was making his name known in Formula Junior racing as the holder of lap records at the Cadwell Park and Mallory Park circuits. Tipped as 'a budding Grand Prix driver', James had driven in a race just one week before the mail train robbery.

Having been found guilty, James was sentenced to thirty years in prison. He was paroled after eleven years, during which he honed his legitimate skill as a silversmith, kept himself fit, and dreamed of resuming his racing career. To this end, James had written to Graham Hill relating his future career hopes. After his release, now thirty-seven, he again contacted Hill. Wishing to help a fellow racing driver, Graham Hill introduced Roy James to Bernie; it was thought that Bernie might be able to find him a place on a team. But however fit, The Weasel's lack of recent racing experience was against him. During a test at Silverstone, he spun off the circuit at 130mph and crashed into a barrier, breaking a leg. His chances of racing again also took a tumble. Bernie was unable to obtain a drive for James, but commissioned him to make a silver trophy.

The kindly gesture has proved to be an irresistible morsel to rumour-mongers, and Bernie himself occasionally finds it amusing to add grist to the mill. It is one of his many curiosities that he sometimes takes mischievous delight in being unjustly credited with misdeeds. He even went so far as to display a model of a mail train in a showcase in his office. But when a book and a magazine suggested that he had taken part in the crime – well, that was different, and he sued. Ask Bernie about the robbery and he replies: 'For that amount of money? You must be kidding!' The sum of £2.6 million in 1963 has a comparative value of about £40 million today. The story of beleaguered Roy James continued when he was sent back to prison in 1994 after shooting his father-in-law and ex-wife. As for Ronnie Biggs, he was later kidnapped and smuggled out of Brazil by the British security service, from that very hotel in Brasilia where some of the Formula 1 team members had stayed before the race. He daringly escaped his captors and returned to Brazil, only to give himself up to the

British authorities in 2001. In 2009, after years of ill health, he was released from prison on 'compassionate grounds', and is living in a care home.

For the 1975 Formula 1 season, Bernie, after a winter of confidence building, managed to secure major sponsorship from Martini, the drinks company, along with support from Italian fuel company FINA. The team, previously entered under the banner Motor Racing Developments, was now entered as Martini Racing and then Martini Racing Brabham, in part because it had been pointed out that 'MRD' in the Grand Prix programmes might draw comparison with a much-used French expletive.

The introduction to Martini had come via David Yorke, a racing manager of long standing whom Bernie got to know at Vanwall in the days of Stuart Lewis-Evans. Later, Yorke took charge of Martini's motorsport interests, and in the mid-Seventies he and Martini linked arms with Bernie and Brabham. Martini was one of the most outstanding sponsors, in terms of the car's presentation: turquoise blue and white against a red background. 'Bernie loved doing the livery on the cars, taking an interest in the layout of the decals' so that the Ecclestone 'Brabhams always used to look pretty cool,' says Gordon.

In 1979, Martini moved to Lotus to be replaced at Brabham by the Italian dairy conglomerate, Parmalat, and the Brabham cars now appeared in simple but elegant white and dark blue, Bernie's favourite combination. After Brabham had completed their first race in Parmalat livery, a representative from Moët & Chandon went round to Bernie's motorhome at the circuit to present him with a crate of champagne. Bernie opened the door and took a look at the 'bubbly'. He smiled teasingly and said: 'We only drink milk now'. Bernie was so proud of his white and dark blue cars that when a future sponsor, Olivetti, 'came along with a cheque' and explained that their colours were green and white, Bernie was polite but firm: 'Well, yes, they were, but they're blue and white now', and so they remained.

As for David Yorke, who had effected the original Martini deal, he stayed on at Brabham as a well-loved advisor, often travelling with the team, until he died 'peacefully in his sleep' in the guest house in which the team was staying in August 1984, two days before the Austrian Grand Prix. Herbie Blash reported the death to Bernie, who said 'stick him in the transporter and we'll take him home the night after the race'. This was a typically joking response meant to cheer up the downcast Herbie, who added 'we could stick him in the bodywork box or in the cabin alongside the driver'. Yorke's body was, of course, sent back to England with all due respect and in accordance with official requirements.

At the circuits, the mechanics, like the cars, now wore sponsorship logos on their backs. The orange overalls were exchanged for an ensemble in lemon and black, and then for sponsor-provided dark trousers, which Bernie preferred to overalls, and Bob Dance specifically remembers: 'Light blue, nice-fitting, cotton, polo-necked shirts'. Even so, the sponsors, for all their essential funding, had not rated the level of VIP hospitality and general nurturing that was being handed out by other teams. At Brabham they simply didn't have time to coddle.

When a sponsor rang the factory asking for photographs of the cars, they were told to 'hold on', whereupon there followed the muffled sounds of whispering in the background: 'What do they mean, photographs?' Whisper, whisper. Then finally someone plucked up the courage to speak to the caller: 'No, you can't have any photographs. Goodbye.' Sponsors were flatly told: 'No, you can't come to the test; no, you can't bring your wife to the Grand Prix, don't be silly.' The bigger teams employed highly paid, dedicated securers of sponsorship, well practised in perfecting the role of Uriah Heep: 'Oh, you want to bring your pet dog along to the race? Yes, yes... delighted. Bring everybody. The school? Marvellous, bring them too. We'll get you tickets.' When, one season, Brabham had been unable to obtain any major sponsorship, says Bob, 'we had to be careful, but we always got paid properly, on time, and expenses'. Gordon adds: 'I don't know where the money came from… whether he [Bernie] put his own money in for a bit, I don't know… but he made it all work.' Bernie was indeed financing Brabham out of his own pocket. 'It cost me £80,000 per year,' he says.

While Bernie was not interested in cuddling sponsors or potential sponsors, he was always eager to attract them by finding or creating opportunities to raise the Brabham profile. Brasilia had been one such opportunity in that the race received considerable television coverage, at least in Brazil. Two years later more publicity was received when Brabham became the first team to 'run a Grand Prix car around the Birmingham street circuit as a test for the police and the authorities', who were considering the possibility of a race in England's second city. Patrick Neve was the driver.

Back on the World Championship trail, the 1975 season started well enough for Brabham, when Carlos Reutemann took third place in Argentina. But he was outshone two weeks later in Brazil, where his team-mate, Carlos Pace, took the chequered flag ahead of the rest of the pack and five seconds ahead of the reigning champion, McLaren's Emerson Fittipaldi, thus achieving his first Grand Prix victory, and in his homeland at that. The crowds went wild, yanking Pace from his cockpit, tearing his overalls then carrying the well-built driver aloft to the podium. In all the excitement an interviewer accidentally hit Pace in the mouth with a microphone. The next victory was Reutemann's, when he won the German Grand Prix in August, and for most of the season the team finished well into the points, putting Carlos Reutemann third in the Drivers' Championship and Carlos Pace sixth, and – perhaps most exciting of all – Brabham was second in the Constructors' Championship, behind Ferrari and ahead of McLaren. Gordon and Bernie, along with the rest of the team, deserved a hefty session of back-slapping, but the season had left them in a somewhat sombre mood. The taint of premature death had hung in the air since the grisly incident that had occurred earlier in the season, in April, during the Spanish Grand Prix in Barcelona.

Most of the drivers had been troubled over the inadequacy of the safety barriers and had boycotted practice in Barcelona. The race organisers had then turned on the pressure by threatening to have the cars impounded in the paddock (a football stadium next to the track) by armed police; the drivers reluctantly returned for the last practice session. On the following day, three drivers refused to race and, as it turned out, theirs was a wise decision. Ten cars were involved in accidents. But the race was not actually stopped until several long minutes after the most serious of these. The carbon-fibre rear wing support broke on the Embassy Hill Lola of Rolf Stommelen, which was leading the race – narrowly – from Carlos Pace's Brabham BT44B. Stommelen's aerofoil flew off his car, which struck the Brabham and careened over the barrier into a controlled area. Five people, marshals and photographers, were killed. Stommelen was himself seriously injured. When the race was finally stopped, several laps later, McLaren driver Jochen Mass was declared the winner, with Jacky Ickx second for Lotus and Reutemann third for Brabham.

For the following race, Monaco, in May, the organisers were anxious to avoid any possibility of a repeat calamity and took the precaution of cutting the field of participants from twenty-five, as in Spain, to eighteen, also spacing out the grid. Even so, there were six crashes and three non-finishers. Of the nine remaining, Pace came in third and Reutemann eighth. The tale of destruction continued at rainy Silverstone during the British Grand Prix when, in a deluge on the fifty-sixth of sixty-seven laps, twelve drivers crashed and, the track being flooded, the race was finally abandoned. Reuteman was mercifully out of the running, his engine having failed in the fourth lap. It was eventually decided that Carlos Pace had finished second behind Emerson Fittipaldi's McLaren. Two races later, in Austria, American Mark Donohue was killed in Roger Penske's March. For Formula 1, it was just one of those years, and all the more a great tribute to Bernie, to Gordon and the rest of the light blue polo-necks that they managed to achieve so much.

But then, as so often happens in motor racing, fate smiled elsewhere. Brabham became plagued with twelve-cylinder fever. Until 1976, the Brabham cars had been running competitively with the V8 Ford Cosworth engine, although Ferrari was winning races using a V12. But now, recalls Gordon, 'it looked like they were going to start running away with everything'. So 'everybody was panicking, we needed a twelve-cylinder engine, and Bernie started talking to various people about it. We ended up with Alfa Romeo'. Unfortunately, it soon became clear that, in fact, the team did not need twelve cylinders to win races in 1976, but by then they were committed. As a result of this experiment Brabham spent three years in a mid-field wilderness and Gordon Murray remains dismayed because 'the design was probably the best Brabham ever had, we could have won the championship. So it was the first engine change brought about by a sort of general (not just Brabham) panic attack.' When, some three and a half years later, Alfa Romeo decided to part company to do their own car, Gordon recalls: 'I got to work and sawed three inches off the back of the V12 car, plugged in the Cosworth V8 and we got straight back on the front row at the first race.'

For the record, Brabham was nowhere in 1976, achieving only three point-scoring finishes, although its results improved a little in 1977, when the team finished fifth in the Constructors' championship, mainly thanks to second places by Carlos Pace in Argentina and John Watson in France. These two seasons brought no more victories, but on balance it should be remembered that the situation during those Alfa Romeo years (1976–9) was not all gloom. Austrian Niki Lauda, who first drove for Brabham in 1978, that year won the Swedish Grand Prix at Anderstorp and the Italian Grand Prix at Monza. Consequently, the team advanced its status to third in the Constructors' championship. In September 1979 Niki finished fourth in the Italian Grand Prix at Monza. A week later, in a non-championship race at Imola, the Alfa engine was used for the last time; Niki won. But victory had seemed unlikely on the morning of the race when he blew an engine. 'There were only four of us at Imola,' says Herbie, 'so Bernie stepped in to help change the engine. He was screwing on nuts and bolts like everyone else.'

Thereafter, unbridled, the 'Brabham boys' rushed headlong towards the next Grand Prix season, propelled by the knowledge that, however small their numbers and budget, they had it in them to become World Champions.

CHAPTER 8

GLORY DAYS

The day Niki Lauda first became aware of Bernie Ecclestone was 6 September 1970, in a photograph printed in a German newspaper. The black-and-white picture showed Bernie carrying away the bloodied helmet of Jochen Rindt, following his fatal crash. 'Who is that guy?' Niki asked, and was told that he was looking at 'the professional adviser to Jochen Rindt'. Niki could not know that, eight years and two World Championships later, he would be working for the man in the photograph.

Lauda was then racing Formula 3 cars, but ambitious to emulate his compatriot, Rindt, he moved on the following year to Formula 2 and thereafter drove in Formula 1 races for March and BRM. In 1974 he was invited to join Ferrari. During his first season with the Italian team he came second in Argentina, and went on to score victories in Spain and Holland. In 1975, Niki Lauda became World Champion; the last Ferrari driver to achieve that distinction had been John Surtees, more than a decade earlier.

In 1976, the world's collective attention was turned to the sport when Niki Lauda battled to retain the championship against a dogged James Hunt, the media's new golden idol, who throughout most of the season had been gnawing at Niki's heels in the title chase. Then there was Niki's horrific accident at the Nürburgring – the accident upon which photographers and, to a lesser extent, television cameramen focused and refocused their lenses, tightening the image of Niki Lauda's Ferrari bonfire. On the second lap of the race, his car had suddenly slammed into the barriers and ricocheted into the path of oncoming traffic, whereupon it was hit broadside and burst into flames while careening down the track. When his Ferrari finally stopped it was left to the heroics of other drivers to pull Niki, unconscious, from the wreckage. He was taken to hospital with massive burns to his head, face, lungs and upper body.

Niki should have died. He was expected to die, but six weeks later, with his wounds far from healed, he was back on the circuit. He claimed an astonishing fourth place at his first post-accident race, in front of Ferrari's fans at Monza, with what TV commentator Murray Walker later described as 'one of the bravest drives in Formula 1's history'. Bernie recalls: 'I was with him at Monza, sitting in a little caravan, with blood running down his face from his unhealed grafts.' This was clearly a man of total dedication who, with a disfigured scalp and lacking an ear (partially concealed beneath a now trademark baseball cap), would carry on, no matter what – the type of man to whom Bernie could relate. He was also unpredictable, a free thinker, someone who, in a deluge during the last race of the season, the Japanese Grand Prix, woke up to fear or reason and pulled out before the end of the race, handing James Hunt – with a single-point advantage – the title. When the Italian press savaged him for his decision, Niki shrugged his shoulders and calmly set about winning, in 1977, a second World Championship. That done, he turned his back on an unappreciative Enzo Ferrari and walked straight into the open arms of the former professional adviser to Jochen Rindt and now Brabham team owner.

When Niki was winning races for Bernie in 1978, he enjoyed, he says, 'a perfect time, no question'. With Bernie, as opposed to Enzo Ferrari, 'it was really fun'. There were, however, moments that were 'pretty weird because [Bernie] had no real idea about the car and nothing worked and he tried to be an engineer, which he wasn't, but it was his dream', so he couldn't help himself. On the other hand Niki also felt that Bernie was 'a risky operator', giving Gordon Murray too much freedom, resulting in car that, during much of the 1979 season, 'was a shit box; I was pissed off with [Bernie] like you wouldn't believe'. But then 'Gordon came along with a new car', and all was well.

Soon after the start of the 1979 season, Niki Lauda had decided that the time was right to begin discussing a pay rise, effective in 1980, with the man who 'never wanted to pay drivers'. During these negotiations it was not, and is not, uncommon for drivers to adopt an open-market attitude and for comparable pay agreements to be taken into consideration. World Champions obviously expect offers that put them at the upper end of the income scale. Niki recalls: 'I wanted a new contract because everybody's salaries were going up. I wanted to triple mine, and I went to Bernie and said, "$2 million", which at the time was a lot of money. He just looked at me and said: "Are you completely nuts or what?" I said, "no, $2 million"... So he went to every team manager [interested in hiring Niki] and said: "Lauda went crazy, you pay him $500,000, there is no way he is going to get $2 million". So then I went to somebody else. I know all these guys and they all said "no way", because they had talked to Bernie. I had about six months' fight with him about getting this contract fixed, and he just said "f--- you, there is no way I am going to pay that much money".'

Rounds one and two to Bernie. But the determined Lauda soon devised a more cunning strategy. With a touch of acquired Ecclestone ingenuity, Niki decided to take his empty pockets to Parmalat, now Brabham's sponsor, replacing Martini. Niki had the upper hand because he had actually brought the Parmalat sponsorship money to Brabham when he signed to drive; sponsors' money had begun to be a factor in the decision over which team a driver would join. For Niki, the prime opportunity came about when a meeting was called to discuss the all-important renewal of the Parmalat contract. Bernie, to strengthen his bargaining position, naturally wanted to take along his two-times World Champion, and Niki was happy to oblige. During the meeting, Parmalat asked the obvious question: 'Who's driving?' 'Lauda's driving,' answered Bernie. Niki now had him pinned down and trumped victoriously: 'No, I'm not driving, he [pointing to Bernie] doesn't pay me.' Bernie, unaccustomed to being outfoxed, communicated his anger by glaring in Niki's direction, 'like he would kill me. But it was clear that in the end he had no choice'. It was agreed in front of the Parmalat executives that Niki would be paid his $2 million, and then the sponsorship deal was put to paper. Afterwards, when the two were leaving, Bernie could not help but let slip a wry smile, approving, if not condoning, Niki's tactics: 'You f---er! But never mind, we did a good job.' Niki still revels in the moment: 'I really did one to him.'

One of the highlights of Niki's two seasons with Brabham had occurred in June 1978 at Anderstorp, in the Swedish Grand Prix, where he and team-mate John Watson got their hands on the extraordinary Brabham BT46B 'fan car'. The cars were fitted with large fans at the rear of the chassis, the action of which Gordon Murray had developed with consultant David Cox, who designed the fan-blade geometry. These engine-driven fans not only served to cool the Alfa Romeo flat-12 engines but also had a more important and highly desirable effect: they sucked out air beneath the chassis and reduced air pressure, thereby enhancing what would become known as 'ground-effect' aerodynamic performance. At speed, the cars gripped the track surface like limpets.

Literally to keep their invention under wraps, the cars had their fans covered with dustbin lids while in the pits. Gordon took it in good part that the cars were promptly referred to as 'loads of old rubbish'. Bernie knew that the 'fan car' was special, so, he recalls, he 'had the cars practise with full fuel tanks, slowing them down so as to fox the other teams.' During qualifying they carried a lighter load and Niki and John got on to the first and second rows of the grid. In the race, Watson went out on lap nineteen, but Lauda achieved a decisive win. The Alfa Romeo mechanics, whose company had not achieved a Grand Prix victory since 1951, were reduced to tears. There were also a few tears of joy being shed by Brabham's mechanics, for it had been almost three years since they had been able to cheer home a victory. However, the 'old rubbish' slingers were up in arms citing, among other things, an infringement of the Technical Regulations. They claimed that the fan was 'a moveable aerodynamic device' – expressly prohibited. Gordon countered by asserting that the 'primary purpose' of the fan was to cool the engine, but everyone knew that its primary effect was to increase downforce. Niki's win was allowed to stand, but the fan cars were withdrawn thereafter.

The good times, for Niki and for Brabham, were not to last. In spite of Gordon's endless attempts to compensate for the faults of the Alfa Romeo engine, the 1979 season became a wearying succession of mechanical mishaps. Niki, the natural shoulder-shrugger, now seemed to internalise every failure of the car, a problem that was exacerbated by a change in his relationship with Bernie. Soon after he had signed his new contract, whatever 'faith' existed between them was allowed to erode in arguments, and, says Niki, 'my driving was suffering'. At the end of September, following the Friday morning practice for the Canadian Grand Prix, Niki resigned. Bernie was horrified: 'Are you mad? Stop, stop think about the $2 million next year… think about it!' But Niki had thought about it: 'It's f---ing stupid and boring driving round and round in circles and I'm not going to do it any more.' No entreaty would alter his decision. 'So I told him to stop,' says Bernie, 'and paid him off.'

Bernie was now faced with the job of explaining why. 'What are we going to tell the press?' he asked the doctor on hand, Professor Sid Watkins, consultant surgeon to the Formula One Constructors' Association. 'Tell them he's got gastro-enteritis,' suggested Sid. 'Maybe he recovers, maybe he doesn't.' The question of who was going to drive Niki's car in the race was settled when Bernie 'found Zunino [Argentine driver Ricardo Zunino] running around in the paddock', and put together a swift agreement for Zunino to replace Niki but, of course, on a much lower salary.

Niki's retirement from motor racing was to last only two years, during which he started an airline company, Lauda Air, before returning to Formula 1 to accept an offer from McLaren. Niki's McLaren pay packet was said to be 'lucrative'.

He enjoyed four successful seasons with McLaren and again showed the force of his determination by becoming World Champion, for the third time, in 1984. He went back to his airline, but still found time in the 1990s to become a special adviser to Scuderia Ferrari and, later, chief executive officer of Ford's Premier Performance Group overseeing the Jaguar Formula 1 team while, along the way, fitting in plenty of Formula 1 television commentary. Niki remains one of the sport's favourite heroes. 'Niki and I had a good friendship and respect,' says Bernie, 'which is as strong now as it was when we first raced together.'

Bernie often found much to admire in the characters of his drivers, as well as their talents, but felt that sometimes they needed reminding of their employee status. Soon after John Watson had signed to drive for Bernie he was treated to a discomforting insight into the mind of his new employer. John had been out on the circuit getting a feel for the car and upon returning to the pit lane Bernie asked: 'How was it?' 'It was great fun.' 'Fun! You're not paid to have fun!' This sort of jesting was also Bernie's way of putting emotional distance between himself and the drivers. But it wasn't effective. John Watson recalls that at Watkins Glen in 1973, when François Cevert was killed during the Saturday qualifying session, the circuit was closed. Subsequently, when it reopened, John was wondering whether or not to take his Brabham out on the track, or to stay in the pits out of respect. Bernie said to him: 'Look, Cevert, up until the last minute of his life, was doing what he loved doing. You get in that car and out on the circuit and drive – fast.' John says: 'That conversation has given me a safety valve that I have used again, when other people got killed.'

In the 1977 Race of Champions at Brands Hatch the Brabham team was running only one car, and John Watson was in it. He was on the grid – in pole position – when an announcement came over the loudspeaker revealing that 'Carlos Pace had been killed in a plane crash in bad weather.' John continues: 'I saw Bernie was very upset, and then I saw him apply the same advice to himself that he had given to me when Cevert was killed.' So the Brabham car raced with John finishing in third place. Even so, it was a very bad blow for Brabham and the team lost some of its zip as Carlos was missed by everybody. 'He was a great deal of fun,' adds John. Bernie says of Carlos: 'He was a really great character, a super chap.' Bernie's attitude to drivers encompassed a broad emotional palette – some would try his patience, others made him laugh, and there were a few that he loved.

At the age of thirty-three, Carlos Pace left behind a widow and two young children. Bob Dance remembers that 'Pace fitted in at Brabham, perfectly. He was one of us, a good tryer, everyone liked him, Bernie, the mechanics, everyone.' Tuana Tan recalls: 'It was very sad, Bernie got very close to him.' Gordon Murray is more specific: 'He took Carlos's death very, very badly, the whole team took it badly obviously, but Bernie took that particularly badly. Because, on two levels, I think he had a very good personal relationship with Carlos and I think, if I remember correctly, he had picked Carlos for Formula 3. He was like Bernie's protégé, he thought Carlos could have been World Champion one day, you only had to look and see how good he was, watch his car control. So, he took it badly on all levels really.'

Nor had Bernie made himself immune to the loss of Pedro Rodriguez, the former Cooper team driver who had been killed in 1971, at the age of thirty, after an accident during a sports car race in which his Ferrari was turned into a blazing inferno. Rolf Stommelen, who had been injured at the Spanish Grand Prix in 1975 after his car had been pitched into the crowd, killing five spectators, would himself be killed, in 1983, after his Porsche crashed in an endurance race at Riverside, California.

Niki's 'old rubbish' victory at Anderstorp in Sweden in June 1978 had been the last Grand Prix held in that country. After Sweden's favourite son, Ronnie Peterson, died from injuries sustained in a crash in his Lotus 79 in the Italian Grand Prix at Monza, the following September, the Swedish authorities, in view of the national outpouring of grief, realised that there would be little support for a subsequent Grand Prix and cancelled the race that had been scheduled for 1979. Since then, despite repeated attempts by the organisers, Sweden has not returned to its customary slot on the Grand Prix calendar. Around the paddock, Ronnie had been well-liked by all the teams for his open, affable manner, and he was a gentleman, holding back his speed on the circuit to allow Lotus team leader Mario Andretti to collect decisive World Championship points. Peterson's tragic accident was part of a series of collisions involving ten cars. The race was stopped and the scene immediately surrounded by a cordon of tough, bludgeon-wielding police and *carabinieri*.

Sid Watkins tried to get to the accident scene by breaking through the cordon, but to no avail, not even with the assistance of a pleading Italian official. Bernie, for his part, tried to get to the medical centre but was stopped by a policeman with a gun trained on him. Fortunately, Bernie had with him, for security, the chief of police at Monza who responded to the drawn pistol by pulling a gun of his own; Bernie was allowed to pass. Meanwhile, Sid was told that an ambulance and doctor were with Peterson, so he then headed for the circuit's medical centre, arriving at the same time as the ambulance with Peterson aboard. 'Ronnie was quite conscious and rational, but both his legs were badly smashed, and he had some superficial burns on the shoulder and chest. We got several intravenous infusions up into the arm veins and his blood pressure was surprisingly normal,' he says. Satisfied that all was well, Sid stayed behind to oversee the care of two other injured drivers, and to be on hand for the restart of the race while Ronnie was helicoptered to a nearby hospital.

At the circuit, there was another accident on the warm-up lap prior to the restart, causing further delay, and the race eventually ended in near darkness. Towards the end, Sid was notified that: 'A threat had developed to the blood supply to Ronnie's legs, and it was thought necessary to try to deal with this crisis by replacing the fractured bones and securing them in the correct position with internal or external pins and nails.' By the time the race had finished it was too dark to travel by helicopter, so Sid, Mario Andretti, Lotus chief Colin Chapman and Bernie drove a tortuous route through the dispersing Monza crowd to get to the hospital.

Sid went straight to the operating theatre to observe the repair to Ronnie's twenty-seven fractures. The surgery went well, and the young Swede was finally wheeled to the intensive care unit for the initial recovery period. But, at about four o'clock the following morning, it all started to go terribly wrong. A chest X-ray showed that Peterson had 'developed multiple emboli [small obstructions due to blood clots or fat globules] in his lungs. His kidney function had also declined, and his urinary output had deteriorated. He was unconscious and a neurological examination showed that he had signs of severe brain damage.' Subsequently, an electroencephalogram showed that Ronnie Peterson was brain-dead. Colin Chapman was notified and left his hotel for the hospital. Bernie also arrived at the hospital 'anxious to know the situation'. He was told that Ronnie was dead. Bernie often went to the hospital when drivers were injured. As Brabham's owner Bernie had automatically become a member of the Formula One Constructors' Association, and had been made the organisation's President. This gave him some say in motor racing safety, a subject that was becoming, for him, and others, increasingly important.

After Ronnie Peterson's accident, Niki Lauda telephoned Sid to find out exactly what had happened. Sid gave him the medical details and then explained that, if he had had a car with medical support on board, there would have been no trouble in getting through the cordon, and the response time would have been almost immediate. It was estimated that the delay in getting Ronnie out of the car and the arrival of the ambulance had consumed between eleven and eighteen potentially vital minutes. After his conversation with Sid, Niki telephoned Bernie to discuss the need to further improve safety. His views were supported by Jackie Stewart who, with Louis Stanley, principal of the BRM team, along with contributions from drivers, had instigated a mobile intensive-care unit during the late Sixties. Jackie continued to campaign for improved safety standards, but in 1978 much remained to be done. Peterson's accident convinced Bernie that Sid's authority 'had to be extended to supervising the rescue arrangements on the circuit, instead of merely being the surgical adviser to Formula 1.'

A Liverpool-born neurosurgeon, Professor Sid Watkins was to become, after what is now thirty-two years of service at the circuits and in the greater Formula 1 arena, another of Bernie's golden friends. It is a relationship that evolved gradually, based on mutual respect. In May 1978 Bernie made an appointment to see Sid in his office at the Royal London Hospital, purportedly about an eye problem. 'I think it was a test,' says Sid. 'I made the diagnosis correctly, and he soon turned the conversation to motor racing. He was aware that I used to take a team of surgical specialists and an anaesthetist to the circuit at Watkins Glen in New York state, where we worked as part of a medical team. I'd done the same thing at Silverstone and Brands Hatch.'

Bernie told Sid that help was needed with the medical intervention at the track, and that there had been worrying incidents with ambulances. In Spain, an ambulance carrying a seriously wounded driver had stopped at every traffic light between the circuit and the hospital in Barcelona, a distance of several miles. There had also been instances of drivers being taken to the wrong hospital, and Sid recalled an incident in the United States when Belgian driver Jacky Ickx, en route to hospital after suffering a minor head injury, was asked by the ambulance driver: 'Have you got any money to buy gas?' After reviewing these and other experiences, Bernie then came to his intended purpose: 'Would you like to take a job coming to every Formula 1 race to try to sort the medical business out?' Sid answered that he would, and Bernie set to work arranging for him to meet the principal drivers, and to be at Brands Hatch the following week during testing.

'He's a very fast responder when he's organising anything,' says Sid, who had attended ten races in 1978, beginning with the race at Anderstorp and finishing with Montreal.

Thereafter, he attended every Formula 1 race until the end of the 2004 season – a total of 424 consecutive races. Of course, when Bernie first offered Sid the job, he couldn't help but make a sharp deal. The pay offered, $35,000, was immediately accepted, and then Bernie added, 'and you pay for your own airfare, your own rental cars, hotel and all costs.' At the end of his first season in Formula 1, Sid totted up these costs. They amounted to about $35,000 – to his accountant's displeasure.

While Bernie is a great talent spotter, he had not realised that the man whose help he had just enlisted, was being hailed in the press as the 'world's leading neurosurgeon'. He was one of only two or three neurosurgeons who had in the Sixties and Seventies pioneered, with dramatic, life-changing results, a procedure called stereotaxis, a deep brain surgical technique for treating tremor. Once the youngest Professor of Neurosurgery ever appointed, he also became neurosurgeon to three American Presidents: Lyndon Johnson, Ronald Reagan and the senior George Bush. Why was such a distinguished figure risking his life at Formula 1 circuits? The answer was disarmingly simple: 'I just love motor racing.' His high standing in the medical community means that he is in touch, often on a first-name basis, with a network of leading specialists from around the world, who can be called upon in an instant.

From 1978 until 2004, Sid – wearing a crash helmet and fire-resistant overalls – was seated in the last car on the grid: the ultra-powerful Formula 1 medical car driven by an ultra-fast driver. Accompanying Sid were a local trauma surgeon or anaesthetist and an FIA anaesthetist – Peter Byles and Gary Hartstein in more recent years. The luggage compartment of the medical car was, and still is, adapted to hold life-saving equipment: ventilators, aspiration equipment, monitoring devices. During the first – and often most dangerous – lap of the race, the medical car with its highly skilled occupants follows the pack so that they are on hand, in seconds, to intervene in an accident. For the remainder of the race the vehicle is parked – engine running – near the pit exit. From here, it might take as long as a couple of minutes to arrive at an accident, whereupon the injured driver(s), marshal(s), member(s) of the pit crew or even spectators receive some of the best medical care the world has to offer. Bernie started this procedure in 1978 at the race following Peterson's accident, the US Grand Prix at Watkins Glen. And it's interesting to note that the medical car has been driven by some of the world's most talented drivers: Carlos Reutemann, Niki Lauda, Jochen Mass, Derek Daly, Frank Gardner, Hector Rebaque, Wilson Fittipaldi, Jean-Pierre Jarier, Jacky Ickx, Vittorio Brambilla, Arturo Merzario, Phil Hill, Chico Serra, Raul Boesel, Jan Lammers and Alex Ribeiro. From 2002 to 2008 the driver was Jacques Tropenat, a doctor who is also an experienced racing driver.

From the beginning Sid found 'that [Bernie] has been as good as his word', which meant sticking to his decisions no matter what the consequences. Because Sid found the medical facilities to be inadequate at Hockenheim in 1978 and at Zolder and Jarama in 1979, Bernie threatened to withdraw the cars and cancel the race. With millions of dollars in revenue – or losses – hanging in the balance, the threat was followed up by swift action and the facilities were improved. In 1978 Bernie and Sid also agreed that the Grand Prix would not return to Brands Hatch until a proper medical centre was built; by 1980 Brands Hatch had its medical centre. Since 1978, new medical centres have been built at every circuit. The centres include major trauma facilities to a standard provided by university hospitals, and all have intensive-care units. Some of the medical centres are also equipped with X-ray and ultrasonic diagnosis equipment, biochemical laboratories and operating theatres. 'Bernie really was the driving force behind the medical services for Formula 1 in the early days,' says Sid. 'I was the instrument that he used. But the concept was his and not so many people realise how much they owe to Bernie for developing that particular strategy.'

However, always quick to amuse or shock, Bernie jokingly had said to Sid: 'If there's an accident to one of my cars and the driver is OK, then don't work too quickly because we want the cameras on the sponsorship!' Niki Lauda feels that there are two sides to Bernie's attitude to safety: on one side the caring individual, on the other the opportunist: 'Because sometimes when the television time is on, he doesn't care a damn, he has only his total view of how Formula 1 should be presented, that's his main issue. I remember one day in Dallas where the [overheated] surface broke up like you would not believe, there was no way we could race. Bernie simply said: "I'm gonna fix it", and he came with trucks full of ice cubes and he just off-loaded it on to the surface so all that happened is it got wet, and that was it! I said, "Bernie, your stupid ice cubes will not fix our problem." Then he got hot water… whatever happened the race had to be on.'

In 1979 Niki's team-mate was Brazilian driver Nelson Piquet, who had replaced John Watson. Piquet will be forever fused with the Bernie Ecclestone/Gordon Murray years of the Brabham saga. He brought them the World Championship – twice. Nelson Piquet Souto-Maior was 'a scruffy little kid' with a mop of dark curls and black eyes that perpetually revelled in some undisclosed amusement, when the Brabham gang first got a look at him lingering about the gate at the new circuit in Brasilia. 'We stuffed him into the boot to get him in free,' says Gordon. Once inside Piquet was happy 'to polish cars all weekend', just so long as he could absorb into every pore the sight and smell of Formula 1. Like many drivers he had raced karts before becoming his nation's Super Vee champion (six victories in ten races), and deciding on an attempt at Formula 3 in Europe, often the base camp to scaling motor racing's heights. In 1977, with the help of Ron Tauranac's Ralt chassis, he won two races and finished third in the European F3 Championship. He won one of the two British national championships the following season, and was the runner-up in the other. Also in 1978, he made his debut in Formula 1 in an Ensign before driving, with competence, a truculent McLaren M23. Bernie now took a closer look at this fun-loving, racing-loving Brazilian, and gave him a trial outing in the Canadian Grand Prix. Satisfied with the young man's talent, Bernie signed him up to partner Niki Lauda in 1979.

Nelson had long since dropped his surname, Souto-Maior, in an attempt to prevent his parents from discovering that their son was partaking in a dangerous sport; they had wanted him to pursue tennis. But just two years after signing the Brabham contract, Nelson would join the ranks of the great motor racing World Champions and all of Brazil would celebrate his name, including his parents. Bernie had his own name for Nelson, 'Pick-it', and there were some who called him simply 'The Admiral'.

However, in the beautiful white and dark blue Parmalat Brabham, Nelson made a less than propitious beginning, being dragged from the wreckage of an eight-car pile-up at the start of the Argentine Grand Prix in Buenos Aires. Along with a stab of disappointment, he suffered a dislocated big toe. In the next race, in front of his home crowd in Brazil, there was more embarrassment when an acute pain in his injured foot caused him to lift it from the brake pedal at a critical moment, and he slammed into Clay Regazzoni's Williams; welcome to the world of Formula 1. Were his eyes still sparkling? They were. Nothing much got 'The Admiral' down, not even the disappointment that followed in South Africa, the United States Grand Prix West (Long Beach, California), Spain, Belgium, France and so on throughout the rest of the season. There was a glint of improvement in September in Canada where, after the departure of Alfa Romeo – at long last – and the reinstatement of Ford-Cosworth DFV engines, Nelson took firm command of third place before his gearbox broke in the closing laps. Ever onward, he put in the fastest lap of the final race at Watkins Glen, which provided some measure of consolation after the drive shaft of his BT49 fractured on lap fifty-three. With only three finishes from fifteen starts, it had been a season for masochists.

Back at the factory it was work as usual – flat out – in preparation for the 1980 season for which Gordon Murray's bag of ingenious tricks included revised aerodynamics and other bodywork revisions for the Brabham BT49, and a new rear suspension layout. His life was one of constant invention and reinvention; racing car designers carry a stress load that is hard to imagine. In testing, the cars looked promising and, when the season opened in Argentina, Brabham hearts heaved with relief and optimism when Nelson Piquet finished in a glorious second place. Brazil again brought disappointment when a tangle with American Mario Andretti's Lotus put Nelson out of the race. In South Africa he came a respectable fourth, but all the attention was on the winner, Renault driver René Arnoux and, more specifically, on his turbocharged V6 engine. The coupling of Renault's mighty resources with turbo technology – now confirmed by the chequered flag – spread shivers through the paddock. Gordon knew that 'the threat was real', and that the race for turbo engines had just begun. But before Bernie could woo additional support Brabham had to win races, lots of races. They had to be seen to be reliable contenders and, somehow, Bernie had to make it happen. If Niki Lauda had found Bernie's interference irritating, he was well out of it, for now Bernie was that much closer to the World Championship and his eagerness to win was searing.

While Gordon was left to his own devices, the mechanics had to bend to Bernie's suggestions, although he tried to be sparing. The man who had put together his own Cooper 500 now needed to meddle, but held back. He needed to pry, to fiddle, to control, but held back. He needed to lay his fingers on engine parts like the laying on of hands, but held back. Until, inevitably, he would give up the struggle and 'do this, do that' and 'let's just *try* it' became his battle cry. 'But he was nearly always right,' says Herbie Blash. Former Brabham mechanic Charlie Whiting remembers the 'intensity' of Bernie's 'enthusiasm', and that 'we were always trying to impress Bernie. If we could do something to impress him then that was cool. But Bernie was difficult to impress.' Yet there were many in the team who loved him. Charlie adds: '[He] commanded loyalty, and you would go that extra bit for him'; some members of the Brabham team would continue to work for Bernie decades into the future.

The atmosphere at Brabham in the early Eighties was taut, but not brittle, Gordon Murray saw to that. Charlie Whiting says that he had also 'gone that extra bit for Gordon who was a brilliant designer and who was the reason the team was so relaxed', although 'Bernie wasn't a relaxing person to be around'. Gordon's stress was kept within, eating away at his health. On the outside he was tranquil. Thus Bernie and Gordon were the perfect combination: fire and ice, power and endurance. They did not yet have a turbo engine, but together they had made the team dynamic. To this, add Nelson, an intelligent, skilful and – to a certain extent – crafty driver. Herbie explains: 'When you've been a long time in motor racing, you've got to try to have the unfair advantage – without everybody else knowing about it. With Nelson it was really every trick in the book, anything he could do to gain an advantage.' Even when he was driving in Formula 3, 'coming down the straights, he used to undo his seatbelt so that he could actually slide down in the car', to reduce the aerodynamic drag and edge ahead. He couldn't see, of course, but 'he didn't need to see as long as he kept the steering wheel straight!' Nelson also had a special affinity with Gordon and the rest of the team that further worked in their favour; and the Cosworth DFV engine was, at least, reliable.

On the twisting circuit at Long Beach, five of the Cosworth-powered cars took points with Nelson Piquet – eyes dancing – at the front; one of the longest losing streaks in Brabham's great history came to an end. Nelson scored points in six of the ten remaining races, and secured two more victories at Zandvoort and Monza, ending up second in the 1980 World Championship behind Alan Jones of Williams. Brabham, with the single-point contribution of Mexican driver Hector Rebaque, who had replaced Zunino, came third in the Constructors' Championship.

For its 1981 campaign, Brabham still had to depend on the naturally aspirated 3-litre Cosworth DFV engine. Gordon had been right in his assessment of the threat posed by the 1.5-litre turbos, and Ferrari now had such an engine, but they were still weighty and, he hoped, prone to mechanical failures. More pressing was the banning of sliding skirts which had made for faster cornering speeds, a matter around which Gordon would soon manoeuvre by devising a hydro-pneumatic suspension system that the rest of the teams would copy. Other restrictions, involving tyre dimensions and indeed which brand of tyre to use, posed a whole ream of variables. So, at the outset of the season, there was much to ponder and the outcome was anybody's guess. Of the fifteen official Grands Prix held that year, the turbo-engined cars, Renault and Ferrari, took five victories between them, leaving the field open for the others. Piquet scored three wins, picked up points in seven races and had four accidents, a bruised leg being the worst of his injuries. The World Championship was neck-and-neck right down to the final race of the season, Las Vegas.

An eruption of concrete high-rise hotels in the Nevada desert, Las Vegas – with its avenues of garish neon lights, fabulous cabarets and gambling round the clock – is Bernie's ideal playground. Toss in stakes that only millionaires can afford to wager and the city encompasses the complete Bernie Ecclestone recreation package. The teams were booked into Caesars Palace Hotel where muscle-bound, toga-wearing porters greeted the guests; and the rooms featured vast ceiling mirrors above the beds. A separate block of rooms was designated 'Fantasy Towers'. It was a long way from Silverstone, and the circuit next to the hotel was well below par compared with the former World War II airfield. 'It was the most appalling track – a car park,' says Charlie Whiting, 'and this was the last race of the season... we were two points behind Carlos Reutemann [in a Williams and the expected winner]. I've never been so nervous in all my life!' Reutemann qualified on pole but, at the start, his team-mate, reigning champion Alan Jones, shot into the lead. Carlos gave chase but soon began to falter and Piquet overtook him. The surface of the circuit, as Niki Lauda has pointed out, was far from ideal, and the layout forced cars into a series of tortuous jerks. Nelson vomited into his helmet, and it was taking everything he had to keep going.

Back in the pits the rest of the team were feeling equally 'gruesome', worrying about Nelson's condition. He was, Charlie says, 'absolutely exhausted... He couldn't put his head upright any more and he was just trying to struggle it round to finish fifth. Jacques Laffite and John Watson, in the last lap, were having a race for sixth and they nearly caught him. I mean coming into the last corner, it was that close, if they'd both caught and passed him, he would have lost the World Championship. He just managed to cross the line.' He had won the championship by a *single* point. 'Nail-biting is not the word… Nelson was completely and utterly wiped out.' Nearly comatose, he had to be helped from the car. The sparkle, the smile, had become vague. As for the rest of the team, 'I think we were all too tired to celebrate'. In the Constructors' Championship, with an eleven-point contribution by Hector Rebaque, Brabham came second behind Williams. As soon as Piquet had dragged himself across the finish line, the moment was opportune for Bernie to offer hugs, slaps on backs, a team party – anything – to convey his gratitude. But he had left the circuit before the end of the race. When, back in England, the team and its owner got together, winning the World Championship was not mentioned. 'Because that's what you're paid to do, you're doing your job, so why get excited about it' – that was Bernie's attitude.

When the Brabham drivers, Nelson Piquet and the new recruit Riccardo Patrese, strapped themselves into their cars for qualifying at the start of the 1982 season their BMW engines were nudging 1,400bhp. They now had their turbos, and they now had to withstand the pressure of increased g-forces as the cars flew – literally, sometimes – around the track at over 200mph. Again, Bernie had turned to a manufacturer, which was still unusual in the early 1980s relative to Formula 1 today. Although he had earlier paired with Alfa Romeo, the usual practice, just as in the heyday of Cooper, was to go out and buy an engine and then build the chassis around it. However, the Cooper-led revolution, which so successfully challenged the domination of grandee car manufacturers, was on the wane – as indeed was the Cosworth DFV. In days to come the involvement of a manufacturer would be all but essential.

But back to BMW, who had fallen under Bernie's spell. Gordon marvelled at his boss's technique: 'Bernie was amazing at getting people on board... and I think the thing that kept it afloat was that Bernie developed good relationships, much more personal... and sociable. When socialising, Bernie preferred, and still does, relaxed chats around the kitchen table. He would often invite Brabham's sponsors and engine manufacturers to his home and they thoroughly enjoyed it, being treated like family instead of important folk or a bank; another example of Bernie being 'difficult to impress', he never acknowledges status. Gordon liked that: 'Bernie had a really good attitude, a mechanic didn't get any worse treatment than a driver, it was absolutely level. I've never known another team owner to do that. If and when Bernie organised a meeting, it was down at the local pub in Chessington, "The Star"... he'd always have half a pint and we'd have a couple of pints and that was our meeting.'

Former racing driver Martin Brundle, who raced for Brabham in 1989, recalls the Chessington pub: 'We used to go down to this pub for lunch. I could never understand it, it was always heaving and there was always one table in the middle that seemed to be spare. That's where we sat. It had a "Reserved" notice screwed to the table, and it was miraculously always available!'

While the turbo engine had become a necessity, it came with a few kinks that required trial and error to remedy, so Gordon wisely continued to develop the Cosworth-powered cars and, during the 1982 season, both types of engines would be used. But despite his best efforts the season turned out to be a disaster, in several respects. It opened, in Kyalami, with a drivers' strike – led by Niki Lauda, abetted by Nelson Piquet. The dispute was over a sub-clause in the drivers' 'Superlicence' application form, essentially tying drivers to their respective teams for the duration of their contracts. Niki and the others didn't care for the proprietary nature of the wording; they would not agree to being owned by the teams. So, instead of getting into their cars for the scheduled practice, they boarded a coach, organised by Lauda, and were taken to the Sunnyside Park Hotel where they lodged en masse in a banqueting suite. The floor of the suite was strewn with mattresses, and the piano players among them – Elio de Angelis of Lotus and Gilles Villeneuve of Ferrari – played throughout the night.

Back at the circuit, the attitude of team owners – Bernie in particular – was stern. He was in a temper and threatened to give the drivers their marching orders; they were employees after all. However, a parting of the ways benefited no one, and the following day the battle ended. The drivers had ostensibly won, and the race was back on schedule. But Bernie still demanded satisfaction of a sort; he was disappointed that Piquet had joined with the strikers. 'Is he crazy?' He asked Professor Watkins, hopefully. 'He's as sane now as he's ever been,' came the reply. Bernie was still miffed. When Nelson stepped into the car, he decided to have his revenge: 'You didn't want to drive when I wanted you to, so now you want to, you can't.' But when Nelson, ignoring Bernie, went out and put the car on pole position, all was forgiven. Yet as far as Nelson Piquet was concerned it would have been better if the race at Kyalami that year had never taken place; he spun off and had to retire. And this was only the opening stanza to another very difficult season.

Next stop, Brazil, where both Brabham cars were disqualified following a dispute over water-cooled brakes. Disqualified, that is, after Nelson Piquet had been declared the winner, after he had swooned on the podium from heat exhaustion. Renault, whose driver Alain Prost had finished third, lodged a protest against Brabham and also against Keke Rosberg's second-place Williams, claiming that they had both raced underweight. They had. A new FIA regulation stipulated that the minimum weight limit was 580kg, and there it was – child's play for Gordon and Bernie and, evidently, their counterparts at Williams. They simply fitted their cars with large water tanks, full to capacity at the start of the race, empty towards the end. In the first few laps the tanks sprayed away their contents and, all being well, the cars – minus their extra liquid – picked up speed and headed for the finish line. Then before the mandatory weight checks, after the race, the water tanks were topped up and everything appeared kosher.

The protest from Renault put FOCA (the Formula One Constructors' Association) on guard for another of their many scrapes with motorsport's ruling body. A month later, an FIA tribunal decided to remove the points gained in Brazil by Piquet and Rosberg. Alain Prost was declared the winner. Most of the other British teams – guilty, as it happened, of the same indiscretion – displayed their outrage by boycotting the race at Imola in Italy, now called the San Marino Grand Prix.

And so to Belgium, where Piquet took fifth. But then he retired in Monaco although his new team-mate, Riccardo Patrese, won there, boosting the team's morale. The race that followed, the USA-East Grand Prix, was this year held in 'Motown' – Detroit, Michigan. In this city, the capital of America's automobile industry, Piquet along with Brabham and BMW suffered the ignominy of failing to qualify. And then came Montreal.

Amongst Formula 1's older generation, the elegant city of Montreal still brings back the spectre of 13 June 1982. The author watched the race from the glass-enclosed control tower overlooking the starting grid. FISA President Jean-Marie Balestre, buttoned up against the unseasonable chill in a black leather trenchcoat and wearing dark glasses, was standing to my left. Bernie, dressed in a crisp white shirt and pressed jeans, was a couple of feet ahead of me, his face to the glass. There were very few non-essential workers in the control tower, thus very few people; I was privileged to be there. The formation lap had been completed and all eyes were intent upon the cars about to start the race.

The green light came on and then suddenly Didier Pironi's arm was raised skyward from the cockpit of his Ferrari, signalling that his engine had stalled. But it was too late. Behind him, unsighted at the back of the grid, Osella driver Riccardo Paletti, shot forward, straight as an arrow at a speed that reportedly equated to 120mph, right into the back of Pironi's car. There was a thunderous impact and both cars were hurled down the circuit, the Ferrari veering in one direction, the Osella in another, coming to a stop below the control tower. Pironi managed to pull himself out of his car, but Paletti was slumped forward, motionless.

Then Professor Sid Watkins – the man I loved and would eventually marry – arrived at Paletti's car, along with other members of the medical team. Sid was bent over Paletti, trying to deal with his injuries, when there was an explosive burst of flames and I lost sight of him behind a curtain of fire. For a few moments I thought I could see Sid's head, then an arm, his back, nothing. It occurred to me that I was watching a funeral pyre. I couldn't look away from the flames. I made an effort to look at the sky, but inevitably my eyes were drawn by the spiral of black smoke, back down to the fire. Beside me Balestre had become hysterical. I didn't look at him, but his shouts filled the room and I was aware of his arms fanning the air, as if to banish the flames.

It has been said that the marshals at the track brought the fire under control within a minute. I do not believe that, it must have been longer. Much longer. About thirty minutes after the crash, Paletti was released from the wreckage. One of the medical crew started pumping the unconscious driver's chest and continued to do so – without pause – as he was moved by stretcher on to a helicopter and taken to hospital.

But I still couldn't see Sid. Eventually the driver of the medical car, Mario Vallee, came into the control tower, and spoke to me across the room: 'Sid asked me to let you know that he's OK, just burnt ankles and feet'; his shoes had melted. I was too relieved to speak. It was only then that I realised Bernie was holding my hand.

Soon after his arrival at the hospital, Riccardo Paletti was declared dead. Two days later he would have been twenty-four. The island track in Montreal had been newly named 'Circuit Gilles Villeneuve' in memory of the great French Canadian driver who, at the age of thirty-two, had been killed the previous month during qualifying for the Belgian Grand Prix at Zolder.

From 1950 to 1977 twenty-two drivers were killed in

Formula 1. From 1978 to 1994 five drivers were killed at Grands Prix and two in private practice. In the sixteen years since 1994 no drivers have been lost, and the most serious injuries have been two drivers with broken legs and Felipe Massa with a freak head injury. Put another way, until the late Seventies one driver was killed or badly injured in every ten crashes in Formula 1; by the late 1990s the rate of driver injury had been reduced to one in every 300 accidents.

In the World Championship points tally at the end of that 1982 season, Nelson Piquet came eleventh with twenty points, albeit in a very closely fought season, only twenty-four points behind the new World Champion, Keke Rosberg. Team-mate Riccardo Patrese went one better, tenth, on twenty-one points. In the Constructors' Championship Brabham was demoted to seventh place. However, towards the end of the season the BMW turbo engines had shown marked improvement, and it should be mentioned that after the wreckage of that dreadful accident in Montreal had been cleared away and the race restarted, Nelson achieved his last victory of the year. There had not been many hurrahs.

In 1983 the time to celebrate would come, for Bernie, for Gordon, for Nelson Piquet and for all the Brabham team, the time of times. The 1982 World Championship had not been won with a turbocharged car, but with a naturally aspirated Williams-Cosworth. The sensitive turbo engines still had a tendency to blow up, but as the season progressed their performance improved. At the start of the 1983 championship, therefore, it was widely believed – and rightly so – that the winning engine would indeed be a turbo. The question was: whose?

Alfa Romeo, Lotus (with Renault) and ATS (with BMW) had joined the turbo club, and McLaren (with Porsche) would soon follow suit, but the smart money was on Renault, who had been tinkering with turbo power since 1977. Renault also thought the championship was as good as theirs. To gain a competitive advantage, the Brabham team would have to squeeze out an extra measure of creative juice. But then they were used to that.

Gordon produced his narrow-bodied, needle-nosed BT52, shod with Michelin tyres. The mechanics, for their part, started rehearsing pitstops – endlessly. It was ballet without the accompanying orchestra, the economics of motion: this one steps here, that one there, one arm up, another down, cross over, turn and – hold – all carefully choreographed. When Nelson Piquet pulled into the pits for a full set of tyres and fuel, it took only seventeen seconds, compared to the more usual twenty; potentially the difference between winning and losing. Another race-winning innovation was to start with fuel tanks half full, so that the cars were lighter, enabling them to bolt ahead for a solid lead before coming into the pits at around half distance, depending on conditions, for fuel and tyres. Nevertheless, it would be another excruciatingly close season.

In Rio de Janeiro they enjoyed a happy beginning when, in front of a 40,000-strong crowd, local hero Nelson Piquet brought his car home to victory amid cheers, chants and the banging of Brazilian drums. Thereafter, his scores zigzagged through points-earning finishes and non-finishes with various mishaps, including crashing into a wall at Long Beach and, at Hockenheim, a terrifying fire in the pits caused by leaking fuel. There were also two more wins. In the penultimate race, the European Grand Prix, that year held at Brands Hatch, the outcome was Piquet first across the finish line followed by Alain Prost in a Renault; fifty-five and fifty-seven points respectively, meaning the World Championship would again be decided in the last race of the season, this time at Kyalami in South Africa.

Bernie decided that the moment had arrived to play his master stroke. He said to Gordon: 'I was talking to somebody the other day about fuel and different additives and stuff. What are the regulations?'

Gordon replied: 'I don't know, we just get the fuel and put it in the car.'

'I think we should look at it.'

'No, BMW would have done that already.'

'I think we should look at it,' Bernie insisted.

So the rules were examined and Gordon was happy to report 'Yeah, we've got a lot of room to manoeuvre here actually.' So they 'went to a fuel company and they mixed up a concoction that passed all the tests but burnt a hell of a lot better. It was a special fuel, but it was totally legal… that was one of Bernie's technical innovations.'

The team got the fuel in time for the race at Kyalami. With only a two-point advantage, Nelson was more than motivated and, starting light on fuel, he burst ahead of Prost at the first corner. On lap eighteen he made a record-breaking pit stop – 9.21 seconds. 'He came out still in the lead,' recalls Charlie Whiting. 'He didn't believe his pit signals because he didn't believe he could still be so far ahead. He pushed and just sped away.' Then on the last ten laps, having been signalled that Prost had dropped out of the race, he backed off to preserve the engine, coasting home in third place to glory and the World Championship; team-mate Riccardo Patrese was the winner of the race. It was a moment Charlie Whiting will never forget: 'It was brilliant, it was one of the best days of my life I would say, it really was… and obviously to do it with a manufacturer!' 'We became the first turbocharged car to win the World Championship,' adds Gordon, 'and with this tiny little team! You could see Renault in the pits staring at us: 'How are these guys beating us so quickly?' I mean Renault had already printed the T-shirts, literally, they had all these T-shirts in boxes, and the badges, a million "World Champion" caps. They were really miffed.'

They were indeed. Along with Ferrari, Renault protested against Brabham's 'higher octane' fuel. FISA, however, drawing on testimony from the French Petrol Institute, the American Society for Testing and Material and the Royal Automobile Club, decreed that Brabham had never exceeded the legal level. Renault and Ferrari decided not to press for the disqualification of Patrese and Piquet; they had, they said, only been seeking a 'clarification of the rules'.

'We thought it was wonderful beating the big boys,' says Gordon, grinning all over, even now. 'We ran Brabham – and when I say "we" I mean Bernie, Herbie Blash and me – we ran

Brabham like a family, everybody got treated equally, nobody skived off because it was run like a family. But, boy, did you get a lot out of people for that. And that was how we won.'

Bernie, of course, left Kyalami before the end of the race. Back at the factory nothing was said, although, 'because we'd done a good job', Herbie felt compelled to ask Bernie if something could be done in the way of celebrations. Bernie capitulated. As Herbie recalls: 'He bought a sandwich for everybody…'

There would be no easing up on the pressure to win again. 'That's just it,' says Herbie. 'That's all you're there for' – to win. Quite simply, they had to stay in front, to get sponsorship, to make money, to develop increasingly competitive technologies, to exist as a Grand Prix team. In Formula 1 racing, the threat of extinction – in all its capacities – is always around the next corner.

CHAPTER 9

READING BERNIE

The 1984 season turned out to be a mixture of ups and downs for Bernie and the Brabham team. For much of the season Italian driver Teo Fabi was Nelson Piquet's team-mate, collecting nine points, which put him in twelfth place in the World Championship. Nelson ended the season with twenty-nine points – having taken pole nine times – and coming fifth in the championship, putting Brabham fourth in the constructors' title. Bernie had wanted to sign Ayrton Senna as the second driver, but Parmalat wanted an Italian and Piquet wanted anyone but a talented fellow countryman, so Teo Fabi was selected.

The year was particularly frustrating for Gordon Murray for, despite his innovations, the BMW engines remained unreliable. Mid-season Gordon complained: 'We've led the last five Grands Prix but we haven't won any of them.' Nelson did manage a victory in Canada and again at the next race in Detroit. Both efforts were heroic. Having burned his foot in the Canadian race, due to the positioning of a new oil cooler, he raced in Detroit with his foot surrounded by dry ice – at Bernie's request. But problems with the BMW engine continued to dog them, coupled with a few miscalculations from Gordon's department.

A miscalculation on Bernie's part was to commit Brabham to a three-year contract to use Pirelli tyres, commencing in 1985. The contract was said to be 'extremely lucrative', but for the cars, says Gordon, it was 'a bit of a disaster… if Bernie had one failing, it was that we would have won many, many more races if he hadn't had to do things for money or hadn't chosen to do things for money', like the Pirelli deal, and 'like paying [sponsored] second drivers. We would have been first or second or winning more races when one car stopped or crashed or whatever, but in the second seat we always had a paying driver who had no chance of winning races.' Thus, with only one skilful, experienced driver at the helm, their chances for the World Championship and Constructors' Championship titles were halved. 'And then he'd sell the cars to make money,' continues Gordon, 'do a tyre deal or an engine deal to make money or to keep the car, to be fair. Maybe it was to keep the company going. But we tended to compromise a lot more for money against performance when you were weighing up both.' Herbie Blash recalls that 'only two BT42 cars were sold to Hexagon and two BT44s to John McDonald for the RAM team. Bernie, however, was happy to hire out cars. John Webb, formerly associated with Brands Hatch, says: 'My first business dealing with Bernie was in 1974 when I persuaded him to hire me one of his F1 cars for Italian girl Lella Lombardi to drive in the Race of Champions at Brands Hatch. She did well until a half shaft broke. I agreed a fee of £5,000. There was nothing in writing, but he kept his word in every way and delivered professional value.'

Swiss driver Marc Surer remembers the Pirelli tyres. In 1985 Surer replaced François Hesnault who had replaced the Fabi brothers. The inexperienced Hesnault was only with Brabham for a few months, during which 'he just couldn't manage to keep the car on the track with the Pirelli tyres,' says Marc. 'It was difficult because BMW was too overpowered and Pirelli tyres obviously didn't work very well.' So, Bernie fired Hesnault and instructed Herbie Blash to get hold of Marc Surer who, although he had never made it to the podium, had, to his credit, some six years of Formula 1 experience; and he could speak German, useful in delivering specific information to BMW's mechanics during engine testing. Herbie duly telephoned Marc at his home in Spain, and after determining that Surer would indeed like to drive for Brabham, asked him to be at Spa-Francorchamps for testing on the following day.

At the Belgian circuit Bernie took over the induction proceedings. Marc had worn his own overalls 'because I had a contract with Barclay cigarettes, who were my personal sponsor. Bernie said "You want to drive for us you have to use our overalls".' He also asked that Marc's own name be removed from his helmet. When Marc hesitated, Bernie promptly 'put the sticker for Olivetti [then Brabham's sponsor] on it. I mean all my life I was driving with my name painted in a special way on the side of my helmet. I've had it all the time, and Bernie said "What's that for, if people don't know you they shouldn't be here". So he put the sticker himself over the name so there was no name left. Then, of course, I learned [that] Herbie is always the man to talk to. "What shall I do?" "Just accept it," Herbie said. "Just accept it, don't argue." So I did, and this was the race that they finally cancelled.' The surface of the circuit had been laid incorrectly and disintegrated during practice. Spa was rerun the following September; Marc Surer finished eighth. Two or three races into the season the situation was still no name and, what's worse – no money. 'I had no agreement, no contract, nothing, it was a sort of race-to-race deal. But it was not even a deal because we never spoke about money, about expenses and so I asked Herbie, and he said "don't worry, expenses will be paid, you just have to speak to Bernie about salary".' Marc later cornered Bernie at dinner.

'We haven't spoken about my salary.'

'What salary?'

'I mean you pay your driver; I know Piquet is earning $1.5 million.'

'I don't pay him at all. When Piquet came he brought some sponsorship, he brought some money the first year, then the second year and now, you're right it's $1.5 million, that's what he earns, but not from me; half a million from Olivetti, half a million from Pirelli and half a million from BMW. I don't pay him, I don't pay any drivers.'

'Yes, but I have to make a living.'

'OK.'

They agreed a sum 'which was fair, but was not a lot, of

course, but I wanted to drive his car. Handshake, that was it... anyway, for the first time in my life, on a Thursday after a race, I had my percentage of the prize money. My salary was per race, came on time; fantastic. I got paid and I didn't even have a contract... so that was a very good experience.' Less satisfying were the 'rumours', reported in the press, about drivers testing in his car 'because I didn't have a contract and people knew that. I asked Bernie about it.

'You know, I read in the newspaper that you let this and this driver...'

'Do you read newspapers?'

'So I never asked him again. I kept the drive to the end of the year, and I remember I learned to read Bernie's questions. That's something I learned in this year.' At Spa Marc had just missed finishing in the points in sixth place. As he stepped out of the car, Bernie asked him: 'Do you like losing?' Marc remembers the moment well: 'What a question!' 'But I knew he really hates losers, and I looked like a loser being side by side with someone for eighth place. I knew when he asked this question that it [was] very dangerous, my position in the team, uncertain. Anyway, for that reason I started to be aggressive, a bit, with the team because I had a chassis where something was wrong, it was weak and the set-up never went right. I found that out because I had the chance to test with Piquet's car and then I put some pressure on and I got Piquet's old car and Piquet got a new one. From that moment on I was quick.' Marc Surer had read Bernie correctly. After his season with Brabham, Surer went on to drive in 1986 for Arrows, the Formula 1 team he had been with before joining Bernie.

Between coded messages Bernie was lavishing humour about the paddock. He couldn't help it, a merry crew was a productive crew, and sharing a joke kept a valve on stress. Except if you happened to be Gordon Murray. Bernie 'used to love to play a joke on me or Herbie when he could,' Gordon recalls. 'One of them was at Nürburgring and race morning was really misty and wet and damp and cloudy, and the drivers were saying "don't know about this because it's dry in some bits and wet in others, and you can't run slicks and you can't run wets and we're not sure". And they've got this lunatic Porsche 911 turbo driver in the safety car, he's done 3,000 laps or something like that. Meanwhile, the drivers are saying "we're not going to start like this", so I'm in the middle of a discussion with a mechanic on something really serious on the car, and Bernie comes and just grabs me. I said, "What's wrong?" "I've got a job for you, come quickly, it's really important, the whole race depends on it." "But, I *really* need to do the set-up on the car." "No, no, come on." So we get to the 911, and Bernie says: "Get in the car with this guy and go round the circuit and tell me if it's dangerous." I get in, off we go, and the guy crashes! Spins off!'

Gordon remembers a similar incident in Argentina. 'Bernie was desperate to get out of the circuit in a helicopter because the crowds were huge and the civil helicopters were obviously spoken for. So, again, race morning and there I am in the middle of a discussion, getting the cars ready, and Bernie comes along – "Quick, quick, quick, you've got to help me, you've got to help me." "But Bernie, the race is starting in a few hours, you know, I've got to make sure the fuel is in, right tyres." He just says, "Come quick, come quick." So off we go to this big wired-off compound where there was a military helicopter. "I can't really explain," he says, "but we've got to go for a ride with this guy." "Why, where are we going?" "We just have to go for a short ride." So we get into the helicopter and there's this guy in his twenties with his feet on the dashboard of the helicopter; flat, polished cap, beautifully polished boots, big cigar, smoking inside the helicopter. Anyway, we get in and Bernie says, "You go in the front and I'll go in the back." "Where are we going, what's this all about? It's race morning!" Bernie doesn't say anything. The pilot keeps his cigar alight, fires the helicopter up, picks it up and flies at the wire fence and then takes both his hands off the stick! I thought: "We're dead!" We just clear the fence and he says: "People say you can't do a loop in a helicopter; you can, watch this." Then we go outside the circuit towards these huge blocks of low-cost flats, tower blocks. So now he flies at the tower blocks. There's all sorts of people on the balconies ready to watch the race, and he just flies at the building, turns, and all these old women were diving for cover, then he flies up the building. He does this for about half an hour; six times, I thought we were dead; and then we went back to the circuit. When we got out, Bernie says: "Thanks, we just wanted to get a lift and the pilot said if we go for a ride, I'll be fixed up for after the race."'

Another prank – or death-defying incident – occurred when Gordon was a passenger on Bernie's jet, flying through heavy cloud over Austria. 'We were flying above mountains, and the pilot says "I can't see anything, I can't fly over these mountains." Bernie answered: "Well, if you get down low enough you can see where you're going." "Yeah, but there's mountains down there." "Well, when you get a break [in the clouds], find a valley and Gordon can sit in the front and read the road signs." We were flying in this jet, you know at 400mph, and I think, oh dear... Fifteen years with Bernie, and there's a story for every Grand Prix... we had fun together.'

The Brabham cars may have entered a new phase of unreliability, but foolery and pranks could always be counted upon – in abundance. 'Just funny things that happened,' continues Gordon, 'like setting motel rooms on fire; running up and down corridors; chucking motorbikes in swimming pools... taking all the wheels off the rental cars that belonged to McLaren, [so that] when they came out in the morning their cars were jacked up and without wheels. And, of course, there was the fire extinguisher under the door... hotel rooms deep in frogs, so when you opened the door... and at every single race there were acetylene bombs'. The technique for the latter was to fill balloons or condoms with the acetylene gas, add a fuse, and BANG! The acetylene ordnance was also deployed at Watkins Glen to blow up the 'disgusting' toilets, known as 'The Bog'. Bernie couldn't get enough of these amusements. His sense of fun is always there, just below the surface, fluttering like a jar-full of butterflies.

In January 1979, the drivers along with their consorts

spent the gap between the Brazilian and Argentine Grands Prix lounging about the pool at the Sheraton Hotel in Buenos Aires. To this relaxed scene Bernie arrived looking all *soigné* in a Gucci suit, accessorised with a Gucci briefcase. Plenty of chatter ensued and, probably, a few smirks, when American driver Mario Andretti, sitting poolside and wearing swimming trunks, motioned for Bernie to join him. 'I've been offered $1,000 by Colin [Chapman] to throw you into the swimming pool,' Mario grinned. Bernie immediately put down his briefcase, grabbed Mario by the arm and exclaimed '$500 each!' while hauling Mario – along with himself – into the water.

Then there was the time Bernie related how, pulling into a tight parking space near his office, he touched bumpers with the car in front. Its female driver was just stepping out of the vehicle and, ruffled by the perceived jolt, rounded on him, saying: 'You've hit the back of my car!'

'I only just touched your bumper.'

'Oh, no you didn't,' she insisted, angrily.

'Wait a minute,' said Bernie, getting back into his car. He started the engine, reversed, and then drove forward, jamming his Mercedes into the woman's car. Having inflicted obvious damage, he turned off the engine and, getting out, said: 'Now, I've driven into the back of your car, and you can get my insurance details from my secretary.' Then he walked away.

The aphorisms are similarly amusing, and instructive, such as 'let's create a problem so we can solve it', 'let's not have a meeting, let's have a decision', 'I don't need to see you, I only need to talk to you' and 'if you're going to rob a bank, make certain there's money in the vault'.

The art of the quick response – in a nanosecond – is all Bernie's. Somewhere in the packed space located on the tip of his tongue, he also stocks a collection of foreign accents. When the need arises Bernie can, without hesitation, grapple with English, sheepishly struggling to do his best in an alien land. Late one night, while overtaking a car on London's Albert Bridge, Bernie described being spotted by two policemen. At some point near the Chelsea side of the bridge, they pulled him over. Bernie rolled down the window of his Mercedes to speak to the men, who began the conversation by pointing out that they had seen him driving over the bridge on the wrong side of the road. Bernie, who carries an assortment of foreign driving licences, produced an Italian licence saying: 'Zees eeza Roma, no?'

'What!'

'Roma, deeza seetee… [gesticulating]… shee eeza Roma, no?'

The policemen gawked at Bernie, then at the Italian licence, then back at Bernie. And finally they said 'Get out of here', or something similar.

Bernie's use of accents is so convincing that when anyone with a foreign accent telephones our home, I now answer: 'Hi Bernie'. He doesn't seem to tire of trying this on so I play it safe. The first time though, he really annoyed me. 'Allo, who eez dat?' he demanded. 'Whayeel who eez eet I am speaking to?'

Of all the impertinance. 'What do you mean, who is that,' I said. 'You rang me. I'm the person who asks who is that.'

'Geet mee Profayzor Vatkeenz.'

'Who is this speaking?'

'Yeew, lehdee, geet mee Profayzor Vatkeenz.'

'Now look,' I said, raising my voice, 'unless you tell me who you are, you're not going to speak to Professor Watkins, not now, not ever. What's more I'm going to put the phone down!'

'Yeew geet heem.'

'That's it!' And as I was about to replace the receiver, I heard Bernie's voice, velvety smooth: 'It's me… Bernie.'

While Bernie appears to thrive on laughter, he can, without warning, plunge into a distant, black space, and then he must be alone. In 'Knollwood', his grand, Tudoresque house, Bernie was sometimes seen sitting alone with a stereo headset clamped over his ears, listening to music – 'all kinds of music from rock to classical' – and shutting out the world so that he could sift, in solitude, through his problems. With the use of his facial muscles and eyes alone, Bernie can shout 'DO NOT INTRUDE'; the voice is superfluous, as is sympathy. He has also been known to avoid conversation by wearing a headset without having switched on the stereo – or portable cassette/CD player as the case may be. Headset on, discourse off.

'Knollwood' and its surroundings were as close as Bernie ever came to anything like renourishing his Suffolk country roots, and he had had enough by 1978 when he sold the country idyll and purchased a colossal, glass box overlooking the Houses of Parliament in the centre of London. He was, hereafter – probably always had been – a confirmed city boy. His new home, the penthouse of Alembic House, situated on the Albert Embankment, had formerly been offices. Under Bernie's instruction it came to resemble a sleek, breathtakingly modern, James Spencerish showroom – no extraneous fluff, no cushions, no mementos, no photographs, no identity; all the comfort of granite. The transformation took two years during which he lived in a modern two-bedroom flat near Crystal Palace. After taking occupation of the penthouse, Bernie remained involved in all decisions concerning its interior design – the glassfibre walls; the minimalist kitchen; spot lighting; music speakers; the style and arrangement of furniture and every other detail right down to fitting the grey carpet. But the carpet, remembers Roy Salvadori, 'had electricity in it, as you walked past you got an electric shock. So Bernie said: "Don't like that, I'll have all the carpet up, have new carpet next time" – and this was an area larger than the foyer of the Hôtel de Paris! That's how he went on.' Nor did Bernie care for the new curtains, which he promptly tore down and threw from the window; a visitor remembers seeing them swirling in the air, like a swarm of banshees heading towards the Houses of Parliament.

Bernie's daughter, Deborah, says that the penthouse designed by her father resembled 'Heals [department store] when it was closed'. While Bernie could not abide bric-a-brac, he proudly displayed – in a large glass case – a collection of ivory and jade sculptures. He also collected, but did not have on show, silver snuffboxes and walking sticks – cheaper by the dozen. He was unable to resist a bargain and added to these were treasures brought home from forages in

Sunday antiques fairs. Bernie was also fond of lithographs by Salvador Dali, and paintings by an artist who 'one day will be famous'; and he filled the penthouse's twenty-five-foot walls with an eclectic collection – Impressionist to Modern – including a convincing forgery of one of the elongated, expressionless portraits painted by Modigliani, as well as others that were said to be 'still wet'. The artist who had faked the Modigliani, a talent that he had thoroughly refined, sold one of his forgeries to a Texan art lover for $2.5 million. When the Texan got back home and showed the painting to experts, he was told that the work was not genuine. The artist was then invited to Texas and asked, directly: 'Who painted this portrait?' To which he responded with a certain amount of pride, 'I did.' The buyer then quietly handed back the work, and that was it, no more was said. The artist later sold the painting to Bernie, who displayed it on the walls of his penthouse, and then enjoyed acquainting admirers of the 'Modigliani' with its provenance.

Beyond paintings and *objets d'art*, Bernie's collections extended to model cars. John Coombs remembers 'a guy who worked for Matra [the racing team] had a big collection of models at his flat in Paris. As soon as you walked through the door, the walls were lined with models on glass shelving.' John, together with race team owner Ken Tyrrell and Bernie, had been invited to the flat for dinner. 'Ken and I were admiring the models when the next thing we know is Bernie bought the whole lot.' The moment money changed hands, a Brabham transporter arrived, the models – in their hundreds – were promptly removed from the display shelves and whisked away; 'that's typical Bernie' – he had distrusted the Frenchman.

At Alembic House, Bernie was no less prone to mood swings, in fact the need for solitude, occasional before, was now becoming prevalent due, in part, to romantic entanglements. When did Bernie discover that he was attractive to women? 'When I took my clothes off,' he jokes. Fine, but it is evident to all that women, lots of women, adore him. The attraction is generally *not* because he is financially powerful. With most women he is always a gentleman, always thoughtful, courteous, warm – and interested. To his friends, male and female, Bernie is an anchor of security, 'someone I know that I could turn to if I were in trouble', has been said dozens of times by dozens of people; as has 'there's something about Bernie, you can feel his presence in a room even before you actually see him'; or 'you walk into a pub, and he's a small guy, but the sea opens up to the bar'. Even his foes acknowledge Bernie's charisma, shaking their heads in dismay over the indefinable 'something'. With women Bernie's heart has definitely been engaged from time to time, and his relationships tend to overlap. Most have come to an end without acrimony because Bernie is usually kind to those he has loved, and generous. The penthouse, with its lack of personal warmth, was eventually sold. 'I paid £500,000 for it,' says Bernie, 'and now it's worth ten million.'

In 1982 Bernie fell in love with a dark Croatian beauty called Slavica Malic. Twenty-eight years his junior and about nine inches taller, she was earning her living modelling sportswear at Monza, the Italian Grand Prix circuit, when they met. He invited her to his motorhome for a Coca-Cola, she accepted, and that was it, the beginning of the paddock's favourite love story, and the most talked about relationship – male/female – in motor racing. 'She's only in it for the money,' they all said. But the fact is Slavica could have walked away with millions long ago, if that had ever been her intention. Instead, she chose to stay on for twenty-six years, sharing a relationship that was, for them both, the most enduring. Standing together they looked a mismatch, and when they met Slavica spoke only a few words of English, but she expressed herself with passion and fire, as one who gives her all – and more – and yet retains a touch of vulnerability. These were the communications to which Bernie responded.

Slavica was born in Rijeka in what was then the Socialist Republic of Croatia, one of the six regions or 'republics' of Yugoslavia. Slavica's family background, like Bernie's, was humble. In Yugoslavia privilege belonged to the League of Communists; for the rest – ninety-four per cent of the population – it was hard work, and learning to grasp at opportunities, which were few. For Slavica, the way forward was through her beauty, wherever that would take her. In September 1982 it took her to Monza. Two weeks after drinking Coca-Cola in Bernie's motorhome, she accompanied a Fila sportswear representative to Las Vegas for the last Grand Prix of the season, and it was there that her friendship with Bernie began to develop into love.

In 1984, Slavica gave birth to their daughter, Tamara, and Bernie, at the age of fifty-four, became a father for the second time. He married Slavica at the Kensington & Chelsea Register Office and, again, following the ceremony Bernie immediately returned to business – no honeymoon. Another daughter, Petra, was born to the couple in December 1988, and Slavica now settled down to devote herself to the care of her children. Bernie would say, to Croatian journalist, Mladen Plese, 'Most important to me is that I know Slavica is a terrific mother, and that I'm sure she will look after our daughters once I am no longer around. That makes me very happy… Slavica is simply the most important thing in my life.'

Some of Bernie's friends believe the marriage to Slavica caused him to cut his ties with the past: 'Bernie changed,' they complain, and for a few of the old gang the door was firmly shut. But marriage would not be the only upheaval in Bernie's life at this time. The relationship with Deborah, the daughter of his first marriage, became distant. He had given her the Dulwich apartment. 'I was married from that flat,' she says, and that was the difficulty – Bernie did not approve of her husband. The young man didn't measure up to his expectations. For Deborah, however, the marriage proved a success and she eventually gave her father a grandson; Bernie 'hasn't seen him since he was seven'; the friction between them at the time of Deborah's marriage has gone, but the distance that it created has been allowed to remain. Nor has Bernie seen his eldest daughter for 'the last twenty years'. Then she adds: 'He has his new family.' One family at a time is all that Bernie can emotionally accommodate. 'But

I know that he's always there for me' and finally, 'I am very, very proud of him.'

By 1986 there would be yet another major break-up, one that left Bernie feeling 'betrayed'; Nelson Piquet split with Brabham to join the Williams team. He was fed up with running on uncompetitive Pirelli tyres and could see that the remaining year of the Pirelli/Brabham three-year contract would not take him to the podium; at the age of thirty-four it was time to be pragmatic. Also, Williams were offering more money. 'Nelson was winding up for more money and it got to the point where he was one of the first superstars earning large sums,' says Herbie Blash. 'Bernie felt very let down.' For Piquet, however, it was – initially – the correct career move. He had a competitive year in 1986 and became World Champion, for the third time, in 1987. Thereafter, his career was less than sensational. He signed with Lotus for 1988 and 1989 following an enormous offer from Camel and Honda, but the Lotus years of triumph had fallen into decay. Nelson then switched to the Benetton team for 1990 and 1991 and scored a few more victories, after which offers of a drive in Formula 1 ceased. But Piquet still had it in him to race, so he plied his talents in the Indianapolis 500 where a huge accident left him with crushed feet and legs; he eventually retired from motor racing in 1993 to attend to his developing businesses and, later, to oversee the racing career of his son, Nelson Jr.

Within the Brabham team the impact of Nelson's departure was compared to 'the breaking up of a family', and it was the final chapter in the noble history of Brabham. In 1986 Riccardo Patrese was joined on the team by another Italian driver – and concert pianist – twenty-eight-year-old Elio de Angelis. He had enjoyed an impressive seven years in Formula 1, but in Gordon Murray's controversial 'low-line' BT55 he drove in the first four Grands Prix of the 1986 season finishing in only one race, Brazil. Then, during a routine testing session, in May, at France's Paul Ricard circuit, there was another tragedy. Travelling at 180mph, Elio suddenly crashed heavily, due to 'a component failure'. The car turned upside-down and was on fire. He was taken to hospital in Marseilles where he was declared dead. Gordon was stunned by Elio's death: 'I think I took that one much harder than Bernie, because I was actually there, and I was the one that had worked with Elio... I don't think Bernie had had time to get that close.' It was a bewildering time for Gordon: the departure of Piquet; the failure of his designs; the loss of Elio; trouble in his personal life – he was dangling at a crossroads. And there was another factor; like Piquet, he wanted more money. After winning the second Championship in 1983, Gordon had started asking Bernie for a rise, and it was always:

'Don't worry about it.'

'But Bernie, I'm only earning the same as the mechanics.'

'Don't worry. I'll always look after you and Stella.'

In any event, Bernie 'bumped the money up', although the amount fell short of Gordon's expectations, and when he complained Bernie pointed out the tax burden incurred by high wage earners: 'Why do you want to pay it all to the tax man? Forget it, you own half the company. It would be better to earn a small salary now, keep the money down now, and you've got the money.' And there Gordon let the matter rest until Ford approached him, offering 'a huge sum for a three-year deal, which was unheard of in those days.' With Brabham he was earning 'thirty-three grand a year' with 'perks... which I really struggled on, a bit'. The Formula 1 grapevine was electrified with the news of Gordon's offer, and Bernie, who has an ear for everything having to do with the sport – absolutely everything – 'obviously heard about it because out of the blue' he invited Gordon for a discussion in his motorhome at the circuit. 'I've been meaning to talk to you about your salary,' said Bernie. 'I think we ought to either put it up or better, we'll sell the company. I've got some Arabs really interested in buying the company. We'll sign a deal where we stay on for five years, you put your bit in the bank, I'll put my bit in the bank and we'll still go racing.' 'Fantastic!' said Gordon, who then turned down the Ford offer 'because I felt so loyal to Bernie and Herbie and the guys... and the Ford deal went elsewhere.'

About three months later, Gordon went back to Bernie to find out how the sale of the company was going. 'Ah, well, that deal fell through,' Bernie explained.

'Well, is the plan still to sell and put the money in the bank?'

'Oh, yeah, yeah, I'm looking for other people.'

'Well, look, I'd like a bigger salary to equal what other people are earning, I've heard this guy's on £200,000, this guy's on £150,000, this guy's on £250,000 – I'd like £150,000 a year until we sell the company. The minute we sell the company, I'll go back to £30,000.' It was not a discussion Bernie enjoyed. 'Bernie hates that sort of thing, he hates being in a situation where he can't deal, so he begrudgingly agreed and paid me the £150,000 a year that was the sort of going rate… well, actually, having won two World Championships it was still a bit low to be honest. He hated it and from that moment on he was far more distant. But he kept coming back and saying "I've still got some other people interested".

'Then we got to the point where we lost Nelson, de Angelis was killed, I tried a really radical car, which didn't work, and we were going to lose sponsorship; we were going to lose the BMW contract. It was all looking pretty bleak after de Angelis, I really was on a low and I went to Bernie and said: "Look, I don't feel I want to continue, you know, I want to stop and get out of Formula 1." "Fine," he said, "we need to sit down and work out the deal." "Yeah, great." So I went into his office, and I was in there for hours… He convinced me that we were so far in debt that if I got my half of the company, I would be paying somebody… and he got me to sign a bit of paper resigning as a director.'

Bernie then promised to 'sort out a one-off payment' for Gordon. 'What about the company deal?' 'Oh, that's not really worth anything.' Gordon was dumbfounded, because he had 'just bought a little house, a ruin, in France and we had like zero in the bank, and I've never borrowed a penny in my life.' As his part of the deal Gordon received £30,000, and, Bernie told him, 'you can keep the company cars'. But, Gordon adds, 'by the end of the day he said "No, you can't keep the cars." After fifteen years and two World Championships… "We'll pay you £30,000 and that's it." Later, he sold Brabham for five and a half million quid. My fault was in believing it wouldn't happen to me… because I watched him do it to everybody else, you know, that's what he's good at, he's fantastic at it. I watched Bernie get the better of me because Bernie loves a deal and to him that's not bad. That's just doing what he does best. He did it to Tyrrell, Chapman, anybody he could, he did the best possible deal… I watched and I thought, "He's never gonna do that to me after fifteen years and two World Championships", and in the end I got exactly the same treatment. So, it's a shame it had to end like that really, but there you go, that's Bernie… I don't look back with any regret, we had some great times together, some good times together, some good fun, a lot of success and it did teach me a valuable lesson.'

Herbie Blash takes a different view of the trouble between Gordon and Bernie. As with Piquet, 'Bernie felt very let down' by Gordon who 'would have been the first designer earning large sums of money, and I think it just got to Bernie and he thought, I don't need this now. That's what really destroyed Brabham,' Herbie says. 'We know about [Bernie's] hard side, the hard negotiator, and he can be very hard, there's no doubt about it. But I like to think Bernie is very honest in his hardness… the one thing you must remember about Bernie is that if you don't deliver, he's not going to look after you, which is what happened with Gordon. He looked after Gordon and gave him everything he required to build the best car. Gordon came up with some very way-out ideas that didn't work. They could have worked but they didn't. So, in the end Gordon didn't deliver. Also, Gordon was having some personal problems at the time, but whatever the reason, the relationship between Gordon and Bernie broke.'

It is Charlie Whiting's conclusion that 'Bernie lost confidence in Gordon' because 'after winning the second championship… his drive seemed to sort of disappear and by the middle of 1985 it was almost as if he couldn't be bothered. He needed something new.' Furthermore, 'BMW had already lost a lot of confidence, the car we had in 1985 didn't perform at all, and Gordon blamed BMW and BMW blamed Gordon and we never got anywhere with it. Then Bernie had to, more or less, force BMW to stay and it was really not the right atmosphere to even think about winning a race.'

Gordon Murray's wife, Stella, still feeling the sting of her husband's disappointment, quite naturally has another perspective: 'Gordon has had a blessed career, Bernie was part of that, quite an extraordinary man... and was always very kind to me.' But 'when he decided to be rid of Gordon, it actually broke Gordon's spirit... I never believed he would do it to us.' Bernie can be very tough and ruthless at times. Today Bernie baulks at Gordon's estimate of the Brabham price tag. 'What! Five million quid? If I had it I'd like to know where the money is!'

Englishman Derek Warwick took de Angelis's place in the Brabham team, but in terms of championship points 1986 was an uneventful year, with Patrese managing only two sixth places. The following year saw a slight improvement with Italian driver Andrea de Cesaris, who had replaced Warwick, taking third at Belgium to Patrese's fifth in Hungary and third in Mexico, putting Brabham in a lowly eighth position in the Constructors' Championship, albeit up one notch on the previous year. But the lustre was gone and in 1988 Bernie decided to dispose of his racing team. He sold Motor Racing Developments and the Brabham name to Alfa Romeo who had agreed to 'employ the majority of the Brabham team to build a new car for a silhouette formula – like a Formula 1 car with a saloon car body' – the Alfa Romeo 164 with a V10 engine. A good idea, perhaps, but it foundered and Alfa Romeo then sold Brabham to Swiss financier Joachim Luthi. The cars resumed racing, using Judd engines, and optimism returned, until Luthi was sent to prison for fraud and other offences. Next in the ownership chain was the Japanese Middlebridge Group which, in 1992, attempted to enliven the team by placing an Italian woman, Giovanna Amati, in the driver's seat, alas disappointingly; Giovanna was replaced by England's Damon Hill, following in his father's footsteps, but even he could not force the car into the points, and in

August 1992 a Brabham was seen for the last time on the starting grid of a Grand Prix. The race was in Hungary, where Patrese, now driving a Williams, was on pole and the winner, in a McLaren, was Ayrton Senna.

Herbie Blash took charge of the Brabham factory at Chessington where the manufacture of carbon-fibre components, Gordon's brainchild, continued in operation, and Herbie remained there, as head of Activa, a company he set up, employing 'a lot of Brabham people'. But Herbie's Grand Prix career was far from over – on Grand Prix weekends he officiates for the FIA.

Charlie Whiting 'went from being a mechanic to a chief mechanic, to an engineer and then from engineer to scrutineer for the FIA' – on Bernie's insistence. Today Charlie Whiting is a vital part of the FIA hierarchy in his roles as Race Director and FIA safety delegate.

Gordon Murray joined McLaren as technical director and race strategist, but only after he had signed a proper contract. 'I tell you when I went to McLaren I had every "i" dotted and "t" crossed... I even had what I could and could not wear in the contract... so there's one thing Bernie did teach me... never to do a deal on a handshake.' Between 1987 and 1989 McLaren, with Gordon's help, achieved an outstanding twenty-nine Grand Prix wins. Thereafter, his need for new challenges placed him four-square in the development of the 230mph, three-seater McLaren F1 road car, and until recently he worked on the design of a totally non-polluting city car among a stream of other brilliant concepts. And Gordon, ever gentle, still enjoys a well-deserved reputation as one of the most respected – and best-liked – designers in the business. What is Gordon's attitude today concerning his distressing departure from Brabham and from Bernie? 'I was pretty upset, I have to admit, but after that you have to get on with life. I base a lot of my life on Mr Dylan, who said "Don't look back".'

As for Bernie: 'When I bought the Brabham team I thought that having given up all my other businesses I would enjoy an easier life as a team owner, but it was just the opposite. We won twenty-two Grands Prix and two World Championships

– I'm very proud of that. At the same time I realised that the sport's administration left a lot to be desired so I became more and more involved with that. But you can't run a team part-time, it's not possible, and when the administrative side of the sport became so time-consuming, I knew that I had to give up the team.' Marco Piccinini, race manager of the Ferrari Formula 1 team at the time, and a man whom Bernie came to know well, agrees: 'Bernie gave up a lot – emotionally not financially – when he gave up Brabham, it's much more fun to be running a motor racing team, rather than negotiating media or promoters' contracts.' But by 1988, when Bernie decided to sell Brabham, the competitive standard in Formula 1 had been steadily increasing while the cost of running a team had sky-rocketed beyond reason; and the sport, like Bernie, had entered a new phase of motor racing history, unlike anything that had gone before.

PART II

CHAPTER 10

FORMULA BERNIE

'There were cars, there were drivers, there were races, there were teams, there was chaos, and then there was Bernie,' said Australian racing driver Frank Gardner, referring to the changes that Bernie has made to Formula 1. Frank, a veteran of some fifty years in and around motor racing, had been working with Jack Brabham when he first observed Bernie, standing about, 'more or less thinking and listening' at the factory in New Haw. This was around 1966 when Jack Brabham won the World Championship and his team won the Constructors' Championship; Bernie was then tagging around with the Cooper racing team and Jochen Rindt. 'That's probably about the first time I took any notice of Bernie Ecclestone,' says Frank, who later drove a sports car for Bernie. He 'would appear from time to time at race meetings'. At the race meetings 'people were talking about contracts for £5,000 or £10,000 and that was a signing-on fee, you found your own way around and you made your twenty per cent of the take. That was a pretty good contract... but the organisation was particularly bad, it was amateur hour... if you didn't get your money, you might not get it until next year and you might not get it even then... there was a very big opening for somebody with an enterprising mind... so Bernie could see all this, he stood and looked and thought and saw.' And after buying Brabham and becoming a member of the Formula One Constructors' Association, Bernie was in a position to take action. 'What Bernie has turned the sport into is like night to day.' He gave Formula 1 a professional structure, a solid platform from which to operate, and from which to build a greater entity.

Before Bernie's reorganisation of Formula 1, it was up to each individual entrant to negotiate an appearance fee with promoters, money for putting a car on the grid. It was always the big winning names, those that had managed to capture the public's interest – Ferrari and Lotus – who took the lion's share of the start money, those with less crowd-drawing power received only a few hundred pounds or nothing at all. Prize money was the money paid by the organiser for 'placed' cars – the first six taking the chequered flag. Thus many teams were restricted to those races that they could afford to attend and, regrettably, absented themselves from the rest. Circuit owners could never be certain which teams would turn up – not even for the big reputation-building events. This was the situation that topped Bernie's agenda for change. 'We're *all* going to go racing,' he said. 'We've got to be fair with the money.' To persuade the race organisers to be even-handed with the money, he had to have negotiating power; he had to have all the teams with him, as a package. He had to control the Formula One Constructors' Association.

The Formula One Constructors' Association (first F1CA, later FOCA) was begun in 1964 by Team Lotus manager Andrew Ferguson to represent the interests of established constructors, particularly the British 'kit car' owners (chassis constructors using purchased engines), meaning not only Lotus but, by 1972, Brabham, of course, and such teams as McLaren, Tyrrell, March, Williams and Surtees whom Ferguson continued to represent with the governing body, then called the Commission Sportive International (CSI) but changed in 1979 to the Fédération Internationale du Sport Automobile (FISA), which governed motorsport on behalf of the Fédération Internationale de l'Automobile (FIA). Anyway, F1CA also negotiated with race promoters, but this aspect of its responsibilities was handled in a rather slipshod manner until Bernie seized control, or rather convinced his fellow F1CA members of the advantage to all in handing him control.

Bernie explained to the constructors that he could improve their finances by negotiating more profitable start money and prize money. This was not entirely a notion that originated with Bernie: Back in 1958 Tony Vandervell, owner of the Vanwall team and Stuart Lewis-Evans's boss, had appreciated Bernie's shrewdness and suggested that he organise the start money. Bernie hadn't forgotten, but now he also offered to improve the prize money and, more importantly, he promised to reduce their transportation costs, particularly for overseas travel, through a package deal, which he had – previously – organised with a freight transport company, saving each team some £4,000 per trip. He had already impressed the constructors with his essential lack of self-interest, and now he deigned to serve the tea while they chatted over his offer.

'Somebody needed to make some investments and take some risks,' says Bernie. 'They weren't prepared to take risks and make investments, so I [offered to do] all that.' The scrappiness of the existing arrangements with organisers had also nagged at Bernie's craving for tidiness, and he needed to put it into order, like the Strood Motor Company, like the Brabham factory, like reorganising the interior of a building, an office, a house; in all things there must be order and logic and then, through this realigned conduit, efficiency would reign and profit might flow. The constructors' attitude was, 'we're racers, we don't want to have anything to do with business', or, as Frank Williams put it, 'I think he probably chose himself because he could see that the rest of us were like a bunch of chickens, more interested in making racing cars than actually looking after our little businesses.' It should be remembered, though, that Colin Chapman had a head for big business and BRM was backed by large industry. It was the convenience of Bernie's proposal that had the broadest appeal, with Bernie handling all the logistics of moving the teams and cars from race to race, and the advantage was in savings and profit. For his services they agreed to pay him two per cent of the prize money – then worth 37,500 Swiss Francs. And why not? It appeared to be a classic 'win win' situation.

For Bernie it was a door unlocked, waiting to be flung wide open. With the majority of the constructors behind him, he could guarantee the promoters a package. There was no show without Punch; Punch could now be expected to turn up in force, absolutely, no question, Bernie would make it happen – at each and every race – even if he personally had to loan money to a team so that they could afford to race. If he said it would happen, it would happen now that he had been given permission to act with the strength of the constructors behind him; permission to take control. What the constructors did not realise was that they had just instigated a revolution – a struggle for professionalism, for power and, eventually, for the commercial exploitation of Formula 1. The authority to act on behalf of the insurgent constructors was given to Bernie on the weekend of the South African Grand Prix in March 1972, in a room at the Kyalami Ranch Hotel – which he would later acquire as well.

In May 1972, at the Monaco Grand Prix, Bernie started flexing his newly augmented muscles when he led the constructors in a dispute over the number of cars receiving prize money that would enter the race. The constructors wanted to increase the number to twenty-six (it had previously been eighteen), while the revered Automobile Club de Monaco, the race organisers, would allow no more than sixteen cars on the starting grid. Bernie and the teams, however, stood firm. There would be twenty-six cars or nothing. Otherwise they would strike. The organisers bristled – this is Monaco, we're special, and we will not be dictated to. Instructions were given for the gates to the underground car park, in which the teams' cars were kept, to be locked, effectively impounding them. Then they underscored their authority by posting police guards at the entrance to the gates, such was the power of the Automobile Club de Monaco, supported by the FIA and the CSI.

However, when the crowds gathered for the practice session, and the teams appeared content to remain tucked up within the confines of the garage, the organisers began to fret. They offered a stopgap solution: if the teams would oblige them by participating in the practice session, then the number on the starting grid would – subsequently – be agreed. Bernie declined. The constructors wanted the number settled first or there would be no entertainment provided by the majority of the Formula 1 teams. And they could tell that to the multitude of Italian visitors camped out in the vicinity of the royal palace on a hillside overlooking the circuit, braving all weathers and deprivations to view for a few hours the teams that were to challenge their favourite team – Ferrari – and their favourite drivers – Ferrari drivers. Anything less would simply not do; in such a circumstance the hill people might become testy. An indelicate scenario loomed before the Monégasque race organisers, who now pleaded that it would be necessary for a CSI representative to sign a document endorsing an increase in the number of starters.

Not Bernie's problem; no agreement, no practice, no race. Within thirty minutes a signed paper was produced authorising a grid of twenty-five cars, which was, in turn, accepted by the teams, and so the cars headed for the circuit. Bernie, with a toss of his Beatle locks, which inevitably came to settle upon the upper rim of his rose-tinted glasses, now part of his uniform (including neat white shirt and well-pressed bell-bottomed blue jeans), likewise stepped into the cockpit of one of the Brabhams, purportedly 'to check it out'. But Bernie still needed to strut his authority, leaving behind a token reminder that there was a new force among the ranks of the kit-car manufacturers. So as he was being pushed by the mechanics towards the track, he accidentally drove up a ramp and over a policeman's foot, causing his hat to fall off. Bernie's satisfaction was now complete: make that two over the bows of the FIA's flagship.

He then dived head-first into negotiations with race organisers for an increase in the constructors' take of the prize purse; and he wasn't coming up for air until he got what he was after – an increase per race from the usual £5,000 or thereabouts to £88,000. Which was roughly proportional to the outrage felt by the constructors after they had purloined a copy of a CSI balance sheet and discovered a gross discrepancy in the level of the profits realised by the organisers and the CSI in comparison to their own. Furthermore, Bernie was demanding that the F1CA be responsible for the distribution of the money, and that they have control of the start money to ensure fair practice. It was all too much for the organisers, and in alarm they turned to the CSI whose members, equally disturbed, agreed to the formation of yet another alphabet organisation, the GPI – Grand Prix International. Dutchman Henri Treu, operating under the authority of the GPI, was appointed to head up a negotiating team to outsmart the brisk persuader, Ecclestone. The wild card in the negotiations was Italian manufacturer Ferrari, and more specifically Enzo Ferrari himself, actually one and the same. Treu believed that Ferrari would always side with the organisers who paid him so much money, and also with the FIA/CSI/GPI or whatever, as long as it wasn't the British kit-car constructors whom Ferrari himself had labelled, disparagingly, the 'garagistes' (garage workers). How and where and when the wild card would be played was of fundamental importance. To improve his chances of winning, Bernie gained political dexterity. Then he would have to convince Ferrari of the strength of his army.

So Henri Treu and Bernie locked horns and the tussle was exasperating if not exhausting, at least for Treu, who then applied various strategies in an attempt to weaken his opponent. These included romancing the constructors individually with increased financial offers. They would not be bought. He then attempted to mitigate the power of the combined constructors by asking the CSI to introduce a new rule allowing Formula 2 and Formula 5000 to race in Formula 1. And so that the kit car assemblers would appreciate the political superiority of the CSI, the new rule was to be announced by the Royal Automobile Club, organisers of the British Grand Prix. The RAC complied, adding that the prize money would be £55,000, unless another amount was agreed the following day, and there was an addendum: entry forms had to be received the next day or all financial benefit would be cancelled. 'We always have trouble with the British,'

Bernie spouts today. But at the time he was unmoved, and confident, reasoning that if the race took place it could not possibly be called a World Championship event, in which case the constructors would not care to be involved. Then he pointed out to the CSI that unless the organisers agreed to the F1CA's financial requirements, they had no business authorising Grand Prix races. 'Henri had his own ideas which actually didn't coincide with ours,' says Bernie. 'He couldn't get his ideas through' because 'we didn't want these other Formulae'. Henri Treu then attempted to attack Bernie on a more personal level, using Graham Hill as his weapon.

The debonair Graham, then in his last season with Brabham, had become a superstar in name only, for his performances on the circuit, following near crippling injuries, were – with notable exceptions – lacking consistency, as were the cars he was given to drive. But making the best of it, Graham found himself, at the start of a race in 1970, positioned at the back of the grid next to the illustrious Jack Brabham, who was also having a disappointing time. He looked across to Jack and smiled, 'Better class of people at the back, don't you think?' Treu took the opportunity to flatter forty-four-year-old Graham – and win him over – by suggesting that Hill race under his own name, like Jack Brabham for instance. It was all the encouragement Graham needed. He left Bernie and the Brabham team, and although he didn't actually race under a 'Graham Hill' banner, he did manage to secure a lucrative three-year contract with tobacco company W.D. & H.O. Wills, and turned up in Barcelona in April 1973 for the Spanish Grand Prix as the entrant and sole driver for the Embassy Shadow team. For extra measure, it was made clear that Hill had crossed over to the GPI camp with the announcement that he had become the first entrant to agree terms with the GPI, and that henceforward he would be heralding the GPI cause. Now Bernie seethed and, it was thought, swatted back by offering F1CA membership to the intended suppliers of Graham's engine – if the engine would never be delivered. Bernie, tongue in cheek, denies interfering, 'I would never use Mafia type tactics… well not every day anyway. It would not be nice to do those things.' Graham received his engine. This episode was only a very minor skirmish in the Ecclestone/ GPI battle, but suggests that the GPI and other bodies were becoming increasingly nervous.

Meanwhile, the travel package arranged by Bernie, for the benefit of his fellow constructors, was made through a shipping company called Cazaly Mills, from which, of course, he received an attractive percentage of the F1CA business. He also perceived a potential for greater gain, so, together with London businessman Ron Shaw, he acquired Cazaly Mills in 1976. Ron looked after the day-to-day travel while Bernie looked after all transactions involving Formula 1. With the purchase of Cazaly Mills, Bernie also acquired Alan Woollard, one of the company's prize personnel. Alan had been responsible for shipping the cars by sea to the races and then dealing with Customs on their re-entry into Britain. When Bernie bought the company he mentioned it to Alan, in passing, one Friday afternoon: 'Oh by the way Woollard, you're working at [the Brabham headquarters] on Monday, I've just bought the company.'

Bernie, however, eventually disposed of his interest in Cazaly Mills. He did so by handing over his share of the company to McLaren boss Teddy Mayer, in payment of gambling losses – 'a five-figure number'. Bernie questions Teddy's memory: 'I gave him a travel company? I never did that.' What is indisputable is the fact that Bernie could not resist gambling, whatever his losses. Disposing of Cazaly Mills was necessary; the company was being drained of profits by one of its employees, an Arsenal fan who was handing out tickets, willy nilly, to members of the Arsenal Football Club. Even so, Bernie was not about to forego travel as a business, for he soon set up the more efficiently organised FOCA World Travel in which Alan Woollard played a prominent role. Alan's duties included, he recalls, not only 'doing all the freight' but also 'everything at Brabhams from driving a truck to – anything. And as FOCA [formerly F1CA] got bigger, I did security, I did the passes, I did everything, and the job was still growing... I had a suitcase that was an office.' Alan also collected, for each race, a complete surgical set from the London Hospital to be transported for Professor Watkins to use at the circuits if necessary.

When Alan, as Bernie's employee, arranged long-distance transport, they switched from sea to air, leasing two CL44 cargo prop-jets; eventually, these would be exchanged for six jumbo jets leased from European commercial airlines. Some thirty years on, Alan would still be working for Bernie, and, looking back on 'those early days when motor racing was changing, we had a few run-ins with various people, but we were all part of the same team by then, we were all trying to work for one end, Bernie's vision. Sometimes we didn't understand because we thought he was going over the top. Only Bernie knew where he was going... I mean he's been tough, but with Bernie, the way he approaches a thing is not the way you would approach it, but at the end of the day he's straightforward, [although] he doesn't explain himself, he just tells you to get on with it. It's his way. In the early days it was all new to me, and it was growing quicker than I could ever imagine.'

In the earlier F1CA days it had been Andrew Ferguson's job to organise the travel. Bernie had him replaced by ex-Red Arrows team manager Peter Macintosh, who had been secretary of the Grand Prix Drivers' Association, and recommended by Ken Tyrrell. Macintosh's role in FOCA, says Bernie, was 'along the lines of general administration', and came to an end in 1978. Another aspect of the travel benefits that Bernie provided was manipulative, but also very clever. He helped the teams' competitiveness by creating an awards structure in which a team's costs could not be covered until it became ranked among the top ten teams, a position that had to be maintained in order to continue to enjoy reduced travel costs. In this way Bernie was not only guaranteeing the organisers a show, but also a quality show; good for the sponsors, good for the media, good for the spectators, and therefore good for the sport.

In the negotiation of prize money and start money with

organisers, Bernie actually reorganised the whole financial base of Formula 1 by instituting a sturdy platform from which he, on behalf of the constructors as a group instead of the entrants acting independently, dealt directly with the organisers. Representing the teams he also agreed a sum to be divided between all the entrants. Then he devised a complicated formula by which money was paid to the teams according to the position of their cars in the race on certain laps. This meant that all the teams received a return for their participation. It also meant that even the teams at the back of the grid gained reimbursement and that the proceeds of the agreement did not all go to the richest and most successful team. This explains why, when cars have lost a lot of time in the pits, they are sent back out on to the circuit to continue to compete despite the unlikelihood of taking championship points. This way, the entrants are encouraged to provide as much spectacle as possible by having as many cars as possible circulating for the entertainment of the public at the circuit and those watching on television. Again, the arrangement was, and is, very good for the sport.

Bernie's early progress in negotiating with race organisers is evidenced by the fact that the average purse increased to $275,000, US dollars having replaced Swiss Francs as the currency for a European race by the mid-Seventies. 'It was 37,000 Swiss Francs [$9,000] when we started,' adds Bernie. Outside continental Europe – due to increased travel costs – he demanded, and received, considerably more, rising to as high as $350,000, by which time he was attempting to tie organisers to three-year contracts. To achieve the figure of $275,000 for a European race Bernie had had to enter into tortuous negotiations with CSI President Pierre Ugueux and Jean-Marie Balestre, President of the Fédération Française du Sport Automobile, France's automobile club. He did so only after Ugueux had declared that the 1976 World Championship would not occur until the financial terms had been agreed between the CSI, the organisers and the F1CA, and that any contracts already completed with Bernie for 1976 would be invalid.

It had been a disagreeable – but necessary – confrontation. As the talk turned hostile, Balestre became increasingly agitated. '[He] broke a pencil and things and then he started shouting,' says Bernie. 'Then I got up and turned the lights off and said "I'm not even afraid of the dark". It sort of cemented our relationship from then on.' Pierre Ugueux finally agreed to Bernie's terms because 'I think he saw common sense in the way we were doing things… because it was fair, honest and reasonable,' Bernie adds. 'Because we had money invested and as usual, those sort of people didn't have any money invested.' Moreover, the additional outlay on the purse would encourage organisers to become more professional. In order to hand on part of the cost via increased gate prices the organisers would have to provide a better product. The entertainment would be good, Bernie would see to that, but now the facilities also had to be good.

Bernie himself carried out the circuit inspections, and whatever was lacking would, with financial pressure, be put right otherwise, he felt, the organisers might become neglectful. Neglectfulness – of any sort – had to be stamped out. When, for example, the organisers and promoters of the Canadian Grand Prix at Mosport Park agreed terms for a race to be held in September 1975, but a few months before the race had not yet signed the contract, Bernie gave them a nudge by increasing the terms and more: 'We said we always get forty or fifty hire cars – free.' The Canadian organisers were not amused and refused to play along; there would be no additional monies, and no free cars!' So Bernie gave them until August to come to an arrangement and, when the contract was still unsigned, he cancelled the race. The Canadians were suddenly willing to renegotiate and sign up. For Bernie, however, the game was over and he would not change his mind. He and F1CA were willing to forego the race on the principle that deadlines must be met – at least by the organisers – otherwise the negotiating position of the F1CA would be weakened.

The following season the Canadian Grand Prix was back on schedule at Mosport Park, the woodland setting some sixty miles from Toronto, where it was held again in 1976. In 1978 the race moved to Île Notre-Dame in Montreal where it has been held – with the odd fracas – ever since, except for 2009. Burdette ('Burdie') Martin, who had been consultant clerk of the course at the Canadian Grand Prix during the mid-Seventies, remembers the race's organisers referring to Bernie as the 'Kidney', because 'his name is Ecclestone and he hurts like a kidney stone'. In 2004 Bernie's $12 million fee would be the cause of the organisers' pain. He again threatened to cancel the race unless they paid up, knowing 'that when push came to shove he could play poker with these guys and clean out the house before his morning coffee,' wrote reporter Jack Todd in Montreal's *The Gazette*. It was further reported that the race day crowd was a 'sell-out', with over 100,000 people in attendance.

There were plenty of disputes with organisers and Bernie relished these conflicts. With the Royal Automobile Club de Belgique he tangled over the choice of a circuit. The Club preferred Nivelles, where it had been held in 1974 whereas Bernie wanted Zolder. The 1975 race was held at Zolder. And in Japan there was widespread consternation when Bernie waited until a few months before the race – the first Grand Prix to be held in that country – to announce that it could not take place. Emperor Hirohito was downcast and the businessmen organisers befuddled. But it was not enough to want a race. The facilities had to meet an acceptable standard as set down by motorsport's governing body and, regardless of continuous admonitions from Bernie, matters improved very little. So to get their attention he hit them with increased travel charges while continuing to decry the circuit's condition. The circuit improved, the race went ahead and F1CA received more money.

South Africa was more complicated, involving world politics and human rights, and the ongoing dilemma concerning the role of sport in such issues – the very issues that had given him cause for a personal grudge against the cruel apartheid regime. In 1968 he had made plans to travel as a foursome with the Rindts to attend the South African Grand Prix, but his

Chinese girlfriend, Tuana Tan, was refused the required visa, because, she says, 'The South Africans said I was "coloured"; if I had been Japanese I would have got a visa.' Still, in 1977 the organisers of the South African Grand Prix paid some £350,000 – then an unusually vast sum – to F1CA to hold a race. Many thought the cost reflected the country's need to divert the world's gaze from the killing of Steve Biko at the hands of the Eastern Cape security police in September 1977; Biko had been detained and interrogated under apartheid anti-terrorism legislation. Six months later the Grand Prix was held as scheduled, but it was overshadowed by fierce shouts from protestors – at the circuit and in the media. The apartheid scourge continued, and still the races took place with objections – from every direction – now being hurled at Bernie and the constructors as well as the organisers and the FIA. Even when the French government (along with those of Finland, Sweden and Brazil) demanded that the staging of a Formula 1 grand prix in South Africa be disallowed, and forbade the Renault and Ligier teams from visiting that country, the Paris-based FIA took no notice.

Bernie was more circumspect, and felt that he must honour a contract – while looking for a way out. With the support of Enzo Ferrari he finally responded to protests within the motor industry and to sponsors who had their logos removed from the cars being televised at the Kyalami circuit. Mind you, these same sponsors' products were in ample supply in shops down the road. 'It is the hypocrisy of it that I can't stomach,' wrote motor racing journalist Nigel Roebuck. In any event, Bernie let it be known that racing in South Africa must come to an end, and after 1985 Grand Prix racing in that country did cease – for a while. Seven years later there was a race at Kyalami, and again in 1993, by which time the apartheid regime was becoming history. The following year Nelson Mandela was elected as South Africa's President, and in 1995 all the world celebrated along with the South Africans – hosting the Rugby World Cup – when he walked into the Johannesburg stadium wearing the Springbok jersey, the Springbok having been the emblem of the ruling National Party during apartheid. Here was true forgiveness. Henceforth South Africa was regarded not only as the freedom-loving 'rainbow nation', but as *one* nation. Bernie met with Mandela in 1998 to discuss the government's interest in financing a grand prix and they became firm friends. But rivalry and corrupt practices amongst promoters stymied progress, to such a degree that it has not been until recent months that a return to South Africa (Cape Town this time) has been contemplated.

All the while, in every race, wherever it happened to be, Bernie was mindful of quality – something very close to his heart – making it his perpetual conscious and subconscious study. Another strategy Bernie devised to improve the racing entertainment was to promise the organisers a minimum of eighteen cars at every race, or the constructors would forfeit half the prize money. He covered this guarantee by penalising teams, financially, if they failed to turn up; and he still continued to enjoy their support – although he had to work at it.

Teddy Mayer, managing director and majority shareholder of McLaren Racing from 1964 to 1983, and a charter member of F1CA, remembers Bernie's support-gaining tactics during those early F1CA meetings: 'Well, I didn't really get to know him in any real sense until we started having FOCA [F1CA] meetings and then you got to know everybody a lot better and very quickly. My impression of him was that he was very clever, good at manipulating people to get what he thought was the right thing to do… I always remember his technique… he would come into a meeting and say that we would discuss on the agenda whatever was the most important project: "Well I think we ought to go south guys," and everybody would look around the room and say: "South, Bernie? You must be crazy, we've got to go north." "Oh, you want to go north? Fine, let's go north." He would just deliberately dangle the bait until the most important people had decided which way they wanted to go and then he'd be with you 100 per cent, knowing that that was the way to go all the time.'

Frank Williams adds: 'At meetings Bernie would begin to

say the funniest things, or when he would run out of funny things to deflect our ire, he would knock his briefcase on the floor, making sure it was open before he did so, or give someone a bollocking who would always respond in a very FU, FU way! Of course he was the master at steering meetings. If we wanted to know about the starting money for Canada or how much the dividend would be – if there was any – and because he didn't want to pay one, he would make sure we went nowhere near money [in the discussions]. Then later, I'd sit back in my car and think, "Damn, he's conned us again." He has quite an amazing technique, time after time he'd throw some remark on the table – knowing that it would get Ron [Dennis] up through the roof, and then they'd all have a go at Ron, and we'd all start fighting amongst ourselves.'

Teddy Mayer agrees about Bernie's ability to run a meeting: 'He was very good at it, he really was. And he was brave. He would take risks personally that nobody else in FOCA wanted to even get near… in terms of promoting motor races or guaranteeing the purse or whatever was required to get a race on in a certain place that he thought we would do well in. And even Ferrari with all their financial muscle would never touch these things and Bernie would say: "Yeah, I'll take it"… It was also interesting in that if you asked him a question about a deal or anything that you're entitled to ask or had the right to ask, he would always tell you the truth no matter what was involved. But if you asked something that you weren't really entitled to ask, he would give you all sorts of answers that may or may not have anything to do with what you were asking… you would get obfuscation.'

Most of the meetings were held in a small conference room in what was then the Forte Hotel near Heathrow airport. The discussions were generally intense, and occasionally 'very arduous'. Teddy remembers a dispute between Bernie and the 'vociferous' Ken Tyrrell who stood about six feet three inches tall. At one point their argument became so heated Ken jumped up on the table, towering over Bernie who, with assertive voice and countenance 'offered to throw him out the window! But I don't think they ever came to blows,' says

Teddy. During those important, empowering years most of the constructors were on Bernie's side, 'because we figured that he was offering the best deal that anybody was going to offer, not particularly for any other reason than we thought it was about – as the Americans would say – "as good as we're gonna do".' Bernie also remembers confrontations – then and later – with Ken Tyrrell, and others: 'There were always the Ken Tyrrells of this world who thought that anybody who was doing anything must be bad for him and particularly if you were making money.' But 'they weren't naïve sportsmen,' says Frank Williams, 'it was that Bernie was on the inside looking out rather than the group all around him, the circle looking inwards... he saw Formula 1 as an entity, as a business in itself and the promotion thereof... and the understanding was stick together and grow this business the best we can – through Bernie.'

Colin Chapman turned out to be one of Bernie's allies; and his support was crucial. Colin's Team Lotus – with variations according to sponsorship – was a crowd-puller, so his opinion held weight with all parties. Colin was also respected for his technical genius. He was criticised for being too experimental, for opting for fragile – lighter – cars to obtain the winning advantage over safer, although heftier, vehicles, but he was nonetheless admired and he was adept at business. Moreover, Colin 'believed passionately in what FOCA [F1CA] was trying to do which was to gain control,' insists Teddy Mayer. Colin 'inspired Bernie to continue the fight... he was a big supporter... he gave Bernie confidence.' It may be recalled that Colin Chapman was one of the three people who Bernie 'admired very much,' the other two being John Cooper and Enzo Ferrari. Colin had taught Bernie lessons in running a team, early lessons in sponsorship and presentation but here was Colin's most important contribution – support at a critical moment. Momentous were the changes to Formula 1 which would, if allowed, also direct the course of Bernie's future – into the stratosphere. It was critical for a few individuals to lean in Bernie's direction in order to maintain the momentum of change. Colin Chapman and Enzo Ferrari were the foremost. If Bernie had not placed himself in this win or lose situation, if he had not risked defeat, even a calculated risk, Formula 1 today would be quite different. But throughout the Seventies he had to keep dancing – maintaining, without a pause, the tempo of change.

So, employing his swift, sharp-shooting, Bexleyheath used car dealer technique, Bernie nurtured his F1CA power and, negotiating from strength with the organisers, he secured races – whole seasons – on his terms. But Bernie's efforts would not continue without further challenges. Henri Treu had been more or less sidelined, but Pierre Ugueux was still after his blood and called in reinforcements to prevent Bernie from becoming the all-out conqueror of Formula 1. The battle – the war – was far from won.

Pierre Ugueux, learning to think like the enemy, decided to unify the organisers by calling upon them to stand behind one Patrick Duffeler, otherwise their licences to stage a Grand Prix might be withdrawn. American born, Swiss-based Duffeler, for six years director of Philip Morris Promotions in Europe – a company that had, through its Marlboro brand, already committed millions to Formula 1 sponsorship – was, like other sponsors, weary of the rancour between the governing structure of the sport and the vehicle constructors. Sponsors sought a neutral, national government-recognised arena for negotiations, instead of a forum dominated by Bernie Ecclestone. Michel Boeri, president of the Automobile Club de Monaco added his voice to the united front, proposing that the organisers pledge their allegiance by putting up a $100,000 bond which would be forfeited should an organiser decide to take his chances alone and negotiate with Bernie directly. Boeri had negotiated the numbers of cars on the starting grid at Monaco with Bernie, and had also been present at the Ugueux/Balestre negotiations in which Bernie triumphed; he was still feeling nettled and so not averse to proposing an arrangement that came to be known as the 'Hundred Thousand Dollar Club' – receiving the unanimous support of the organisers. Shoulder to shoulder with Michel Boeri were Baron Fritz Huschke von Hanstein, a former SS

Colonel who became Public Relations Manager for Porsche and Sports Secretary of the Automobilclub von Deutschland; Jean-Marie Balestre, said to be a former Nazi collaborator, who was also a publishing magnate and, as has been mentioned, President of the French automobile club, the Fédération Française du Sport Automobile (FFSA), as well as a host of other heavy-weights who together represented the traditionalists: Monaco, Germany, Austria, Italy, Spain, Argentina, France and Holland. Bernie represented Britain and Belgium along with the relative newcomers to staging a Formula 1 race: Brazil, Sweden, USA-West (Long Beach), USA-East (Watkins Glen), South Africa, Canada and Japan; he wanted to take Formula 1 to the world and – eventually – vice versa.

Bernie snatched up the FIA/CSI gauntlet, by promptly organising the 1977 Dutch Grand Prix. Holland, it seemed, could not decide on which side to stand, nor could the Belgians. F1CA then brashly declared that it would be producing its own rulebook for the 1977 season, and as for Duffeler, Bernie would have nothing to do with him. Duffeler returned fire with a full complement of artillery announcing, with CSI support, the creation of World Championship Racing, WCR, based in Monaco and to which organisers – wishing to hold grands prix under a three-year contract – must transfer their negotiating authority. Argentina, who already had a contract with Bernie for 1977, decided to cancel by omitting to pay outstanding funds owed for travel. Bernie, in turn, cancelled Argentina. Only months away from the start of the season, Formula 1 stood on the brink, with organisers almost equally divided between the two factions.

Would there be a 1977 Grand Prix season or not? The situation for motorsport was dire, so dire that the Guild of Motoring Writers set up peace talks – actually a press conference held in December 1976 at the gentlemanly Royal Automobile Club in Pall Mall, London – so that Ugueux, Duffeler and Bernie could, at last, meet to decide upon the coming season. The talks, lasting three hours, ended in a stalemate. Never mind the coming season, what was the future for Formula 1? Had Bernie gone too far? Was he feeling remorse, would he bend and sway rather than allow Formula 1 to break? Three weeks later, at a meeting held in the Paris headquarters of the French automobile club, Bernie – to everyone's amazement – backed down. The constructors agreed to attend the Argentine Grand Prix on WCR's terms. What is more, Bernie also agreed to the start money and prize money put on the table on behalf of the organisers the WCR represented.

But Bernie, in reality, was just squirming out of a hard place, playing for time, waiting for what he perceived would be the inevitable opportunity to seize, once more, the upper hand. He knew that the organisers, with all their geographical, cultural and economic differences, could never achieve lasting solidarity; they could never, like the constructors, speak with one voice. F1CA attended Argentina and then Brazil under WCR terms, but that was it. Bernie would not commit F1CA to the European races without new negotiations. 'We might have stopped to get people to persuade us to get going,' he says because 'there wasn't enough money'. At the time he cited 'serious disagreements' with the sport's governing body, and with the season well under way the CSI and its cohorts were unlikely to jeopardise it. The terms of the three-year contracts were now adjusted to be more favourable to the F1CA. The WCR eventually dissolved. But the threat to the F1CA had not disappeared, their unity had to continue, cast in iron, or the revolution would fail. Bernie was often heard quoting the declaration made by John Hancock and Benjamin Franklin to the Continental Congress meeting in Philadelphia during the prelude to the American War of Independence: 'We must all hang together or most assuredly we shall all hang separately'. Except, he didn't say 'most assuredly'. Still, it was an accurate assessment by all three – Hancock, Franklin and Ecclestone. And there was yet the wild card – Enzo Ferrari – to be played.

Teddy Mayer recalled: 'In the late Seventies we were going through a piece of FOCA war and Bernie, of course, was heavily involved and... he didn't have Ferrari's undivided support, that's for sure, but he did have some support. I would have to say that probably Ferrari was doing one thing privately and saying things publicly that were more appealing to the FIA... So I think there was a certain element of yes, we're backing you Bernie but we're going to tell the world we're not... I think Bernie learned a lot about the politics of motor racing in that period.' In fact Enzo Ferrari was quite candid with Bernie, saying: 'On top of the table (hitting, with his fist, the table upon which they had been lunching) this is the sport; under (pointing below) is the business.' And, Bernie says, 'he was more interested in under the table than the top, but as far as the world was concerned he was an on-top-of-the-table guy!' Bernie and Enzo first met in 1978, introduced by Marco Piccinini.

At the age of twenty-five, in 1977, Marco Piccinini became Ferrari's sporting director/team manager, and Enzo Ferrari's spokesperson in dealing with F1CA. Charming, soft-spoken, Marco was the son of a Roman banking family who had studied architecture at university but also loved motorsport. With a group of friends he had 'built a few Formula 3 single-seaters'. His father, who knew Enzo, had paved the way to the Ferrari headquarters, and Marco soon found himself involved 'in the conflict between Enzo and Bernie... it was my role to start negotiating, and when you negotiate you must always start from a difficult position – a bit confrontational – but, of course, Bernie is definitely the master at that.' The 1978 season began with Argentina, which was Marco's first Grand Prix in his new role; an initiation that he would never forget. In Argentina, Bernie says, 'we had taken the piss out of Marco in the biggest way'.

Enzo Ferrari had had an association with Alfa Romeo since 1919, as a driver turned salesman turned racing manager. He was sacked by Alfa in 1939 and had felt unkindly towards them ever since. In 1978 Brabham's engines were supplied by Alfa Romeo, therefore Brabham was also out of favour. Nor did Enzo Ferrari find it endearing that Bernie, the previous year, had attracted Niki Lauda – the Ferrari World Champion – to Brabham with a pile of Parmalat money and, worse still,

Lauda had brought with him Ferrari's chief mechanic. And Ecclestone was one of those upstart 'garagistes', whereas Ferrari was one of the 'grandees', a builder of thoroughbreds, though he often belittled his grandness by belching in public. Marco Piccinini would have to keep a close eye on Ecclestone and Brabham – and their Alfa Romeo engines – and then report back all that he saw, every detail. Enzo Ferrari, who never went to races, needed to be informed.

In Argentina, Bernie immediately determined that Marco was a tattler, and so put together a plan to 'goose' him. Bernie explains: 'The Alfa Romeo engine was well known to be heavy on oil, so I went to the clerk of the course or the stewards and told them to reduce the race length quite a bit, like about twenty per cent or something. They knew it was a joke. So they put out a paper saying that they were reducing the race. Of course Marco got hold of it and, being very efficient and wanting to prove to Ferrari what a good guy he was, went apeshit… Colin Chapman and Teddy Mayer, all of us English guys were all in my garage, which was next to Ferrari's… and we saw Marco flying with this bit of paper out of the garage up to the stewards, and when he came back we all clapped and cheered [Bernie actually clapping and laughing]. So poor Marco… The reason that I changed the length of the race was that we'd have run out of oil… It was a joke anyway. The race director said, "I'm sorry Mr Piccinini, but Mr Ecclestone insisted we do this" [more laughter, but louder]… he reported it all to Ferrari'. Marco's recollection of the incident is also 'quite vivid'.

Following the race, and before the next grand prix, which was to be in Brazil, Bernie went to visit Enzo Ferrari at his headquarters in Maranello, near Modena in Italy. The reason for the visit included the race-shortening business, but more importantly Marco, in his very first exposure to Bernie, had begun 'preparing the ground for an understanding' between FOCA's power broker and Enzo, and there 'were still some points which were unclear'. Bernie's notions on diplomacy are more simplistic, he felt that it was time to get to know the 'Old Man' in person. To Bernie, he is always, affectionately, the

'Old Man' and, respectfully, 'Mr Ferrari'; he keeps a portrait of Enzo Ferrari in his office. The old man, aged eighty when forty-eight-year-old Bernie headed for the Maranello summit, was well turned-out with professionally coiffed white hair (he visited the barber every day), immaculate dark suit of the type and quality Bernie still admires, and dark glasses worn at all times concealing deep-set, drooping eyes. He oozed power, as prevalent as an over-indulgence in cologne.

His was the most famous name in the automobile industry, and the yellow shield carrying the prancing horse was the most famous symbol, the red cars the most celebrated vehicles. Enzo Ferrari was motor racing made manifest; John Frankenheimer had featured this doyen – dark glasses, the whole kit – in his 1966 film, *Grand Prix*. Frankenheimer knew to exploit the fact that a race without at least one Ferrari on the grid was not a race; and if the car should win Enzo Ferrari knew how to exploit the victory by turning it into money-gathering publicity. An autocratic team owner, Ferrari scrimped, he underpaid, and his drivers were treated as employees – rarely more – yet they grace the holy firmament of motor racing. Ferrari's drivers included Tazio Nuvolari, José Froilán González, Mike Hawthorn, Juan Manuel Fangio, Harry Schell, Peter Collins, Dan Gurney, Phil Hill, Richie Ginther, Ricardo and Pedro Rodriguez, John Surtees, Jacky Ickx, Mario Andretti, Carlos Pace, Carlos Reutemann, Niki Lauda, Gilles Villeneuve and Jody Scheckter. It was González, the 'Pampas Bull', who holds the distinction of breaking, in 1951, Alfa Romeo's stranglehold on grand prix racing when his Ferrari, emblazoned with the number 12, won at Silverstone. Bernie had watched that race, and later bought the car number 12, which he still treasures. Enzo Ferrari also ran a team of motorcycles. He had a knack for picking the right people for the right job and referred to himself as 'an agitator of men'. Bernie was mesmerised.

Even so, he played it cool at that first meeting in Maranello. Marco Piccinini, who speaks three languages, was not at the meeting so it was necessary for Bernie to speak through Franco Gozzi who, among other duties, acted as Ferrari's interpreter and translator. 'Why did you employ that idiot, Piccinini?' said Bernie through Gozzi. 'Because he's cheap,' came the answer. They were off to a good start. They settled their differences – those that had arisen in Argentina – and thereafter Bernie went to visit Ferrari in Maranello or Modena, where Enzo also kept offices, 'about three or four times a year, for lunch'.

Within days of that first meeting, Piccinini was summoned to Ferrari's office where the young team manager was fixed with a glowering stare – if such could be perceived through dark glasses. 'Mr Ecclestone has been to see me and you've been upsetting him a lot' (according to Marco's translation). Marco immediately began sputtering apologies, but Ferrari cut him off. 'That's what I've employed you for.'

About once or twice each year the constructors would hold a meeting at Maranello, travelling down by private plane – hired by Bernie. 'And one year we had a very nice FOCA meeting and afterwards, the old man gave us a splendid lunch,' Teddy Mayer recalls. 'At the end of the lunch a huge wheel of Parmesan cheese – I mean it must have weighed thirty pounds – was served by a guy passing it around. Bernie, who doesn't eat very much, he's not terribly interested in food, said: "No thank you." And Enzo said, "Oh no, Bernie, you must have some of that, it's good for the libido." Bernie duly took a piece of the cheese and ate it.'

Frank Williams adds: 'Bernie always took his troops, including me, down to Maranello in the Seventies and Eighties, ten of us ganging up on Enzo – he didn't give in – and I think Bernie respected that.' Marco Piccinini always attended the F1CA/FOCA meetings, wherever they were held, and he and Bernie soon became very good friends. Enzo Ferrari came to treat Marco like another son, for Marco was quick to learn – after a few harsh lessons – the skills of a consummate negotiator and politician. Marco now laughs at Bernie's initial 'suggestion that Mr Ferrari get rid of me. Ferrari thought, "Ah, if he wants me to get rid of Piccinini then he must be doing just exactly what I told him to do." I was then locked in with Ferrari as long as he was alive.'

The 1978 season continued to be a crowded, head-butting one – as usual – for Bernie. What was pivotal was his formal appointment as president of administration and chief executive of the Formula One Constructors' Association, which now became FOCA; Enzo Ferrari had mentioned to Bernie that F1CA resembled a rude Italian expression. 'You had better change the name,' said Ferrari through Gozzi, and so it was done. Bernie's appointment as president had taken him six years to achieve, and with it he became a member of the establishment, albeit an establishment that he himself created and he now had status. Whereas, in the past, he had been a user or borrower of authority, his authority was now *bona fide* and in his possession. To Bernie, this made a difference, a big difference. It was confirmation of his success in restructuring the financial base of Formula 1. It was a vote of confidence – Bernie was now the accepted master. Also, the door to a future of fantastic – and lucrative – possibilities had just opened considerably wider.

The new 'Establishment Bernie' emerged in the aftermath of the Swedish Grand Prix of 1978, in response to the 'fan car' controversy. In compensating for the Alfa Romeo engines, Gordon Murray had managed to produce a car that would win races, that achieved improved downforce and faster cornering speeds and, consequently, beat Colin Chapman's Lotus 79, along with the rest of the teams. That was the problem. 'Was the fan intended to cool the engine or to create aerodynamic advantage by creating a suction drawing the rear end of the car to the track?' Colin Chapman, Teddy Mayer, John Surtees and Ken Tyrrell wanted to know. Mario Andretti said Gordon's fan-assisted car must 'be stopped for safety reasons,' because it was picking up stones and other debris, and throwing them on to other cars. That's 'a lie' responded Brabham driver, John Watson, while the constructors ruminated over the very real challenge now posed by Brabham, annoyed that they hadn't thought of it first.

The objections to the BT46B turned into a storm of angry accusations, and threatened Bernie's newly won security as president of FOCA. Although everything in his nature rebelled, Bernie gave in, and the fan car was sacrificed in order to maintain the all-important FOCA unity. The Swedish result was allowed to stand, but the car was withdrawn thereafter. Gordon was devastated, as was the rest of the Brabham team. 'Bernie was always supportive of anything that was new and anything that gave us an advantage,' says Herbie Blash. But 'when we had the fan car, that's when Bernie had to think about the future of the sport as well as Brabham. We were desperately upset, but that was Bernie, Bernie was looking at the overall picture and knew that if it continued Formula 1 would have been a different place completely.' All the same Brabham probably would have won the championship two years earlier if they had kept the 'loads of old rubbish,' which had reputedly cost Bernie £500,000; the price of joining the establishment.

The changes that Bernie brought to Formula 1 were manifold. Apart from the financial restructuring, medical support and safety, he was responsible – through various means – for the continual upgrading of all the paddock facilities, introducing passes and more rigorous circuit security; regularising scrutineering; introducing the warm-up lap to be sure everything worked; the starting light procedure; fixed numbers on cars; and for bringing to grand prix racing, and its personnel, a crisp, professional, larger-than-the-role appearance, equipped to impress, and to take on the world. Formula 1, in all aspects, simply became more efficient. When he could delegate responsibility he did so, handing over a portion of the detail work to trusted, hand-picked, employees. Herbie Blash recalls 'dealing with passes, sorting out testing and we had to do hotel arrangements. Bernie was always wearing two hats, but I wouldn't say he walked away from Brabham to look after Formula 1 because he had a team around him who looked after Brabham right from the start.'

Gordon Murray's attitude is slightly different: 'By the time of the de Angelis period [1986] he was circuit signage, FIA, FOCA and his sights were somewhere else.' Both agree that Bernie made the sport 'what it is today'. His greatest strides in improving Formula 1 were achieved by developing close relationships with 'people like Ferrari and other teams,' continues Herbie. 'Because he had such a close relationship he could manipulate, no, direct teams in various ways; Bernie started doing all the orchestrating... he would be a chess player putting all the pieces into place.' To motor racing journalist and author Nigel Roebuck, Bernie said: 'People may not believe it, but I'm still a racer, and if I had the time I would still have a race team. But it's impossible to do both jobs properly, which was why I started to neglect Brabham. You're competing against people who think of nothing else for twenty-four hours a day, seven days a week; you can't pop in on a part-time basis against that.' Bernie was consumed with the greater picture, involving the necessary drudgery of persuasion and negotiation – this was the performance that mattered above all others – to achieve the sport's potential, as he saw it.

Frank Gardner, who knew Bernie since the Cooper 500 days, summed up Bernie's metamorphosis: 'I don't think Bernie was ever looking at becoming a manufacturer, even running a race team, even Formula 1. My perceivement [sic] was that he was there to gain experience, to understand the actual infrastructure, in detail, of what teams had to do to achieve some sort of professionalism...You had to be a hero, in the first place, to think you could get all that rabble together in that era, so I suppose that was Bernie's forte – he could see the end product. There has not been a Bernie appear ever before. There's been some shysters, some conmen and the sport is basically riddled with pretenders, but the real people who stood up and were counted, I can only think of one and his initials are B.E. For the first time there was some structure to achieve something, and because the group had a unified position, there was access to some of the best technical people in the world... it attracted more sponsors... and television – x number of minutes on television of identifiable signage.

'Bernie was the one to think up the whole concept. So it doesn't matter how you join it up, if [the words] "Formula 1" hadn't been used, you could have called it "Formula

Bernie"... In my fifty years of observation I have not seen anyone come close to the Ecclestone way of thinking. You look at various facets of it and no matter what facet you look at, somewhere along the line there's a Bernie link to it and he's holding all the dog chains and the hounds go so far and then they pull back – that's by design – because he's thought about it. While everybody else has been wandering around, wondering how they can promote themselves, Bernie's promoted the sport.'

Of course, there continued to be strong resistance to Bernie's methods of promoting the sport. Many believed that his shaping of FOCA into a powerful, cohesive organisation was preliminary to the all-out hijacking of Formula 1. Many believed that Bernie's authority was far too broad – which actually formed the specific line of engagement in the final phase of the war, and the breakneck battle was about to be waged.

CHAPTER 11

WAR AND A CONSTITUTION

During most of the Seventies the likes of Henri Treu and Pierre Ugueux had been really no match for Bernie who, while fighting for the betterment of the sport, was at the same time fighting for his own future; the stakes were quite different. Treu and Ugueux had demanding occupations outside the blazer and cravat club of motorsport's governing body, the duties of which they fitted in to their day-to-day lives, for little reward. To Bernie, matters concerning Formula 1 were everything. So it is not surprising that objections against his ascendancy were crushed. There was one man, however, the acerbic, pencil-breaking Frenchman Jean-Marie Balestre, who was determined to thwart Bernie's dominance, and he almost succeeded.

In October 1978, fifty-seven-year-old Balestre was elected president of the CSI in place of Pierre Ugueux, who had decided to step down, perhaps persuaded by Bernie who felt that Balestre might be better suited to carrying forward the further restructuring he anticipated in Formula 1. 'Ugueux is a good guy,' said Bernie, after they had mended their quarrels and became friends. As for Balestre, friendship with Bernie Ecclestone was not on his agenda. Upon becoming president he had the name of the Commission Sportive Internationale changed to the Fédération Internationale du Sport Automobile (FISA). He had already made the CSI independent from the FIA; now this new attitude was reinforced with a new name.

Balestre had a distinctive – and easily lampooned – style with his black leather, Gestapo-type trench coats, his tinted glasses, tall and solid in physique as well as in gesture. He was fond of melodrama punctuated with arms slicing the air and pounding fists and nothing would slip by without his notice. 'Where is my Tuesday?' he demanded of his minions on examining his travel documents for Australia, unaware that due to crossing the date line a day would be lost, only to be regained on the return journey to France. The misplaced Tuesday had to be recovered double-quick, requiring nervous, painstaking explanations. Another flight was summarily cancelled when it was discovered that the commercial airline he had intended to board was not equipped with his favourite brand of mineral water. And the noise of a tennis ball was too distressing to contemplate, for the manager of the Brazilian luxury hotel at which he had planned to stay was required to measure the distance from the hotel's tennis courts to the proposed room before any reservations could be entirely firm. If the distance were judged to be insufficient, his room, his travel plans, would be disengaged.

If, there was something of 'der Führer' about Balestre, it was enhanced by allegations that he had served in the SS – with photographic evidence to prove it. Photographs showing Balestre in Nazi uniform were published in a book. Balestre sued in French courts and was awarded one franc in damages. He would have it that he worked for the French Resistance and was arrested in 1944 by the Germans, spending from August of that year through to May 1945 in a concentration camp before being released and sent back to France. This was sometimes a ploy undertaken by collaborators who had themselves arrested in the final stages of the war, later to be released by the Americans and thereby considered innocent; Jean-Marie likened himself to James Bond. Sport, particularly motorsport, had been a life-long interest. He founded the magazine L'Auto Journal and established a publishing company before becoming a founder member of the French national motorsport authority, the FFSA, in 1952. He was created president of karting in France in 1959 and held administrative positions in another dozen sporting-motoring-publishing organisations. He is also the recipient of France's Légion d'Honneur and Monaco's Ordre de Saint-Charles. Such a man would not hold much truck with Bernie Ecclestone. Jean-Marie Balestre would be the voice – singing solo – of Formula 1 forever more if he had his way.

In his dealings with Treu and Ugueux, Bernie had called upon advice from two lawyers, both FOCA members – Englishman Max Mosley of the March team and American Teddy Mayer of McLaren. Teddy actually had a degree in law but had never practised it. Max teased him saying: 'You're like someone who's read all these dirty books but has never actually done it.' Even so, Teddy's advice was listened to. 'Bernie was the leader and Max and I were sort of his henchmen in that it sometimes needed three of us to effect something, and Max would do the legal work. Then it would get passed to me to sort of eyeball... Bernie wanted two legal opinions,' says Mayer. But upon becoming president in 1978 Bernie appointed Max Mosley – only Max – as FOCA's official legal adviser. Teddy continued to make a contribution until he left McLaren and thus FOCA in 1983, but it was Max who really worked in concert with Bernie, forming the most unlikely – and yet the most commanding – duet in motor racing.

By 1977 thirty-seven-year-old Max Mosley, tall and slender with graceful patrician features, had sold his interests in the March team to his partner Robin Herd, and was ready to pursue new challenges, preferably those linked to motorsport. He was an ideal choice for the job, which of course Bernie knew, so they clasped hands and leapt towards a power-climbing future together. That they ever met and, what is more, fused, is utterly astounding. Max is the product of aristocratic stock, and his parents were both glittering and notorious. His mother, Diana, was the daughter of a peer, and one of society's adventurous 'Mitford girls'. She admired intellect and possessed a natural talent for writing, becoming a successful author, editor and reviewer. But Diana Mosley is, perhaps, better remembered for her beauty and, moreover, for her attachment to Adolf Hitler. She and Max's father, Sir Oswald Mosley, were married at the home of Joseph and Magda Goebbels and Hitler attended their wedding.

Max's father, Oswald Mosley, a politician and founder of the British Union of Fascists, was devilishly handsome – of the silver screen variety – and a philanderer until after his marriage to Diana, who became a willing helpmate in his fascist cause. A firebrand orator dressed in black, fashioned after his fencing clothing, or in a facsimile SS tunic, jodhpurs and jack-boots, Mosley was unsettling, and while many of his economic policies would – years later – receive praise, these were all but obliterated by his Nazi-saluting, black-shirted followers who instigated riots in London's East End. Oswald and Diana Mosley, in the supposed interests of national security, were incarcerated in Holloway prison in London, in June 1940. Diana left behind her young sons, Alexander and ten-week-old Max, whom she had been breastfeeding and on her way to prison she was permitted to stop at a chemist's shop to purchase a breast pump.

During the next three-and-a-half years, Max and his brother saw their parents for only a few, brief visits. After the Mosleys were released from prison, the family eventually settled in Ireland, although spring and summer were spent in France where the Duke and Duchess of Windsor (the former Edward VIII and Wallis Simpson) became an important part of their circle – a social circle that included Randolph Churchill, Cecil Beaton, John Betjeman and Evelyn Waugh. August was spent in Venice where they stayed at the Europa or the Cipriani – de rigueur for the rich and famous. In Ireland Max developed a passion for riding. Perhaps it was the freedom of being carried – at speed – by a power other than his own that led him to motor racing and, in time, to Bernie Ecclestone; motor racing had been 'a hobby' when he was a little boy.

Max's education, before university, was problematic. After the war most schools in Britain would have nothing to do with the sons of Oswald and Diana Mosley. On the Continent, the same mood generally prevailed and, although the boys were admitted to boarding schools in France and Germany, their troublesome behavior – a propensity for fighting among other things – often saw them packed off back home. Much of their early education, therefore, was undertaken at home, and a good education it proved to be. Multilingual Max won a place at Christchurch College, Oxford, where he concentrated on physics and also debate, becoming Secretary of the Oxford Union. While at Oxford he campaigned for his father who in 1959 stood as a parliamentary candidate for Notting Hill. Oswald Mosley's campaign centred upon opposition to unrestricted black immigration, and he favoured a unified Europe, as did Max. Oswald was defeated in 1959 and again in 1966, after which he retired from politics. Max's interest in politics has continued to this day.

After Oxford, he read law at Gray's Inn in London because: 'I realised fairly early on that I wasn't going to be the next Einstein and win a Nobel Prize... if I couldn't be really good, I didn't want to do it... also the pay was pitiful.' He was called to the Bar in 1964, eventually specialising in patents and trademarks. His biggest case was a dispute over the rights to 'the Bayer cross' logo, which he won on behalf of his German clients. But Max's work life soon became too routine, presenting a wearying sameness: 'I used to walk across one of the squares in the Inns of Court, and I'd see some old boy coming the other way, probably about sixty and I would think, "that's me in thirty-five years' time, I don't want to do that".' Instead, he turned his attention to motor racing, becoming involved in club racing where after two seasons he had won several races and set lap records before buying a Formula 2 car 'with a bit of help from a sponsor'; Frank Williams 'looked after' the car. But after only a season and a half he needed still more motor racing challenges, and in Frank Williams's workshop he met engineer Robin Herd who was modifying a vehicle of his own. Max and Robin had known each other at Oxford where Robin came away with the second highest mark ever scored in the engineering final; small wonder Bernie and Jochen Rindt had attempted to lure him into a Formula 1 partnership. But by then Robin was committed to Max.

Soon after becoming reacquainted they started talking over 'the idea that maybe we needed a racing car company,' says Max. So, as 1969 approached, Max and Robin together with two other partners, Graham Coaker and Alan Rees, set up March; although 'Robin would probably have been better off if he'd gone with Bernie,' Max now concedes. For all its early promise, within a few years the March team, like so many others, ran out of money. But Max still held motorsport ambitions, ambitions that would soon embrace all of his talents. Like Bernie, Max's early career had been a process of defining, then refining, his future.

In 1971, when Bernie began attending F1CA meetings, their nodding acquaintance developed into a firm friendship – based on mutual respect. 'It was obvious to me that he [Bernie] was somebody who understood business and I didn't have a lot of time for the other members of the association,' says Max. 'When I first joined in 1969 there was a lot of resentment against March because nobody believed that you could just come along, find a factory unit in September and turn up the following March in South Africa with a working racing car, and we not only did that but we were at the front of the grid.' But the FOCA members weren't so blinded by jealously that they could not appreciate the value of an 'in house' legal opinion. So, stifling their resentment, the constructors encouraged him to continue to attend the F1CA meetings, and Max soon discovered that much was awry in Formula 1.

'I remember sitting in the first meeting... in Brussels or Paris, and I just couldn't believe that a world sport was run like that,' says Max. 'I mean I was only twenty-nine, but I just sat there amazed. I thought "this isn't possible, that people would do something as big as this as badly as this". Then a couple of years later Bernie appeared on the scene and he was obviously in a completely different league, and it very rapidly ended up with the two of us doing all the negotiating' – Bernie doing all the dealing, Max advising. Max was impressed by Bernie: 'He was cleverer than the others and obviously very good at business, and... he sees things differently.' And Max would continue to be impressed: 'In ordinary everyday life he will create a problem just to entertain himself. I remember his lawyer once saying to me that Bernie is brilliant at getting himself out of trouble which he got himself into in the first place... it is that combination of an unconventional approach and very quick thinking that gives him the ability to turn situations to his advantage... that's why he's a formidable negotiator.'

Even then, Bernie was a perpetual – if not habitual – deal-maker, which included imaginary transactions. 'I remember sitting by a swimming pool in Rio with him,' says Max, 'and he'd say things like "What would you give for that hotel?" And left to himself with nothing in particular to do, he'd sit there working out how many rooms there were, what the occupancy rate was, what they were charging and what the overhead was, and therefore what the hotel was worth. He just thinks things like that, that's what interests him and, as a result, when it comes to dealing, he can get closer to 100 per cent than anybody I know.' He's brilliant at the old poker thing of knowing when to hold and knowing when to fold, he knows exactly the feel and if it's necessary, he will fold and walk away. He will never be stubborn about a deal, he would do what was in the interests of the business and wouldn't care if, as a result of that, he appeared to have backed off or backed down.'

After Max had disposed of his interest in March he was urged by the FOCA members to stay on because he had 'always acted for them as their Deputy Representative on the FIA and so forth'; the title of legal adviser was invented by the members – and endorsed by Bernie – to maintain Max's involvement. 'Although it wasn't really legal advice at all, I was just going on doing what I've always done with Bernie,' says Max. 'By the end of the Seventies FOCA, well me, Bernie and I suppose Teddy were practically running Formula 1, making all the rules and deciding what was happening and everything. Then Balestre came along with the mission of getting control back... and this rapidly led to conflict which became worse and worse. But it was really about who ran Formula 1.' With Max's intelligence, his knowledge of physics, law, languages and European culture and every aspect of motor racing, together with Bernie's experience and abilities they would provide stout resistance against anything Jean-Marie Balestre would hurl at them; and they were eager for the fray.

Balestre would primarily engage them upon technical points. To rail against Bernie's dealings with organisers and promoters had proved fruitless; Balestre would venture into that territory only when it became absolutely necessary, such as in making a full declaration of war. For now, challenging Bernie/Max on technical issues had a better chance of success because Formula 1's governing body, more specifically Balestre, had the support of the 'grandees'. Among these principally were the big manufacturers such as Ferrari, Renault and Alfa Romeo – Ferrari had always held the most influential position, supporting or even suggesting technical rules or formulae that favoured their own innovations, which in turn would destabilise the lesser-financed, mostly British, teams. But then Ferrari also 'acted like the fulcrum of a balance,' says Max, 'moving a little bit this way, a little bit that way to help [one team then another]. Therefore they exercised power out of proportion to their size as a single team.'

Enzo Ferrari, like Bernie, realised the importance to the sport of maintaining a full, competitive grid which, however, did not prevent him from finding fault with teams using the Ford Cosworth engines when they were beating the then unreliable turbos – including Ferrari. But Lotus with the Ford Cosworth engine won the World Championship in 1978, after the competitive Brabham BT46 'fan car' had been banned. Lotus achieved its success that year through the reliability of their normally aspirated engines and, more importantly, through the use of ground effect created by a device making the bottom of the car resemble an inverted aircraft wing, producing a vacuum that was controlled by 'skirts' – sliding plates attached to the sides of the car. So Ferrari, together with Renault, soon commenced lobbying FISA/Balestre to remove ground effect – which Bernie and the other British constructors soon had as well The dispute raged over the next two years, with FISA arguing that the cornering ability of ground-effect cars was too great and that the cars' speeds going into the corners created safety problems, which would need to be accommodated by creating suitable run-off areas. Indeed the safety of circuits was a justifiable issue and was of increasing concern to drivers. On the other hand circuits needed to keep pace with technical developments.

Meanwhile, against this background Balestre mounted a ceaseless barrage of squabbles aimed at undermining Bernie, who relished these encounters while contending: 'there was never any personal animosity between us... I had a good relationship with him even when we were in conflict.' More determined conflict came in 1979, when Balestre took it upon himself to fine John Watson, then driving for McLaren, £3,000 for his part in a collision with Ferrari driver Jody Scheckter during the Argentine Grand Prix. Watson would not be allowed to compete in further races until the fine had been paid. FOCA expressed their outrage and an inquiry followed which gave Balestre the opportunity to attack Bernie – via the press – for allegedly prohibiting the drivers from giving evidence at the inquiry; Bernie denied this. Thereafter Balestre attempted to denigrate Bernie's character by accusing him of selling passes to the pit lanes while discouraging the issuing of International Racing Press Association (IRPA) passes for which there was no charge, and further, that he had levied a £600 tax on foreign radio stations. Bernie ignored these charges, being more concerned with Balestre's unilateral decision to fine John Watson.

In Brazil, the second Grand Prix of the season, Bernie and Max called a meeting with Balestre, held in the basement of an office at the Interlagos circuit. During the meeting Bernie and Max attempted to define the bounds of responsibility, pointing out that Watson would be racing in Brazil without paying the fine imposed by Balestre, and that the race organisers – Bernie through his financial contribution being one of them – supported the decision. End of story, unless Balestre – who had demonstrated his fondness for the press – would care to make the decision public and risk humiliation. He chose, instead, to write a statement: 'The fine inflicted on

Watson was paid by the FOCA within the delay prescribed by the sporting code.'

To be certain that Balestre understood his FISA perimeters, Bernie announced during a FOCA meeting in Maranello that the governance of the World Championship was not the provenance of FISA; car specifications, safety, race regulations and driver discipline would be overseen by a committee appointed by FOCA. Moreover, Enzo Ferrari supported him. Balestre, of course, was swift to make a counter-declaration adding that financial negotiations with promoters and organisers were henceforth under FISA control. And then he trod upon the sensitive area of television rights, suggesting that these were also within FISA's domain; he was stoking the blaze. Thereafter, he set about interfering with Bernie's arrangements with race organisers.

When an attempt was made to reinstate the Swedish Grand Prix, with money actually being found to support it – $25,000 advanced to FOCA – Bernie happily announced that the race was back on the calendar; Balestre decreed that it was not. The circuits at Long Beach and Watkins Glen were suddenly instructed to make costly improvements on the grounds of safety because, it was thought, the organisers of these circuits were on friendly terms with Bernie. On it went with increasing venom. John Hogan, head of Marlboro racing, vividly remembers the conflicts: 'The fights [Bernie] used to have with Balestre were legend, I mean there was Balestre, this awful bully, cunning as a fox and devious to boot. He didn't speak any English, and there was Bernie who didn't speak any French, and they used to have these monumental rows, it was ships passing in the night. I mean if you spoke French and you listened to what was going on, Christ... And there was Max, always sitting there like his eminence, "Well, Bernard, shall I f--- him now or wait?"'

At Zolder in May 1980 the hostilities culminated in open warfare. The declaration of war had been delivered the previous February when Balestre – assured of support from Ferrari, Renault and Alfa Romeo – proclaimed that an all-out ban on 'skirts' would come into effect on 1 January 1981.

The threat had now become reality. He had stripped the 'garagistes' of their best weapon against the turbo onslaught. What has become known as the FISA-FOCA war had begun in earnest, with the first shot being fired during the weekend of the Belgian Grand Prix at Zolder.

Balestre had decided to make mandatory the drivers' attendance at pre-race briefings. A driver's absence from these meetings would result in a $2,000 fine in the first instance, $5,000 in the second. The constructors were pretty relaxed about the briefings, and official rules had not been established to make attendance a requirement. Bernie, always ready to rebuke a command from Balestre while at the same time casting about for a strategy against the 'skirts' ban, instructed his drivers – as did other constructors – not to attend the briefing at Zolder. Thus, at the pre-race meeting only drivers from Ferrari, Renault and Alfa Romeo turned up. This scenario was repeated in Monaco, and so far no fines had been paid. By the following race, the Spanish Grand Prix at Jarama, the offending drivers had still not paid their fines, so Balestre ordered them not to compete, and their licences were revoked. The teams responded by offering to pay the fines for them. 'No,' said Balestre, 'each driver will have to pay his fine'. Bernie dug in his heels, the drivers would not be paying anything, and unless the licences were reinstated the constructors would not take part in the Spanish Grand Prix.

Now, King Juan Carlos stepped in. His country would not be used as a stage for their bickering and he wanted to protect the future of his country's premier event. He ordered the Spanish automobile club to pay the outstanding fines and to go ahead with the race, with a full grid, no matter Jean-Marie Balestre's views. 'Non,' said Balestre. Now, the race organisers came up with a complex solution, inspired by Max and Bernie, to circumvent FISA's president. It was decided to run the race under the rules of the FIA (then still the superior authority to FISA), making Balestre's position immaterial. The legal footwork required the Spanish organisers, the Real Automovil Club de España, to swap, back and forth, their sporting powers to the Federación Española de Automovilismo, but it was enough for them to declare confidently that the Grand Prix would commence as planned.

Balestre became apoplectic, announcing in return that a race in which drivers were not licenced to compete could not be considered an official World Championship event. More to-ing and fro-ing ensued before Max announced that FOCA 'fully support the position of the Real Automovil Club de España and will participate in the race,' and 'the Spanish Grand Prix will count for the official 1980 Formula 1 World Championship'. Police then escorted the FISA officials off the circuit grounds. The fracas had caused delays in practice, after which Ferrari and Renault withdrew. They 'could not compete in an illegal race and lose their entrants' licences'. So the constructors raced amongst themselves. Alan Jones was the winner, and it turned out to be – from the spectators' point of view – one of the best races of the season. But as Balestre had already declared, it did not count in the championship series. After more confrontations the constructors were allowed, or rather ordered, to pay the drivers' fines. The biggest casualty was Formula 1 and the acrimony of Belgium and Spain threatened to taint the entire season, if not destroy it. The level of the carryings-on had become childish and distasteful, and should have been fought in the boardroom, not at the circuit. The sponsors, as well as the spectators, began to have serious qualms about the sport's future.

Balestre then tried a divide-and-conquer tactic, making an attempt to depose Bernie and place Colin Chapman on the FOCA throne. Journalist and FISA technical adviser Gérard 'Jabby' Crombac was invited to be present at a 'private discussion' which Balestre held with Colin in a caravan at Le Mans. According to Jabby, Balestre was blunt: '"You [Colin] get rid of Bernie and become FOCA president and we'll make a deal together. Instead of getting rid of the skirts, you'll keep the skirts, we'll have different tyres [also contentious], but you have to get rid of Bernie." The deal was that Colin would go the next day to visit Ferrari and together they would mount a coup to get rid of Bernie. Colin said, "yes, yes, yes". But then something happened, and Colin changed his mind.' The attempted coup never took place. Instead Colin, along with Bernie and the other 'garagistes', threatened to boycott the French Grand Prix, the land where Balestre was king. Balestre, anxious to avoid at all costs a public quarrel on his home ground, offered to push back the deadline for the imposition of the ban, permitting the constructors a reasonable period of time to make the necessary technological changes – if all the teams, including those of the manufacturers, would agree. The vote was to be taken after the French Grand Prix – which was allowed to run, incident-free.

In the meeting that followed Bernie put forward an agreed set of proposals including a five-year delay on the 'skirts' ban, but allowing 'reduced cornering speeds through less efficient tyres'. Balestre appeared to approve of what he heard, and a resolution to their struggles seemed at hand. It was thought that grooved tyres would reduce grip and therefore have a similar effect to removing the 'skirts'. It was decided to discuss the matter at Brands Hatch in July, in a meeting with the Michelin and Goodyear representatives. Jabby Crombac chaired that meeting, and when he proposed grooved tyres the representatives 'just laughed'. The tyres could be grooved with an application of soft rubber, but after a few laps 'it would be back to slicks', it was too dangerous. Balestre and Bernie were back to deadlock.

By the autumn of 1980 the constructors felt they had no choice but to threaten, as they had done in the past, a breakaway series. But this time they drew up a calendar and Colin Chapman wrote the rules and regulations; they were meant to be taken seriously. The Constructors' World Championship, organised under the auspices of a new governing body, the World Federation of Motor Sport, WFMS, was to be run by Bernie Ecclestone; he already had contracts in place with the circuits. However, even as Bernie announced the WFMS series he knew that reconciliation was vital. 'In more than a dozen meetings,' he had tried to make Balestre see reason, at least his version of it, supported by legal precedence from Max, and indeed statutes existed which allowed for a minimum two-year transition period before major technological changes could come into force. Bernie would agree to the two years, but again Balestre was steadfast, there could be no agreement as long as Bernie remained powerful, although he cited safety grounds as his reason for avoiding compromise.

Without a resolution the reproaches – public and private – continued; sponsors began to drift away. British constructors were on the verge of bankruptcy, and as they relied upon a network of subcontractors, the whole motor racing industry was coming under threat. The future of Formula 1 – Bernie's future – was looking tentative. This was the moment Balestre had been waiting for, the economic conditions that would see Bernie ousted and bring the dissident constructors crawling back home to an official governing body of motorsport – FISA.

Now the 'below-the-table' wild card, the 'fulcrum' that was Enzo Ferrari, was ready to sway. In mid-January, at a meeting in Monza, Enzo gave Bernie the future that he desperately needed. Marco Piccinini explains how this came about. 'Alessandro Buzzi, CEO of Philip Morris, Europe, invited Teddy Mayer and me to one or two confidential meetings – always perfectly coordinated and inspired by Mr Ferrari – to prepare a framework to be discussed by Jean-Marie Balestre and Bernie. Then we had a meeting at the Ferrari offices in Modena, between the two sides of the teams but without FISA, and the result of this meeting – which was called the Modena Agreement – was then submitted to the FISA.' The Modena Agreement, signed by both factions – garagistes and grandees – was a peace treaty. Formula 1 – and Bernie's role in it – was once more safe. The document, which was delivered to FISA at the end of January, set out a compromise solution by which FISA could work with Formula 1. It not only covered the technical conflict but also the workings of the Formula 1 business as a whole in the hope of preventing future hostilities.

The constructors agreed to the banning of 'skirts' for which a minimum period of two years notice would be given to cover technical changes, and on all major changes the time allowed would be four years. FISA received the governance of the technical rules. But it would be another two months before Balestre would release the agreement, having signed it. 'It will be good for us to pretend we're in conflict for another few months,' he said to Bernie. In the interim Balestre still clung to the hope that, with the support of Renault, he would yet see the back of his adversary – former or otherwise – Bernie Ecclestone.

Bernie was well aware that the constructors must race or perish, so he announced that during the first three races of the 1981 season – USA West at Long Beach, Brazil and Argentina – the constructors' cars would be entered with 'skirts' attached, defying Balestre's 1 January deadline for the enforcement of the ban. Bernie's contracts with the organisers and promoters made it plain that the races would be run with the technological specifications that existed when the contracts were signed – before 1981, thus his position was legal. Now Balestre was on dangerous ground. His disagreement could possibly result in more than the ruin of Bernie, it might bring about the final destruction of Formula 1 as a whole. Bernie now turned up the heat by holding a pre-season race, on 7 February, at Kyalami.

This is the race that Max calls 'a big bluff'. The idea for the race was conceived earlier that winter when Max, Colin Chapman and Teddy Mayer were dining in a restaurant in Kitzbühel, where they had been skiing. On the wall they noticed an unusual picture, depicting a cow being painted by a group of people. They asked the waitress about the picture and were told that it illustrated the story of an ancient siege that had left the villagers with only one cow. So as to convey the impression they had plenty of food and, hence, plenty of fight, the villagers painted the cow – in different attitudes – every day, making sure it was well within view of their enemies. 'That's it,' shouted Chapman. 'That's what we need to do – we need to organise a race!' They then telephoned Bernie – in the middle of the night – and, after they had convinced him they weren't drunk, he agreed to the 'cow plan'. The next step was to hold a press conference at the Hôtel de Crillon – only footsteps away from the FISA headquarters – where they announced that there would be a race in South Africa. As it turned out, the major constructors did not attend the race and without crowd-pulling Ferrari it was a skimpy affair, and failed. But the point was that it had received good television coverage and had been watched by the teams loyal to Balestre, stirring more than a pang of unease. 'You see,' says Max, 'it destabilised the manufacturers, who realised that we could put on a race but Balestre couldn't.'

The first official race of the 1981 season, Long Beach, was scheduled for the late date of 15 March due to all the dramas. Balestre favoured cancelling the race in the belief that it would bring about the collapse of the dissident constructors. He was confident of support from Renault and, the Modena Agreement aside, hoped the other manufacturers would follow. With this view in mind he met in New York with members of the Sports Car Club of America who sanctioned the Grand Prix at Long Beach. Balestre asked them not to authorise the race, adding that should it go ahead the manufacturers' teams would not participate. It was a fatal error. Renault owned American Motors and wished to avoid criticism from wealthy, car-buying Californians. Renault made it clear that 'with or without Balestre they would be going to Long Beach,' said Jabby. 'That's when Balestre knew he'd lost.'

He made, however, a last request, that the Modena Agreement be known as the 'Concorde Agreement,' the most likely reason being that the FIA shared offices with the Automobile Club de France located in Paris's Place de la Concorde. Next door to the French automobile club is the building in which Benjamin Franklin signed the peace agreement that ended the War of Independence; Concord also resonates as the name of a town in Massachusetts and a few miles away – the shot fired that was 'heard round the world'. Furthermore, the Place de la Concorde is the grisly, blood-soaked site where so many heads had been severed during the French Revolution before anything like a concorde could be achieved. Perhaps Balestre was disposed to ponder such historic points; perhaps he was more concerned with confiscating Ferrari's glory. In any case Jean-Marie Balestre signed the Concorde Agreement on 11 March 1981. Through either his recalcitrance or in the better interest of the sport – probably both – Balestre had in fact achieved the secure right to govern Formula 1's rules and regulations. No small achievement against the fortitude of a Bernie Ecclestone and a Max Mosley.

Beneath Max's somewhat strained countenance – suggesting a complex tangle of emotions – there is a well of laughter that readily bursts forth. He loves jokes and jokesters, his mimicry of foreign accents is, like Bernie's, hilariously better than the original. 'You know he and Bernie [were] such naughty boys,' said Max's mother, Lady Mosley, remembering their shenanigans when France's government – opposed to apartheid – had tried to discourage French teams and the FIA from participating in the South African Grand Prix; Balestre had insisted that the race would be run with a full grid. For Max and Bernie the situation positively shimmered with mischief-making potential. They decided to ring up Balestre and torture him. Bernie, playing the part of an international operator, informed Balestre that there was a person-to-person call on the line from Nelson Mandela (then incarcerated in Pollsmoor prison where he had been transferred from Robben Island). Now Max took over and, assuming the voice of the South African, said: 'I hear you are coming to my country, president. I would like to invite you to my home [the prison].' Balestre was nonplussed, and started spluttering a response: he was most honoured and so forth, but owing to... ughhhh... the demands of his pre-arranged schedule... ughhhh... Whereupon Bernie cut in saying, 'It's all right Jean-Marie, it's only Bernie and Max.' 'This is not a joke!' Balestre shouted, slamming down the receiver.

Practical jokes had soon become a fixture of the Bernie-Max double act. At one point they discovered a way to create counterfeit Telex messages (in the old-fashioned pre-fax machine days) so that Telexes appeared to have come from the FIA. They sent one of these to Teddy Mayer informing him that he had been banned – for life – from all the circuits.

Teddy immediately rang Bernie and in 'a complete panic' read out the Telex. 'That's OK,' soothed Bernie, 'I'll just make it into a transfer for psychiatric treatment.' The arrival of the fax machine presented even more fun-filled opportunities. In a hotel near one of the grand prix circuits, Bernie had a fax machine installed in his room. Balestre, who was staying in the same hotel, also had a fax machine in his room. So Bernie and Max then whiled away the hours sending Balestre a steady stream of nonsense faxes, also resulting in a certain amount of mental disturbance.

Humour had provided a cushion of comfort amid the frustrations of battle and, in that sense, further bolstered their determination; ten years after Balestre had signed the Concorde Agreement, Max Mosley would have his job. In 1986, Bernie and Max 'hatched a plot' to make Max chairman of the FIA Manufacturers' Commission – on which all the big manufacturers have a seat. In this position Max automatically received a seat on the World Motor Sport Council, an important political power base. To achieve this, Bernie and Max had needed Balestre's agreement. So they met with him at his home in the South of France and, over dinner, explained 'that it would really be good for the FISA, for me, to have the job,' says Max. 'Balestre sat there, and you could see he sort of knew this wasn't the right thing to do. And yet, he knew the person that would then be incumbent wasn't ideal. Anyway, against the will of the manufacturers, Balestre agreed, so I held that job for five years.'

Toward the end of those five years, Max was getting fed up with the inefficiency of decision-making by committee and was considering quitting. But then he thought better of it, deciding instead to stand against Balestre for the election of FISA president. To win the election required Max to engage in plenty of behind-the-scenes machinations, such as promising New Zealander Ron Frost reinstatement on the FIA World Council – if he were elected. Balestre had got rid of Frost and in so doing created an enemy – and a Max Mosley campaign supporter. Rallying in New Zealand would also be put 'back in the world championship. That's how it works,' says Max, who defeated Balestre by forty-three votes to twenty-nine.

'Now to begin with it was a terrible blow [for Balestre] to lose the FISA presidency, he thought he'd be there for life,' says Max. While still president of the FISA (and the FFSA) Balestre had also become president of the FIA and was wont to brag: 'I am a triple president!' But two years after becoming FISA president Max became president of the FIA, and Balestre 'actually stood down'. This too, says Max, was 'a terrible blow for him, but he's been big enough to overcome it, so I've got a lot of time for him... I admire him. I think he's done the best he could and he was a formidable opponent for Bernie and me at the time. But I suppose in the end, we got just about everything we wanted out of it. To his [Balestre's] credit – that was the beginning of the separation of the commercial [rights] from the sporting [rights] because the Concorde Agreement spelt out how the rules could be changed and what role the teams played in that, and gave the right to exploit Formula 1 – commercially – to Bernie, on the assumption that it actually belonged to the FIA which, of course, is debatable. But that's how it worked.' Balestre became president of the Senate, the judiciary body of the FIA, from which he later retired although he still attended meetings of the World Council. Until his death in 2008 he could often be seen – still resplendently attired – at grands prix in Monaco and, of course, France.

When Max became president of the FISA in 1991, Lady Mosley was 'so pleased' that her son had 'got a proper job at last'. Gone were Max's shaggy hair-do, bell-bottom jeans, white patent-leather belt and shoes, replaced by a tailored, immaculate presidential look and – later – bearing. He reigned as the FIA's president until October 2009. But had Bernie not been at Max's elbow and vice versa, throughout the years of negotiations with organisers, throughout the disputes with the governing body and its offshoots and through the final struggles with Balestre, the future for both of them would have turned out quite differently. Their ability to focus with such clarity on the same goal was energised by friendship.

'Personal relationships are important to Bernie,' says Max. 'You notice the people that he gets on with, he never abandons, even when they cease to be useful to him... if you ask him for help of some kind (I'm not talking financial help), but of all the people I know, that you could most rely on to be there if you needed him, it's Bernie, and I think that it's important to him, and that he feels people would do the same for him is important to him. Strange person... Bernie's the softest-hearted person I know.' Not everyone shares Max's opinion, but a remarkable number of people do. The fact that Max felt he could depend upon Bernie – and Max is not the trusting sort – was the foundation of their relationship. In years to come their friendship would seemingly falter for a time, but the FISA/FOCA war and all that led up to it had created an indissoluble bond. Yes, Max was useful to Bernie, and despite the disparity in family background and upbringing, they understood each other, completely. That's what mattered, adding a kind of super-dynamism to their combined talents.

Also essential to the equation for success was Enzo Ferrari. 'I think that he thought I was a little bit like him,' says Bernie. 'He loved to argue about money, so I always used to put on $20,000 for him to knock it off, this was a game he liked to play... he enjoyed it, he was basically a very good used car dealer, when he sold his Ferraris he was a very good salesman.' Max agrees: 'Enzo had this very funny relationship with Bernie, one of those men like Helmut Kohl, Nelson Mandela... they had a sort of paternal instinct towards him... there's a real sort of affection there.' And a sense of fun too. Max relates another version of the Parmesan cheese story, told from the point of view of one who understands Italian: Enzo cut a lump of the supposed aphrodisiac cheese, and when Bernie was looking the other way, he put the cheese on his plate. 'This will get the little man going,' Enzo laughed.

Sometimes Bernie and Max would have a private meeting with Ferrari, just the three of them. Without an audience to entertain, Enzo's attitude was more serious, more conspiratorial: 'Now, we'll do something useful,' he would say, setting the mood. Max liked these get-togethers. 'We'd

ABOVE LEFT: *Bernie, aged three. It was about this time, 1932–3, when the defect in his right eye was discovered. 'I couldn't see out of one eye, that's all,' says Bernie.* (Marian Tingey)

ABOVE RIGHT: *More Christmas capers at the Youngs. The increasingly successful 25-year-old challenges all-comers with a snooker cue.* (Alan Young)

BELOW: *Bernie and his father – wearing trenchcoats – pose in front of motorcycles to be raced at Brands Hatch.* (Marian Tingey)

ABOVE: *Bernie in his 500cc Cooper at Brands Hatch, 9 September 1951; at that time the circuit was used in the opposite direction and today's daunting downhill plunge at Paddock Hill Bend was a steep ascent. The car was the product of Charles and John Cooper's Surbiton factory, with some hands-on assembly from its owner. These low-cost single-seaters heralded a new era in British motor racing.* (LAT)

BELOW: *Bernie, Cooper 500, Brands Hatch, 20 October 1951.*
(Guy Griffiths Collection)

ABOVE: *The starting grid at Thruxton, 3 August 1953. Bernie grins as he – among others – flaunts the rules and deliberately creeps his Cooper-Bristol (73) forward from the third row.* (Quentin Spurring Collection)

BELOW: *Bernie's fun-loving friend, Stuart Lewis-Evans, was considered 'a rare talent' on the circuit. After years of 500cc racing in the UK and on the continent, he was ready to try Formula 1. Seen overtaking Harry Schell's Maserati, Lewis-Evans, driving a Connaught, finished fourth in the 1957 Monaco Grand Prix.* (LAT)

ABOVE: *Connaughts entered by Bernie finished fifth (Stuart Lewis-Evans, car 14) and sixth (Archie Scott Brown, car 12) in the Glover Trophy, Goodwood, 7 April 1958.* (Ludvigsen Library)

OPPOSITE: *Brands Hatch, 25 May 1972. Bernie and his co-driver, Graham Hill, discuss tactics ahead of the Ford Capri 'celebrity' race. Bernie drove in the entrants' race, and Hill in the drivers' race. They finished in fifth place on aggregate.* (TopFoto)

BELOW: *Roy Salvadori (left) and Jochen Rindt, who had three years together at Cooper, seen at the German German Grand Prix, Nürburgring, August 1965.* (LAT)

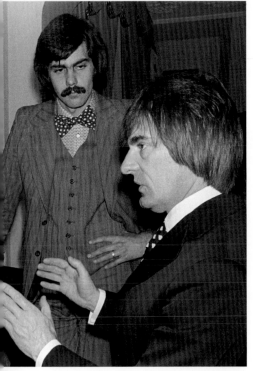

ABOVE: *Buenos Aires,
23 January 1972, Argentine
Grand Prix. Bernie talks to
Brabham driver Carlos
Reutemann.*
(sutton-images.com)

LEFT: *Gordon Murray and
Bernie at the Brabham BT44
launch in 1973.*
(sutton-images.com)

ABOVE: *Caesars Palace, 17 October 1981. Nelson Piquet wins the first of two world titles for Brabham – with a fifth-place finish.* (sutton-images.com)

BELOW: *Bernie and Gordon Murray discuss the new Brabham BT50 at the factory in 1982. The BT50 was designed around the BMW four-cylinder 1.5-litre turbocharged engine.* (Rex Features)

ABOVE: *Bernie and Max early in their power-climbing future together. That they ever met and, what is more, fused, is utterly astounding.* (Schlegelmilch)

BELOW: *Carlos Pace, Frank Williams and Bernie at Silverstone, 25 August 1975, for the British F3 Championship.* (sutton-images.com)

RIGHT: *Bernie talks to Colin Chapman at the Swedish Grand Prix, Anderstorp, 17 June 1973. Bernie admired Colin's genius as a designer and engineer as well as his entrepreneurial risk-taking.* (sutton-images.com)

RIGHT: *FOM President Bernie with Ken Tyrrell in 1990.* (sutton-images.com)

RIGHT: *Bernie was Jochen Rindt's 'guiding light' when they first met, and Ron Dennis (right) was Jochen's mechanic. While still a teenager in the early sixties, Ron began his career in motor racing with Cooper before moving on to Brabham; by 1968 he was chief mechanic.* (LAT)

ABOVE: *Bernie talks to FIA President Jean-Marie Balestre in 1987. Although his principal battles with Bernie and Max were settled by this time, Balestre was not a spent force.* (sutton-images.com)

OPPOSITE: *Niki Lauda takes Bernie for a snowy ride at the annual Kitz Charity Trophy weekend at Kitzbühel, Austria, in January 2004.* (Getty Images)

BELOW: *Bernie in the paddock with Juan-Manuel Fangio, 1986.* (LAT)

ABOVE LEFT: *With Ronnie Peterson,*
British Grand Prix, Brands Hatch, 1978.
(Getty Images)

ABOVE RIGHT: *With Sir Stirling Moss,*
Monaco Grand Prix, May 2006.
(sutton-images.com)

BELOW: *Bernie talks to Ayrton Senna, at the Canadian Grand Prix, Montreal, June 1991.*
They met in 1983 when Ayrton tested for Brabham, and soon became good friends.
(sutton-images.com)

ABOVE LEFT: *George Harrison at the Australian Grand Prix in Melbourne, March 1997.* (Getty Images)

ABOVE RIGHT: *Bernie with Victoria and David Beckham, Silverstone, British Grand Prix, 2007.* (sutton-images.com)

BELOW: *Bernie with fellow co-owner Flavio Briatore at Queens Park Rangers football ground, Loftus Road, 2008.* (Rex Features)

ABOVE: *Bernie and family at the 2008 Great Ormond Street Hospital F1 Party.* (sutton-images.com)

BELOW: *Prof Sid Watkins, Bernie and Susan Watkins at the Motorsport Safety Fund Watkins Lecture at the Autosport Show, NEC Birmingham, January 2006.* (LAT)

ABOVE: *Bernie with Jenson Button at the 1998 Spanish Grand Prix at Barcelona. It was Jenson's first visit to an F1 paddock after Bernie agreed to give him a pass.* (sutton-images.com)

BELOW LEFT: *Helping Michael Schumacher to celebrate the 100th Grand Prix of his career, the Luxembourg Grand Prix at the Nürburgring in September 1997.* (Getty Images)

BELOW RIGHT: *With Lewis Hamilton at the Great Ormond Street Hospital F1 Party in 2007.* (Getty Images)

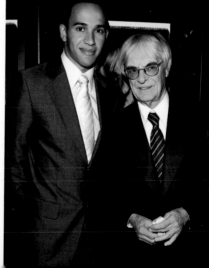

ABOVE: *Bernie gives Sebastian Vettel a little advice at the 2010 Turkish Grand Prix.* (sutton-images.com)

BELOW: *After endless attempts to establish Formula 1 in Russia, Bernie and Prime Minister Vladimir Putin signed a contract for a World Championship race to be held in the Black Sea resort of Sochi from 2014.* (Rex Features)

have a very sensible discussion about the fundamentals…
he was a real strategist.' In a conversation with the head of
Marlboro racing activities, John Hogan, Bernie talked about
Ferrari. 'You know that old bugger, he's got a mind like a steel
clamp, you can't get anything past him.' John adds: 'I think
Bernie respected Ferrari because he'd kind of met somebody
as intellectually adept as he is. And his survivability, how
he [Ferrari] sucked in Gianni Agnelli [president of Fiat],
because he told Agnelli he was gonna sell it [a partnership in
Ferrari] to Ford, and Agnelli came down there [to Maranello]
with a cheque.' The transaction had ensured the continuity
and development of Ferrari automobiles. 'Bernie just loved
that, just loved it. Agnelli zapped down with a cheque in
five minutes and the old man sold it. Ford had, from what
I know, no intention of buying it. And Bernie admired the
fact that the old man used to go to the office every morning
in a Renault, chauffeur-driven, a poxy old Renault 11, light
purple, with a loaded shotgun on the back seat. Yeah, Bernie
loved that too, and the power – the power that Enzo Ferrari
had was just extraordinary. He would have anybody in the
office within hours from the Pope downwards. Except he
didn't like the Pope, he didn't get a Christmas card.'

The decor of Enzo Ferrari's office was sombre to garish,
with purple carpeting and green, flocked wallpaper. On the
walls were several prints of 'Old Masters' in ornate frames.
One of these depicted a gambling scene. 'This is Ecclestone
doing the prize money for FOCA,' said Ferrari to John Hogan
over an impromptu lunch. 'I keep it on my wall to remind
me.' Bernie remembered the 'Old Man' with a 200-year-old
bottle of brandy for his birthday. Herbie Blash also harbours
warm memories of Bernie's relationship with Ferrari: 'Enzo
treated Bernie as one of his very close friends,' and in turn
Bernie 'respected' Enzo, 'he was the same sort of fighter…
and I think deep down it's not just being a businessman, the
other thing that comes into it – he was a racer… he really
loved his racing… always striving for that extra little edge
just to go quicker and quicker, Bernie appreciates anybody
like that.'

Their friendship was such that Bernie was one of the first to be told of Enzo Ferrari's death on Sunday 14 August 1988. Bernie was staying at his recently purchased home in Sardinia next to that of Silvio Berlusconi, when the call came through informing him of Enzo's death. Bernie then shared the news with Herbie, his houseguest. 'Enzo's died,' he said, 'but obviously we can't tell anyone.' During the dinner party that followed not a word was said about Enzo's death, not even when the chatter turned to Ferrari and Ferrari folklore, not even to Berlusconi who had joined them; because Enzo Ferrari was worshipped in Italy, 'he was bigger than the Pope and the Prime Minister and the President,' says Herbie. Ferrari's death was a milestone in modern Italian history, just as it was in the history of motor racing, and yet nothing was said because Enzo Ferrari had not wanted any fuss, no outpourings of grief, no public ceremony – silence. So Bernie was quiet, noticeably less animated, and kept his sadness, as usual, to himself. Ferrari was buried at seven o'clock the following morning. Only six people – his immediate family, the faithful interpreter Franco Gozzi and two others – had attended the funeral.

With the third figure Bernie admired, Colin Chapman, the relationship became a little thorny. Max Mosley believes that Bernie had blamed Colin for Jochen Rindt's death, which may have made genuine closeness impossible. But they appeared to enjoy each other's company, and there was mutual respect. They were, however, both racers, competition was in their bone marrow and on the circuit they would give in to snarling. There was the matter of the Brabham fan car and it had not been easy for Bernie to bury it. Then there was Colin's twin-chassis Lotus, first revealed at Long Beach in 1981; it was time to redress the balance. Colin, like Bernie with the BT46, had found a loophole – which was perfectly legal. But Bernie was incensed: his fan car had had to go, and so too would Colin's twin-chassis car. All of the teams wanted to be rid of Colin's newest innovation and made no secret of their feelings. But it was Bernie who was particularly influential in persuading the stewards to declare the car illegal. Colin had no recourse but to respond with the traditional form of outrage, demanding a lawyer – he would see them all in court. The twin-chassis car was disallowed in Brazil (where Bernie was a race promoter) and in Argentina, and the case finally went to the FIA Court of Appeal; Colin lost. The 1981 World Championship went to Brabham's Nelson Piquet.

Many argue that the outcome of the 1981 World Championship was determined by Jean-Marie Balestre's new-found, post-Concorde support for Bernie, specifically in allowing Brabham to equip their cars with the contentious hydro-pneumatic suspension system, while disregarding cries that it was 'a misinterpretation of the rules'; Renault who came third behind Brabham in the Constructors' Championship being among the most vocal. But then Balestre had his own scores to settle – with Renault – for their determination to go to Long Beach, thereby ending the battle with Bernie, and leading to the signing of the Concorde Agreement. 'Balestre should have stepped in and excluded the car,' said Jabby Crombac, 'but he was still smarting from being let down.' So he allowed the complaint against Brabham to gather dust 'until three months after the finish of the World Championship. What sort of World Champions would there have been then? It would have been bad for everything, so they didn't protest, and that was that.'

One thing is certain, 1981 was a year that only the stoutest of hearts could endure, and a unified FOCA, allowing for a certain amount of infighting, was essential. Bernie and Colin would continue to have 'a love-hate relationship', as Max calls it. On the love side, Jabby believed that 'Colin, being a money man, admired Bernie enormously for the savings he was making'; and Bernie admired Colin's technological ingenuity, his ambition, enthusiasm and his opportunistic ability to attract sponsorship. But most of all he was grateful for Colin's influence within FOCA at a critical time which, although Colin would not have realised it, was to have a bearing on Bernie's future.

Nine months after the signing of the Concorde Agreement Colin died of a massive heart attack. He was fifty-four. It has been suggested that had he lived, he may well have been implicated in the De Lorean fraud. Between 1981 and 1982 American John De Lorean had obtained some £53 million of British taxpayers' money to fund the production, in West Belfast, of a stainless-steel, gull-wing sports car. Lotus had provided the project's technical expertise. But for all its financial resources, the De Lorean 'supercar' project ran out of money, money that, it was suspected, had found its way into the bank accounts of John De Lorean and Lotus accountant Fred Bushell. Both Bushell and De Lorean were to serve jail sentences, the latter for drug dealing. Colin had been short of cash at the time of his involvement with De Lorean, when the Essex Overseas Petroleum Corporation, sponsors of Lotus, owed him several million dollars, a situation that was not eased by the Lotus car's lack of performance. The years of triumph in the Sixties and Seventies were well past, replaced by financial confusion. Lotus seemed to lose its sense of direction, as did Colin. 'We used to turn to Colin for technical details,' says Bernie, 'and in the end we used to turn to him to ask which was the best restaurant.' After Colin's death the Lotus factory struggled on, with the gifted Ayrton Senna bringing a brief but welcome revival in 1986 and 1987. Ayrton drove a Lotus to victory – for the last time – in June 1987 at the USA East Grand Prix in Detroit.

Some FOCA members believed that Bernie and Colin would have fallen out – permanently – had Colin lived much longer, for Colin was becoming uncomfortable with Bernie's seeming omnipotence. Ken Tyrrell was also wary, but then that was part of Ken's nature, a combination of bluster, charm, and affection which, with regard to Bernie, was offset by distrust. Bernie, likewise, had his reservations about Ken. 'The Defector' he still calls him, raising his voice. The defection occurred in 1982 when the FOCA teams had voted to boycott Imola following the disqualification of Nelson Piquet and Keke Rosberg from Brazil after Piquet, in a Brabham, had won the race. Ken Tyrrell later decided against standing with his comrades; his was the lone British team at the Imola Grand Prix.

If money kept FOCA together, competition pulled them apart. But there was always a tendril, and Bernie could work with that, for more than anyone he understood the value of the union. As FOCA President he had received a mandate for power, giving him access to the structure and operation of the sport. Then he wanted more, and would fight to get it until, at length, his power was further enhanced with the signing of the Concorde Agreement. 'I take a lot of satisfaction in what we achieved in those early years leading up to the creation of the Concorde Agreement,' says Bernie. 'Everything since then has been built from that.' In that hard-won agreement motorsport's governing body now joined FOCA in granting Bernie the exclusive right to negotiate with organisers and promoters on all commercial aspects of Formula 1 – including television; the last door was not just opened, it was ripped from its hinges, never to be closed again. Beyond were opportunities prime for exploitation, endless riches to be gathered. But Bernie was not the only beneficiary. Through his efforts the FOCA teams saved money, but also many would eventually be in a position to *make* money – by the millions – and Formula 1 would become transformed into an outstandingly successful, world-class, professional sport.

'I think the most important date in the history of motor racing is when the Concorde Agreement was signed,' said Jabby Crombac, 'when Balestre was clever enough to realise that there was nobody at the FIA who was able to handle the television rights as well as Bernie.'

CHAPTER 12

SHOW BUSINESSES

Tall, blond and tanned, James Hunt would have been perfect to play the role of a fairytale prince, or a Viking bold of legend. Neither character would be burdened with the twenty-nine-year-old Adonis's handsomeness, nor was James. He was as open and approachable as a child, absolutely straightforward, sometimes explosive but always full of fun. The press adored him, and in return he showered them with copy. For journalists and reporters it was Christmas every two weeks because James gorged on life and was blissfully emancipated from guilt. It was a matter of which headline-capturing story to produce, which to discard – regretfully – for such manna is infrequent. 'Hunt the Shunt', his nametag, was bantered round the world, affectionately approving the enthusiasm which often got the better of the machinery he was given to drive. And the stories – take your pick. There was the gorgeous young journalist who made it her mission to sleep with James and then report – in detail – their nocturnal activities; there was the wife who left James to marry actor Richard Burton, either before or after his marriage to actress Elizabeth Taylor had come to an end; there was the riotous lifestyle; the starlets. But more than this, there was the fact that he was a fine driver and in 1976 carried all of Britain's hopes for the World Championship – a near impossible long shot until Niki Lauda was dragged from his blazing cockpit at the Nürburgring where James won, putting himself fourteen points behind the favourite.

With the first-degree burns to his face and wrists, severely scorched lungs and windpipe, Niki was not expected to live.

The doctors could do no more and he was given last rites. James, extremely distressed by the accident, sent Niki a message – it said, in essence, 'fight'. And through the force of his unstoppable will, Niki recovered, ignorant – for a time – of the German newspaper headline with the words: 'My God, Where Is His Face?' Six weeks after the Nürburgring inferno, Niki took his face of broken tissue back to Formula 1 and the Italian Grand Prix at Monza; the media went with him. Although he had been absent from two Grands Prix – Austria and Holland – he was more than eager to resume the title challenge; and there was the challenge within his brain – fear – that had to be resolved. While Niki was in hospital, James had picked up points in Austria, had won in Holland and would win again in Canada and at Watkins Glen, so that at the Mount Fuji circuit in Japan – in sheet rain – Niki and James would come together to decide the championship.

Never before had a race attracted so much media attention. Here were scores of news writers, gossip columnists, sports writers, armies of photographers and television cameramen all huddling from the deluge, but not in the least daunted. For some of the drivers, however, the weather conditions at the circuit were intolerable. They – including Niki and James – refused to race. As the delay ran to an hour, then an hour-and-a-half, the thousands of Japanese race fans began blowing whistles – part of their race paraphernalia – exhibiting frustration as a prelude to riot. It was high drama, complete with the song of the sirens. Would it be tragedy? Would our heroes be swept by the sound to their doom? The tension was that fantastic. Bernie, who had arranged for international television coverage, was among a contingent keen for the race to proceed, and darkness was only a few hours away. Then, piercing the gloom, a voice crackled through the loudspeakers: 'The race will begin in five minutes'; there would be a full grid after all.

Television had been an occasional visitor to Formula 1 circuits during 1976. By October and the Japanese Grand Prix where Niki Lauda and James Hunt met to decided the title, television – on an international scale – had come to stay.

Prior to 1976 organisers and promoters had been known to pay for television coverage, certainly promoter John Webb had had to pay the BBC to cover a Formula 1 race at Brands Hatch. French television was slightly more accommodating if the Grand Prix could be scheduled to fall on a viewing black spot such as Bastille Day. In Italy, full coverage was provided for the Italian Grand Prix – once per year. But then, in 1976, Formula 1 became transformed from sport to theatre. The gods came down from Mount Olympus to tantalise us with tales from mythology, with heart-melting drama and life and death struggles – the whole of the playwright's panoply. The leading players: the bravest man in the world (Ferrari driver Niki Lauda) versus the most beautiful man in the world (McLaren driver James Hunt).

The drivers came out on to the lake of a circuit, and when the starting flag dropped James shot away dividing the water like a speedboat, creating a curtain of spray that obliterated the vision of those in his wake. Niki retired, voluntarily, after the second lap, making James Hunt – when he had ploughed his vehicle into third place – the new World Champion; James had a total of sixty-nine points to Niki's sixty-eight. The photographers click, click, clicked away in the rapid repetition of machine gun fire, the television cameras shifted focus, then zeroed in on a close-up: a dazed, race-worn James Hunt who had just delivered the performance of a lifetime and in the effort accorded film star status to future Formula 1 drivers. Niki Lauda, James's co-star, had been an essential contributor to the transformation. Like the stars the sport itself had been similarly recreated, becoming a stage as tangible as any Adelphi, Theatre Royal or Roxy; and it was now primed for exploitation.

Bernie was lip-smackingly gratified. It confirmed what he already knew, intuitively – glamour and drama could be converted into money, big money, flowing from various streams. One of these was the income potential of James Hunt's fame. In 1977 he offered James Hunt a million dollars in return for all of his earnings for the year. James declined, on the advice of his accountant brother who believed that

James's earning potential was now rather more. The same year, the BBC began live broadcasts of Formula 1. In 1982, three years after James had retired from Formula 1, Bernie attempted to woo him back into the sport with an offer of £2.6 million for sixteen races, which was the value Bernie placed on James's celebrity when the sport's superstars had – temporarily – thinned out. Again, James refused, as he no longer wished to risk his life on the circuit: 'You can't spend a fortune if you're dead,' he said. So James carried on working as a tutor to young, talented drivers such as Mika Häkkinen who eventually became World Champion, twice; and for thirteen years 'laid back' James worked as a commentator in partnership with the more animated Murray Walker for BBC's *Grand Prix*; a programme begun in 1978. To the abiding regret of his friends, James, at the age of forty-five, died suddenly of a massive heart attack on 15 June 1993.

If Formula 1 sometimes lacked the celebrity conferred by a Niki Lauda or a James Hunt, Bernie created the fairy dust by energetically perpetuating, within the sport, glamour and style and, yes, drama when he could to achieve, overall, entertainment. For Bernie sees the world as a film director, in images. Then he sets about adjusting the picture to fit the view that he holds in his head. Every detail of the image must be perfect. The teams in clean, smart uniforms; the circuit signage eye-catching and well-positioned; the arrangement of the teams' transporters in apportioned parking zones; and team motorhomes, in scale and well-aligned, conveying Wall Street boardroom finesse along with the impression that Formula 1 is the most efficiently run sport in the world. 'It was all under strict instructions as to how I wanted it done,' says Bernie. 'People know that if they don't [maintain the prescribed appearance of the circuit and its surroundings] they're going to lose their event, so if they want to keep it that's what they have to do. With education a lot of the people are very proud of what they do now because we opened their eyes to all sorts of different things, and we keep changing things and they see they benefit from it financially as well by doing things in a particular way.'

Paddock passes for the press, VIPs and so on are controlled to avoid not only an obstruction to the mechanics' work and the danger posed by congestion, but also to avoid a bulky, over-populated appearance. To maintain order it is necessary to exercise discipline, as Bernie has already explained. This extends to pit passes, which he may brandish as an instrument of punishment – by withholding them; or approbation – by making the passes available. Both gestures deliver a message, and it comes across the mists louder than a foghorn. Former driver Martin Brundle is fully aware of the system and how it functions: 'I remember when I was the chairman of the GPDA [Grand Prix Drivers' Association] and making noises, I turned up at the first race and my passes weren't available. I'm a grand prix driver and I can't get in! And it was "Mr Ecclestone's got them in his briefcase." "Why's that?" "Oh, he needs to talk to you." Well, Bernie didn't turn up for about three days, so there I am blagging my way in to talk to my engineers and when I finally get in front of Mr Ecclestone in a little room, there's a little table, my passes were nicely presented in the middle of the table. "Martin," says Bernie, "let's have a word about the GPDA shall we?" Yeah, I got my collar felt as chairman of the BRDC [British Racing Drivers' Club] as well. But, you know, that's the law of the jungle.' Today, as a polished, much-celebrated race commentator, Martin's collar is still vulnerable.

The same goes for journalists and other members of the media. It is Bernie's show and he is in control of the overall presentation of the sport, no detail is too insignificant, not even the vendors' displays outside the circuit gates. The whole production must be first-class, the best of the best, throughout. So, the image needs constant readjustment, to which Bernie is at all times attentive, always on watch, always masterminding or puppet-mastering. He is the great impresario overseeing the entertainment, and for the sponsors, the crowds, the television audience, the roving theatre – the greatest show on earth – comes to town like a circus. The acts are the teams and, as with all forms of theatre, actors compete for the leading roles.

The money made from Formula 1 images falls into countless

categories from T-shirts to television; wherever a Formula 1 or related image is displayed, or Formula 1 precincts are occupied, Bernie needs to know about it and, in most instances, he receives a fee – small to massive. Likewise, when a sponsor displays advertising – anywhere – associated with Formula 1, money must be paid, be it in marketing brochures, in a Grand Prix programme or on trackside advertising. With regard to the latter, cost is calculated according to size and then, if required, according to the number of seconds a television camera focuses on the image.

Since the French Grand Prix at Dijon in 1983, signage has been the responsibility of Geneva-based Allsport Management, run by former journalist and marketing executive to Philip Morris, Patrick 'Paddy' McNally. He had first come into contact with Bernie through buying advertising on behalf of Marlboro at Grand Prix circuits where Bernie had the rights. At Philip Morris Paddy was specifically responsible for circuit signage, and he soon realised that the signage at the circuits – then in disarray – would benefit from his expertise. So he took the bold decision to leave Philip Morris, where he had worked for ten years, and go into business on his own. At the time, Bernie had his hands full with running the Brabham team and FOCA along with other business interests, including the running of what McNally colourfully refers to as 'the lame-duck grands prix,' those held in Holland, France and Austria where the promoters were then struggling to pay the fees. Bernie needed these races – and more – to continually increase the profile of the sport, and thus increase demand, keeping it uppermost in viewers' minds or expectations as part of his plans to exploit the potential of the television market. So he had to dip into his pockets – the loss leader again – in anticipation of future recovery; and future profit, the level of which perhaps only his mind could encompass. But there were limits, if not to his prospects, then to his time. Paddy McNally, proposal in hand, appeared right on cue. Also a risk-taker, Paddy sensed that he had reached one of those life-changing moments when the choice is to play it safe or go for broke, the lady or the tiger. He got both.

Paddy explained to Bernie that starting with the 'lame ducks' he wanted to acquire the rights to the signage. Bernie listened politely, then he laid down three conditions: 'You must have a limited number of advertisers; not more than one tobacco company; and no advertising between the camera and the action.' In fact the state of the advertising had begun to rankle with Bernie, falling short of the film director's crisp requirements. Paddy offered to tidy up the image with panels in a standard size, making certain that no extraneous clutter would be allowed to render imperfect the view delivered through the television cameras. However, 'doing a deal with Bernie is never easy,' adds Paddy. 'It was only when I was getting cold feet about leaving Philip Morris that we struck a deal. I still have the one-pager where he wishes me luck.' Walking away from a Bernie Ecclestone transaction, emotionally bedraggled but still retaining a sense of accomplishment, is luck enough.

Hereafter, trackside perimeter advertising at grands prix circuits was transformed, and from those first few circuits and early struggles the business grew so that McNally eventually had extensive rights at most of the Formula 1 races – Monaco, Brazil and Canada excepted – with contracts directly with the race promoters. He also had an overall, long-term agreement with Bernie's company Formula One Administration Ltd, which in addition to a large fee – 'plenty of money,' says Paddy – obliged him to provide a range of services, including paying for the official timing and IT, as well as the provision of the safety and medical cars – on behalf of the FIA – and the organising of the podium and prizegiving ceremonies. But then Allsport rakes in a substantial profit. Blue-chip, global companies have gradually replaced many of the automotive suppliers and national advertisers that formed Paddy's customers when he first started out. One company spent some $40 million annually on trackside advertising, race sponsorship and hospitality, but then corner sites cost up to $1.5 million, according to industry report *Formula Money*, and race title sponsors typically pay around $7 million per race for a package that includes title branding. Over the years since 1983 Bernie helped make Paddy McNally wealthy, the possessor of multi-million pound property holdings, but woe betide him if a sign was not in the right place or not in keeping with Bernie's idea of the correct Formula 1 image.

With the trackside signage cleaned up, Bernie suggested that Paddy turn his attention to corporate hospitality and, at the 1984 French Grand Prix at Dijon, the Paddock Club was born. On a terrace above the pit lane or a tented and turfed village inside the track, guests are pampered with extraordinary cuisine, superb wines, and optimum views of the track and pit lane action. According to a recent Club brochure 'a guest's journey in the Formula One Paddock Club will be a series of quite exceptional entertainment options peppered with the highs of Grand Prix action, creating a weekend to savour for years to come'. During the course of this luxurious 'journey' business talk is encouraged. Indeed, opportunities for mingling with key corporate decision-makers are such that the race often becomes a by-product of the business conducted at grands prix circuits. 'Each guest will be accommodated in a private suite dedicated to a particular client, or on tables of ten in the Formula One Paddock Club Restaurant. Suite décor may be customised to suit the host's personality or style through branded gifts, decoration panels and a choice of flowers and furnishing colors'; and as a little added indulgence guests can treat themselves to a neck and shoulder massage or a quick trim in the 'hair and beauty salon where our international stylists are on hand for some extra grooming or even a whole new look'. The journey might also include some retail therapy in the Club's boutique or its Siemens shop. Should the race be entirely forgotten, Paddock Club guests are reminded of the event with a programme; Paddy McNally also produced the official race programme.

But it wasn't always smooth sailing. The Paddock Club began as a loss leader with high costs, disappointing tickets sales and, more importantly, opposition from the teams. Paddy was ready to give it up, until Bernie told him that 'it's all part of the package, that's how it is, try and make it work'. Then he helped him turn it around. At a team meeting in 1986, Bernie made an announcement: 'Sorry, but McNally is thinking of closing down the Paddock Club. What do you think?' There was pandemonium. 'He mustn't do that! We're going to use it more!' Paddy says: 'The teams needed the Paddock Club to continue as it had come to form an integral part of their sponsorship programmes.' The ploy worked, Paddy McNally was back in business, and with success the Club's ambience became further refined. During that time the cost of Paddock Club pampering was $200 per person for the Friday, $200 for Saturday and $1,560 for the day of the race, Sunday. The capacity of 1,000 to 4,000 – depending on the circuit – was often full. Not so today. Lavish consumption is out of tune with the recession-weary, causing corporate leaders – sensitive to their public image – to forgo the Paddock Club. While Bernie was instrumental in the setting up of Allsport Management, he claims to have 'no financial relationship at all, Patrick took the risk and did all of that on his own.' Yet he still keeps an eagle eye on everything that Allsport produces, always striving for 'perfection' and 'faultless attention to detail', as was also mentioned in the Paddock Club brochure, in accordance with Bernie's doctrine.

But the 'plenty of money' paid by Allsport Management was not the most lucrative part of Bernie's image empire, the big money-maker was television. Formula 1 was becoming a hugely expensive enterprise as individual teams budgeted for ever-increasing technology and its attendant research and development. Greater funding in the form of sponsorship was required. But to attract the big sponsors international television coverage – beaming their product images around the world – was essential. As a result of the FISA/FOCA war, resolved in 1981, Bernie was granted commercial control of Formula 1, including the negotiation of television rights. But even before 1981 Bernie had started acquiring television rights, preparing for what was to come.

Max Mosley, in a press conference held on 10 July 1999, explained that Bernie 'started buying the rights in the early Seventies. Back at the beginning of the FOCA, when I was on the other side of the political dividing line, Bernie had realised that it was essential for the future of Formula 1 to have all the television rights in one basket. In the Seventies to find the results of a major motor race was extremely difficult. Either you telephoned a news agency or looked for the occasional few minutes of TV, tucked between the cricket and the hockey. In those days British TV might show extracts of Monaco, Monza and the British GP, and that was all. Bernie's approach [on behalf of FOCA] was [to] make an offer to [the] race organiser: FOCA would offer to race for a stated fee while also taking over the TV rights to the race, at least outside the country. Gradually, through the Seventies, he acquired the TV rights to all the races. This enabled him to reach an agreement with broadcasters for them to show the entire championship. This allowed him to build up the largest possible audience and obtain the widest possible TV coverage. As a result, the TV rights gradually became valuable. By the time the first Concorde Agreement was signed in 1981, Bernie had acquired the TV rights to virtually every Grand Prix. One of the most important provisions of the Concorde Agreement was that those rights should be handed over to the FIA, and then ceded back to Bernie.'

During the same year he set up FOCA TV in a move to fix Formula 1 on – initially – European television screens. And then the world. In the basement of Brabham's Chessington headquarters, FOCA TV produced video coverage of the races, the rights of which were then sold through Eurovision, a branch of the European Broadcasting Union, responsible for co-ordinating all the efforts of the mostly national, public service European television networks such as the BBC and Germany's RTL. When there was an event of international interest, the host country was charged with the responsibility for broadcasting it. 'We were the first sport to go to the European Broadcasting Union,' says Bernie. In 1982 he secured a three-year contract with them, and the EBU 'agreed that they would broadcast advertising,' which contributed to the restrictions in Bernie's contract with Paddy McNally.

Bob Lobell, associated with Goodyear and who has worked

in motorsport, motorsports promotion and 'just about every aspect of Formula 1 you could imagine' for some twenty-six years, remembers the beginnings of Bernie's television enterprise. He saw the rights were 'going to the EBU and he lobbied them to coordinate the transmission of the television signal for the grands prix. This was a major step forward because before that individual countries would go out and try to pedal this crappy signal. Sweden would try to sell to Germany, Germany would try to sell to Sweden, Spain and whoever else. Bernard thought: "This is all going to be together one day. Maybe I can get them to put it together on one big schedule – that country is responsible for, say, the German Grand Prix and they're gonna give the signal to this, this and this." And that is how he came upon owning the television rights, because before 1981/82 there were no television rights. The host broadcaster sold the rights to whoever came along and bought the damn thing [*ie* Bernie], so he put a lot of order into what at the time was total chaos.'

Bob Lobell goes on: 'It was a major contribution in gaining international acceptance for Formula 1 as a global sport. Before that, it was an event that was the Swedish Grand Prix or the Spanish Grand Prix, whatever. Then, it became the Grand Prix season. When Bernie did that, he created a total international quality to the thing, made it an international sport. At the same time, when you start putting drivers on international television then even the guys in Canada know who a Jacky Ickx or a Niki Lauda is.'

Bernie also formed International Sportsworld Communicators (ISC), through which he marketed, from 1982, the television rights of non-Formula 1 events. For his television operations Bernie sought out some of the most experienced people available, but inevitably there were those who found that they could not tolerate his hands-on approach, his need to control every detail. But then, perhaps, only Bernie understood the astronomical financial potential of his television enterprises. To achieve that potential required careful manoeuvring.

In September 1987 he hired Swiss media consultant

Christian Vogt, who had handled television rights for all major soccer events on behalf of Lucerne-based ISL Marketing, formed after the 1982 World Cup. Bernie had complete confidence in this talented thirty-six-year-old and, uncharacteristically, decided to put him in charge of marketing Formula 1 and later all ISC events, now expanded, by Bernie's appointment as FIA vice-president of promotional affairs, to all motorsports authorised by the FIA. Christian was also given responsibility for marketing the motorcycle world championship series, MotoGP, 'that Bernie had acquired from FIM [the governing body for motorcycle racing] to consolidate his position in sports,' says Christian.

With regard to Formula 1, Bernie realised that the arrival of privately owned commercial television stations presented new income potential and he wasted no time in authorising the like-minded Christian Vogt to negotiate 'single-handedly' with host broadcasters rather than through the EBU. Christian explains: 'My personal aim was not only to increase revenue for F1 but also F1 exposure on TV and, as a result, viewers.' It was a big risk, but Christian was confident – and enthusiastic: 'It was more work but also more fun, when TV could be reinvented. We were the first major sport [Formula 1] that jumped ship from Eurovision – we were pioneers. I even continued to negotiate with the EBU for months even though we had already signed major European territories… we handled things very close to our chests.'

He began with Canale 5 in Italy, owned by Silvio Berlusconi, who later suggested in an interview that signing the Formula 1 contract had helped provide the impetus needed to amass his television empire. The Canale 5 contract was followed by a contract with TF1 in France and RTL in Germany.

To ensure the most effective coverage, Vogt's contracts with television companies stipulated that coverage was for an entire season's races and that these would be broadcast live, as would qualifying and the post-race commentary. Then he further multiplied Formula 1's television exposure by making certain that the contracts permitted him to sell 'again' Formula 1 broadcasts 'to different TV viewers and different stations.

It really put F1 on the map, it was an explosion of revenue, territories, hours of F1 on TV and TV viewers.' In time, public-service broadcasters realised that their bargaining ability was not enhanced through their membership of the EBU and, accordingly, they began their own negotiations with FOCA TV; the EBU's monopoly of the marketing of Formula 1's television rights was over. Remarkably, 'during the Eighties and early Nineties only two [people], plus three for administration, worked for FOCA TV', although the production staff would eventually increase to twenty. In Europe, the television viewing audience would eventually exceed forty-five million viewers per race weekend.

Christian stayed on Bernie's payroll until 1995, leaving because of 'exhaustion' from the relentless tempo of negotiations – 'I had to put a brake on it' – and because 'Bernie and I had a different interpretation of how, and especially how much, I should have been paid… but we're still friends', and on various projects 'we still work together'. They were still working together in 1997 when Christian Vogt constructed his biggest deal for Bernie: 'A ten-year pay-per-view contract with France's Canal+ for $500 million.' Between 1985 and 1990 Bernie's contract with the EBU – covering the whole of Europe – was, says Christian, 'about $5 million yearly', reiterating with well-deserved pride that the 1997 contract was 'the biggest TV deal in F1 in those days… and, again, Bernie gave me the trust and support to pioneer something in TV.'

With some motor racing events outside Formula 1, however, Bernie's endeavours failed to fulfil expectations. What is more, there were those who had strenuously objected to his promotion as the FIA's vice-president of promotional affairs, wary of the spread of his power. The members of the Automobile Club de l'Ouest (ACO) were particularly anti-Bernie. The ACO organised the Le Mans 24-hour endurance race, first held in 1923. Until Bernie's appointment the ACO had enjoyed financial rewards gained from sponsorship and television rights, track signage and off-track trade, all of which now came under Bernie's control. The ACO refused to relinquish their earnings without a fight, and so ensued a three-year battle, in and out of court. The race was ultimately threatened with cancellation – not for the first time in its carnage-prone history – bringing the ACO to heel, and in 1990 they agreed to hand over their television rights. In return, Le Mans was assured of World Championship status for the next five years and television coverage at least equal to that achieved previously by the race's organisers. Two years later, however, the ACO complained that due to a failure on the part of the governing body, the numbers of cars entered had fallen to twenty-eight from the anticipated fifty, and that television coverage was paltry, with the race being shown in only four countries compared to the previous twenty-six. The ACO again took their complaints to court, where it was found that the contractual obligations with regard to television coverage had not been met; the ACO was awarded damages and interest totalling 1.65 million francs. Both parties then appealed with the result that the ACO's award was increased to three million francs. Bernie was oblivious to the acrimony: 'Le Mans asked me to distribute the signal but something went wrong with the contract and so it was cancelled, and that was the end of it. There wasn't any serious dispute.'

Bernie's endeavours to promote the Production Car World Championship (Procar), for unsponsored silhouette saloons, were similarly unsuccessful. Heralded as an arena for manufacturers to test their latest technology, one of the most enthusiastic supporters of the series was Alfa Romeo – purchasers of the Brabham team – who then got busy designing and building the Alfa 164 Procar with the aim of getting other manufacturers interested. It was basically a Formula 1 concept under a production car body. But without the financial cushion provided by sponsorship money, the manufacturers ultimately found the venture far too costly. The Procar series, scheduled to start in 1989, failed to live up to its hype and simply faded away. Bernie said the manufacturers were afraid of being outshone by their competitors.

However, the manufacturers were squarely behind Bernie – and Max Mosley – in their enthusiasm for the Sports-

Prototype World Championship, which had been in existence, under a variety of names, since 1953. By 1969, Max says, 'sports car racing was mega... there were obviously Ferraris, the Porsches, there was Ford and so on and the money was huge compared to Formula 1... the sports cars were much more important. In some Formula 1 races there were only thirteen cars on the grid and four or five of them were just there for the start money, and the money was tiny compared to sports cars. In 1969 if you could have chosen sports cars or Formula 1 and you could have it to run, you would have chosen sports cars.' But all that changed when Bernie came along two years later and Formula 1 became properly managed, as a business. Then Formula 1 was completely turned around and sports cars went 'skint'.

But would Bernie cast the same magic over the Sport-Prototype World Championship? He would not. According to Bernie, he was as keen as anyone, having 'built a car at the Brabham factory with an engine that was quicker than the then-current Formula 1 cars. All the other manufacturers agreed to provide cars like that, but they copped out because of the cost.' In addition, several changes to the rules and regulations were made, and the calendar was continuously altered. The fiddling and inadequate media coverage and spectator interest had added to the financial worries of the manufacturers – Daimler-Benz, Nissan, Alfa Romeo, Peugeot, Mercedes, Jaguar and Toyota – and they, along with the privateers, simply drifted away.

Bernie and Max, among others, voted for the cancellation of the series, which came to an end in 1992; they had wanted the manufacturers to contribute to a promotional fund, but nothing was forthcoming. The glorious history of sports car racing was sadly over. The only place remaining for the manufacturers to test their wares and show off to consumers was in Formula 1. Many hold the belief that this had always been Bernie's intention. Bernie sees it another way: 'There are too many non-Formula 1 championships, they are too fragmented and too many people are inferring about them something that they aren't. But in the long run, market forces will deal with this condition, and manufacturers who come in with their own series will go out as soon as it suits them.'

In his office at Princes Gate in London, Bernie's own day-to-day operations are a sight to behold. Sitting behind a huge desk with an enormous commercial paper shredder situated to his left, he goes through paperwork like a scythe. Vast clumps of documents – with over-sized paperclips attached – are consigned to fragments. Asked if the paperclips might damage the machine, he replies: 'It's built to do that.' Telephone calls – never-ending – he dispatches with one or two words, and the record for the shortest telephone conversation belongs to Bernie. If he can't take a call, he will respond when he can, always, without fail. He is monumentally precise in all things. Face-to-face he is equally quick, but accurate. Years ago when the then FIA safety delegate, Derek Ongaro, along with Prof Sid Watkins, visited Bernie to persuade him to change car design to make it safer, he quietly listened to their arguments, and then he said: 'OK.' Just like that, the decision had been made, and as he was escorting them to the door he said 'We never had this conversation.' The design changes were immediately put in train for the next season. No hesitation, no nonsense, no wastage of words. Another of his aphorisms is 'Just do it, and we'll sort it out after.' That's power.

In 1993, with forthright optimism, Bernie took control of the promotion of another non-F1 event, the World Rally Championship. His company, International Sportsworld Communicators (ISC), was appointed by Max to market rallying commercial interests. Until then, the four principal teams – Ford, Mitsubishi, Subaru (Prodrive) and Toyota – had managed quite well and they were happy with their television arrangements, which appeared to work to everyone's advantage. But then ISC became involved and required the teams to sign an Event Accreditation Agreement acknowledging that the global commercial rights belonged to the FIA, and under a new rule, Article 28, it vested in the FIA all film and picture rights and authorised the ISC to claim them on its behalf. The manufacturers could either sign up or lose their World Championship status. They signed, and the World Rally Teams Association became responsible for the commissioning of television coverage for the series, to be distributed to broadcasters worldwide; the ISC was responsible for negotiating the all-important financial terms.

The contract for providing coverage was won by BBC Worldwide Ltd, an independent television production company whose predecessor, BBC Enterprises Ltd, was set up in 1979 to develop a coordinated approach to the BBC's worldwide production costs – thought to be in excess of £2 million per year. ISC's marketing operation then began selling the film to national and international broadcasters, reaping a handsome profit while creating mass appeal. In addition, the ISC profited from film footage of the event, which might be used as part of a manufacturer's campaign, and on the hiring of a film crew to shoot manufacturers' cars as part of a special marketing promotion. However, television viewing figures dropped, and the sport similarly ceased to capture the public's imagination, although it was agreed that the quality of the coverage, as a result of ISC's participation, had definitely improved. In 2000 interest in the World Rally Championship revived and viewing figures surged accordingly, maintaining the 2000 level ever since – although another increase is anticipated due to political changes within the FIA.

But Formula 1 was still the greatest show on earth, and to keep his show on the road Bernie was in constant motion. He didn't walk, he flitted – checking this, adjusting that – and dealing, dealing, always dealing. It consumed him. By the time he sold Brabham in 1988, Formula 1 had swallowed him whole. 'I needed to devote my energies to the wider picture,' he wrote in the foreword to *The Great Challenge, The Lauda Era*. He was now unable to step away from the intensity of Formula 1; for Bernie the Grand Prix weekend was never over. It was seven days a week, twenty-four hours a day, with no breaks. In perpetual motion, his travels took him across North America, South America, Europe, Asia, Africa and Australia – wherever the Formula 1 circus could set up its big tent. Home was becoming the inside of an aeroplane.

In his private jet he acts as his own host, handing out the

Coca-Cola and crisps to those accompanying him; he doesn't go in for exotic nibbles or anything that smacks of lavish cuisine. Back in his seat, music headset on, he'll flip through magazines quickly, skipping over anything as long as an article, or longer. 'I don't read books,' he says, although 'the good eye is still very good, small print is OK', and 'TV is no problem'. On board his jet Bernie can unwind. 'I like it up there,' he says, 'beautiful sunshine all the time and no telephones!'

Once, flying from Biggin Hill airport to Magny-Cours for the French Grand Prix, Bernie gave a lift to my stepdaughter, Jessica, who is an experienced commercial pilot. During the flight he suddenly said to her: 'Let's fly the plane, you get in the left side [captain's side] and I'll get in the right.' The two pilots who had been flying the plane until that point were now made passengers. Later, en route to France, a brief stop was planned for Gstaad, and as they were approaching the snow-covered peaks of the Swiss Alps, Bernie said: 'It's getting dangerous, we'll go and sit in the back and let the real guys take over.'

Officialdom on the ground rarely presents delays. Sid Watkins recalls that 'coming into Biggin Hill was fun. Bernie flashed through customs and immigration, telling the officials "The doctor's got the drugs in his bags!" By the time I got through Bernie had vanished.' Of course, on arrival at any airport a chauffeured car or helicopter is always waiting to transport Bernie on to the next phase of his travels, usually to set-up – again – the big show.

The big show was, and is, a pricey item. By the end of the Seventies a Grand Prix reportedly cost organisers about $3 million; towards the end of the Eighties that figure would rise to $15 million; and more recently Singapore spends $100 million on its Grand Prix, including a reputed $48 million fee to Bernie's companies for the privilege. The direct and indirect financial returns to a city or country hosting a Grand Prix can be hundreds of millions. These include the multiple benefits to the hotel and tourism industries along with spillover effects in all aspects of the motoring industry, as well as the raised profile of the host country or state.

Except, it would seem, in America. After 1980 Bernie was looking for race venues to replace Watkins Glen, as its organisers could no longer afford the circuit changes – on safety grounds – necessitated by the changing technology of the cars. Also, they were finding FOCA's fees impossible to meet. Anyway, Bernie disliked the remoteness of the woodsy upstate New York circuit – 'not the right image' – and the organisers, the Grand Prix Corporation, had failed to pay FOCA a debt of $800,000. For the man with the mission of increasing the constructors' revenue and one who professed to prefer cement to grass, Watkins Glen was not endearing.

Finding new places to race in the United States was not, in the early Eighties, a problem. Bernie already had Long Beach. By 1982 Las Vegas, Nevada and Detroit, Michigan had been added to the Grand Prix calendar, and what could be more logical or desirable: the gambling capital of America coupled with the home of its automobile industry. The gambling Mecca made no secret of its mobster foundations, which Bernie found intriguing, and there was a James Bond element to his dealings with Clifford Perlman, Chairman of Desert Palace Inc, and Billy Weinberger, president of the casino and Caesars Palace Hotel where they sealed the race deal – literally – in a fireproof, bombproof, soundproof, basement boardroom.

But the Las Vegas organisers had not adequately marketed Formula 1, had not played up the international celebrity of the race to the audience of gamblers unaware whether it was night or day, so obsessed were they with shaking the hand of a 'one-armed bandit' or gazing, relentlessly, at the numbers on a turning wheel. For this crowd the race was just a lot of noise on an oven-hot car park. The television interviewers were no more interested or knowledgeable, scratching around for questions to ask on – what was it – Formula 1? Amazingly, the Las Vegas Grand Prix was held twice – 1981 and again in 1982 – before it was finished for good; or at least until Bernie can acquire a lucrative new contract. But at the time Bernie still managed to walk away with a handsome profit for the FOCA coffers and for himself. Once the teams' prize fund and travel expenses were taken care of, the remainder went to Bernie. However, Las Vegas had had the last say, for Bernie lost his stake at blackjack or roulette and then proceeded to dispense with a rather long line of credit provided by casino owner Teddy Yip. The next day at the circuit Bernie repaid his debt, by handing over a large paper bag full of $100 bills.

The street race in downtown Detroit had a reasonable run with seven races being staged between 1982 and 1988. The organisers had signed a contract for four races which contained an option on a further three. They were hoping to add impetus to the revival of the downtown ghetto, where the Renaissance Center – a high-rise hotel along with a convention centre, shopping mall and offices containing General Motors' headquarters – had been built, and around which the cars zoomed. It was an extraordinary idea and an extraordinary sight. Sadly, by the end of the seven years, goodwill between the organisers and Bernie had become strained. Bernie decried the facilities. 'Detroit promised to build a proper pit complex, but then they didn't do it and the roads were so bumpy and the manhole covers were so difficult to deal with, because of the extreme temperatures you get in Detroit, that the circuit eventually became unusable,' he says. The organisers were equally fed up with Bernie's eleventh-hour increases in the FOCA fees. So America's car capital and Formula 1 parted.

Long Beach, California, went one better. Somerset expatriate Chris Pook, the race's principal organiser, managed to hold eight races there. Long Beach was home to the recently dry-docked Thirties ocean liner turned hotel, the *Queen Mary*, which became a home away from home for the teams and race personnel. Nearby was Howard Hughes's *Spruce Goose*, a vast, wooden cargo-carrying aeroplane. Other attractions nearer to the circuit included the revealingly attired *Penthouse* girls. The cavalier, bearded Pook established the Long Beach Grand Prix as 'America's greatest street race'. He had also helped to promote the race at Caesars Palace, but his attention was clearly concentrated on Long Beach where the crowds and press coverage were more encouraging.

Chris Pook radiated entrepreneurial verve and, like Bernie, a telephone was glued to each ear. This may be one reason why America's greatest street race came to an end – Pook couldn't compete with the master or, perhaps, the master recognised a would-be usurper. Bernie says that he 'gave up Long Beach because they shortened the circuit'. Pook also had a valid practical reason for calling it quits with Formula 1: loss of income. He had smarted when giving over the rights to signage and corporate hospitality, and profits at the gate were outweighed by FOCA's trans-America travel costs, always on the increase, as were the demands for prize money. Furthermore, the television coverage, produced by Grand Prix Teleproductions, was syndicated through cable television and, seen through this narrow funnel, the audience was, at the time, meagre. Chris Pook could get more money out of Champcars and so he switched to CART.

The year after Long Beach held its last Grand Prix, Bernie's circus went to Dallas for a one-off wonder in 1984. The race that meandered through the uninspiring streets of Dallas Fair Park, situated south of the city, attracted 90,000 leisurely elegant visitors, an encouraging turnout that topped the gate numbers in Detroit and certainly in Las Vegas. The organisers had put in the legwork of attending European grands prix, holding press conferences that conveyed well-packaged optimism while selling the international chic of Formula 1 to Texans back home. The craze for the television series *Dallas* was at its peak, blending a smattering of amusing kitch into the cocktail. One of the sponsors booked a price-is-no-object get together at Southfork Ranch, and on race day J.R. Ewing and Sue Ellen agreed to put in an appearance. If an Oscar were to be awarded to the Grand Prix demonstrating the highest level of showbiz glitter, Dallas would have been a serious contender; Monaco, coinciding with the Cannes Film Festival, would be a close second; recently a Formula 1 car, its nose-cone studded with diamonds, was used to promote a Hollywood film.

So why did Dallas schedule their race for July? Accepting the convenience of a North American slot following Montreal and Detroit, the choice of Dallas in July was suicidal. Temperatures reached a steamy 107, melting the circuit into sticky rubble. Most of the drivers were of the opinion that to race in such conditions was lunacy. And yet they made the best of it, driving hard, and it turned out to be an exceptionally engaging grand prix, albeit a testing one with eleven crashes. The fastest lap was set by Niki Lauda, who also had an accident; Britain's new hero, Nigel Mansell, took sixth after climbing out of the cockpit and pushing his car across the finish line before fainting. But it was the heat-acclimatised Finn, Keke Rosberg, who was presented with the trophy and a kiss from the smiling Mrs Ewing, Sue Ellen. All in all, the Dallas Grand Prix had been a success and, if it could have been scheduled for a kinder time of the year, was bound to continue. However, the financial details of the race are clouded in mystery. It was said to have cost organiser Donald R. Walker $6 million, and the takings mysteriously vanished. Walker was later jailed for tax fraud. Bernie sizes up the race as 'OK', and he 'got paid for that', regardless of Walker's doings.

Despite all, Bernie remained cheerful regarding Formula 1's prospects in America, and had developed, it seemed, a fondness for hot climates; he always enjoyed visiting Brazil where the circuit temperature regularly reached forty degrees centigrade. In which case it may not be so surprising that Phoenix, Arizona, staged three grands prix from 1989 to 1991. Bernie, as promoter, invested £12 million in the venture, such was his keenness to develop a Formula 1 foothold in the American market. But the first race, held in June, was, again, climatically ill-judged. Phoenix in June appeals mostly to rattlesnakes. There was no chance of enticing the citizenry to leave their air-conditioned houses overlooking air-conditioned swimming pools set in gardens composed of gravel and cacti. The second race, held in March, was somewhat better in terms of spectator numbers, but not profit; same again in 1991. Phoenix proved to be one of the few gambles that Bernie walked away from – empty-handed.

Thereafter, he tried his luck down south where his offer to buy a circuit in Atlanta, Georgia, failed. The so-called Road Atlanta circuit was purchased by commercial developer Don Panoz, who spent $30 million upgrading the track and facilities to meet Formula 1 standards. But it was not enough. 'Too dangerous' said Bernie, who by then was thinking of a move to Indianapolis, Indiana, home to America's famous oval, the Indianapolis Motor Speedway. Bernie had put practically all of the United States under a microscope in his search for suitable Formula 1 venues. He had even considered hilly San Francisco, presumably nostalgic for a flavour of Steve McQueen, and there were musings of a street race in New York City. But there was nostalgia galore at Indianapolis, where for eleven years, from 1950 to 1960, the oval circuit had held a slot in the World Championship series. Purchased in 1945 by tycoon Tony Hulman, it eventually became – on film and in reality – one of the world's best-known racing circuits.

In the early Nineties Bernie began talks with Hulman's grandson and heir, billionaire Tony George, who after much discussion persuaded Bernie that the time was right, and the facilities more than adequate for Formula 1's return; also the deal was reported to have involved $30 million. In September 2000 a quarter of a million spectators turned up at the speedway to watch the Formula 1 cars loop the inner field and swerve round part of the oval. And even though it's in Indiana, what the locals call 'Hoosier Country' and 'Middle America', it works. Or rather worked until race day of 2005 when seven teams, on safety grounds, refused to compete; their Michelin tyres were puncture-prone in the banked turns twelve and thirteen. Bernie and some of the team principals had worked tirelessly to pull a decent show out of a complex set of circumstances, but the governing body's president, Max Mosley, would not allow any of their proposed track alterations and that was that. The fans at the circuit, not surprisingly, went berserk, but an estimated 205,000 of them returned in 2006, encouraged, perhaps, by 20,000 free tickets supplied by the errant Michelin.

The manufacturers wanted Indy to provide them with all the cosiness of a fixture; Ferrari, for example, sells most of its cars in the US, and much of the teams' sponsorship originates there. But without an American team and an American driver on the podium, it is an ongoing struggle to increase the American viewing audience. On the other hand the revenue enjoyed by the city of Indianapolis is substantial, thought to be somewhere between $100 million and $170 million. These were among the factors that came into play when Bernie negotiated with Tony George to renew the Formula 1 contract beyond 2007. But, Tony George said in an official statement, 'after several discussions Bernie Ecclestone and I were unable to agree how to keep F1 in Indianapolis for the near term'. By then Bernie's attitude was: 'It's not vital to Formula 1 to be in the United States' – which grated upon the ears of the sponsors and manufacturer teams. Still, Tony George added a hopeful note to his statement: '… we have both agreed to leave the door open for a potential future date.'

We're still waiting. Meanwhile, after a lapse of twenty-eight years, Texas beckoned: not Dallas, but Austin, where a Formula 1 Grand Prix will be staged for ten years, from 2012, on a purpose-built circuit. The Internet hummed with news of the deal Bernie concluded with Full Throttle Productions, whose managing director, Tavo Hellmund, commented: 'This is a case of the right timing in the right place. As many Americans know, Austin has earned a reputation as one of the "it" cities in the United States.' It only remains for Formula 1 to become one of America's 'it' sports.

On the other side of the globe, the Grand Prix round in Australia has been an astounding success. Home to some of Formula 1's greatest drivers, Australia extends welcoming arms when Bernie's travelling extravaganza comes to their country. In sleepy but cosmopolitan Adelaide, the circus was staged between 1985 and 1995. Then, due to economic and political pressures, the race was moved – amid considerable controversy – to Melbourne. Bernie is always courted by politicians and businessmen eager to reap the benefits of holding a grand prix event along with every possible related programme and publicity attracting scheme that can be latched on to it. Actually, to say the weekend becomes an extravaganza is an understatement. It is not unlike annually hosting the Olympics, but obviously on a much smaller scale; and for cities hoping to stage the Olympics it becomes a useful exercise in laying on efficient transport, creating sporting facilities and accommodation to test the water.

The Premier of South Australia, John Bannon, was instrumental in persuading Bernie to sign the contract that awarded Adelaide the Australian Grand Prix. Bannon was looking for a means of focusing world attention on South Australia with its population of two-and-a-half million, and decided that Formula 1 was the answer. Bernie had been impressed with this unassuming politician who had personally travelled to his offices, then still at Brabham's headquarters in Chessington, to put the deal together. The Adelaide race, which was said to have paid FOCA $9 million per year, was actually agreed over a few pints in the pub after which Premier John Bannon flew back home with the assurance that as long as he remained in office the Australian Grand Prix would remain in Adelaide. But in 1993 Bannon's popularity took a dramatic dip and he was eventually thrown out of office, due primarily to the collapse of the State Bank of South Australia. Whereupon Melbourne business supremo Ron Walker stepped in.

Ron 'pursued Bernie all around the world' explaining the merits of Melbourne, which along with the rest of the state of Victoria had a population of five million; attendance at a Melbourne Grand Prix would be 'enormous'. But Ron was working against stiff competition: Sydney wanted the Grand Prix and various other Australian entrepreneurs were romancing Bernie with their proposals. But Ron then cleverly pointed out: 'the only thing to do, is to do business with the government because you get paid… an entrepreneur who comes along and loses money they'll blow the game and you'll start over again'. Ron was preaching to the converted (although Bernie's position regarding government backing of the British Grand Prix would waver). 'But in order to get the race from Adelaide I told him I would fund it myself until the government was convinced,' Ron recalls. Either way, Bernie liked what he heard, and on a handshake the Melbourne Grand Prix was agreed; and Ron did not have to reach into his deep pockets.

Victoria's Premier, Jeff Kennett, decided 'to put the money up' for a contract that was, Ron says, 'the same as Adelaide'. With that settled, Ron was left with the unenviable task of consoling South Australia, as the people of Adelaide were angry at losing their race. Upon leaving the city in his private plane, Ron attempted to refuel, but when the driver of the refuelling truck recognised him, he spat on the ground, turned his back and drove away; Ron had to travel back home on a commercial flight.

Nothing, however, would dampen Ron Walker's determination. 'The state was about $23 billion in debt, we had lost the Olympic games bid to Atlanta, we lost everything we tried for and the people in this state were getting sick and tired of losing'. So '100 million' Australian dollars were spent upgrading Melbourne's 300-acre Albert Park – a place where people walked their dogs and the site of a former rubbish dump – to create a Formula 1 circuit with stands that could be dismantled and reconstructed every year along with the appropriate infrastructure.

The result was, at the time, one of the most visually appealing circuits on the calendar, its track winding round a lake where yachts of all colours and sizes are anchored. Even so, Ron Walker had not selected the park for the beauty of its lake and landscape, but for its backdrop – 'of the city to be advertised throughout the world'. Previously Lord Mayor of Melbourne, Ron had also been the Liberal Party's federal treasurer and fundraiser, and he was a close friend of Prime Minister John Howard. It was soon confirmed by the Treasury that the total payments to Bernie/FOCA would be underwritten by the taxpayer and made through a company called Melbourne Grand Prix Promotions Pty Ltd, which was later replaced by the Australian Grand Prix Corporation (AGPC), Walker being chairman of both.

However, not all the taxpayers were delighted. Environmentalists were up in arms, as were neighbouring residents; a series of protests ensued with more than 600 people being arrested. On safety grounds, legislation was enacted making it a trespassing offence for members of the public to enter sealed-off sections of the park while construction was under way. Yet opposition continued to rage and became so caustic that Bernie actually received death threats. When the first race was held in 1996 protestors threatened to let loose an offensive of homemade oil bombs, targeted at Bernie, or rather the aircraft in which he was flying. An explosion shook the private jet that was taking him from Melbourne to Adelaide, destroying an engine and impairing the hydraulics. The pilot was forced to make an emergency landing. Bernie was, as usual, unflappable, being far more engrossed in the magazine he had been reading and, after the fireworks, he was perturbed by the inconvenience.

While Bernie demonstrated yawning indifference to personal danger, he was as alert as a hunting spaniel when he got a sniff of humour. He particularly savoured the amusing and much-publicised story of the then State Premier Kennett's publicity photo shoot in Albert Park. As Kennett smiled for the photographers, with television cameras capturing every moment, a person on a bicycle rode past, shouting 'f--- you, Kennett'. To which the Premier of Victoria replied, 'f--- you too'. 'He's a great guy,' Bernie had said, grinning all over himself. 'We could do with him being Prime Minister of England.'

The Australian press reported that 400,000 spectators turned up to watch the opening race of the 2002 season at Melbourne; the spectator numbers in 1996 were roughly the same. To put that into perspective, it was twice the number that attended the football World Cup in Paris in 1998. Corporate guests numbering 86,000 sat down for a gourmet lunch, combined with 19,000 international and 27,000 interstate visitors. And such is Melbourne's appeal that the Australian race had become traditional as the opening race of the Grand Prix season. In 2006, the city lost this coveted slot due to a clash with the Commonwealth Games, and attendance dropped to around 302,000 over the uniquely long four-day jamboree. But for three more years, 2007 to 2009, the Australian Grand Prix once again opened the season, and Melbourne has continued to attract 'the focus of the world', which is what Ron Walker and the government were after. Speaking in 2004, Ron said 'we actually make 135 million [Australian] dollars in economic benefit because all the hotels are booked up within a fifteen-mile radius, and we collect another twelve million in tax, so if you add that to everything people spend, it's just been an absolute bonanza for us. So whatever I pay Bernie and the others is chicken feed compared to what we get back in advertising Melbourne to the world… and it's the biggest corporate event on the globe.' Ron was particularly pleased with his negotiations with Paddy McNally: 'I insisted that as part of the deal we have Melbourne Australia [on a sign] at the start of the race and over the life of our contract with Bernie that's worth over 100 million a year to us in free advertising, so it was great.'

For many the financial rewards are not always so great and *caveat emptor* is very much the rule, particularly for organisers and promoters with limited budgets and lacking government support. Even the Melbourne Grand Prix weekend, with its state backing, lost money in 2006 and 2007, but the overall benefits to the city are such that a new contract has been negotiated with Bernie to take the Albert Park race through to 2015. As for new races, the prospects are far from rosy, and Bernie now makes it a practice to warn organisers that immediate profits are not guaranteed; losses should be expected. Indeed, losses of between $5 million and $20 million per race are not exceptional. Malaysia was warned, before the government put up the funds for the construction of the Sepang International Circuit near Kuala Lumpur, where the race has been held since 1999. By 2002 it was 'contributing about RM500 million in the form of tourism and related activities', according to government Minister Datuk Pandikar Amin Mulia. The Deputy Prime Minister, Datuk Seri Abdullah Ahmad Badawi, reported: 'The organising of this event in Malaysia is good for the country's economy... thousands of foreigners have come and are staying in hotels and spending their money... they eat, travel and visit places and all these are bringing returns to Malaysia', and 'Malaysia has become more famous as its name as the host nation has been aired all over the world through the international media coverage of the event.'

This reflects the prevailing attitude as new circuits are introduced, the aim being far broader than the numbers of people passing through the gate – it's about tourism and promoting a country. Once a country has achieved an acceptable degree of prominence, staging a grand prix may no longer serve the purpose originally designated by its government officials. With regard to Malaysia, ticket prices are relatively cheap, but the number of spectators at the Sepang International Circuit had failed to meet the organisers' initial target of 120,000, which, in any case, doesn't begin to cover fees paid for the privilege of holding the race and television rights. That said, it's probably the most spectacular event to come to this country and as long as it continues to draw the world's attention, along with a flux of new business and revenue, the show will go on. The financial strategy of the organisers of the Malaysian Grand Prix required fortitude. And patience. It took several years for the crowd numbers to reach the anticipated target. By 2008, however, the number of spectators amounted to an impressive 185,382 over three days, and the event has a renewed contract with Bernie's FOM.

According to recent television viewing figures, each round of the Formula 1 World Championship is telecast to a worldwide audience of approximately 527 million viewers in over 187 countries. 'The awareness of Formula 1 worldwide was entirely dependent on broadcasting TV worldwide, and that is the thing that developed the current interest,' says Bernie. In the process he has become a billionaire, while always striving to perpetuate the sport's appeal. At the same time he created the means for making the FOCA team owners massively rich – by causing the sport to become more professional, by attracting more sponsors and/or directing sponsors to teams and teams to sponsors, and by increasing revenue through the marketing of countless Formula 1 products. The key to success in all of these areas is Bernie's guarantee that the show – picture perfect – will go on. Even if it means that he, himself, must become the promoter. Many times over the years Bernie has asked other FOCA team owners to go into partnership with him. Herbie Blash recalls: 'He would say so-and-so Grand Prix, they don't want to pay us, so we'll become the promoters, but we need some money up front. "No, no, too risky," was the usual response from the FOCA members. Bernie would then "go and do it on his own". Not for nothing is he called "Mr Big".'

Amid all this capitalist commerce it must be remembered that – before perestroika, before the Berlin Wall was toppled – the Formula 1 show travelled behind the Iron Curtain, in 1986, to raise the big top at the Hungaroring near Budapest in Hungary. The VIPs attended a welcome dinner held at the Communist Party headquarters. In the squelching Budapest August heat, the KGB operatives could be readily identified: they were the quiet gentlemen wearing wool suits in which they sweated profusely. The enchanting city of Budapest was something of a Soviet experiment, more economically flexible compared with other 'republics'. Take away the wool suits and the machine guns trained on the Danube and there lingered a sense of bygone grace from a pre-1914 era. There was a dignity about the place and its people that one must now search a little harder for, away from the German invaders and their strings of neon-coated sex shops. But then, as now, everyone has heard of Bernie Ecclestone and appears to be glad that he came to Hungary. The road to the Hungaroring is named after him and he has been awarded the Hungarian government's highest honour – even though the number of spectators at the circuit is dwindling.

In contrast, on 23 September 2004 the Chinese Grand Prix made its debut near Shanghai. The circuit is a work of art of awesome proportions; one stand alone holds 35,000 spectators. In a country with a population of 1.3 billion they tend to think in large numbers. For the first race all 150,000 spectator tickets were sold at an average cost of 2,000 yuan ($241), the equivalent of a month's wages for most Chinese. The track is built over a 300-metre swamp, so its foundations had to be raised – fourteen metres high in some places – on polystyrene (the whole of the Asian market having to be bought out for this purpose). The cost of the circuit was 2.6 billion yuan plus 3.35 billion yuan for the surrounding infrastructure (roughly $700 million in total), and Shanghai will have reportedly invested, overall, about $600 million annually in hosting the Grand Prix. 'I've been trying to get into China for ten years,' Bernie told reporter Grant Clark in a telephone interview from Shanghai, reported in the *International Herald Tribune* of 24 September 2004. 'Shanghai is the obvious place for us. I'm very much pro-Asia. Europe will be a Third World economy within ten years, and Asia will rule the world, assisted a little bit by America.' Yet, in recent years, spectator turnout at the Shanghai circuit has dropped dramatically. Still, its economy continues to do well. Reflecting in 2011, Bernie underscored his Third World predictions about Europe, adding: 'The problem is their social systems. That's what will ruin them. It's a little different in America because the people there are always willing to work. China is going to take over Africa and run Africa. It will have a massive influence. We should have maybe two races in Africa. One in South Africa and one somewhere else on the continent.'

To make way for new circuits, some of the old fixtures have been sacrificed, particularly in Europe with its clampdown on tobacco advertising. And economic viability has certainly taken its toll. In Germany, the financially strapped Hockenheim runs on alternate years with the Nürburgring, and Magny-Cours in France could no longer pay its way, while Imola has been replaced by the Grand Prix of Europe in Valencia, with its street circuit skirting the Mediterranean along Port America's Cup. At the height of Fernando Alonso's success, Bernie had felt the time was opportune to negotiate for a second Formula 1 venue in Spain. The seven-year deal is reputedly worth $42 million per year. Although the traditional circuits are diminishing, pro-Asia Bernie has not yet allowed the overall numbers of circuits in Europe to likewise decrease. In 2010 and 2011 there were still eight European races on the Grand Prix calendar. Asia has seven, counting Turkey with its circuit on the Asian side of the Bosphorus. Making up Asia's numbers, 2010 newcomer South Korea joined Shanghai, Malaysia and Turkey, and Japan's Suzuka returned after alternating with the rain-soaked Fuji Speedway for two years; Singapore's Marina Bay first made its appearance in 2008 – at night; and India made its debut in 2011. Canada's Circuit Gilles Villeneuve in Montreal returned in 2010, and Brazil's Interlagos remains a fixture, as does Melbourne, Australia, although in 2010 it again lost the coveted season-opening slot, which it regained by default in 2011 with the cancellation of Bahrain. The last race of the 2010 season, aimed to leave us breathless, was Abu Dhabi. The country's Yas Marina track, the costliest – at a reputed $1 billion – on the Formula 1 calendar, is the *Avatar* of motor racing, a meeting of imagination and wealth overseen by the artistically talented Philippe Gurdjian, formerly in charge of the Paul Ricard circuit-cum-hotel complex in France. In 2011, however, Brazil returned to its traditional season-ending slot.

Should Bahrain make a comeback in 2012, the Formula 1 World Championship calendar will comprise a historic twenty-one races. Bernie feels that sixteen makes for a more comfortable season and the teams' mechanics would certainly agree with him. But then in October 2010, after endless attempts to establish Formula 1 in Russia, Bernie and Prime Minister Vladimir Putin signed a contract for a World Championship race to be held in the Black Sea resort of Sochi from 2014. With the addition, too, of the race in Austin, Texas, in 2012, expect a continuous reshuffling of circuits. Could there be too many Formula 1 circuits? What is certain is that tough and/or frenzied negotiation is Bernie's ideal condition, stretching out the striped canvas of Grand Prix racing's global – maybe universal – big tent. Come one. Come all.

The negotiation process doesn't happen overnight. Bernie, remember, likes to take his time, improving his position as the days, months, years roll by. Factors such as a local champion, a competing event, viewing potential or markets for manufacturers and sponsors are variously taken into consideration. Once a circuit secures a slot on the Formula 1 calendar, war, politics and the ebb and flow of economics can come into play. These Bernie will use, dismiss or rectify. Actually, in Valencia, politics entered the mix at the negotiation level. It's a recurring trend. The regional president, Francisco Camps, who had negotiated with Bernie to bring the race to the city, was up for re-election. In a press conference he seemingly made a connection between obtaining the Grand Prix and a successful outcome to his campaign. 'Thank you Mr Ecclestone for putting so much faith in me,' he said, 'linking the Formula 1 Grand Prix to my continuation as Premier of the Generalitat.' He later denied tying the two together. Nevertheless, Spain's Deputy Prime Minister, Maria Teresa Fernandez de la Vega, was outraged: 'It is frankly insulting that a private businessman should travel to a foreign country and seek to influence the democratic will of its people.' Bernie also thought there had been a misunderstanding – and a lot of fuss over nothing. He had simply developed a business relationship with Premier Camps, a meeting of the minds, which is essential for a transaction to proceed. 'With Valencia, perhaps, if the current people are not in power any more then I am not sure who I will be dealing with. So until I know who that is going to be I am not prepared to enter into a contract. It is normal business I would have thought.' After all, the annual appearance of the Formula 1 in Adelaide had been dependent upon Premier John Bannon – its negotiator – remaining in power.

In Turkey, the situation was a little more complicated. The Formula 1 travelling circus first went to Turkey in 2005, and in spite of the August heat the race at Istanbul Park was superb. Just as it was in 2006, apart from the dispute that followed the awards ceremony when a gentleman – a Turkish Cypriot – made his way to the podium and handed out the trophies. It was thought, by the FIA, that the appearance of this individual was part of a gambit to focus the world's attention upon the ongoing problems in Cyprus. The FIA, therefore, handed down a fine of $5 million to the promoters and organisers of the race; the fine was later reduced to $2.5 million. Formula 1's governing body, the FIA, maintains that the sport must be apolitical, so a political infringement is a violation that must incur a fine.

What is interesting is that many hold the opinion that there was another flag being raised in Turkey during the race, specifically that of the European Union, which many Turks would like to join. Successfully staging a Formula 1 grand prix may have been part of their European Union agenda, although the location of the circuit is technically in Asia. Enter economics on a national scale. But it was economics of a more personal nature that concerned the organisers. Just as in the early years of the Malaysian Grand Prix, spectator numbers in Istanbul had failed to meet expectations, threatening the future of the race. Bernie's solution was to become the owner of the lease to the circuit, in 2007, for around $131 million. At the same time he confirmed a place on the Formula 1 calendar until 2021 at least – there would be no stingy five-year contracts for him. Another feature of the race at Istanbul Park is, and always has been, security. Their painstaking screening against terrorist attacks is worthy of study by other countries.

For his part Bernie, the man who went galloping through the Iron Curtain, shrugs his shoulders at any pertaining threat to world security. In the days after 9/11 the teams were expected to follow his cue, travelling nonchalantly through eerily abandoned airports across Europe and North America to reach Indianapolis for the race. Similarly, while the Middle East was suffering with war and terrorism, the first Bahrain Grand Prix was held in April 2004, and it was fabulous – the circuit, the race, the whole enchanting entertainment. Nothing will stop Bernie's theatre on wheels. The show must go on.

Except, that is, in February 2011, when the opening race of the season – Bahrain, scheduled to run in March – was postponed. As in South Africa in 1977, human rights lay at the heart of it. In the wake of uprisings in Tunisia and Egypt, civil unrest in the tiny kingdom of Bahrain had become rampant, with scores of pro-democracy protesters slaughtered in the streets by the ruling Al-Khalifa regime's security forces. During the following weeks and months some hundreds of others were imprisoned, many of them allegedly suffering torture while awaiting trial in military courts. On what should have been race day, March 13, a thousand Saudi troops were deployed to assist the government, and two days later martial law was declared.

Bernie, as with South Africa, was anxious to honour a contract – while looking for a way out. The financial figures involved a race fee of around $40 million along with a premium of $20 million for the season's opening slot. Bahrain had already spent $50 million on a revamp of the circuit following criticism of the 2010 race which, in entertainment terms, had been less than fabulous, indeed it had been regarded as positively dull – not good for a season-opener. But in 2011, what was more important to the Bahrain government was the propaganda opportunity inherent in hosting a Formula 1 race, to promote – worldwide – a favourable image of the beleaguered kingdom. The teams were against reinstating the race on moral and security grounds. So the FIA decided the best course was to send a delegate to Bahrain to assess the situation close at hand. The delegate had a seemingly thorough look, with the assistance of government officials; he came away with the opinion that conditions in the country had returned to normal. Two days before the FIA's World Council was to decide on the fate of the race, martial law in Bahrain was ended. On 3 June, in a somewhat vague show of hands, the FIA voted in favour of reinstating the race. A revised calendar was posted, moving India from 30 October to 11 December in order to make room for Bahrain.

During the week that followed, controversy squeezed the sport – and the FIA – by the neck. The FIA's new president, Jean Todt, declared that the FIA's decision reflected 'the spirit of reconciliation in Bahrain... Reinstating the Grand

Prix is a means of helping to unite people as the country looks to move forward.' Unfortunately, there was little evidence of reconciliation in the reports being broadcast on the nightly news. Max Mosley's position on the Bahrain race was unequivocal: 'I absolutely wouldn't go.' He went on to explain: 'I'm virulently anti-torture. But if you start saying we're not going to go to any country where there are human rights abuses, you'd find very few places you can go. A classic example is America: Guantanamo Bay is a breach of human rights by any ordinary standards. That would be illegal here [Britain] under the Habeas Corpus Amendment Act of 1679; putting people outside the reach of your courts by the Executive has been prohibited here for more than 300 years. It's a question of degree. America is at a fairly low level. China is probably at a bit higher level. Where I would draw the line is where you have a regime that is going to use the Grand Prix in order to present a face to the world that is, on the best evidence available, a complete travesty of what's going on. If you go to Bahrain you are directly helping the government in what they are doing. Conversely, if you don't go you'll then make it more difficult to continue what they're doing. To be fair to the Bahrainis, they're doing this under instruction from Saudi Arabia... If F1 does go [to Bahrain] it's going to be a major public relations disaster. And I think it will have a very negative impact on all the sponsors. But that shouldn't be a reason you decide not to go. For me, if I were still in charge, it would be an absolute no-no. It would be a resigning issue.'

The teams agreed with Max and wholly rejected the FIA's decision to reinstate the race. In a letter to the FIA the teams made it clear that they would not allow the alteration to the championship calendar that moved the Bahrain race to October and India to December. One must also spare a thought for the race organisers in India whose inaugural Grand Prix was being shoved about. Bernie's own position can only be described as wavering. Always preferring to stand by a contract, he had supported reinstating the Bahrain race then changed his mind, saying it was 'not on', before changing his mind yet again, suggesting a date somewhat earlier in December. This is also a reflection of Bernie's soft spot for Bahrain, a country that he feels has heretofore been good for Formula 1. In any event the refusal of the teams to reinstate the race finally put an end to the saga. According to Article 66 of the International Sporting Code the championship calendar cannot be changed without unanimous agreement of the teams.

The creation of the $180 million Bahrain International Circuit was the work of designer Hermann Tilke. He recalls first meeting Bernie in 1994 to discuss drawings of Austria's A1 Ring: 'Bernie looked at the drawings and then said: "It's okay, but this and this is wrong, you have to shift this here, this here", and that was it, done in two minutes.' Since then Tilke has designed a new grandstand in Barcelona and a plan for the redevelopment of the circuit at Estoril in Portugal. He has also planned changes at Hockenheim and the Nürburgring. Moreover, he designed, among others, the circuits for Shanghai, Abu Dhabi and Istanbul, the latter one of the drivers' favourites thanks to it having challenges on par with those of Spa. Hermann shows his circuit sketches to Bernie, and then they discuss them: 'He has a very, very detailed knowledge about everything. It is good to have the opportunity to get his opinion about things. Sometimes he caused problems and says "this is rubbish, make it another way round". It is not a problem when it is in a very early stage of the building of the design, but if it is in a late stage, then it causes problems... He is always very clear... and sometimes you know what he said is right!' It normally takes Hermann Tilke about four years to produce a Formula 1 circuit.

In 1999 Bernie, through his family trusts together with the renowned Philippe Gurdjian, set up Excelis SA for the purchase of the Paul Ricard Racing Circuit and adjacent Le Castellet Airport, located in the heart of Provence between Marseille and Toulon. Opposite the airport they built the luxurious Hôtel du Castellet, designed by the multi-talented Gurdjian, with forty-seven rooms and suites facing the

Mediterranean, along with a restaurant that boasts 'the most refined cuisine in the area'. Both airport and circuit have been completely redeveloped and, by 2004 the circuit that saw its first grand prix in 1971 had been remade into an ultra high-tech track – for testing only. 'I don't want any crowds dirtying up the place,' Bernie said. Now, the facilities and services include a medical centre with a 'medical video control room', the provision of a rescue team, the 'Blue Line Concept' (a Pop Art design around the circuit for a better tracking system), twelve three-level pit units (comprising a telemetric pit for the engineers, garage for the mechanics and a hospitality room for the reception area), a track video control room, a conference room, a 500-seat restaurant and an exhibition hall. There is also a kart testing track on site.

Although the Paul Ricard test track is a masterpiece, it is the circuit in Bahrain that gave Bernie a particular sense of achievement. And while it seems somewhat ironic in view of recent events, it was at Bahrain's inaugural Grand Prix on 4 April 2004 that Bernie fell in love – that isn't too strong a word – with what he saw. He was beaming as he walked around the circuit that he regards as the perfect theatre for staging his show, for displaying to advantage all of Formula 1's glamour, its unique razzle-dazzle, its camera-ready image – the greatest show on earth. 'Not bad for a lad from Suffolk,' he said. Happiness was evident in his voice and features. Absolute happiness.

CHAPTER 13

FATE AND NUMBERS

Bernie's path to power had been paved a little smoother after Max replaced Jean-Marie Balestre as president of FISA in October 1991, although to Bernie a change at the top had seemed – initially – a potential detour. After all, it had been Balestre who, in 1987, had conferred upon him the FIA's vice-presidency of promotional affairs, purportedly out of gratitude for the revenue Bernie was adding to its coffers. Max Mosley as president – unlike Balestre – was an unknown quantity. Yes, Bernie and Max had an important bond, forged during the years of the FISA/FOCA war. But now that the war was won Max appeared to be developing independent ambitions, and Bernie was presented with – rare for him – a quandary. He canvassed his friends, forming a question in his typically detached style couched to manipulate the response: 'Do you know they're going to make Max president of the FISA?' The replies ranged from complete indifference to: 'What are you, out of your f---ing tree?' Meanwhile, Max was gaining support for his presidency from other member countries with a comparatively recent motor racing history. He comforted the traditionalist Europeans, wary of his connection with Bernie, with the promise that he would resign after a year in office should they be dissatisfied. So, what Bernie had suspected soon became apparent, Max was making headway, quietly, in the background, picking up significant support. At seven o'clock on the morning of the election Bernie telephoned Balestre:

'Jean-Marie, you're gonna lose the election.'

'Bernie, why you phone me like this, I have a list, I know, don't do this.'

'Jean-Marie, you're gonna lose.'

'No, no, no! I've seen the list!'

'Well, you're gonna lose, why don't you go up on the podium and say "I'm not going to stand, but I'd like my friend Max Mosley to stand and I'd like you to support him".'

'Oh, but Bernie.'

And that was it. Balestre, confident of another term, disregarded the idea. Max won the election, taking forty-three votes to the soon-to-be former president's twenty-nine.

Upon taking office, Max, true to his word, formally submitted his resignation, effective in one year's time if he failed to please. A year later he was re-elected by a comfortable margin. By that time Bernie had come to favour Max over Balestre because Jean-Marie 'was getting a little bit out of control and used to do silly things, but in fairness to him, if he'd done something that he thought was a bit silly, he'd always ring me and say: "Bernie, you must help me, you must save my face," so that's probably the difference between him and Max.' Then in 1993 Max determined to attain the top prize, the presidency of the FIA (a federation of over 200 national member clubs in 125 countries worldwide), and Bernie envisaged a way to shape the future. Although Balestre had lost the FISA presidency, he was still president of the FIA and would – with white-knuckled intent – hold on to that office. To prise him loose called for equal resolution – and shrewdness.

Bernie gave Max two suggestions, and Max decided to listen. First, he suggested the formation of an important, decision-making FIA Senate to take over the function of the finance committee; he had previously made this suggestion to Balestre. Second, that Max offer Balestre the presidency of the Senate, with offices in the Place de la Concorde, in exchange for standing down as president of the FIA. Balestre agreed. Bernie then threw his support and influence behind Max to become the FIA's new president. This involved a form of dialogue aimed to confirm Max's election with member organisations. Jeffrey Rose, chairman of Britain's Royal Automobile Club and an FIA vice-president, recalls being contacted by Bernie who set up an 'urgent' breakfast meeting – a threesome including Max. During the ninety-minute meeting Max said little, allowing Bernie to lead the discussion, informing Jeffrey that 'Max is going to be the next president of the FIA' and explaining his merits; Bernie then invited the RAC's support.

Jeffrey Rose was both surprised and discomforted, reasoning that as a basic qualification for the office a candidate should be president of a leading club, which was customary. At the time Max was not even a member of the RAC. (The RAC, incidentally, has existed since 1897 and was one of the thirteen founding members of the FIA.) Max's lack of motoring club leadership was 'brushed aside by Bernie,' but Jeffrey regarded it as 'highly relevant,' although he undertook to present Max's proposed candidacy to the committee of the RAC. This he did, and while the committee members appreciated the advantage of Max's cultural and linguistic capabilities along with certain personal qualities, they were 'not prepared to support, for the presidency of the FIA, an individual who in effect represented no member club within it', says Jeffery. What's more, there was general unease over the perception that Max's main role was as FOCA's lawyer and, in a sense, Bernie's man. Bernie, who was well placed, 'and well qualified', continues Jeffrey, 'to exploit the coverage of Formula 1 on television. Already the commercial dominance of the Formula 1 television rights was recognised as a most important issue in the interface between Bernie and the FIA, and it seemed inevitable that some realignment of ownership of those rights – as between Bernie and the FIA – would take place.'

But could two individuals as close as Max and Bernie actually take opposite sides in negotiations? The members of the RAC thought not and put forward a candidate to stand against Max, the eminently qualified Jeffrey Rose himself. At least opposition made it possible for the matter to be ventilated through debate. But it soon became clear to candidate Rose – and to the electorate, the FIA's General Assembly – that the presidency was 'a done deal', predicated upon patronage and a fear of backing the wrong horse. 'The FIA has all the appearance of a democracy but none of the reality,' says a prominent member of the FIA, 'and that's as true today as it was then.'

In any case, Jeffrey Rose, realising that the quest was futile, withdrew as a candidate. On 10 June 1993, in an exquisite room belonging to the Automobile Club de France, the ballot papers were collected from the representatives of the member countries that made up the General Assembly. Bernie and Marco Piccinini observed the formalities from the back of the room. Thirty minutes later it was announced that Max – unopposed – had been elected to, nominally, the most powerful position in motorsport.

After being elected Max did indeed form the FIA Senate. Jean-Marie Balestre was appointed president and the other members – eight in total – included Max, Bernie and Marco Piccinini, who had become a director at Ferrari and would later become a director in Bernie's principal trading company, Formula One Management (FOM). Max also implemented a restructuring – introduced by Balestre – which effectively merged the FISA with the FIA so that the latter now became responsible for all sporting and technical rules, circuit inspections and approval, scrutineering, safety and medical support. Since the Seventies Bernie has been a member of the World Motor Sport Council (World Council) or as it was then known, the Executive Committee. It is composed of representatives of the national sporting authorities concerned not only with Formula 1 but all forms of FIA World Championship motor racing; Bernie has never missed a meeting. He has also, since the Seventies, been a member of the Formula One Commission, which receives proposals from the FIA, from the teams and other quarters pertaining to the sport; the Commission is Formula 1's ultimate ruling authority.

Thus the combined FIA, in which Bernie then maintained his vice-presidency of promotional affairs plus his roles on the FIA's governing bodies, and now the Senate, allowed him to thoroughly infiltrate – and influence – the elite ranks of the rule makers. He could now clutch the teams in one hand and the sport's mandarins in the other, encircling the war-inciting FOCA – of which he was still the leader – and the body politic in the same mental corral. This was, still is, the real Bernie, a paradox to everyone but himself. He perceived no conflict of interest, no having it both ways, no poacher turned gamekeeper, but rather a single-minded approach to achieving total control of Formula 1.

This also meant taking the incremental steps – improved circuits and facilities, global interest in the sport through television, commercial success – that would push Formula 1 towards the zenith of professionalism while swirling in ever more money. Down to his bone marrow Bernie cared about the professionalism of Formula i. Dig even deeper and it is power; the acquisition of money was not – since the irrational decision to buy Brabham – the essential quarry, it just happened, like Midas but with purpose.

The Concorde Agreement signed in 1981 was renegotiated for the period 1987–91 and again for 1992–96. In each renewal sections were added in order to address new problems, but ultimately the result was a document with regulations between the international federation, the FIA; the commercial promoter of the championship; the teams; and the promoters or organisers of the event. There are, in essence, four parties, all of whom need written certainties upon which they can preserve their businesses and/or their financial stake. In the renewal of 1992 FOCA members agreed to transfer management of their commercial rights to Formula One Promotions and Administration (FOPA), one of Bernie's companies, for a royalty split of television revenue along the lines of what had been agreed in 1987: thirty per cent to the FIA, forty-seven per cent to the teams and twenty-three per cent to FOPA, which also put up the prize money.

The FOCA members further agreed that the race promoters and organisers' fees would be kept by FOPA as compensation for Bernie's financial risk, for he bore all the expense. This was an interesting situation considering that Bernie participated in the promotion of several grands prix including Brazil, Belgium, Germany and France. So for those races that he promoted he was negotiating with himself. Again he did not perceive a conflict, it simply didn't matter. To Bernie it was more important that a guaranteed number of teams turn up at a guaranteed number of races – even if he personally had to fund them – across a spectrum of countries, which in turn would attract sponsors and require more television coverage. This is what really counted in the revenue departments of the FOCA, the FIA and Bernie Ecclestone.

Many times he had invited FOCA members to join him in investing in races but, always fearful of losing money, they shunned the opportunity. 'You see,' says Bernie, 'the teams, in the early days, had the opportunity – which is what I wanted – to form a company that I would run and manage, and I think at the time I agreed to manage the whole bloody lot for thirty per cent, have all the expenses paid and the company would have the rest. That would have meant everybody had to put some money in because we had a few races that were losing money. We all had to put some money in, and they said: "No, no, no, we want to go racing, we don't want to be promoters and we don't care if you want to do it. If you want to make money, you do it, but we don't want to do these sorts of things".'

In 1992 FOPA reportedly had the best profit ratio of any British company, making a profit of more than £15 million on a turnover of some £18 million. In 1993 it was declared in *The Times* newspaper that Bernie was Britain's highest-paid employee with a pay packet of £45 million, which he again achieved in 1994. Events in 1994 would contribute to a massive upsurge in television viewing figures – and another bonanza. But before that the business of television broadcasting would take its toll of losers.

Back in 1990 Jean-Marie Balestre had entered into negotiations with Paddy McNally, who promised Balestre that in return for the FIA's thirty per cent of the television revenue, Allsopp, Parker and Marsh Ltd (APM) would guarantee the FIA an annual fixed royalty payment of at least

$3 million; Paddy says that his 'family trust owned APM' of which Allsport Management – associated with the lucrative Paddock Club and trackside advertising – is a part. Balestre seriously considered McNally's proposal, influenced by the demise of Canal 5, the French television company owned, as it happened, by a close friend. So any guarantees having to do with the risky business of television merited interest. Paddy explains: 'Balestre was worried – and he had an inside track – that the TV rights wouldn't be worth anything. With my background in Philip Morris, I knew they would. So what I did was guarantee him a fixed amount and took the risk!'

The deal was done, and Balestre had seemingly backed a winning proposition. However, between 1992 and 1996 Bernie negotiated an estimated $341 million in television royalties of which thirty per cent – $102 million – went to APM. The FIA received $37 million; had they not done the deal with APM they would have gained a further $65 million. Bernie, as vice-president of promotional affairs, participated in the negotiations with Paddy. 'We did a deal with McNally, like an insurance policy,' says Bernie. 'We said "you give us a set figure and you own them" [the FIA's share of the TV revenue]... all the TV rights worldwide were crashing. I really didn't know that Canal 5 in France was going to close down and he [Balestre] thought that... the revenue would drop and everything would drop – and that's all the money the FIA had – so he thought "better have a fixed sum" rather than take a chance. Maybe it's good or bad, but he didn't want to take any risks.'

Even so, Bernie had advised Balestre against the contract with Paddy, but his was a lone voice. The FIA Finance Committee supported Balestre in his decision to accept the McNally/APM offer. 'That was Jean-Marie's style,' adds Bernie. 'In his case it was correct because they [FIA] are not in the business – and still shouldn't be – of taking risks.' However, Balestre's 'timing was wrong', concedes Paddy. 'I mean he could have been a 100 per cent right – look what's happened to some of these commercial chains!' McNally, experienced in marketing and promotions, was aware that what had worked commercially for the World Cup could soon be applied to Formula 1. 'I was so impressed by the way Philip Morris had been marketing the TV rights to the World Cup, and I could see that Bernie was doing the same. I'm not even sure it wasn't for the same reasons, *ie* he'd seen how it was done – so obvious at the time.' But it wasn't obvious to Jean-Marie Balestre: he missed out, with the result that 'lots of people raised lots of eyebrows'.

Does Bernie have a vested interest in APM? 'No,' says Paddy. 'No,' says Bernie. Still, the raised eyebrows ultimately drew the attention of investigative journalists, including Mark Killick, who questioned Paddy about an APM/Bernie link in preparation for the BBC's *Panorama* broadcast in November 1998. The programme focused on the maze of Formula 1 finance. 'The early relationship with BCE [Bernard Charles Ecclestone] has stood APM in good stead – opening doors and giving the company credibility in the marketplace,' Paddy told Mark Killick. McNally was thereby able to 'market on an international basis, ensure uniformity in advertising... consistency in service and standards in keeping with the high standards of Formula 1 generally,' and so on, but Bernie did not receive from APM the financial benefits of an owner. In an article in *The Economist* of 14 July 2000, investigating Bernie's companies and finances, several paragraphs are devoted to the subject of APM, comprising APM1 (a British company incorporated in 1983) and APM2 (the same company reformed for tax purposes in the Republic of Ireland in 1988).

In the article it is revealed that Swiss lawyer Luc Argand was a director and the legal owner of a share in APM; he later became a trustee of an offshore trust set up for Slavica Ecclestone to whom, in 1996, Bernie would transfer two of his companies. Although Bernie insists that the article in *The Economist* is 'rubbish', he admits to an association with Luc Argand. 'I know Luc Argand very well,' says Bernie. 'Anything to do with Switzerland we use him. We met through Jochen Rindt.' Argand had, after Jochen's death, helped to set up the Rindt Trust for the benefit of Jochen's daughter. Bernie is a trustee. Around the time that the Rindt Trust was set up, Luc Argand introduced British lawyer Stephen Mullens to Bernie, 'because I think they needed somebody in England' to deal with certain matters pertaining to the Trust. Stephen Mullens has also acted on behalf of APM. Both Argand and Mullens are directors of Excelis SA, which owns the Paul Ricard racing circuit along with the nearby hotel and, until recently, the airport. Excelis SA is ultimately owned by the Ecclestone family trust.

In the year that Bernie became vice-president of promotional affairs of the FIA, 1987, APM was given – by the FIA – the right to exploit the broadcasting rights to its championships other than Formula 1. Two years later APM passed on the administration of some of these rights to Bernie's company, International Sportsworld Communicators (ISC). Then in 1996 ISC obtained from the FIA the rights that had been held by APM; and four years later ISC was sold, according to *The Economist*, 'for an undisclosed sum, but certainly many millions of dollars' to David Richards. How much was the amount? 'It's not for me to discuss other people's business,' says Bernie. 'But it was your business too.' 'Yeah, well.' According to ISC accounts the headline figure was $28 million. As a former rally co-driver, Formula 1 team principal, head of Prodrive and part-owner of Aston Martin, this was a logical acquisition for Richards, who, like ISC's previous owner, is a successful entrepreneur. The television rights acquired with ISC have since been sold to North One Television.

The pace of Bernie's business life is maintained at a constant fever pitch as he moves with stealth among, around, through and beyond deals, displaying a financial dexterity that is breathtaking. Added to this is another skill, or perhaps a God-given talent – which is his incomparable pre-emptive capacity. To Bernie's way of thinking holidays are a punishment, any situation in which he is starved of transactions is a demoralising wasteland. His idea of recreational activity is to buy buildings, improve them, and then discard them – through sales or leases – for a profit, when the fun of rethinking the interiors and exteriors has come to an end. Buildings by the score – office blocks, shopping malls, houses and hotels – have passed through Bernie's hands. One hotel project that Bernie didn't discard is the fifteen-bedroom Olden hotel in Gstaad, Switzerland. He and Marco Piccinini bought the hotel together. Marco, who had studied architecture at university, marvelled at Bernie's ability to instantly analyse and reconfigure space, seeing not what existed but what could exist; straddling the present and the future is his natural posture, and the source of his creative ability. Bernie 'can read volumes and space,' says Marco, reflecting upon Bernie's transformation of the traffic patterns within the hotel and restaurant, he shuffled walls as easily as furniture to achieve optimum efficiency. After that he attacked the interior design choosing colours, fabrics, and staff uniforms, all contributing to a pleasing cohesion. Indeed, Bernie has an enhanced ability at 'reading' buildings; the visual impairment that he was born with doesn't enter into it. Bernie 'is very fond of properties,' adds Marco, 'not only from the merchandise point of view, he understands property, what a building can do.' The Olden cost Bernie and Marco £4 million. The refurbishment cost considerably more.

Bernie bought another building in Gstaad, a £4 million luxury chalet so that Slavica and their daughters, and Bernie himself in more recent years, could enjoy winter holidays skiing on the mountain slopes that made the resort town famous. Slavica and the girls delighted in their Swiss home, while Bernie tried to fit in a few business meetings because 'I couldn't wake up to a day without anything planned.' He regards all non-work as idleness that inevitably gnaws on his nerves, making him irritable; within twenty-four hours, a desperate man, he'd fly away for a deal-making fix. If he couldn't decamp due to Christmas or some family commitment, he played – swapping and selling over the telephone – with his car collection, part of which was housed in Gstaad, though the majority of his cars are at Biggin Hill. He eventually purchased a hangar at Biggin Hill where he also keeps his Challenger, two Learjets, two BAe 146 jets and a Falcon 2000. For travelling by sea he has a £60 million yacht called *Petara*, named after his two younger daughters.

With regard to Bernie's road car collection, he would like to acquire former dealer/driver John Coombs' 1937 BMW 328. 'That old BMW, I could maybe do a swap,' he said to John, making it sound like a favour. On the other hand there were 'about five cars' in Bernie's collection that John wanted to buy. John had his chance in October 2007, Halloween to be precise, when fifty of Bernie's cars – spanning European vintage cars to the ultimate chromed-up machinery of the Fifties and Sixties – were put on the auction block. The auction itself was a glittering event worthy of Formula 1's impresario. With a touch of James Spencer showroom razzmatazz, Bernie's elegant Marlene Dietrich of a car, a 1937 Mercedes-Benz 540K Special Roadster, was lifted to the stage, accompanied by suitably dramatic music. It went for £3,967,125, becoming one of the most expensive road-going Mercedes-Benz cars ever sold at auction. There was also a touch of nostalgia in the gull-wing Mercedes – of the type driven by Bill Whitehouse and Bexleyheath's bus-encountering Bernard Ecclestone – that attracted a bevy of bidders, as did Bernie's Ford GT40, the latter sold for a mere £938,400. Its colour? Metallic blue. These cars, in a sense, represented the early history and aspirations of the car dealer who had mastered Warren Street etiquette. And here was a quick turn-round to impress even that shrewd young man.

The history of grand prix racing is charted in Bernie's collection of racing cars. Twenty-four of them went on public display – for the first time – at the Bahrain circuit in 2009. Most notable were two 'Silver Arrows' dating from 1937: a Mercedes-Benz W125 and a rear-engined Auto Union V16. Closer to Bernie's heart are the 4½-litre Ferrari 375 V12 driven to victory in the 1951 British Grand Prix by José Froilán González and the Vanwall four-cylinder 'teardrop' cars as driven by Stirling Moss, Tony Brooks and Stuart Lewis-Evans – Bernie's close friend. And there's James Hunt's McLaren-Cosworth M23 made famous in 1976, along with the Ferrari 312T2s driven by Niki Lauda, Clay Regazzoni and Carlos

Reutemann. Special tenderness is reserved for the Brabham-Alfa Romeo BT46B (the 'fan car') and the turbocharged Brabham-BMW BT52. These cars represent Bernie's life, the ongoing story, and are, thus far, not for sale.

In London, Bernie's principal residence continued to be a transitory process of upgrade and move on until he finally settled into a five-bedroom, Georgian-style home on a quiet Chelsea street. After departing from the Thames-side penthouse with its view of the Houses of Parliament, he moved to a rented apartment in a new, high-rise block, Pier House, near the river on Oakley Street, Chelsea. He later bought this and an adjoining flat with the intention of knocking out the intervening walls to create one large apartment. Having modified the space, he sold the property to his friend Flavio Briatore, then boss of the Benetton Formula 1 team.

Frank Williams remembers visiting Bernie at the Oakley Street apartment, 'not long after I broke my neck, and it [the flat] was quite large then'. Frank's broken neck was the result of a road accident near Marseille in 1986 that left him quadriplegic, paralysed from shoulders to feet. After the accident he spent eleven weeks in hospital. Frank also remembers that Bernie visited him in the hospital, 'every Sunday after every Grand Prix for all the time I was there. When the accident occurred, Nelson Piquet had been on hand and immediately telephoned Bernie who, in turn, got hold of Professor Sid Watkins. Bernie then arranged for a plane to take Sid to Marseille, and another plane to take Frank's wife to be at her husband's bedside. Finally, after Frank's condition was made stable, in l'Hôpital Timone in Marseille, he was flown back to England, accompanied by a British anaesthetist, and then taken by ambulance to the London Hospital, also at Bernie's expense. 'He wouldn't take any money for the hire of the planes,' says Frank. 'No, I can afford to pay for it, there's no question about that,' Bernie had said, end of discussion.

Somewhere between the rental and ownership phases at Oakley Street, Bernie and his family moved into an apartment over offices that he had acquired in 1985 in Princes Gate,

Knightsbridge, opposite Hyde Park. He liked to say that he 'lived over the shop'. Bernie bought the office block from Saudi financier and arms dealer Adnan Khashoggi. The asking price for the building was £8 million; Bernie reportedly paid £7 million, but the story around the paddock said Bernie paid less than that, much less. At the time Khashoggi was supposedly nervous, fearing arrest for his alleged involvement with Philippines president Ferdinand Marcos and his wife, Imelda. The Marcoses, suspected of siphoning off hundreds of millions of dollars from the Philippines, were deposed in 1986 and fled to Hawaii, where Ferdinand died in 1989. The millions had apparently disappeared into various offshore banks and real-estate transactions.

There was more than enough reason for Bernie, in 1985, to have sniffed the delectable aroma of a ripe bargain. He met with Khashoggi and discussed purchasing the office block, concluding their conversation by supposedly opening a briefcase containing his deposit offer for the property – three and a half million, in cash. Adnan accepted the contents of the briefcase, whatever that amounted to in reality, and Bernie now owned a nine-storey office block in Knightbridge. Four years later, in 1989, Adnan Khashoggi was arrested, and in 1990 both he and Imelda Marcos were put on trial in New York. Imelda was charged with fraud and racketeering, Khashoggi with concealing the Marcoses' ownership of four buildings in the Manhattan area of New York City; both were eventually acquitted.

Meanwhile Bernie spent £2 million refurbishing his new headquarters. Outside, a skin of black glass sets it apart, making the unadorned stonework of the adjoining offices appear naked. Inside, a larger-than-life, boldly uncorseted figure, the work of a Mexican sculptor, stands guard near a comparatively demure reception desk. Other artwork – an eclectic collection of paintings, ceramics and sculpture – is displayed throughout the offices that are as blank as an uptown gallery, where it is art – and nothing else – that is meant to be noticed. But there is a taut energy, one can feel, without seeing the corridors and floors of offices where teams of lawyers, media experts, marketing geniuses, financial wizards, masters of public relations and secretarial staff are all busy spinning threads in the labyrinthine web of Bernie's businesses.

However, the whirligig tempo at Princes Gate nearly faltered as a result of the incidents that occurred at Imola during the San Marino Grand Prix weekend of Friday 29 April to Sunday 1 May 1994. Bernie's Formula 1 businesses – and the sport itself – became threatened as never before. On the Friday afternoon shortly after the start of the first qualifying session, Rubens Barrichello, driving a Jordan, hit the kerb of a chicane at 140mph, flipping his car. Marshals, arriving on the scene, just ahead of the medical team, rapidly turned the wrecked vehicle upright and as they did so Barrichello's head swung, ominously, to one side. Professor Sid Watkins cut the chinstrap of the driver's helmet, which he removed, to find the Brazilian unconscious, with profuse facial bleeding and obstructed breathing. Sid immediately thrust a plastic airway through Rubens' teeth and rotated it until he obtained an airflow. A cervical collar was then wrapped around the driver's neck and he was carefully extricated from the cockpit. From the trackside he was transported by ambulance to the circuit's medical centre and from there to the Maggiore Hospital in Bologna. During the minutes following the accident, spectators, reporters, other drivers and the paddock crews waited, anxious, fearing the worst. But, remarkably, Barrichello soon regained consciousness and, suffering only a broken nose, cuts and bruises, was able – the next morning – to return to the circuit to make his farewells before flying home to rest-up for the next race. With him went Formula 1's luck, all used up.

At 1.18pm during Saturday's qualifying session, Austrian driver Roland Ratzenburger, competing for the Simtek team, in only his third grand prix, lost control of his car and crashed at 314.9kph into a concrete retaining wall. He lay slumped and motionless in the wreckage. Less than a minute later when the helmet was removed, Sid knew, with a quick glance at the driver's eyes that 'the situation was grave. Intravenous infusion, intubation, ventilation and cardio-pulmonary resuscitation were performed,' before the ambulance took Roland to the intensive care unit at the medical centre. From there he was flown, along with a resuscitation team, in one of the larger designated helicopters, to Bologna. En route, his heart, with assistance, was kept pumping until, soon after arriving at the hospital, Roland Ratzenberger was officially declared dead.

When Roland's accident occurred Bernie had been sitting in his motorhome talking to Lotus team principal Peter Collins, while at the same time watching the qualifying on television. Seeing the accident, he immediately got up, grabbed his walkie-talkie in order to keep in touch with race control, and headed for the paddock. He knew, all too well, that it looked bad, and he knew the drill, convey a confident, business-as-usual attitude. Formula 1 would go on, no matter what. The television networks and the sponsors had paid for a guaranteed race. And, of course, work, keeping busy, would restore some level of normality, some degree of comfort.

One who was unable to continue, just then, was three times World Champion Ayrton Senna. When Ratzenberger was taken to the medical centre, Ayrton jumped out of his car and followed. There, after being told that Roland's condition was hopeless, he openly sobbed on Sid Watkins's shoulder. Ayrton had also shed tears the previous day when fellow Brazilian Rubens Barrichello was injured. He had, since 1987, advised Rubens on his career. But now he was utterly distraught.

'The wonder of the motor racing age', Ayrton Senna was an intense competitor with exacting standards which led him into famous arguments with fellow competitors, notably Alain Prost and Nigel Mansell. On the track Ayrton simply would not compromise. When asked why he drove with such an all-or-nothing swiftness, he answered: 'When I go very, very fast I feel my spirit is in front of my body.' Nor would he give an inch on his principles; or his sense of justice; or his religion – prayers and reading from the Bible eventually became part of his daily routine – and he tried very hard to shape his life to his beliefs. But more than anything there was about Ayrton Senna a humanity that he communicated to those with heart enough to understand, touching the shy ones like Rubens Barrichello and perhaps Roland Ratzenberger; certainly Bernie Ecclestone.

In 1983, twenty-three-year-old Ayrton Senna, as he was known professionally, having dropped his surname, da Silva, had tested for Brabham at the Paul Ricard circuit in France. Bernie had been informed – in a flurry of exclamations – of the young man's talent, and now, with his own eyes, he could see what all the fuss was about; Ayrton Senna was sensational. He signed him up, there and then, as the team's number two, filling the vacancy left by Riccardo Patrese. On returning to England – in Bernie's Learjet – Ayrton and Bernie talked about the future. But back at the Brabham factory another Brazilian, his number-one driver, Nelson Piquet, soon opposed the idea. Any challenge to his throne would not be tolerated, and his veto was supported by Brabham's sponsors, the Italian conglomerate, Parmalat, who wanted one of their own countrymen on the team. Bernie had no choice: it was either submit or risk losing both Piquet and Parmalat. Teo Fabi, assisted by his brother, Corrado, was handed the number two slot.

Bernie then offered Ayrton a contract for a year of testing with the inference that it would eventually lead to a place on the team. But Ayrton did not want to wait, he wanted to race in the 1984 season, and accepted an offer from Toleman. So, Ayrton Senna was never to be employed by Bernie. Instead, they became firm friends. He was always welcome in the Ecclestone household and soon won the affection of the whole family. The girls thought of him as an uncle. Likewise, the Ecclestones visited Senna's home at Angra dos Reis on the Brazilian coast. 'He was a charming, charming, charming guy, sincere about things he thought about,' says Bernie, 'and obviously still, I think the best driver there's been. Had Senna been in the same position that Michael [Schumacher] got himself into, best team, best car and not any challenge from a number two, but somebody riding shotgun, maybe Senna would have won eight world championships, we don't know.' We don't know because during the race on Sunday 1 May 1994, Ayrton Senna, driving a Williams Renault FW16B, crashed into a concrete barrier at the circuit's Tamburello corner, and died four hours later in hospital.

The previous day – when the loss of Roland had left him emotionally fraught – Senna had been urged not to drive. 'Why don't you withdraw from the race tomorrow,' Sid had pleaded. 'In fact, why don't you give it up altogether. Give it up, let's go fishing… I don't think the risk is worth continuing – pack it in.' Ayrton listened, silently, calmly. He gave Sid a 'very steady look,' and then answered: 'There are certain things over which we have no control. I cannot quit, I have to go on.'

On race day the sun was shining, the paddock was, as usual, in immaculate order, and the morning's warm-up went off without concern. But there was nothing like the heightened anticipation that usually energises the atmosphere of a grand prix. The mood at the circuit was palpably sombre. During the drivers' briefing, held at 11am, Bernie – uncharacteristically – asked the drivers to stand to observe a minute's silence in honour of Roland Ratzenberger. Ayrton, who was at the back of the room, had tears in his eyes. However, by the end of the briefing he had managed to pull himself together, and initiated a discussion on safety issues with a few of his fellow drivers. Then he secured their agreement to meet again – with all the drivers present – in Monaco, prior to the next race. After that, Ayrton went off to the Paddock Club for a chat with Williams' sponsors during which he appeared more relaxed, and enjoyed a light lunch in the Williams motor home before heading for the garage to prepare for the race.

From the front row of the grid, he appeared preoccupied, although the familiar half-smile rested upon his lips. His smile broadened when the grid was announced and the San Marino crowds cheered to the heavens at the mention of Ferrari driver Gerhard Berger, a close friend. Then, balaclava on, helmet on, visor down, he focused on the business of winning. At 2pm, right on time, the cars pulled away for the warm-up lap around the circuit and back to their grid positions. Then, the lights turned red – four seconds – then green and the cars screeched ahead towards the first turn, but almost immediately the yellow flags were waving. Pedro Lamy, in a Lotus, had smashed into the back of JJ Lehto's Benetton which had stalled on the start line. Both drivers were unhurt, but debris from the accident had scattered across the circuit and a wheel from the Benetton went into the crowd, injuring nine spectators.

The rest of the cars were continuing round the track as the pace car came out in front of the leader, Senna, to slow the pack while the wreckage from the accident was cleared. About twelve minutes later, after the clean-up was completed, the pace car pulled off the circuit and into the pit lane. Ayrton, closely followed by Michael Schumacher and Gerhard Berger, burst ahead, clocking 1 minute 24.887 seconds on his sixth lap. Then, twelve seconds into his seventh lap, turning into the Tamburello curve at nearly 200mph, his car suddenly veered to the right, off the track, and slammed heavily into a concrete wall.

When the medical team arrived, Ayrton was slumped in the cockpit. Repeating the procedures of Friday and Saturday, his chinstrap was cut, helmet removed, airway inserted. He was deeply unconscious. Sid Watkins raised Ayrton's eyelids and it was evident from the appearance of the pupils that he had suffered a massive brain injury; he was seeping blood. Ayrton was carefully lifted from the cockpit and laid on the ground, a tube was inserted through his airway, an IV infusion inserted into his arm, and a helicopter – for transport to the hospital – signalled. As the medical team worked on Ayrton's inert form, another helicopter – in which a television camera was rolling – hovered overhead, zooming in on the tragedy which was being broadcast – minute by minute by minute – to 200 million viewers on television screens across the globe. It was replayed, incessantly, for the next twenty-four hours. Ayrton Senna, who had received constant media scrutiny when he lived, was receiving it again – magnified – in death; and every front page of every major newspaper in the world carried news – and pictures – of his accident. Even in America, Formula 1's black spot, the story was everywhere reported; on the NBC Nightly News Nigel Mansell, interviewed about the tragedy said: 'I thought he was bulletproof, it hurts, it hurts big time.'

For Bernie, the loss of Ayrton Senna, like the deaths of other close friends – Bill Whitehouse, Stuart Lewis-Evans, Carlos Pace, Pedro Rodriguez and particularly Jochen Rindt – was a personal grief that he felt, profoundly, but also felt compelled to conceal, something to be internalised so as not to betray a weakness. After Ayrton had been lifted into the medical helicopter for transport to the Maggiore Hospital in Bologna, Sid Watkins was radioed by Martin Whitaker, the FIA's press delegate, to ascertain the seriousness of Senna's injuries. What Sid had said about Senna's condition was: 'It's his head.' Over the radio lines crackling with static, Martin Whitaker mistakenly heard: 'He's dead,' which he then relayed to Bernie who was in his motorhome. With Bernie was Ayrton's brother, Leonardo da Silva. Bernie thought it best to immediately tell Leonardo so that he could make some sort of preparation for the press deluge that would soon follow.

'I'm sorry, he's dead,' Bernie told him, in an even tone, forcing calmness into his words, 'but we'll only announce it after the end of the race.' A shattered Leonardo now completely went to pieces, overcome by the news and angry that the race would be restarted. What Sid had actually said was soon confirmed, but Leonardo da Silva was beyond consolation, small though it may have been. Bernie called for others to assist the young man while he headed for the paddock. It was now his duty to assert stability for he had immediately understood the wider magnitude of Senna's accident. First, he conferred with the control tower. Then he walked about the pit lane expressing confidence that Ayrton was receiving the best possible care. That the show would go on went without saying, as it always does.

Thirty-seven minutes after Ayrton Senna's crash, the race was restarted; Michael Schumacher was the victor. At the hospital in Bologna a brain scan confirmed that Ayrton's condition was beyond hope. He had major skull fractures probably due to a detached wheel and suspension assembly striking his helmet, causing his head to impact with the carbon-fibre headrest. At 6.17 that evening Ayrton Senna was officially declared dead. Bernie was on his way to Croatia to comfort Slavica and the girls who were vacationing there.

'For Formula 1, his death was as if the sun had fallen from the sky,' Gerhard Berger later wrote in the foreword to Rainer Schlegelmilch's pictorial chronicle, *The Senna Era*. It was an accurate description of the sport in the aftermath of Ayrton's accident. Not since the death of Riccardo Paletti at Montreal in 1982, some twelve years before, had there been such a tragedy during a grand prix. The death of Elio de Angelis, felt so deeply by Brabham's Gordon Murray, had happened – away from the cameras – during testing, at Paul Ricard in 1986. During the ensuing years Formula 1 – and its global television audience – had become complacent. Now the viewers – even the Vatican – roared with outrage. 'This must never be allowed to happen again,' became their universal chant. The demise of major motorsport in Italy seemed a very real possibility – and with it Ferrari. Take away the prancing horse and Formula 1 could dwindle. There was much to consider, and at the core was the continued existence of Formula 1.

Meanwhile there was Ayrton Senna's funeral to endure. Brazil was paralysed by grief, the schools were closed and three days of national mourning had begun. The plane carrying Senna's body arrived in his hometown, São Paulo, at dawn and already an estimated one million Brazilians had lined the route through the suburbs to the legislative assembly building in the city's Ibirapuera Park where the flag-draped coffin would lie in state. Downtown the streets became gridlocked in a surreal standstill, as 8,000 mourners per hour – day and night for twenty-four hours – made their way to the procession that passed by the catafalque. Brazilian television and radio networks broadcast coverage of the event round the clock. Countless members of the Formula

1 fraternity – drivers, team owners and some of the most famous names in the sport – attended the twenty-minute funeral ceremony.

Conspicuous by his absence was Max Mosley, who had chosen not to travel to Brazil for the funeral. Bernie was also missing. While the ceremony was taking place he sat in his room in São Paulo's Intercontinental Hotel, watching the coverage on television. The previous morning Ayrton's brother, Leonardo da Silva, had held a press conference in which he expressed the family's anger over the handling of the events surrounding the tragedy: the restarting of the race when, in their view, Ayrton had died upon crashing into the wall. 'The motorsport authorities are only interested in money,' he said; and he attacked the FIA for the dangers of the Imola circuit's Tamburello corner. 'If they'd taken correct precautions, my brother would be alive today.' Leonardo made it clear that neither Max nor Bernie would be welcome at the funeral. Slavica Ecclestone, accompanied by the Mayor of São Paulo, attended the ceremony without her husband. Ayrton's coffin was carried by fire engine to the Morumbi cemetery, 200,000 people – weeping, clapping – lined the route while overhead planes from the Brazilian air force's aerobatic display team made smoky patterns in the sky. There was a military salute, another service, then he was buried. By 1.30pm the family, VIPs and other mourners were gone.

A little while later Bernie made his own visit to the grave. He too was grieving, and it hurt him still more that Ayrton's family had excluded him from the funeral. After leaving the cemetery, Bernie went to see the state governor, Luiz Antonio Fleury, to explain, in detail, what had happened at Imola. One year after Ayrton Senna's death, after the emotional storms had eased, the rift between the da Silva family and Bernie mended.

For Formula 1, reparations were more complicated. The changes in the design of the cars, the design of the circuits and crash barriers, the introduction of frontal crash tests and improved medical facilities were such that it had been eight years since Elio de Angelis had been killed in an F1 car. It was a great achievement. But much remained to be done. In Monaco, following the tragedies at Imola, Austrian driver Karl Wendlinger crashed during official practice, suffering a severe head injury, and would never race seriously in Formula 1 again. Max Mosley immediately introduced changes to the cars to reduce speeds, and announced the formation of an Advisory Expert Group, headed by Professor Sid Watkins, to research and develop means of achieving greater safety in cars, circuits, barriers and spectator protection. In addition to his medical eminence, Sid is also a scientist. Tragedy has time and again resulted in improved safety, particularly since the expansion of media interest in the sport. Senna's death, however, provoked a worldwide reaction of such ferocity that Formula 1 was threatened with extinction unless safety was given the highest priority. Back in London, the publicity-shy Bernie agreed to be interviewed by David Frost on his BBC *Sunday Morning* television programme. During the interview he – and Max – discussed the immediate, post-Senna safety measures and the aims of the Advisory Expert Group.

In Italy there was another pressing issue. Italian law required that someone be held responsible for Ayrton Senna's death. State prosecutor Maurizio Passarini duly charged not one, but six individuals with manslaughter in the Senna case: They were three members of the Williams team, including Frank Williams, two Imola circuit officials and one official from the FIA. During the nine-month trial that began in 1997 Bernie was called to testify, but he didn't appear in person, evidence was delivered on his behalf by FOCA-TV personnel: Alan Woollard, previously so essential to Bernie's travel company and the Brabham team in general, now FOCA-TV's director; Eddie Baker, the company's production manager; and Andy James, the engineer.

Formula 1 was the first major sport to have onboard cameras – another of Bernie's innovations. By 1987 the talented crew at Bernie's FOCA-TV had solved the technical complexities of not only speed but also space restrictions on F1 cars. Eddie Baker recalls: 'One of the biggest changes was that we moved away from the camera being built up of lots of components spread all over the car… and built the camera all as one unit. Bernie gave me a lot of support in that, it was a very difficult task… we had to make everything that much smaller, and obviously putting a camera on any kind of lightweight, high-speed, high-vibration, high-heat environment is very difficult. That whole development programme really started back in the 1980s and more especially in the 1990s'. In 1994, at Imola, thirteen of the twenty-six cars in the race carried FOCA-TV's onboard cameras, including Senna's Williams Renault. The signal from the cars was picked up by the FOCA-TV helicopter and relayed to equipment on the track. There were only four channels, so only images from four of the thirteen onboard cameras could be recorded at any one time. It was Alan Woollard's job to switch the signal between them.

State prosecutor Passarini demanded to see the nine minutes of footage from Senna's car. It had been delivered to the Williams team within a week of the accident. Six months later, due to a misinterpretation of the request, it was given to the prosecutor who, after viewing it, contended that it was incomplete because it stopped 0.9 seconds before the crash. With Ayrton leading the race and nothing ahead of him to interest the viewers, Alan Woollard had decided to switch to the camera onboard the car of Japanese driver Ukyo Katayama. During the changeover he accidentally pressed the button for the camera on Gerhard Berger's car, then immediately corrected his mistake so that indistinct images were, momentarily, seen. But there was nothing of the crash, and although the prosecutor was dissatisfied over what he considered to be the missing 0.9 seconds, he also came to the conclusion that Bernie – previously expected to be called as a witness – was not directly involved with the investigation.

The testimonies of Woollard, Baker and James were ultimately accepted. On 16 December 1997, the trial came to an end, and the six charged with the manslaughter of Ayrton Senna were all acquitted. State prosecutor Maurizio Passarini appealed, but his appeal failed. The Williams team also appealed. The court had cited that a modification in the steering column had caused the column to break and in turn caused Ayrton's accident. In this instance the appeal was successful, the defendants and indeed all the Williams team were completely exonerated. Formula 1 racing in Italy would be allowed to continue.

In the years since Senna's death the work of the Advisory Expert Group has resulted in lives saved and injuries reduced. Every year there have been serious crashes in which either serious or fatal injuries would have been expected. In fact the most serious injuries, as mentioned previously, have been leg fractures on two occasions and one head injury. There has also been one case of minor lumbar spine fractures and, in other drivers, mild concussion – although the analysis of the cars' individual accident data recorders had shown high deceleration forces normally associated with serious head injuries. What is more, the safety measures introduced in Formula 1 were subsequently brought into use in the Formula 3000 FIA World Championship and, in 2005, measures to reduce the risk of head and neck injury were also implemented in the FIA World Rally Championship and other closed-car series as well as Formula 3.

To be sure, Ayrton Senna's legacy has been to make Formula 1 and other forms of motor racing safer, and it is hoped that automobile manufacturers will also study the FIA safety measures and adapt them, as appropriate, for use in road cars. Beyond this Ayrton's legacy is the hundreds of thousands of Brazilian children and adolescents whose lives have been transformed by the Ayrton Senna Foundation. Before his death Ayrton had wanted his fortune to be used to help impoverished youngsters achieve – through access to better education and healthcare – productive and successful lives. The Ayrton Senna Foundation, administered by his sister, Viviane Lalli Senna, has converted Ayrton's aspirations into reality. And his legacy continues in education programmes that reach not just the needy, but have also begun to nurture in the general population a sense of co-responsibility. The charity is funded by profits from products bearing Senna's image or trademark, a cartoon character, 'Senninha', and even Senna credit cards, which collectively bring in some $53 million per year. The official advisers to the Ayrton Senna Foundation are Frank Williams, Alain Prost, Gerhard Berger, Julian Jakobi (Ayrton's former manager) and Bernie. In addition, Bernie has become close to Viviane, enabling him to help the charity in 'big ways'; and he has given £150,000 to the Leonard Cheshire Foundation in São Paulo for the building of a new home for disabled people and he has also given 'a substantial donation' to the children's hospital. When asked about these hospitals, he replied:

'I've visited them, but I don't know exactly where they are. I did several hospitals.'

'How many?'

'I can't remember, it's not important.'

This is an example of his generosity and humility.

Senna's death also meant that the Formula 1 circus had lost its superstar. Alain Prost had retired at the end of 1993, so Bernie's big show, lacking drivers whose crowd appeal could be measured on the Richter scale, was barely lukewarm. And with so many fists being shaken in indignation against the sport, Bernie feared that viewers would start to turn off. An application of the tried-and-tested tonic – celebrity pizzazz – was urgently required. He got to work and spent $10 million brokering a deal for Nigel Mansell, who was racing Indycar in America, to return to Formula 1 for a few races in 1994 as Damon Hill's team-mate, filling the vacant Williams-Renault seat. Nigel went on to win in Australia, the last race of the season, but the attraction value of his occasional presence was academic because, in fact, viewer numbers following Senna'a death increased by a staggering thirty per cent. The upsurge was partially attributed to the rivalry between Damon Hill and Michael Schumacher, but the primary reason was a massive increase in new viewers whose attention – macabre or otherwise – had been drawn to Formula 1 by Senna's tragic accident. No one was more surprised than Bernie and, of course, his pockets became even heavier as a result. This latest leap in revenue to Bernie's companies again raised a few eyebrows – particularly among some of his FOCA colleagues.

The next renewal of the Concorde Agreement was signed in 1996, effective from 1997. Among other things it included a new financial arrangement – not to everyone's liking. The stirrings of disagreement were rooted in 1995 when Bernie revealed that he had invested vast sums in a multi-channel digital television company. It commenced operations in July of 1996 at the German Grand Prix at Hockenheim, following a £50-million deal with the KirchGruppe, a major German television company that owned the satellite channel DF1. Pay-per-view coverage of the Hockenheim race was broadcast by DF1 (later Premier) into Germany, Austria and Switzerland. Similar deals were subsequently made with Canal+ of France, broadcasting into Europe and South America; Telepiu of Italy; RTL Plus, also in Germany; and there were plans to introduce the service via BSkyB into Britain in 2002.

In 1995 Olivetti and Longines had closed their time-keeping operation in Formula 1, and the following year Bernie initiated an in-house time-keeping team, making significant advances in the data that was available for television graphics. A digital television company had seemed the next logical step. That same year digital television was making its first appearances around the world, and, although the numbers of broadcasters were few, the opportunity for pay-per-view television – through digital transmission – had started to become a reality. Bernie has always been entranced by technology and its possibilities, now it was bordering on an obsession. At the Belgian Grand Prix he set up a test to create a multi-channel feed. The success of this experiment led to the contract with DF1. In 1996 he spent some £35 million to build a broadcast centre at Biggin Hill. The facility integrated seven in-house cameras with those of the international feed to produce a multi-channel programme specifically for digital television.

By 1997, Bernie invested even more money to build a complete independent broadcast system, which meant that the cameras for the digital feed were entirely separate from the cameras for the international, free, over-the-air feed. Thus 1997 was, effectively, the first year of digital programming in Formula 1. The 300-tonne mobile production centre was moved from race to race by twenty-seven metallic grey Mercedes trucks lined up in the paddock like a platoon of Grenadier Guards for inspection, and – reminiscent of the motorcycles displayed nearly fifty years earlier at Compton & Ecclestone – in order according to the numbers on their license plates. The trucks carried a cargo of about 100 containers which, dismantled, created the external walls for the temporary, air-conditioned broadcast facility called 'Bakersville' after the man responsible for it, Eddie Baker, along with another 250 staff. Eddie has actually worked for Bernie since 1978, having moved from Brabham to FOCA-TV to the digital television company.

Bakersville was transported to overseas races by three 747 jumbo jets. Eddie, along with the rest of the principal production crew, travelled to races in comfort aboard Bernie's BAe 146 jet; the irregularities of commercial airlines cannot be countenanced in the exacting world of television. And after all, Bernie's digital team had created the most sophisticated, highest quality television feed for any kind of sports programming then in existence, a mini technological revolution.

The greater revolution that Bernie brought to sports broadcasting, overall, was an accumulative process begun back in the early Eighties when he brought cohesive television broadcasting to Formula 1 in terms of host broadcasters. Later on he created a special technical team producing more sophisticated onboard cameras as mentioned before, followed by the time-keeping operation and advances in television graphics. Then, in 1996/7, he introduced to Formula 1 the multi-channel digital feed. Added to these technological advances was the huge increase in television viewing numbers, particularly following Ayrton Senna's death. For example, in 1997 Britain's ITV paid £30 million for a contract that expired in 2005, ten times the amount previously paid by the BBC for the rights to broadcast Formula 1. In total 120 broadcasters have contracts with Bernie to show grands prix. But Bernie's success was contributing to a certain amount of anxiety on the part of some team principals who wanted a greater share of the profits; and, it was thought, Bernie was taking advantage of an opportunity that they had given him.

Then there was the matter of what was perceived to be his turncoat entrenchment at the Place de la Concorde, allowing him to seize the financial upper hand. Grumbling among the teams – always a Formula 1 tradition – now assumed a different character, and it had Bernie's name on it. In this latest Concorde Agreement, the FIA's commercial rights were directly transferred – in a fifteen-year lease – to Formula One Management, Bernie's company, whereas in previous Concorde Agreements the rights were licensed to FOCA, who in turn subcontracted them to Bernie, personally, or to his company, Formula One Promotions and Administration (FOPA), which also kept the promoters' fees.

Ken Tyrrell, Frank Williams and Ron Dennis refused to sign the new agreement. Ron Dennis explains: 'Everybody I know who has ever had any dealings with Bernie feels that, at the end of the day, you've been taken to a point beyond what I would call the comfort zone. When you reflect on a deal with Bernie you feel that he's managed to squeeze that extra five per cent out of you to create the rub, but you never feel that warmth of a fair deal. I know that he does many great things for many people, but I wish he'd be a little more appreciative of the extensive contribution that all the teams have made to building Formula 1... He's always done a wonderful job of orchestrating, but I don't think he's ever appreciated, properly, that a great conductor can only be there if he has great musicians, and I think the role of the teams has been that of the musicians. Why, when you've made such a phenomenal success of Formula 1, and taken such tremendous commercial gain from it, why continue to squeeze so hard? Bernie effectively stole Formula 1 from us. He stole it by concealing from the teams the significant increases that were coming to them as a result of better television contracts. He used this commercial benefit to persuade the teams to accept a contract [Concorde Agreement] that eliminated them from the passing of rights as had previously existed. Not having a team put him in that position. The way he swerved the situation, I mean some people would say it was brilliant, but in essence it was pretty deceitful because the teams were trying to say "Hold on, Bernie, we own these rights".'

But Bernie held the trump card – Ferrari. 'Ferrari broke ranks and did a deal with Bernie,' adds Ron. 'The moment that Bernie had Ferrari in his pocket, some of the other teams capitulated, and it ended up with three teams outside the Concorde Agreement.' These teams were McLaren, Williams and Tyrrell. Max Mosley, in his capacity as president of the FIA, obtained the approval of the World Council and decreed that the new agreement could be implemented without the signatures of the recalcitrant three, important though they were. The three teams would, however, be allowed to take part in the championship series, albeit with less income – and political power – if eighty per cent of the other signatory teams (eight) agreed. The new Concorde Agreement also gave the signatory teams a greater say in the sporting and technical regulations of Formula 1 by allowing for changes to be made if eighty per cent of the teams were in agreement. Furthermore, the top five signatory teams – according to the previous year's World Championship – were given votes on the Formula One Commission, one of the most powerful political entities in the sport. The team that had appeared in the greatest number of World Championships since time immemorial – Ferrari – was also given a vote.

Bernie, slipping into the shoes of 'the Old Man', Enzo Ferrari, held a meeting at the Ferrari headquarters in Maranello to discuss the possibility of a compromise with the three outsiders. They weren't actually at the meeting, but Bernie, encouraged by a previous discussion with Ron Dennis and Frank Williams, spoke on behalf of his old comrades, explaining the compromise that they had put to him. By the time that the Maranello meeting was finished, the compromise proposals – undisclosed – had been accepted. But for Bernie it had two important outcomes. First, he continued to maintain a seat on the newly composed Formula One Commission alongside Max Mosley (four promoters, two sponsors and six team representatives including Marco Piccinini from Ferrari) and second, he himself, became a signatory of the Concorde Agreement.

But, alas, there were to be no celebrations of peace. Indeed, the squabble was set to continue across a wider battleground, continuously reignited by the flow of money. Of course, the teams' share of the commercial revenue had, through Bernie's efforts and the power they had entrusted in him, made 'everybody', says Ron, extremely rich, and there were certainly more sponsorship opportunities available. But now their expectations had been raised. Frank Williams acknowledges Bernie's contribution in transforming the sport and the teams' futures. 'Bernie generally attracted good money because of his power in FOCA, but all the time his focus was on making Formula 1 a very rich business which he felt he should control since he had half created it. Principally created it and pushed it towards new horizons.'

But then there was the irksome business of the promotions revenue – the teams weren't getting any. 'It's only when things started to look good and I invested the money and it started to work that they thought maybe they should have done it,' says Bernie, and 'yeah, if people couldn't make a circuit work, we'd [Bernie's company] take it over and run it and put it in good condition and give it back to them.' Back in the late Eighties revenue received by Bernie's companies from promotions and organisers' fees was estimated to be around £120 million per annum. In addition there was the money paid to Bernie's Formula One Administration (FOA) by Paddy McNally's Allsport – under the APM umbrella. Paddy says, 'I had a monthly contract with them [FOA] and it was a massive contract.' He was unwilling to specify the amount in figures, preferring adjectives, reiterating 'massive' and then 'very substantial'. Over to Bernie.

So, 'Bernie, how much did the company or companies represented by Paddy McNally pay to FOA?'

'We looked at buying Allsport [for £100 million] a while ago.'

'That's nice, but how much?'

'Big fee.'

'Wouldn't you like to say how much?'

'Rather not!'

By now Bernie is grinning to his ears and showing his teeth – like the Cheshire Cat perched above a crossroads in Wonderland.

CHAPTER 14

SMOKE ALARM

In February 1980 Essex Petroleum, sponsors of Colin Chapman's Formula 1 Lotus team, held a dinner extravaganza for a thousand guests at London's Royal Albert Hall to introduce the Essex-Lotus 86. Hocus-pocus, the car levitated above the stage amid clouds of dry ice while the plush *voce fortissimo* of Shirley Bassey cloaked the hall with song. Prime Minister Margaret Thatcher popped by for pre-dinner cocktails, and Brabham team manager Herbie Blash, also among the one thousand, was introduced to the Prime Minister by her son, Mark, who was clad in a white dinner jacket blotched with red wine. Mark Thatcher was then pursuing a career in motor racing and his attendance at various motorsport gatherings and official dinners was part of the job. Herbie appreciated Mark's conviviality in making the introduction to Mrs Thatcher so he politely declined to mention that this was the second time they had been introduced. The Prime Minister, for her part, appeared to have forgotten the previous occasion, but she distinctly recalled the times she had met and conversed with Herbie's boss, Bernie Ecclestone. 'I'm pleased he's not involved in politics!' she said, before the talk moved on. 'For me, that was maybe one of the highest accolades that Bernie could ever have,' says Herbie, still relishing the memory. Seventeen years later it would be politics or, more specifically, a political scandal that would be linked forever more with Bernie – the so-called 'Ecclestone Affair'.

In January 1997, during the run-up to the general election, Bernie donated £1 million to the Labour Party – 'no strings attached'. In which case it should have been a colourless story not worth printing, or at most a back-pages gap-filler. After all, it was commonplace for the Tories to receive donations of this size – or considerably larger. But the gesture turned into a front-page drama that wouldn't go away when the Government, under the new Prime Minister, Tony Blair, suddenly decided to renege on its election manifesto commitment to ban, comprehensively, tobacco advertising. Instead, Formula 1 was made exempt from the proposed legislation. The pedantically inclined argued that Labour's pledge had not specified a ban on tobacco sponsorship in sport, but that didn't change the outcome. A few days later Bernie's donation became known, making his generosity look suspect. 'Bribery!' shouted the news-writers. 'Cash for favours!' shouted the Tories. 'We demand an inquiry!' shouted Old Labour.

It all began early in 1996 when Tony Blair's chief of staff, Jonathan Powell, contacted David Ward, previously an aide to former Labour leader John Smith, and who, after John Smith's death in 1994, became the Brussels director of the FIA and, later, director general of the FIA Foundation. Jonathan Powell asked Ward if, in his opinion, Bernie could be approached to make a sizeable donation to the Labour Party. Ward explained that the best way to get to Bernie was through Max – himself a financial donor to Labour although his contributions were comparatively modest. Max had already become well-acquainted with the Labour leadership, beginning with John Smith in 1993 and, subsequently, with Tony Blair, whom he invited to the British Grand Prix at Silverstone in July 1996. The then would-be Prime Minister and his family were invited to Bernie's circuit headquarters, the dark metallic-grey motor home parked at the entrance to the paddock, where they chatted for about fifteen minutes.

Mr Blair's interest in Bernie was very likely twofold – income and an endorsement from big business. In the matter of income, the earnings of the publicity-shy former used car dealer from Bexleyheath were becoming widely discussed. And with good reason, for in the tax year to March 1996 his salary was reported to be £54.9 million. 'Bernie Ecclestone' was becoming a synonym for wealth. Labour's election war-chest barely jingled compared to that of the Conservatives. So New Labour fund-raisers began focusing their efforts, rather aggressively, on that segment of society so often associated with the Tories, big business, and the more entrepreneurial the better. Bernie Ecclestone naturally came to mind. Mr Blair also wanted to reduce his party's dependence on donations from the trade unions, and an association with big business underscored New Labour's changing ideology.

In January 1997, six months after the Silverstone get-together, Bernie handed Labour the £1 million. It was his way of showing approval for the party's decision not to put up income taxes at the top rate. Actually, Bernie had been reluctant to make the donation. Max had tried to persuade him and, when that failed, Max teased, 'Your friend Tony Blair saved you millions.' Bernie gave instructions to issue the cheque. The following May, the Labour Party won the general election by a landslide, and Labour ministers, buoyed by victory, were eager to put in train their election manifesto pledges. Health Secretary Frank Dobson, addressing the annual conference of the Royal College of Nursing on 19 May, stated that 'sponsorship is a form of tobacco advertising' and would therefore be outlawed. But there was only limited parliamentary time available during that first year's legislative programme; precedence had to be given to larger issues and the tobacco advertising ban was not among them. The Ministry of Health, probably frustrated at the inevitable delay, turned to Brussels.

Back in 1985, the European Economic Community (EEC), as it was then called, began to seriously consider tobacco product regulation as a means of fighting tobacco-related illnesses. The European Council of Ministers, the legislative body of the EEC, approved a programme called 'Europe Against Cancer', which led to a series of Directives (binding measures to be implemented by all member states) designed to regulate tobacco consumption. In 1989, the Council proposed a draft Directive prohibiting tobacco advertising and sponsorship. This was met with a full-scale lobbying campaign by the tobacco industry – resulting in modifications and amendments to the Directive until, in 1991, it was blocked from passage. In 1997, the Directive was being reintroduced and now specifically included the area of sports sponsorship, with provision for advertising tobacco products from 'third countries' – those outside the European Union (EU), as it was now called. It gave Labour the means to obtain early action on tobacco legislation, but this latest proposal was likely to trigger a process that was self-defeating.

In Britain a ban on cigarette advertising on television had existed since 1965, and countries in Europe and elsewhere followed suit. In order to keep their brands on television, cigarette companies started to sponsor sports. In 1997, everyone agreed that smoking was damaging to health, so a tobacco advertising ban across the EU was attractive to all parties apart from the tobacco industry. However, to pursue the removal of sports sponsorship would destabilise competitions that relied on income from tobacco sponsors – not only motor racing, but sports such as ice hockey, greyhound racing, motorcycle racing, rugby, billiards and snooker. Embassy cigarettes, for example, had supported the snooker championship for twenty years. Furthermore, the proposed Directive became nonsensical when applied to global sports – particularly Formula 1. The reason was simple: you can't stop people from watching television. If sponsorship by tobacco companies were immediately banned at circuits in Europe, the companies would move their investment to circuits in Asia, the Pacific and South America – countries where, in any case, they wished to increase their sales. The television audience would follow the circuits overseas, along with the unrestricted tobacco advertising being picked up by television cameras. As a result Formula 1 fans, young and old, would be exposed to more tobacco advertising rather than less. Technology existed to block certain advertisements as they appeared, and there was legislation in place that enabled races to be rebroadcast without tobacco advertising, but these measures were considered either too costly or too impractical. While it was true that demand for foreign circuits made it inevitable that the number of circuits outside Europe would increase, in 1997 twelve (including Hungary) out of seventeen Formula 1 Grands Prix were still held in Europe. Time was needed to manage the logistics of removing tobacco sponsorship from sport, particularly Formula 1.

And there was another consequence of hasty action – job losses. The Royal Automobile Club estimated that 50,000 people were then employed in the motorsport industry in Britain, with around 8,000 involved in the supply side of Formula 1. Harder to calculate was the financial benefit of synergy between Formula 1 and myriad associated businesses. What's more, the motorsport industry had become an institution with a history stretching back to the days of Charles and John Cooper. By 1997 it had grown to the point where British companies controlled ninety per cent of race car manufacturing worldwide, with a turnover estimated at £1.5 billion. Bernie puts it his own way: 'Well, I mean, this country has always been conceived as the home of the industry because basically most of the teams are there [Britain], most of the things have come out of there, even the teams that have raced abroad have got British input, and I'm English, living in England – at the moment – so I suppose that's it. What's it done for the country? That's exactly what it's done, it's done a lot for the industry. But it hasn't done much for us, the country, done nothing.'

To the Formula 1 teams alone, sponsors such as Philip Morris, Benson & Hedges and British American Tobacco (BAT) contributed around $200 to $300 million. Thus any possibility of compromising the status of the industry by rushing to adopt the EU Directive in the – faulty – belief that it would serve to carry out Labour's election pledge was irresponsible. It would result in job losses along with the loss of teams and circuits, threatening the viability of race car manufacturing and countless related businesses. The best way forward was a phased withdrawal carried out over several years.

How many years? When Luxembourg assumed the

Presidency of the Council of the European Union in July 1997, a compromise was added to the proposed Directive, allowing for a three-year 'derogation' period. But this was scarcely long enough. Engineers, designers and businessmen with an eye to the future would waste no time in moving to less restricted countries, so the threat to the existence of teams and circuits on the Continent as well as in Britain remained the same. While in the short-term the removal of tobacco sponsors' logos at races held in EU member countries was ineffective due to the transmission of international events, it was expected that, in the long-term, non-tobacco sponsors would come on stream as the number of Bernie's television deals continued to increase and, with them, the opportunity for the worldwide display of their advertisements. The commercial branch of Formula 1, Bernie's territory, was about to be floated on the stock market. Much of the resulting revenue was to be ploughed into the further expansion of digital television – with its company based in the UK – and into expanding coverage. Along the way a range of companies would, it was anticipated, be clamouring to advertise their wares, but a complete changeover from tobacco sponsors could not realistically occur within three years or even six years – the aggregate period of time allowed for existing sponsorship of certain global sports – before the Directive became law. A longer period of grace was more realistic.

That said, there was 'no problem at all' with a domestic Bill against tobacco advertising and sponsorship. At televised sporting events, such as the British Grand Prix, a ban had existed – on a voluntary basis – since the mid-Eighties, and only the colour schemes of tobacco companies were displayed. This was also the case at races held in Germany and France. All that was needed was to 'turn the voluntary agreement into legislation', according to an FIA official.

With regard to the proposed EU Directive, Max and Bernie felt that the phased approach – apart from anything else – was more feasible. When a tobacco ban had suddenly been implemented in France, it created difficulties, such as when the Williams-Renault team, in 1992, had been fined a combined

FF35 million for displaying on its cars the Camel cigarettes logo during Grands Prix in Japan and Australia. The races were broadcast on French television and thus in violation of France's anti-smoking legislation. The law in France had to be amended to exempt the promotion of tobacco in motorsport events held outside the country. With races scattered across the globe, a ban on tobacco sponsorship and advertising became futile. Unless, that is, the ban was enforced worldwide. The only practical and fair solution was 'a phased withdrawal' – aiming towards a worldwide ban. That is what the FIA and Bernie wanted and attempted to achieve.

During the autumn of 1997, FIA officials wrote to all the European Union members proposing a worldwide phased withdrawal, beginning with the removal of tobacco company logos from drivers' overalls and the clothing of the pit crews, followed by trackside advertising and, eventually, the cars. They then focused upon the political decision-makers in the European countries that hosted grands prix, while Max, along with Ron Dennis and Frank Williams, argued Formula 1's case with members of the House of Lords. Their lobbying campaign continued with Max and David Ward engaging in discussions with the Minister of State for Public Health, Tessa Jowell, whose position was staunchly anti-tobacco, and with Sports Minister Tony Banks. Max and Bernie then sought support from the Italian Prime Minister, Romano Prodi, and from German Chancellor Helmut Kohl who had, in recent years, become a close friend of Bernie's. During all of their discussions the FIA and Bernie never asked for any sort of unique arrangement in the handling of the tobacco issue – or anything outside Labour's manifesto pledge as they saw it. Indeed, they considered it a matter of finding a sensible way forward.

With that in mind, on 16 October 1997, Bernie and Max, along with David Ward, attended a meeting with Tony Blair at Downing Street. Jonathan Powell was also there, and the Prime Minister's private secretary, who took handwritten notes that, with subsequent recollections, were later made public. Meeting with politicians is not Bernie's idea of a good time. However, as a representative of Britain's Formula 1 industry he felt duty-bound to put the case before the Prime Minister for a long-term phased withdrawal. It seems the Prime Minister was generally of the same opinion as he duly listened to what Bernie, David Ward and Max had to say. During their discussion, lasting about twenty minutes, Max began by stating: '[The] Proposals for [an] EU Directive put forward by [the] Luxembourg Presidency make no sense. If Formula 1 leaves Europe, you will get more, not less sponsorship on TV. A perverse consequence... national legislation [is] better.' There was 'great pressure for Formula 1 to move to [the] Far East', and he ran through a list of countries wanting a Grand Prix, adding: 'Tobacco companies [are] building circuits.' Finally, Max pointed out that he 'had been to see Tessa Jowell and Tony Banks', but was 'not sure [they had] understood'. The Prime Minister put forward his own position by saying that while he did not 'need persuading about the basic case in favour of Formula 1', he was 'also in favour of a ban on tobacco ads'. It seems the private secretary was then asked why the Government was 'pursuing a Directive and not national legislation'. To which he responded: 'Because it is [the] best way of getting [a] ban quickly.' Bernie now joined the conversation: '[The] FIA has made Formula 1 very high-tech. If tobacco money goes...' this would be lost. He went on to say that he had 'put a lot of effort into developing TV. Digital technology [is] coming. TV will go with the races.' When asked if alternative sponsors such as car manufacturers could be found, he responded 'no', saying that they did not have the resources. It was explained by the private secretary that the European Directive had a four-year phase-in. '[It] would not come into effect for another two years, so six or so in all.' Bernie informed them he had 'met Kohl, in Luxembourg, and Prodi. They agree with us, it is [an] impractical Directive and will say so.' 'Why do other countries not see the problem?' asked the Prime Minister. Bernie and David Ward took it in turns to respond, which the notes recall as follows: 'Some of them do, which is why we cannot understand why they are arguing for the

Directive. Italy had [a] ban in place, but it did not stop [the] Grand Prix taking place. At the beginning of [the] Grand Prix weekend the organisers paid a fine of about $10,000 and that was the end of it.' The private secretary pointed out the 'hard stance' taken by health ministers in other countries. David Ward then queried the position with regard to other sports such as motorcycling. The Prime Minister seemed concerned about this: 'Do other sports have the same scale of dependence?' There followed a 'general discussion'. 'Some did have tobacco sponsorship, but not on the same scale.' Mr Blair then brought the discussion to a close. He thanked them for coming to the meeting, and said they recognised the problems and 'would think about' what had been discussed.

What is not recorded in the notes of 16 October is that both Max and David Ward had reiterated a point previously put to the Prime Minister in a letter: the proposed Directive was 'almost certainly illegal under EU law'. It would be better for the Government to introduce domestic policy and thereby keep its election manifesto pledge. That meeting of 16 October was their last dialogue with the Government.

Bernie loves to prevaricate. When asked about the substance of his meetings with the Prime Mininster at Silverstone and Downing Street, he casually responds, 'The state of the economy, religion, everything, open and frank discussions.'

'Did you want a change in policy?'

'What policy?'

'The policy to ban tobacco advertising in sport.'

'Did I want that? Oh, if they wanted to do that, I'm happy with it, I'm not controversial, I'll sort of go along with what people want [rather] than try to fight people.'

The day after the Downing Street meeting, the Prime Minister wrote to Tessa Jowell. When later being interviewed by John Humphrys during the BBC's *On the Record*, Mr Blair paraphrased the essence of his letter: the Government needed to 'protect the position of sports in general and Formula 1 in particular.' Whatever his exact words to the Health Minister, by 4 November she was putting the Government's argument to Brussels where it was regarded as 'a disaster, a complete

U-turn. This could spell the end of the Directive, obliging the Commission to withdraw the proposal.' Even so, the next day it was announced in Britain that Formula 1 would be exempt from the ban on tobacco advertising and sponsorship – permanently. The news came 'without warning' says David Ward, and neither Bernie nor Max were pleased. They had not asked for – nor wanted – a total exemption, but rather a phased reduction carried out over a period of time long enough to allow the teams to acquire alternative sponsorship. The Government had misunderstood their lobbying and, what is more, the decision would be seen as special treatment, leaving other sports – including other types of FIA World Championship motorsport – out in the cold.

Reporters were off at a dust-churning gallop for the story behind the story. Top of the list was the obvious – Tessa Jowell. Wasn't her husband, David Mills, connected with Formula 1? He was. Mills had been a non-executive director of a company that ran the Benetton racing team. The previous May he had resigned. Ms Jowell, acting with probity, had been quite open about her husband's Benetton connections and had sought the appropriate clearance before becoming involved in the tobacco-advertising proceedings. End of story. No matter, more tantalising pickings were available – in the form of large donations. It was known that in the past Bernie had given mega-money to the Conservative party, but then Bernie became 'fed-up' with Prime Minister John Major. He had, said Bernie, 'lost the plot', and consequently Mr Ecclestone dried up as a source of Conservative campaign funding.

Tony Blair, meanwhile, had been making political capital, accusing Major's Government of deferring to the 'squalid monetary interests of the Conservative Party'. New Labour, by comparison, would be 'purer than pure' when they came to power. So it is not surprising that while questions were being asked about financial donations, it was purportedly a member of the Conservative Party who seized the opportunity by saying 'Bernie Ecclestone is now a Labour donor', or similar words. Of course this titbit, following on the heels of the U-turn in Labour's tobacco policy, seemed too coincidental. *The Sunday*

Telegraph reporter Tom Baldwin started making enquiries about Bernie's donation, and the other broadsheets followed his lead. A little more digging would reveal that Bernie had met with Prime Minister Tony Blair twenty days before the announcement exempting Formula 1. All the ingredients for a major political scandal were now ripened to perfection.

Panic reigned in the Labour Party as they scratched around for ways to mitigate the inevitable mud-slinging. The Prime Minister's chief press secretary, Alastair Campbell, favoured revealing the amount of Bernie's donation, getting it out and over with. The Minister Without Portfolio, Peter Mandelson, felt otherwise, as did the Prime Minister. When political correspondents became pressing in their questions about a possible Ecclestone donation, they were told the Labour Party had changed finance directors, therefore details of donations were difficult to verify. Anyway, all donations over £5,000 would be revealed when the Party's accounts were made public – nine months hence. For extra measure the reporters were given a gentle reminder concerning Bernie's fondness for litigation. The next day in *The Sunday Telegraph*, the existence of the donation was questioned, squeezing the Prime Minister to set the record straight.

Two days earlier the inner circle at Downing Street had chosen the path of righteousness, putting the matter before the Committee on Standards in Public Life. In their letter to the Committee's chairman, Sir Patrick Neill (later Lord Neill of Bladen), it was mentioned that the Labour Party had received 'a substantial donation' from Bernie, and it was explained why they had sought an exemption for Formula 1. But the decision was not 'in any way influenced by Mr Ecclestone's contribution some months before'. This, however, was not the point upon which they were seeking clarification. The letter went on to state that 'Mr Ecclestone has, since the election, offered a further donation' (thought to be around £500,000) and what the Prime Minister wished to be advised upon – 'in the light of our approach to the Directive and to avoid any possible appearance of conflict of interest' – was whether the second donation 'may be properly accepted'.

Bernie's position on the second donation is emphatic: 'False! I wasn't going to give them another penny but they would have taken it if I offered it to them!' It seems Labour fund-raisers had had expectations since the previous May that Bernie would make an additional contribution to their coffers. Sir Patrick advised the Government not to pursue the second donation and, with regard to the larger donation (he didn't know the amount), said it should be returned in order to avoid 'even the appearance of undue influence on policy'. This must have come as unwelcome advice as the £1 million had, by then, been spent. What's more, by seeking guidance from Sir Patrick Neill and his Committee, the Government had achieved the very circumstance they had wished to avoid – making Bernie's donation appear tainted.

Of course reporters were just as quick to hammer on Bernie's door. His lawyers issued a statement denying – even though it was blatantly wrong – that their client, Mr Ecclestone, was a Labour donor. Bernie was determined to honour a pact of silence, the details of which were revealed in *The Sunday Times* nearly three years later. 'If someone puts me up against the wall with a machine gun, I will not confirm or deny anything about the donation,' he said. 'They said "okay, okay, we will do the same".' The Labour Party, however, became fairly relaxed about the oath, and with Sir Patrick Neill's advice in hand they confirmed they had received a donation from Mr Ecclestone – of over £5,000. And in accordance with Sir Patrick's advice, the money would be given back. They had no choice but to come clean. Not squeaky-clean, mind you, as it was hoped that by revealing a portion of the truth they would satisfy the now ravenous media.

What the Government actually achieved by the revelation was to make an enemy of a friend. Bernie's blood boiled, as it does when he senses he is being treated unfairly. If Labour were going to be cagey about the amount of money they had received, then he would take it upon himself to handle the matter, even if it contradicted his lawyers' statement. The whole business was becoming absurd. After five days of evasion by the Government, Bernie, when queried, told motor racing journalists that he had given Labour £1 million. Of course, he wasn't happy about revealing anything to do with his financial affairs, for his contributions – to whatever cause – were not for public consumption. Not then. He *had* agreed that his name could appear in the party's accounts, in October 1998, but Downing Street was jumping the gun and Bernie wasn't prepared. 'I was hung out to dry,' he told reporters. 'It was third-rate behaviour by a bunch of clowns.'

Bernie's verbal fisticuffs barely registered at Downing Street, where the Prime Minister's advisors ruminated over enquiries – now laced with implications that could bring about Mr Blair's resignation. The Opposition Health spokesman, John Maples, had tabled a parliamentary question asking the Prime Minister when he had informed the Secretary of State for Health, Frank Dobson, about 'the decision to exempt Formula 1 from the proposed ban on tobacco sponsorship'. Should there be an investigation into the 'disturbing story of an apparent ministerial conflict of interest?' On 12 November the Prime Minister told the House of Commons 'at the beginning of last week [3 November] there was the decision to seek a specific exemption for Formula 1, and then to seek a worldwide voluntary agreement so as to avoid Grands Prix in other countries being shown here without restriction. Once that route was chosen, I recognised that there was obviously an appearance of conflict of interest.' The Government had sought Sir Patrick's Neill's advice. 'He gave it; we followed it to the letter… Can anyone imagine the Tory party ever returning a donation?' John Maples, in answer to his earlier question, was referred to the Prime Minister's statement. Conservative MP William Hague pointed out that leading governing bodies of sports other than Formula 1 were feeling ill-treated. Was the Prime Minister happy to meet with them 'on the same basis as his meeting with Formula 1?' Of course he was.

Later that afternoon Labour's highly respected Director of Communications, David Hill, was instructed to hold a briefing. He explained to journalists that the decision to exempt Formula 1 had been made – collectively – between Ministers and Mr Blair, during 24 and 31 October. Never mind about the time discrepancy, he was ready with a chronology of events including the fact that Frank Dobson, as early as 17 July, had written to the Prime Minister outlining a strategy to the EU Directive, which included a suggestion that the Government 'must keep options open on sport'. By 14 October Dobson was pointing out the need 'to seek a longer transitional period for F1'. On 24 October Health Minister Tessa Jowell, who had been taking the lead on this issue along with her boss Frank Dobson, set out various options 'for helping Formula 1'. The purpose of the briefing was 'to dispel any misapprehensions that the decision to exempt Formula One was tied to the meeting the Prime Minister had with Ecclestone on 16 October.'

The purpose of the briefing failed. The Government's media strategy was in tatters and the Prime Ministers's reputation was getting into a similar condition – giving impetus to the controversy that now raged at fever pitch. It remained centred upon a series of problems involving timing – the backbone of this saga from start to finish. These comprised: the wisdom of meeting with Bernie (after his massive donation) when it was likely he would discuss proposed legislation that had a direct bearing on his business interests; the lack of a formal record of that meeting (which also occurred at a time when they were seeking a second donation); the Government's decision to exempt Formula 1 (after the meeting but before seeking guidance on the propriety of the donations from the Committee on Public Standards in Public Life, along with the fact that they only wrote to the Committee after reporters had started asking questions); and the dribbling-out of information, one partial piece at a time, leading to the appearance of dissembling. This, in turn, formed the basis of John Humphrys' soon-to-be famous interview with Prime Minister Tony Blair during the BBC's *On The Record* programme of 17 November 1997. By this time Mr Blair felt compelled to apologise for his handling of the affair. In a drawing room setting at Chequers, Mr Blair's eyes – fawn-like – glistened. He was 'hurt and upset' by suggestions that he had been influenced by Bernie's million, and hoped that people realised he would never do anything improper. 'I'm a pretty straight sort of guy,' he said. He was happy 'to supply Sir Patrick Neill with a list of donations and the amount', provided 'the Conservatives do it as well'. He was even willing, under the same arrangement, to have, say 'a five thousand limit' on the amount. The country could rest assured he remained 'the same person they believed in' at the general election.

But while his interview may have placated the general public, rumblings continued within the Government over what was seen to be a policy U-turn. Two members of Labour's National Executive Committee, Ken Livingstone and Diane Abbott, called for an independent inquiry. Ms Abbott 'wanted to know who took what decision, when, because the whole party has been compromised, but the party as a whole has not been involved in this'. Mr Livingstone believed that 'only an investigation like the "arms for Iraq" hearing' would remove suspicion surrounding the change in policy. Suspicion was equally rife among members of the Health Select Committee, its chairman, David Hinchliffe maintaining 'the Government have had the wool pulled over their eyes by Formula 1'. Norman Baker, a Liberal Democrat member of the Select Committee on European Legislation, had noticed that Ms Jowell was 'uncomfortable' with the exemption. Had she been the instrument of the Prime Minister's bidding? Both committees felt that Formula 1 'should be placed under the same pressure as other sports to seek alternative sponsorship'. Besides, there was 'no very exacting assessment' of sport's – any sport's – dependence on tobacco sponsorship. As to the number of jobs that would be lost, Ms Jowell admitted: 'It's very difficult to isolate a precise number... above 8,000.' The Department for Trade and Industry believed it was 'unlikely that if F1 should leave the UK there would be an immediate effect on industry as a whole.' There were many who believed that Max and Bernie were pawns of the powerful tobacco industry, and now this belief was extending to Tony Blair. One of Labour's worst weeks in power was becoming one of its worst months, even two months.

On 3 December, Tessa Jowell told a House of Commons Committee that rather than a permanent exemption she would press for Formula 1 to be excluded from the tobacco advertising ban for only a few more years – beyond the three (effectively six) in the draft Directive. The next day, in Brussels, she was arguing for a ten-year exclusion for Formula 1. This was rejected, and it was only after heated negotiations that a compromise could be reached: Formula 1 would be given a period of grace of nearly nine years, taking the deadline to 1 October 2006.

Meanwhile, the teams were being flooded with data from their tobacco sponsors demonstrating that advertising in Formula 1 was about brand loyalty, not about attracting smokers. This distinction prompted Max, in March 1998, to announce that the FIA would act immediately to remove tobacco advertising and sponsorship from Formula 1 if evidence were presented demonstrating a direct link between tobacco advertising and smoking; such evidence could lead to a worldwide ban as early as 2002. It could even be included in the Concorde Agreement, negotiated in 1997 and soon to be signed. The FIA also wrote to the Ministers of Health in every country hosting a grand prix to request evidence 'that young people, and people who otherwise would not have smoked, took up smoking as a result of the promotional activities of the sponsored teams in Formula 1'.

The results received by the FIA were disappointing – to say the least – as only two governments, Germany and the UK, made the effort to respond. The Concorde Agreement, lacking the signatures of Frank Williams, Ron Dennis and Ken Tyrrell, had already become a highly inflammable item – with or without cigarettes. It was, however, finally resolved and all the teams signed the Agreement in May 1998. The tobacco issue was not included. 'The 2002 date has slipped with the signing of the 1998 Concorde Agreement,' said Max, 'which prevents us from introducing such a ban before 2006.' Bernie was once more emphatic: 'If I honestly believed tobacco advertising made people smoke, I would definitely be saying it should be banned. But, without any shadow of a doubt, nobody has ever proved that it does. Maybe it makes people loyal to a brand or they change brands, but it certainly does not make people smoke.'

'And you think Labour changed their policy because...?'

'I think they thought it was the right thing to do.'

In July 1998, the European Union adopted the Directive on advertising and sponsorship of tobacco products, envisaging a total ban on sponsorship of international sport and cultural events by 1 October 2006. Some two years later, on 5 October 2000, the European Court of Justice declared the EU Directive null and void, following litigation brought by Germany. The EU could only legitimately introduce a ban on certain types of tobacco advertising and sponsorship with cross-border implications on the basis of an Article having to do with internal markets, not on the basis that it involved public health issues – expressly excluded from the European Union Treaty, and exactly as the FIA had warned Tony Blair. Internationally, the World Health Assembly adopted the Framework Convention on Tobacco Control, negotiated under the auspices of the World Health Organisation, on 23 May 2003, establishing an international legal instrument aimed to reduce tobacco consumption by proposing that every party to the Convention 'undertake a comprehensive ban of all tobacco advertising, promotion and sponsorship'. The effect of the Convention was to put pressure on countries – everywhere – to ban advertising. The FIA, for its part, participated in an ongoing dialogue with the World Health Organisation to pave the way for a tobacco-free Formula 1.

But within the narrower confines of Europe, the story of the Directive took yet another twist. In December 2002, the European Council of Ministers voted through new (legal) anti-tobacco legislation banning tobacco sponsorship in EU countries from 31 July 2005 – some fifteen months earlier than what had been agreed in December 1997. Max was outraged – as was Bernie. The Austrian Grand Prix was dropped from the 2004 championship calendar, putting all Formula 1 races in EU countries under threat. Still, they could hardly have been surprised, for the Grand Prix calendar had often been vulnerable to this kind of political tempest. The previous year the Belgian Grand Prix had been removed from the calendar after the teams voted against taking part in the race; the Belgian Government had decided to adopt legislation ahead of the EU ban and that was that – until the legislators reconsidered and the race returned in 2004. Nor was this hard-line attitude restricted to EU countries. The organisers of the Canadian Grand Prix were informed their race would not take place in 2004 due to the Canadian Government's ban on tobacco advertising. After negotiating with Bernie the race in Canada was reinstated – for an additional $20 million. Bernie said: 'All our contracts with promoters and organisers worldwide state that if any country brings in legislation that in any way affects any of the teams' sponsors – not just tobacco, whatever it might be – then we have a right not to be in that country.'

Back in Britain, legislation or no legislation, Bernie's donation to the Labour Party had remained a hot topic. On 25 November 1999 in an interview with the BBC's *World at One* programme, the vice-chairman of the Conservative Party, Tim Collins, acknowledging that the Conservatives received foreign donations, then energetically informed the public that Labour also received money from people overseas although in his example he rather stretched the point: 'Look at Mr Bernie Ecclestone who gave a million pounds to the Prime Minister and secured a change in government policy. And most of his money, of course, is generated overseas because his money [is] from Formula 1, and as you all know there is one, or at the most, two Formula 1 races in a year in Britain.' Bernie was furious. He shot off a letter to William Hague, then Leader of the Opposition.

'Mr Collins' claims are totally false,' Bernie wrote. 'I have lived in this country all my life and remain a tax-paying resident. Before making these outrageous comments Mr Collins made no attempt to check the facts with me. The only evidence Mr Collins offered in support of his false statement about my status is the absurd comment that my business activities involve Formula 1 races held overseas. In fact my business successfully exports British technology and expertise and helps to generate substantial earnings for a wide range of companies based in the UK.' Having got rid of his anger, he injected the kind of flippancy that so easily trips off his tongue or the nib of his pen. In the final paragraph of his letter, he wrote: 'In the wake of the Jeffrey Archer affair I understand that you will no longer allow people who lie to hold office in the Conservative Party. Can I now assume that you will, therefore, be requesting the resignation of Mr Collins?'

In September 2000, Bernie's £1 million donation to the Labour Party was still capturing headlines after the Shadow Chancellor, Michael Portillo, called for Chancellor Gordon Brown's resignation. An extract from the book *Servants of the People* by Andrew Rawnsley of *The Observer* had just been published, revealing that Mr Brown knew of the donation two days before his interview on the BBC's Radio Four *Today* programme. During the interview, Mr Brown claimed that 'I've not been told and I certainly don't know what the true position is,' regarding Bernie's donation. Mr Portillo was quick to point out that the Chancellor's spokesman later mentioned a meeting – that had actually occurred before the interview – in which Mr Brown and the Prime Minister discussed the donation. A spokesman for Gordon Brown denied that the Chancellor had misled the interviewer. He had spoken with the Prime Minister about the donation, but not about details – such as the amount. 'The facts are, Mr Brown never met or discussed any aspect of finance with Mr Ecclestone nor did Mr Brown ever see any papers or documents related to Mr Ecclestone's donation,' the spokesman said. Tony Blair stuck by Gordon Brown and dismissed calls for his resignation.

The Tories weren't satisfied. Andrew Lansley, Shadow Minister for the Cabinet Office, wrote to Lord Neill (chairman of the Committee on Standards in Public Life) concerning the questions surrounding Mr Brown's statement. And there was the fudging over Bernie's donation(s) that needed clearing up: 'New disclosures show to a greater extent than before that the basis on which your advice was sought and the way in which public statements were made by Ministers, were destined to mislead the media and the public over the circumstances of the original Ecclestone donation, the influence over Labour policy on tobacco advertising which resulted, and the circumstances in which a second donation from Mr Ecclestone was solicited.'

Would the Committee undertake a specific investigation into the circumstances of this affair? They would not. The Committee was not empowered to investigate individual allegations of misconduct.

It irks Bernie that the Conservatives still use his donation like a cosh in their sparring matches with Labour. 'Oh, they do it all the time, they did yesterday probably. I mean people always refer to that don't they?' says Bernie. 'My friend Lakshmi Mittal, the steel man, gave a lot less money [£125,000] and got a lot more for it. They helped him get the steel concession in Romania or somewhere. Blair helped him to bail out the steel companies and everything when they were sort of gonna deregulate.' Former Conservative Party leader Iain Duncan Smith called for an inquiry into what looked like 'a trail of cover-up and deception'.

David Ward had become disgusted by the Tories' readiness to resort to Bernie's donation at every opportunity. 'Through malevolence, the Conservatives treated Bernie as badly as Labour,' he said. Nor was he happy with the media's 'cash for favours' treatment of the 'Formula 1 tycoon'. He decided to set the record straight by initiating an interview, reported in *The Times* on 15 April 2002. In the interview David gives his account of Bernie's donation, making it clear that it had been motivated by personal tax benefits and not to achieve an exemption for Formula 1. Today, David admits that the meeting he had attended with Max and Bernie at Downing Street, on 16 October 1997, 'was a big mistake' leading to 'a series of disasters', although 'Bernie had acted in perfectly good faith'. The whole episode was really 'a cock-up rather than a conspiracy'.

Bernie also wrote to *The Times* pointing out that he lives in England and pays UK taxes – £27 million – which led him to think that he could give his money to whomever he wanted. But the Government's handling of the matter was a 'big mistake'. The other big mistake the Government made was to introduce new gun controls –'so that only the criminals could have guns, a licence to criminals, effectively,' Bernie now says.

He was getting beyond weary with the whole business. Unlike the worker bees at Whitehall, who were enthusiastically rolling up their sleeves, ready to become immersed in a wide-ranging investigation of the tobacco industry and the Government's policy. In January 2000, Max and Bernie were invited to give evidence to the Parliamentary Select Committee on Health. The committee members were 'particularly concerned at the Government's proposal to seek an EC directive which contained provision for a permanent exemption for Formula 1.' What, they wanted to know, was Max and Bernie's understanding of the circumstances that had led to the proposal? Max, perfectly at home in this arena, did most of the answering. The most important point, Max said, 'is that we never asked for an exemption for Formula 1 only. It would have been a mad thing for us to ask for... It was an invention somewhere in the Ministry of Health.' He went on to explain the unique problem presented by globally televised sport, as well as the negative impact the ban would have on the motorsport industry. He also discussed the 'divergence of interests' between the FIA as the governing body on the one side and teams on the other, 'because the teams get the money from the tobacco industry and we [the FIA] try to run the sport... The difficulty is that we are dealing with commercial entities whom I have to persuade. If I could just say "that is it" and dictate – but I cannot. We can on rules, on things like safety, but we cannot on things which would interfere with their commercial affairs. We have to carry them with us.' During his meetings with the teams Max had argued that they 'risked being down a cul-de-sac with the tobacco industry, while the mainstream of sports sponsorship continued and would eventually overtake Formula 1. Far from having more money, they would have less. The teams responded with two arguments: firstly, there was nothing illegal about what they were doing, based on the lack of evidence proving tobacco sponsorship in Formula 1 caused people to start smoking; secondly, if the EU was 'serious about trying to stop the publicity from tobacco, they could do so overnight because the EU currently subsidises the growing of tobacco to the tune of 998 million ecus [roughly $883 million] which was probably in the order of two to three times as much money as the whole sponsorship of Formula 1.' The total EU budget for combating cancer was '14 million ecus and for health initiatives generally – 37 million.' Confronted with these statistics, Max had had difficulty convincing the teams that their position was morally precarious.

The Committee then turned to Mr Ecclestone. 'The suggestions in the media that your donations to the Labour Party influenced this whole area, this very important area, are nonsense from your point of view?'

'Absolutely.' The case made itself – as it had in other EU countries. Bernie's donation didn't come into it. When the Committee made its report the following year, it condemned the Government for failing to match anti-smoking rhetoric with action.

Six years on, Bernie's donation continued to capture the headlines – this story had more legs than a centipede. In 2008, under the Freedom of Information Act, Government documents – faxes, letters, minutes, briefing notes – relating to 'the Affair' were made available. The press could now gorge on factual data, making up for the near-starvation rations of 1997. Overall, the bureaucratic paper trail is mind-numbingly tedious. The dogged reporters at the *The Sunday Telegraph* focused on the hours from the meeting of 16 October to the 'collective' decision announced by the Prime Minister – the recent proof compared to the earlier statements. *The Sunday Times* was similarly reporting on the evidence. The documents support what had been widely suspected, that the Prime Minister had personally intervened in the decision to exempt Formula 1, a decision that appears to have taken place within hours of the meeting on the 16th rather than during the period 24–31 October. The appearance of a conflict of interest had sent the Prime Minister's advisers into a tizzy, leading to statements that were 'disingenuous' – as one civil servant had feared.

In 2000, Williams-BMW became the first major team to run without tobacco sponsorship. Thereafter the visibility of tobacco advertising and sponsorship in Formula 1 steadily diminished. After the 2006 season only three countries organising Grands Prix still allowed tobacco sponsorship – Monaco, China and Bahrain. These circuits are now tobacco-free. The final controversy, culminating in 2010, concerned Philip Morris's sponsorship of the Ferrari team, a ten-year deal to 2011, reputedly worth $1 billion. The lettering used on the cars had been replaced by stripes, which eventually morphed into the 'bar code' – strongly associated with the Marlboro brand. The team and Philip Morris were accused of subliminal advertising. At the European Grand Prix in Valencia this too disappeared, after a legal struggle.

Bernie muses on politics, or rather his political beliefs, like a memory one might waft into the ether on a halo of smoke. 'My father was always very conservative-minded and took certain newspapers, so as I grew up that's what happened. And we always supported Oxford for the boat race. These are the sort of things you grow up with so you stay with them.'

'Did you ever want to go into politics yourself?'

'Definitely not!'

'You wouldn't like to be Prime Minister?'

'I can't think why anyone would want to be Prime Minister. It's very hard for a politician who is going to be elected for five years to do all the things that are good for the country in that time... so they've got to try to balance everything. It's difficult.'

'Better if they had a longer term?'

'Or a dictator.'

Bernie's Christmas card for 1997 featured an illustration of a £1 million note in red, with a depiction of a bat-eared, toothy Tony Blair sporting a green bow tie. The Formula 1 crowd were much amused and saved it as a memento to be enjoyed years later, just as Herbie Blash had done recalling his brief chat with Mrs Thatcher in 1980. Bernie's actual £1 million was eventually returned to him. He was 'very happy' to have his money back: 'I'd like to have more arrangements like that with people, I thought it was very generous of them.' From a distance humour is easy. Up close the donation was the catalyst to a very convoluted episode that caused a great deal of embarrassment to all parties.

From the comfort of 2011 Max Mosley reflects on the fiasco: 'The idea was that Bernie should give the money, we would then have access to lobby at the very top level so that we could get things done. Serious assistance from the British Government in Brussels would have been very helpful with road safety, Encap, environmental things. That's what it was all about. Tobacco didn't really come into it, that's what's annoying... The awful thing about politicians is their number one priority is not to do the right thing but to get re-elected. So if you give them money it helps them get re-elected and makes them more inclined to do the thing you want. Very few people who get to the top of politics are still idealistic.'

In any event it will be a long time – if ever – before Bernie donates money to politicians. Dictators excepted. The returned cheque lay on his desk gathering dust until he could exert himself to deposit such a trifle. By which time the notion of the Ecclestone million had entered into the parlance of frisky wheeler-dealers in London's financial district, where emoluments of one million – dollars, pounds, dinars, whatever – became known as 'a Bernie'.

CHAPTER 15

THE JACKPOT

International motorsport promoter Wolfgang Eisele considered himself the victim of unfair practice and it had rankled him for the best part of a year. Then, in the early spring of 1997, the merchant bank Morgan Stanley leaked the news – which made headlines – that Bernie Ecclestone was about to float his company Formula One Holdings (FOH), whose primary assets were pay TV and free-to-air contracts. For Wolfgang Eisele it was the prime moment to thoroughly redress his grievances. And he seized it by arranging a clandestine meeting that was held at the Sheraton Hotel in Frankfurt on 21 March 1997. Invited to the meeting were representatives of non-Formula 1 events – the touring car championship, rallycross and 'others'. Everyone signed a confidentiality agreement, whereupon Eisele's lawyer, Dr Wolfgang Deselaers, got down to business – planning an 'anonymous solidarity action' – against Bernie and the FIA. The mighty Mosley/Ecclestone combine, as they saw it, would not rumble on unchecked.

Listed on the meeting's agenda was an item entitled 'Objectives in Brussels'. This concerned a formal complaint that Eisele planned to put before the European Commission's Directorate-General for Competition – the anti-trust division of the European Commission. The complaint – lodged two months later – alleged that the FIA and Bernie's company International Sportsworld Communicators (ISC, which he then still owned) were in violation of European Community competition laws. In 1995, the FIA had adopted its broadcasting rules (Article 24 of the International Sporting

Code and the associated general prescription Article 27) stating that the television rights of all international motor racing championships were the property of the FIA.

In 1996, ISC had obtained from the FIA the power to exploit its broadcasting rights to championships other than Formula 1. There were criticisms of this policy, most notably from Wolfgang Eisele, who from 1983 had built up a business marketing international motorsport championships, particularly the European truck racing championship. But the rights to cover these races, as of 1996, belonged to ISC. Consequently, Eisele's company, AE TV, which he had nurtured to success, was threatened with failure. After direct entreaties to Bernie had come to nothing, Eisele lodged formal complaints – first in Germany, then in Brussels – arguing that Mr Ecclestone in his executive role(s) was monopolising the FIA, and that as the commercial rights holder he had control over promoters, organisers and broadcasters. More importantly, he alleged that the FIA had 'used its power to seize total control of the broadcasting of international motorsports for its benefit and for the benefit of Mr Ecclestone', according to a Commission press release, bringing ownership of the television rights into question.

Four months after Eisele had delivered his complaint to Brussels, the FIA wrote to the European Commission's Directorate-General for Competition to lodge a 'notification' to ensure that Formula 1's broadcasting rights would be exempted from the European competition rules. The same month, the FIA made a notification on behalf of Formula One Administration (FOA), the subsidiary of Formula One Holdings PLC (FOH) that directly runs Formula 1. It was a formality – Bernie thought – that would help facilitate his flotation of FOH on the Stock Exchange. After such heavy investment in digital television, Bernie had decided to capitalise on FOA, whose assets included revenue from Allsport's activities, circuit franchise fees and video game makers, but FOA's principal assets were indeed Bernie's extensive pay-TV and free-to-air contracts. He had seen the revenues from his television deals grow beyond even his wildest expectations, and a public offering seemed the next logical step, a kind of 'topping out' ceremony – laying the last brick on the skyscraper that Formula 1 had become – and thus allowing him to extract maximum wealth.

Formula One Holdings had been incorporated, the previous year, as the designated company to be floated; Formula One Administration then became its subsidiary. The Ecclestone trusts and companies form a complex pattern, with the names of the companies seemingly swapped back and forth. FOH became the wholly owned subsidiary of SLEC Holdings Limited, the family trust registered in Jersey in the name of Slavica Ecclestone and, in October 1997, SLEC Holdings became a subsidiary of Bambino Holdings Limited. Much of the reasoning behind the structuring of these companies, and the flotation of FOH, was to make Bernie's wealth secure for the benefit of his family after his death, which also meant reducing the tax impact. While he was still alive he intended to amass as much wealth as possible, then it was a matter of preventing the Ecclestone fortune – and his Formula 1 businesses – from being squandered after he was gone.

Two more subsidiaries of FOH are Formula One Management Limited (FOM) and Petara Limited – named after Bernie's daughters, Petra and Tamara. Not even the financially astute Paddy McNally was certain to which company he paid his monthly fees. 'FOA, SLEC, call it what you like but I [had] a contract with them which is very substantial' – that is all Paddy would say. And on it goes: Formula One Productions Limited is a subsidiary of FOA that, in turn, owns Petara. There are others.

As part of the FIA/FOA notifications of exemption from the competition rules, copies were supplied of the 1997 Concorde Agreement. The Agreement included the amendments sidestepping FOCA and surrendering the commercial rights – and the FIA's thirty per cent share of the television revenue – directly to Bernie's company Formula One Administration for fifteen years in return for an annual payment of $9.5 million. It was a red rag to a bull, the bull in question being Karel van Miert, head of the Directorate-General for Competition.

His attention, which had already been drawn to Bernie, was now rapt – thanks to Eisele's efforts. Should the European Commission favour Eisele and decide that the television rights were not Bernie's to exploit, Bernie's financial plans would be in serious jeopardy, for without the television rights he had much less to sell.

Eisele's case had a kind of David and Goliath appeal, at least to van Miert, as one small voice against the might of Big Business Sport. What followed was – for Max and Bernie – an intimation of disaster. For in July 1997, two months before the FIA/FOA applications to Brussels, a Frankfurt district court had ruled that the FIA, through its handling of the television rights to European truck racing, was in violation of European competition law; the rights had to be returned to the organisers. This was a worrying development that, left unchallenged, could potentially see the rest of the FIA's television rights fall like ninepins. The hour had come for Max to take his barrister's wig out of mothballs and for Bernie to marshal his own, personal squad of lawyers. Max commenced by cancelling the 1997 FIA truck series; if the FIA didn't own the television rights then – no series. But Max relented, saving his energies for the more powerful opponent – Brussels. And the most valuable prize – the television rights to Formula 1.

Max informed the Commission that if they found the central marketing of Formula 1 to be illegal, then this aspect of the FIA would move outside the European Union. He foresaw several negative ramifications to their meddling, among them the loss of viewing races free of charge, an outcome that would affect some forty-five million European households – imagine American boxing promoter Don King and the heavyweight championship restricted to Pay TV. In such an instance Europe's viewers would drastically diminish – which in turn would affect the viability of the teams whose sponsors relied upon the broad impact of free-to-air coverage. While the bureaucrats were taking their time to mull this over, Max strengthened his arm by announcing that the FIA had joined, in September 1998, a working group of the

International Olympic Committee (IOC) which was actively supporting sports federations seeking, from the Commission, a broader understanding in the application of its competition rules; and either an exemption or a modification of the European Union Treaty. Then, to keep them shivering, Max made it clear that should the FIA and the Commission fail to reach a satisfactory agreement, the FIA would be obliged to file a complaint with the European Court of Justice.

Bernie, for his part, had kept busy exercising his own weapon-of-war par excellence – dealing. He offered Wolfgang Eisele a partnership in Motormania, a pay-per-view channel he'd been negotiating with Canal+. There was only one condition: Eisele had to withdraw his complaint with Brussels. Eisele declined Bernie's offer, but apparently took advantage of the cooperative mood by proposing a settlement he considered to be in line with the damages/costs he had incurred: $5 million. Bernie – concerned with protecting the much larger financial strategy – decided to agree. A down payment of $500,000 was transferred to Eisele's bank account, the rest would follow when all was well with Brussels; but first Bernie wanted the name or names of those who had helped him in his German court action, along with all relevant paperwork. Both Bernie and Max suspected that Eisele was being supported by Mercedes-Benz, who had been heavily involved in the truck series. Bernie was on friendly terms with Jurgen Schrempp, a familiar face around the paddock who as the then chairman of DaimlerChrysler, the parent company of Mercedes, was a big participant in Formula 1, but not – according to Schrempp – a supporter of Wolfgang Eisele.

The Frankfurt district court then surprised everyone by ruling that if there was a violation of the television rights or of European competition law, an action could only be brought by the organisers, not by a third party. Wolfgang Eisele, immediately appealed, but to no avail – nine months later, on 15 December 1998, his appeal was dismissed. So Eisele – ever dogged – lodged a final appeal with Germany's Federal Court of Justice in Karlsruhe. As it happened, Eisele's complaints had already triggered change – although not exactly what he was after. Before the Frankfurt verdict, the FIA, to appease Brussels, had returned the television rights of all non-Formula 1 championships – and their marketing – to the organisers, not to third-party Eiseles. But he didn't walk away entirely empty-handed; in exchange for dropping his final appeal in Karlsruhe, Wolfgang Eisele kept the $500,000, although he never received the additional $4.5 million he had hoped for.

Eisele, however, hadn't been the only player stirring up the European Commission's investigation. There was also Frenchman Patrick Peter to contend with, and he wouldn't go easily. The complaint was similar in that it centred upon television rights. Peter wanted to claim them for endurance races for GT cars. Bernie explained that the rights went to ISC, or no GT series, at least not Patrick Peter's. The FIA announced the formation of its own GT series, the World Grand Touring Car Championship. Bernie then offered Peter's organisation, BPR, in which he had two associates, the opportunity to organise the new series and receive the competitors' entry fees. The two associates liked the idea. Peter didn't and, alone, filed a legal action against Bernie and ISC, claiming damages of around £14 million. BPR, incidentally, had been represented at the Frankfurt meeting, which suggests that Patrick Peter may have been a co-conspirator.

Peter followed up his legal action by lodging, with the European Commission, a formal complaint against Bernie's FOA and ISC and against the FIA alleging a violation of the European Commission's competition rules. Commissioner Karel van Miert appeared to take a particular interest in the case, and it appeared that Patrick Peter had become rather fond of spending time in Brussels. So much so that he began to consider himself something of an influential expert in the workings of the Directorate-General for Competition and he reportedly offered to represent Bernie in Brussels – after a settlement of $15 million had been agreed ($10 million to Peter and $5 million to the lawyer representing BPR). By coincidence – or not – John Temple Lang, director of information, communication and multimedia for the

Directorate-General for Competition wrote to the FIA's lawyer, Stephen Kinsella, saying that the FIA can 'give Mr Peter more favourable treatment than is normal'. Max's attitude was, 'I'm not going to do anything.' Bernie had interpreted the letter as: 'Better pay up'; and, consummate negotiator that he is, Bernie talked Peter down to $2 million. Peter allegedly wanted the money to be distributed in a way that would avoid tax, which Bernie's lawyers refused. The $2 million was paid – quite transparently – from ISC to Patrick Peter's organisation, the name of which had been changed to GTR. It was just business, and for Bernie a pragmatic means of untangling the snarls in Brussels.

Patrick Peter's next offer was to use his Brussels expertise to help ease Bernie's difficulties with the Commission. For his services Peter reportedly required a mere $2.5 million (his lawyer's fees included) to be paid to his company, plus $50,000 as a monthly allowance – excluding expenses. But this time Bernie wasn't buying. On 3 June 1998, Patrick Peter withdrew his complaint. Otherwise, there was no change, the investigation of the European Commission continued unabated. The fact remained that many considered that Max and Bernie had overreached the bounds by granting all the television rights to Bernie's companies, although another benefit, claimed by the FIA, was to improve the quality of the minor championships. In the end it had given Wolfgang Eisele and Patrick Peter a chance to gang up on them. Bernie says: 'They were just two guys trying to do the best that they could for themselves.'

Actually, Eisele and Peter were not the only thorns in Bernie's tender side. There was a much bigger, and infinitely more complex problem to be sorted out – the teams. As of August 1996, Ron Dennis, Ken Tyrrell and Frank Williams had not yet signed the 1997/98 Concorde Agreement, so Bernie decided to create a crisis – always a favourite ploy – by offering the signatory teams an equal division of the television revenue that would otherwise have been allocated to their three non-signatory colleagues. Now it was the turn of the rebel trio to play hardball. Either Bernie would allow them to return to the fold on equal terms or they would file a complaint with the European Commission on the grounds of unfair competition; and lawyers had been engaged to see it through. What's more, the teams – all the teams – were annoyed that they had not been notified of Bernie's intended flotation, and they were also shocked by the valuation put on the business – $2.6 billion. They had no idea it was worth anything near that sort of money, and they wanted a stake in it. Bernie was, for once, vulnerable, as the teams well knew, and they used the tension emanating from Brussels as leverage in negotiating terms before applying their signatures to the final document. Bernie ranted, but eventually he could see nothing for it but to capitulate.

He offered the teams ten per cent equity in trust, with the right to dividends but not share ownership. This was to be taken out of Bernie's own shareholding in FOH, leaving him with thirty per cent; another ten per cent was allocated to the FIA, with the remaining fifty per cent on offer to the public. He also offered the teams nearly fifty per cent of the television revenue. But then Bernie always keeps a card up his sleeve. In exchange for his compliance, he required that the 1997/98 Concorde Agreement be extended from the usual four or five years' duration to a period of ten years – until the end of 2007 – which would please potential investors. Ultimately, all the teams agreed, and in May 1998 the Concorde Agreement – having undergone some fifty revisions, including negotiating a larger share for the teams from Internet activities, video game rights and rights over the advertising on cars – was finally signed. Now it was up to Brussels.

Bernie hadn't put *all* his eggs in the television basket, but nearly all; it made the difference between wealth and extreme wealth. Yet there was more to it than money, much more. He was going for the big one, the big granddaddy of a deal. All those years since Compton & Ecclestone and at Warren Street, working the street to turn over cars as fast as he could lay his hands on them, looking smart and acting smarter with calculations gushing through his brain. Then in Bexleyheath where he became the hire-purchase king of the James Spencer showroom, moving the flashy 'specials' – 'Jags, Mercs, Rollers' – selling to some of the biggest names in show business during the day, gambling at night – gin rummy, chemmy, backgammon, roulette – for ever-higher stakes. The Brabham team was a gamble too, and the heavy losses always came to mind though he tried not to think about it – Stuart, Jochen, Carlos, Ayrton – so many. And the battles – battles with Balestre, battles with the FOCA teams, dragging the sport to the pinnacle of professionalism. He had done it, shown them the way, shown all of them, and still there were battles with race organisers, with broadcasters, with banks and financial advisers, even with governments, and deals, deals, never-ending deals. It had all brought him to this, this moment. He had graduated, he was ready to move ahead – far, far ahead, away from the rest of the pack. But a Brussels bureaucrat, Karel van Miert – 'who didn't know what he didn't know,' says Bernie – was standing in his way.

His way was also obscured by the political stench of tobacco, which, by November 1998, had thoroughly settled in clouds around Brussels. The exemption of Formula 1 from the EU Directive on tobacco advertising was not well received by the Commission, so Karel van Miert was even less disposed to look upon Bernie Ecclestone with anything like favour. Indeed, some argued that he was 'incredibly prejudicial' against Bernie and the FIA. In addition, van Miert's case against them was further overshadowed – or encumbered – by a dispute concerning the Belgian Grand Prix at Spa-Francorchamps. The Flemish Socialist Party of Belgium secured a ban on all tobacco advertising and sponsorship to take effect by 1 January 1999, as distinct from the EU-wide phased elimination that was then still under consideration. Bernie reacted by cancelling the 1998 Belgian Grand Prix unless the ban was lifted. Spa is located within the French-speaking region of Wallonia whose government was eager to continue hosting Formula 1 races – which generated so much revenue – and so declared the federal ban did not apply to them. In Wallonia they were determined to make their own legislation regarding tobacco advertising which, in this instance, meant they supported tobacco advertising and sponsorship at the Belgian Grand Prix. Bernie then announced that the race would go ahead as scheduled. In the end it was ruled by an independent judiciary that the ban on tobacco advertising should not be imposed prior to the Directive being considered, or rather reconsidered, by the European Commission; the Walloon Government won their case. And Karel van Miert tightened the screws.

During the course of the Commission's investigation, now approaching its third year, potential investors lost confidence in Bernie's Formula One Holdings. Why was the investigation taking so long? How secure were Bernie's television contracts and, more importantly, was the FIA the *bona fide* possessor of the television rights that they had handed to Bernie to exploit? The answers to these questions had not been resolved by the Commission, still heavily into its investigations, so prospective investors drifted away and the flotation effectively failed. Bernie then resorted to an alternative plan for capitalising on Formula 1, a $2 billion Eurobond offering by Formula One Finance BV, listed on the Luxembourg Stock Exchange. To launch the Eurobond deal it had been necessary for the FIA to alter its commercial rights contract with Bernie, for which he agreed to pay $60 million. Even so, investors wanted the blessing of the European Commission. As long as the acrimony with Brussels continued there would be doubts about the future strength of Bernie's – mostly television-based – Formula 1 business and, to further rattle investors' nerves, there was a global economic downturn.

In March 1999, the size of Bernie's Eurobond issue was reduced to $1.4 billion, and even then a successful launch seemed increasingly unlikely until, that is, American financial expert and former ballerina Robin Saunders, of Westdeutsche Landesbank (West LB), came along to save the day. West LB had joined investment bankers Morgan Stanley as principal managers of the Eurobond issue, which represented a securitisation of future revenues generated from the sales of

Formula 1 television rights. Miss Saunders and her team at West LB offered to underwrite two-thirds of the issue and Morgan Stanley one-third. Their willingness to subscribe for any bonds not sold off to investors was a measure of the banks' confidence in the future of Bernie's television revenues. Even so Bernie had to lodge $400 million as security against a shortfall in those revenues and, if necessary, to eventually pay off the bonds – which were further propped up by the Ecclestones' Petara Limited, registered in Jersey. Then Bernie and the banks braced themselves for the decision from the European Commission's Directorate-General for Competition.

But before that, Karel van Miert and his staff created more headaches by releasing to the *Financial Times* information pertaining to the Commission's – supposedly confidential – 'warning letter' sent to the FIA, FOA and ISC. The purpose of the warning letter was to highlight every conceivable objection of the Commission, throwing the metaphorical book at them – all part of the formalities. The recipient was then meant to respond. However, before the response could be formed, a press conference was held during which – for the ultimate public assault on Max and Bernie – the Commission's deputy official spokesperson revealed the contents of the warning letters. Journalists from four major newspapers – the *Financial Times*, the *Wall Street Journal*, *The Times* and the *Sunday Times* – referred to the contents of the letters in subsequent articles. Karel van Miert certainly appeared to be enthralled by the high-profile nature of Formula 1 and the publicity it attracted.

Max was outraged at this public disclosure of confidential information – still under discussion. He responded by bringing proceedings against the Commission in the European Court of Justice in Luxembourg. And he won. The Commission issued a formal apology and was forced to pay 40,000 euros towards the FIA's legal costs. In legal circles the decision of the European Court was seen as something of a landmark. 'The trouble with van Miert,' says Bernie, 'was he'd been dealing with very large companies and the world was quite clear where they were – anti-competitive. In our case he never bothered to find out what we were about. So he really pulled the gun out and started shooting and he didn't know what he was shooting at.'

On 30 June 1999, the long-awaited 'Statement of Objections' was issued from Brussels. The 188-page document alleged that the FIA along with Bernie's Formula One Administration and International Sportsworld Communicators had violated European Union antitrust laws. Of particular concern were contracts involving broadcasters. FOA it must be remembered sold the television rights to Formula 1, and ISC marketed the broadcasting rights to other FIA motorsport events. It was argued that the FIA had appropriated ownership of the commercial rights – including television – to FIA events, the rights of which it then assigned to FOA and ISC. The Commission also argued that the FIA abused its licensing power to authorise FIA events, thus thwarting the development of non-FIA motorsport series. Unlawful contracts would 'have to be renegotiated' and, just to be extra menacing, Karel van Miert added: 'We have found evidence of serious infringement of EU competition rules, which could result in substantial fines'. However, the Statement of Objections was 'a preliminary procedural document and not the Commission's final verdict on the case'.

Van Miert had expressed particular difficulty with the length of Bernie's commercial rights contract with the FIA – fifteen years. The Commission preferred contracts with a duration of five years. Then there was the most recent Concorde Agreement, effective for ten years, and Bernie's contracts with broadcasters some of which were also for ten years, and eleven years in the case of various pay-television companies. Nor did it help that a few of the contracts offered discounts of up to fifty per cent to broadcasters who agreed to show only Formula 1, and that promoters had to agree that Formula 1 and Formula 3000 races would be the only televised single-seat car races held on their circuits; Bernie also promoted Formula 3000. In any event Bernie and Max ultimately rejected the Commission's criticisms, which they decided to challenge in an oral hearing.

The oral hearing was scheduled for 10 May 2000, but Karel van Miert would not be there. He, along with nineteen other commissioners – the entire executive of the EU – resigned following a report by independent investigators into fraud, nepotism and mismanagement within the European Commission. Karel van Miert was not among the four persons named in the report, but the allegations were such that all the commissioners decided that it was better to jump before being pushed. Professor Mario Monti, a noted scholar in economics and a businessman, replaced van Miert as the Commissioner for Competition. Under the new regime, Max looked forward 'to a phase of rational discussion, rather than a continuance of the confrontation' that had predominated in their dealings with the Commission. And as Max had predicted, a phase of 'rational discussion' did indeed ensue. Mario Monti was more conciliatory than his predecessor.

The Commission eventually reached a compromise with Max and Bernie that, in January 2001, formed the basis of a 'peace deal'. The oral hearing became unnecessary. The FIA agreed to amend its regulations 'to strengthen the rights of motorsport organisers, circuit owners and participants', according to a statement put out by Mario Monti; in essence, the FIA would be restricted to the role of 'impartial motorsports regulator'. It would thereby have no 'commercial interest in the success of Formula 1, and the new rules [would] remove any obstacle to other motorsport series competing with Formula 1'. However, 'the FIA [would] retain its rights over its championships and the use of the "FIA" name and Trade Marks'. But it would 'remove from its rules any claim over the broadcasting rights to events that it authorises' and agreed to 'waive any claim to broadcasting rights under the relevant clauses' in the Concorde Agreement – this was the crucial point. What Max had agreed with Mario Monti was to split away the commercial side of motor racing from the sporting side; the division had been allowed to grow obscure since the signing of the first Concorde Agreement in 1981. Now the arrangement was as definite as the separation between church and state. Its effect with regard to Bernie was to make it clear for all to see

– and for Brussels to acknowledge – that in Formula 1, Bernie represents the commercial segment of the sport and the FIA represents the sporting regulations. Together, they make up Formula 1 – which cannot exist, of course, without the teams. The foundation of his financial restructuring was now solid as far as potential investors were concerned.

The fact that the provision restricted Bernie to the commercial activities of Formula 1 was fine because, by the time that Mario Monti had issued his statement, Bernie had sold ISC – reduced to rallying only – to David Richards. In the compromise with Brussels Bernie also agreed to limit the duration of the FOA's free-to-air broadcasting contracts to three years, except for those in which specific investments justify a length of up to five years; all provisions penalising broadcasters who wanted to broadcast other forms of open-wheel racing were also removed. Nor would Bernie be allowed to continue as the FIA's vice-president of promotional affairs. He became an honorary vice-president instead (there are fourteen of them), which he remained for some time. 'I'm just a vice-president,' says Bernie. He, likewise, left the Senate because 'the European Commission had said that it was a big conflict of interest my being on the Senate, in a position where I could damage other championships... Max said to me, "What we'll do is, we'll put John Large [then the representative from Australia] on for a year, and then you come back".' John Large remained on the Senate, until his recent death, because 'Max was a bit reluctant for me to come back'.

The Commission had also argued against Bernie organising the Formula 1 Championship calendar, interpreting this as control over who holds grands prix, and where. But apart from exerting influence over 'who' and 'where', it seems that he had a special aptitude for organising dates. Burdette (Burdy) Martin, president of the Automobile Competition Committee for the United States (ACCUS) and America's delegate on the FIA World Council, remembers that Bernie always, without fail, attended the Calendar Commission, which was overseen by the World Council.

'Bernie would try to work on his Formula 1 Calendar with the FIA,' Burdy says. At one meeting 'the commission's chairman said: "Ecclestone, give out the schedule you've got," and Bernie read out the schedule for Formula 1. But immediately, the Italian delegate jumped up: "Oh, we cannot do it at that time, we cannot do that, that's a holiday in Italy, we cannot, we always have had it at another time." Then somebody else jumped up – Belgium – "It's impossible, we can't do it." Bernie said: "You're so right, and I'm so wrong, I should have known all this (to the Italian), I apologise to you terribly (to the Belgian). Just work out what you would like to have." Well, the Italian delegate got into an argument with the Belgian, and then there were a whole bunch of arguments. We went on for probably a half hour or so, and nobody was happy with the schedule. Then they started piecing it all together and, finally, they said: "Here Mr Ecclestone, here is the schedule". And it was exactly the one he had given to them in the beginning! That's so typical of him. He's so hard to figure out, and he'll come out with things just the opposite to what I expect most times.' For example, continues Burdy: 'Somebody will say something in the World Council, and I think: "Bernie's going to blow his top about this." But Bernie will say: "Wonderful, I think it's a great idea." Then, at other times, I think: "Oh, he'll like that, it's good for Formula 1," and he says: "No, that can't be done that way." But the interesting thing about it is, that as time goes on – and it could be six months, it could be a year – you'll see what's happened, and you'll see why he was able to figure it out that far ahead of everybody else, how it would work out the way he wanted it to work out.'

As it happened, there was another development – inspired by Max – concerning the television rights. But to say that it worked out the way Bernie wanted it to would be a gross understatement. On 28 June 2000, the FIA General Assembly met in an extraordinary session and voted, unanimously, to approve a deal recommended by the Senate to grant the FIA's commercial rights in Formula 1 to Bernie's company, SLEC Holdings – for a period of 100 years! Indeed, it was an extension of the fifteen-year contract to 2110. Considering that the head of the European Commission's Directorate General for Competition had objected to Bernie's fifteen-year contract with the FIA on the grounds of its lengthy duration, how would a 100-plus-year contract be received? No problem at all. Commissioner Mario Monti felt that 'a longer duration of exclusive arrangements can prove to be justified, particularly when an operator wishes to enter a new market with an innovative service or to introduce a new technology requiring very high risk and heavy investment' – such as Bernie's investment in digital television.

For his 100-year contract with the FIA, Bernie agreed to pay $313.17 million. After all, by selling all its commercial rights – actually the right to the Formula 1 name and logo – for such a long period, the FIA further prevented a conflict of interest. But in spite of all the goodwill that was being handed around, it seems Max then insisted on a condition: that $60 million – as part of the whole sum paid to the FIA for the 100-year rights – would be due for payment the following month, and he meant it; Bernie wasn't the only one who could play the tough negotiator.

Bernie, through his principal family trust, then SLEC Holdings, put the $60 million in escrow until Mario Monti had signed the final settlement approving the deal. This was not received until six months later, on 21 January 2001. But even then, some six months past the due date, Bernie continued to delay making the payment. Max was getting impatient. He thought of taking Bernie to court but chose instead to offer the 100-year deal to the Formula 1 manufacturers – Fiat (Ferrari), Ford (Jaguar), BMW, DaimlerChrysler (Mercedez-Benz) and Renault. Max knew the manufacturers were getting anxious about the amount of money Bernie was making through his Formula 1 companies. None of the team bosses benefited from the Eurobond sale; and their split of the television revenue was forty-seven per cent shared between them, while SLEC received fifty-three per cent. Max then decided to offer Bernie an ultimatum – pay the $60 million by 22 March – reasoning that this would allow the manufacturers time, just, to make a bid. Their bid, however, failed to materialise, so Bernie was granted another opportunity to complete. The money was finally paid, plus $4.6 million that the FIA estimated it had lost in interest, on 24 April 2001.

What was so intriguing, for observers, about the outstanding $60 million is that it was tattooed with all the hallmarks of a genuine dispute between Max and Bernie. Amazing, astounding, shocking – it was all of that. It was also utterly scrumptious. Paddock soothsayers have spent many a delightful hour pondering the Max/Bernie relationship, looking for angles. Could these blood brothers – still crowned with their somewhat bedraggled laurels from the FISA/FOCA war – possibly be at odds? Everyone wanted to know. They still want to know. Max and Bernie like to keep people guessing. Anyone wishing to take sides would be well advised to proceed with caution, if at all. These two are the best – absolute tops – at political intrigue.

'So Max, how is your relationship with Bernie?' I asked in 2001.

'It's fine.'

'Healthy?'

'It's relaxed, jokey. I mean we have to, both of us, defend particular interests. I can't do things that are against the interests of the FIA, and he can't do things that are against the interests of his shareholders. He only owns twenty-five per cent of the company, but we both recognise that we can help each other a lot in a way that is in the interests of our respective organisations. And my part of it works fine... It's now like it has been for the last thirty years, sort of making jokes, permanent sort of rivals... it's all quite enjoyable.'

And to Bernie: 'What kind of a relationship do you now have with Max?'

'Good.'

'Still good friends?'

'Yes.'

'What do you think Max's contribution to motorsport has been?'

'Well, he's worked extremely hard, given up an awful lot of his private time to the sport, and sincerely and genuinely wanted to see aspects of the sport changed. For example, he was very much pro-safety which was what I started a long time ago with the Professor, and he sort of continued with this and, hopefully, because he believed that we should save people's lives, which is what I'm sure he did. So from that point of view he did a good job and made people aware.'

'Any other big contributions?'

'Um, he tried to rationalise different things, but a little bit of a problem with Max is, he has very fixed ideas and won't move away from them. And I said recently, (I don't know how we're going to put this but) if you go to a doctor, and he prescribes some tablets to cure whatever it is you've got wrong, and you're not cured, you change the tablets. That's what Max doesn't do... He keeps the same old tablets and hopes one day they're going to work.'

'The 100-year deal produced a huge amount of income for the FIA.'

'Yeah, which it managed to lose, thirty-odd million a year.'

The FIA didn't actually lose the 100-year money, at least not all of it. In fact 'seventy-five per cent of it was quickly converted into euro-dollars, making a surplus of $11 million,' according to David Ward. Chunks of it went into equity markets that were hurt by the economic downturn following the 9/11 terrorist attacks, and damaged further by the Enron scandal. So the FIA only lost $20 million. But, happily, 'long-term we'll be OK,' adds David, 'it's coming back.' But would Max?

During the slow, sultry weekend of the French Grand Prix at Magny-Cours, in early July 2004, the paddock – normally drowsy at this race – was all a-chatter with talk of Max's sudden resignation as President of the FIA. He had had enough of the quarrelling within Formula 1, making his days long and stressful. He needed fresh air and preferred to devote his efforts to motor safety and its legislation in Europe; perhaps he also needed more time to drive racing cars and to parachute from aeroplanes, both of which Max, then aged sixty-four, still enjoyed. But the Senate and officials from various clubs would not let him go, not like that. Stay on, they pleaded, see your term through; and Max, 'pleasantly surprised', relented. He would remain as their president until the election scheduled for October 2005. Then we'd see. Nothing like quitting to settle the dust, by mid-July he had grabbed the reins with new vigour; and those who sought to replace him had become vapour. In 2005 he again secured office, where he remained – despite the occasional challenge – until October 2009.

During his presidency, Max has brought many benefits to motorsport, primarily his acquiescence to the definitive separation of the commercial side of motor racing from the sporting side. Beyond this, income from the 100-year deal between Bernie and the FIA has led to the endowment of the FIA Foundation for road safety that examines wide-ranging safety-related issues, including the impact of cars on the environment. And there is the FIA Institute of Motor Sport Safety, responsible for safety research in open-cockpit racing, closed-car racing, karting and medical services. Max was also behind the creation, in 1997, of the European New Car Assessment Programme (Euro NCAP), a crash-assessment system by which new road cars receive a star rating of between one and five, according to their safety performance. Manufacturers have been quick to appreciate the marketing value of these ratings, improving the safety of vehicles receiving only one or two stars in order to increase sales. Today many new road cars receive four stars, and there are even a few fives. Max has other achievements to his credit, but in 2008 his successes became overshadowed, sadly, by a lurid sex scandal, the details of which were read around the world in newspapers, magazines and on the Internet – complete with graphic photographs. But the fact remains that he has helped to keep alive more racing drivers than ever before in the history of the sport, along with the general public. That's what one must remember about Max Mosley.

Back on the business front, in 2001 Max, in his dialogue, referred to Bernie's ownership of 'only twenty-five per cent of the company' – SLEC – in whose name the 100-year commercial rights deal with the FIA had been contracted. What Max was actually referring to was the stake Bambino Holdings still held in SLEC, which through a complicated series of transactions expanded – enormously – the Ecclestone family wealth. But there was no way Bernie was going to lose control of SLEC, no matter who owned shares or sat on the board; it had been written into the shareholders' agreement that he would remain in command. 'I'm the Chief Executive of the Company,' he pointed out. With that established beyond any doubt, he rolled up his sleeves and started dealing, dealing tough as only Bernie Ecclestone knows how to do. It was not for amateurs.

By the middle of February 2000, Morgan Grenfell Private Equity had paid $325 million for a 12.5 per cent stake in SLEC Holdings and, with the help of Bernie's behind-the-scenes manoeuvring, Hellman & Friedman, an American private equity firm paid $712 million for a 37.5 per cent share. Then, the following month, Hellman & Freidman together with Morgan Grenfell sold their combined fifty per cent shareholding to the German media company, EM.TV & Merchandising for $1.8 billion in cash and equities. Part of the EM.TV agreement included an additional twenty-five per cent share option to be taken up within a year, which would then give them shares in SLEC totalling seventy-five per cent. However, EM.TV soon suffered crippling financial setbacks sending the value of their own shares into freefall. Instead of taking additional shares in SLEC, EM.TV was forced to sell part of its existing holding.

Meanwhile, watching all of these transactions with emotions hovering close to alarm were the manufacturers, who were worried about the security of their scores of millions pouring into Formula 1. They were particularly anxious over the prospect of a media company – involved in promoting pay-per-view television – owning a controlling interest in a company that held the commercial rights to Formula 1; the sport's free-to-air coverage – across the globe – was essential to the teams' multi-national sponsors. Paolo Cantarella, chief executive of Fiat, approached Bernie, on behalf of the manufacturers, to discuss the purchase of EM.TV's fifty per cent stake plus a further ten per cent share. Bernie welcomed the involvement of the manufacturers, especially as they had begun to talk about a breakaway series, just as Bernie had done during the final months of the FISA/FOCA war. The manufacturers' stake in SLEC would ensure the future of Formula 1. But inevitably, that old alluring caress – of a more profitable deal – overcame him. The dealmaker had to keep dealing, he had to keep playing for a better hand, and a better hand and – still a better hand – until he clutched the jackpot.

And so Bernie agreed a deal with Kirch Media, a subsidiary of the KirchGruppe, which bought 36.75 per cent of EM.TV's shares for $619 million; and for EM.TV's twenty-five per cent option it paid SLEC $987.5 million. EM.TV retained 38.25 per cent, so that, between them, the two media companies effectively owned a seventy-five per cent stake in Formula 1. The manufacturers were livid, and an article in *The Sunday Times*, on 5 August 2001, did little to soothe them. In the article Thomas Haffa, founder of EM.TV, was reported to have said that he intended to 'hand control of the marketing rights to Formula 1 racing to broadcaster Kirch to help repay EM.TV's debts'. Bernie did his best to assure the manufacturers that free-to-air television coverage was safe, and their sponsors would continue to enjoy massive, revenue-generating, worldwide exposure.

'EM.TV have a fifty [38.25] per cent share, but no control. No control whatever,' Bernie had told *F1 Racing* ten months earlier. Thomas Haffa 'could sell his shares to whoever he wanted, and it wouldn't make any difference because they wouldn't have any control. Their fifty per cent is like having five per cent. The control rests with the trust, and I am still the chief executive of the company that the trust own.' But the manufacturers felt his words were hollow, and soon began making definitive plans for a rival world championship series – and their own television transmission.

Yes, Bernie was worried, and he knew that the saga with the manufacturers was poised to continue, like a scratched LP stuck in a groove. 'It's an ongoing thing,' says Bernie, 'what they want to do, I don't know. I don't think they know. I think it's one of those things where somebody said something and wished they hadn't, and don't know how to get out of it.' But, in the meantime, Bernie could console himself by counting the family billions. In less than two years, the Ecclestone fortune had increased by more than $3 billion, bringing their overall wealth to an estimated $4.1 billion. That's $4,000 million, or, in 'City' lingo, 4K 'Bernies'.

CHAPTER 16

ODDS AND ENDS

Bernie's billions along with the tobacco controversy and the theatre of Formula 1 established, for all time, a condition in his life that was already becoming an uncomfortable reality: he was a world figure and, hence, public property. Living with that burden would be an ongoing battle, and, worst of all, it would throw into question the genuineness of his relationships. But the private man also had the everyday burdens we all share – grief, illness and loneliness among others. Bernie, as always, would work his way out of anything he couldn't understand, or couldn't cope with, by ratcheting down his anxiety with activity. 'If I don't acknowledge it, it doesn't exist' is often his attitude in response to the most painful crises, like love affairs that have unexpectedly come to an end, the deaths of friends, or the deaths of his parents.

On 30 November 1990 Bernie's father, Sidney William Ecclestone, nearly eighty-seven, had died from heart disease. On the death certificate his occupation is given as 'car salesman (retired)'. To the end Sid had remained proud of Bernie's success at trading in cars – thousands of them, from Reliant Robin to Rolls-Royce – and the fact that his son had enabled him to exchange blue-collar work at Seamans foundry in Dartford for white-collar James Spencer Limited in suburban Bexleyheath where he had acted as Bernie's 'eyes', sizing up customers as they crossed the forecourt. When, five years later, Bernie's mother, Bertha Sophia, died at the age of eighty-nine of bronchopneumonia, her occupation on the death certificate is noted as: 'widow of Sidney William

Ecclestone, Car Showroom Manager (retired)'. Bernie's sister, Marian Tingy, had registered the deaths of both parents.

Bernie 'deeply cared for his parents,' said Marian. 'He looked after them in their old age, always came up to see Mum when she went into hospital and the nursing home… he was very upset when they died.' But Bernie was never physically affectionate with his parents, nor did he use words for love. Instead, he demonstrated love by looking after them. For the widowed Marian and her three children Bernie bought a house in villagey London Colney near St Albans in Hertfordshire; and he bought a house in the same neighbourhood for Sid and Bertha. During his father's funeral Bernie had lingered outside in the churchyard, too upset to join the service. Then he went home. He didn't attempt to go to his mother's funeral service, knowing that he would be unable to cope with it, and knowing that his daughter Deborah would be there and her family, and Tuana Tan; the gap between his personal past and present was more than he could emotionally breach. When Marian died in 2005, Bernie had attended the funeral, urged there by his daughters Tamara and Petra, who accompanied him. While she lived, Marian, like Deborah, was content with the knowledge that 'if ever I needed anything Bernie would help, I only had to ask'.

Bernie's generosity towards his parents and family is mirrored in the countless kindnesses towards his friends, even acquaintances. Over the years he has often called upon Formula 1's medical chief, Sid Watkins, to manage the health problems of, well, almost anyone Bernie has come into contact with – team mechanics, secretaries, family members, colleagues. His request is always the same: 'Please, just sort it out and send me the bill.' But even Bernie occasionally gets weary of the outstretched palm. There was a certain Austrian gentleman who, on arriving at Heathrow Airport, telephoned Sid, complaining that he was bleeding from his bladder and wanted to be admitted to a National Health Service hospital. Sid explained that admission to an NHS hospital was not possible because, first of all, he was Austrian and, secondly, he was resident in Spain. The only option was to be admitted to a private hospital. 'Can you afford that?' 'No,' said the Austrian, 'but Bernie will pay.' So Sid telephoned Bernie, giving him an account of the man's condition.

'How much will it cost?' asked Bernie.

'For a stay of three to five days in hospital, it will cost four or five thousand pounds.'

'How much will it cost to keep him in there forever?'

More recently, Bernie asked for Sid's help in finding the best specialist to treat a member of his staff who was suffering from a skin tumour. And, as usual, he picked up the tab.

Generosity is one of Bernie's principal traits, although he remains shy on this point. Most of the beneficiaries are glad to talk about his kindnesses. Bernie says not a word. Ever. A business associate estimates that Bernie has spent around £100 million supporting hospitals and other medical facilities. In particular he has helped disadvantaged children – in Brazil, Argentina, South Africa, Croatia – and he has helped people in many other ways, impossible to detail.

Ron Dennis, on the other hand, argues that Bernie is not *always* a silent benefactor. 'Anybody that is absolutely down, at the very bottom – and he knows them – he will step in and help them back to a point of self-respect. The problem is it's always difficult to know whether that's true because people he's helped rarely tell you about it. But strangely enough, he does. I mean, a while ago he said to me: "Oh, by the way, just to let you know, I've got Tom [Walkinshaw] out of trouble, I've managed to get Cosworth off his back and I've settled with Cosworth", and Cosworth are the people who were going to go absolutely to the end with Walkinshaw, even if he went to prison. Bernie might say "Well, it's bad for Formula 1." But in some ways, you think if he sees the individual as a racer, then he's there to sort of help. But I just hope I'm never in a position where I have to receive that sort of help, because I've always felt that Bernie functions a bit like most people think the Mafia functions, and you can ask Bernie for anything, and if it's in Bernie's power, he'll do it. But then you're made. That's it. Then you owe him forever.'

Back in the late 1980s I telephoned Bernie at his

Knightsbridge office to ask him to fund a gala evening at the Royal Academy in London. After a brief word with Ann, then his PA, Bernie was on the line. 'What do you need?' he asked; Bernie always gets straight to the point.

'Ten thousand pounds,' I answered, 'for a fund-raising event in support of the Royal College of Occupational Therapy.'

'OK, give me their account number. The money should be in there later today.'

'Thank you, Bernie', I said, adding, 'there are just a couple of minor details I need to tell you about.' I told him where the gala was to be held and that Anne, the Princess Royal, was the patron. 'She'll be there, and Bernie, I'd like you to stand next to her in the reception line.'

Silence.

'OK?'

Silence.

'It will be nice,' I continued, increasing the level of enthusiasm in my voice. 'You like art,' I went on, 'we'll be viewing an exhibition of Mantegna's drawings... victorious Roman armies... superb.'

Silence.

'And there's going to be a concert... Russian violinist... she's had marvellous reviews... and dinner.' Now there was a perceptible groan, so I changed tactics. 'Well, I'm sure Slavica will enjoy it, and the girls.'

'OK,' he answered. 'Gotta run.'

On the night, Bernie was flawlessly attired in evening dress as he stood next to the Princess in the grand entrance hall of the Royal Academy, greeting the paying guests like old friends. There was no stiffness in his manner, no self-conscious tugging of cufflinks. He was all ease and gladness, affecting a general *bonhomie*. Indeed, while cocktails were being served Bernie actually made small talk with Princess Anne, chirruping away, occasionally laughing. I was beginning to feel giddy. Then, in the exhibition room, he fell upon the Mantegnas with the ardour of a connoisseur whose particular passion just happened to be Renaissance drawings of sinewy soldiers. I couldn't see him during the concert, for I was sitting near a pillar, but somehow I felt that he was conveying the impression of being entirely pleased with the world. At dinner we were seated next to each other, and Bernie consumed each course with – what was for him – gusto while, between mouthfuls, entertaining the table. He was the toast of the evening, and I was succumbing to a lofty sense of self-congratulations. 'Oh, Bernie, it's all been so wonderful,' I gushed. 'Thank you for coming, thank you for everything you've done.'

'Susan,' said Bernie, stern of voice, 'I would have given you £20,000 if I didn't have to come to this thing.'

For Bernie, gratitude – expressed by either party – is excruciating. For his sixtieth birthday, the office staff at his Chessington premises got together to throw a little surprise party for him, with cake and champagne. 'He hated it and it was very embarrassing afterwards!' says Penny Whitaker, who, since 1989, has worked as the administrator of, first, the Formula 3000 championship series and then GP2, which replaced it. Begun in 2005, GP2 has become one of the stepping-stones to Formula 1, turning out drivers such as Nico Rosberg, Lewis Hamilton, Timo Glock and Heikki Kovalainen among others. It was set up by Bernie along with former Renault boss Flavio Briatore and Bruno Michael, who was the series promoter and was formerly the managing director of Ligier. This trio should form a brand, 'Triple B' (Bernie, Briatore, Bruno), and stamp it on a hefty muscle of motor racing's haunch. In 2006 they sold GP2 to CVC Capital Partners for an estimated $300 million, then turned around and set up GP2 Asia in 2008. Not content with that, in 2010 'Triple B' launched GP3 as the feeder series to GP2.

'Bernie is very, very demanding,' continues Penny. 'He rarely gives praise and is quick to point out mistakes. But, he's exhilarating to work for' – as long as the office routine is strictly observed, 'nothing out of place, no boxes under the desk', nor should anyone object when 'he leaps on to desktops to reposition the blinds'. As for the privilege of being driven by Bernie… Penny describes his driving style as 'controlled recklessness'. Before it was illegal to use a mobile phone while driving, Bernie used to 'rest the steering wheel on his leg while dialling... he must have an angel watching over him.'

Perhaps the same angel was watching over Bernie on the night, in 1997, when he and Slavica were tackled by burglars outside the Princes Gate office – above which they then had an apartment. On arriving home with Slavica, he got out his keys and was about to unlock the front door when two hefty thugs sprang at them from inside. Bernie tried to hold them back by pushing on the door, while shouting to Slavica to give him a hand: 'Come on, push, try to close it. Push!' 'I can't,' she said. 'I'm wearing high heels.' Bernie, between blows, yelled back: 'I told you not to wear those bloody shoes!' And then just as suddenly the burglars were gone. Bernie and Slavica were badly shaken but, luckily, Slavica was only bruised and Bernie suffered nothing more than a broken nose. Their attackers managed to get away with Slavica's £600,000 diamond ring; and neither ring nor burglars have since been traced. A string of similar robberies targeting the rich and famous had occurred throughout 1997. Scotland Yard called the thugs 'Rolex Robbers', employing a technique that was always 'smash-mouth and grab'. Being rich and famous has brought with it a number of death threats and kidnapping threats. Bernie doesn't worry about his own safety, the street savvy acquired in Dartford and in Warren Street has served him well. His only concern is for the well-being of his family.

The decade of the Nineties was a time when Bernie, in his sixties, would frequently confront his own mortality, although he is not afraid of dying. 'I'm not afraid of anything,' he says. That is the key to Bernie's life, he has never been afraid to take chances because he obliterates fear by the sheer force of his will. And he is not just the Evel Knievel of the financial world, he once sat in the last car in a row of Formula 1 cars while some American daredevil on a motorcycle zoomed up a ramp and flew out above the cars before landing – just the other side of Bernie, the only person brave enough to sit there. It even took a certain amount of bravery to attempt the flotation, and then to see the Eurobond sale through to completion, hating all those prying eyes intent upon the Ecclestone company ledgers; and he was not too fond of the controls imposed by the trust. But following the deaths of his parents he had begun to realise that he must make the future secure for his family, particularly in a world he no longer inhabited. Otherwise it didn't make any sense, all that effort, the empire he had built, would not matter, and that was intolerable.

Bernie was also concerned about the future well-being of Formula 1 itself, as were the team bosses, anxious to see an arrangement in place that would involve them – directly – in the commercial aspects of the sport, while seamlessly connecting the Bernie and post-Bernie eras. Then there were the physical reminders, the punch-up with robbers and, more significantly, the chest pain that led, in 1999, to a triple-heart-bypass operation. But even then he made light of it, cracking jokes on the way to the operating theatre, making the nurses laugh. After his surgery, as the staff in the intensive-care unit were struggling to get his chest drains working properly, Bernie leaned over the side of his bed and enquired politely: 'Would you girls like me to get up and help you with that?' Alarmed, one of the nurses telephoned John Wright, the cardiac surgeon who had performed the operation. 'Mr Ecclestone has got brain damage,' she said. 'No, no, that's just his sense of humour,' John Wright assured her.

The obverse to Bernie's blazing energy is the idle happiness of laughter. He doesn't laugh out loud, his is the quiet smile, an attempt at earnestness, while those around him are falling about. His jokes are retold from one end of the paddock to the other, then taken home and shared out. Sid continues to savour his vintage stock of Bernie's stories and cracks. 'Bernie's sense of humour, like his kindness, is paramount to his character,' says Sid. All of Bernie's friends and most of his acquaintances would agree.

Ten days after his heart operation, Bernie was back in the office putting in his usual 8am to 6.15pm day, 'feeling like I've always felt, no change'. He still took time for lunch at the 'Swag and Tails', the pub (which he now owns) near his Knightsbridge office, although the old egg and chips washed down with half a pint of beer has been exchanged for lighter fare. When he was not jetting around the world, evenings were spent, until recent years, with Slavica and their daughters, Tamara and Petra. Tamara now has her own mews house, a gift for her eighteenth birthday, but she continued to enjoy evenings and weekends with her parents and sister. Petra, likewise, eventually moved out of the Ecclestones' compact Georgian mansion, but it remained the essential 'home'. For Bernie, time with his family was fundamental to his happiness. When his daughters were younger, he made every effort to drive them to school, in Slavica's Audi estate car.

And school, or rather education, was to become something of a sticking point. Both girls attended Francis Holland School, after which Tamara – with much encouragement from her parents – headed for University College, London, which she left in order to work on Bernie's *F1 Magazine* and as a sales assistant at Armani. One can almost hear the echoes of Mr Ecclestone senior's frustration when Bernie dropped out of school; the compromise then was Bernie's employment at the gasworks laboratory in Dartford. If Bernie had hoped that life as a member of Britain's nine-to-five workforce, starting at the bottom, would cause Tamara to yearn for academia, he may have been right – initially. She returned to university to read sociology and social policy at the London School of Economics, but then left after a year to take up a brief course in television presenting. This led to a job presenting Channel 4's *Red Bull Air Race* followed by work as a presenter and host for Sky Sports Italia, covering the 2008 and 2009 Grand Prix seasons. But rather than be pegged as a female sportscaster, she has turned her hand to refurbishing – another Ecclestone tradition – the 'Swag and Tails' pub, which she owns with her father and intends to manage. Both young women receive a generous allowance – some £100,000 per annum – but it hasn't snuffed out their determination.

Petra, like her older sister, was similarly eager for the wider world. After achieving three grade As in her A-level examinations, Petra attended art college, but left to start work, which, in this instance, consisted of designing and promoting her own fashion collections. Bernie's tailor of more than thirty years, Edward Sexton, trained her in the basics, just as he had with Stella McCartney. Using some of Sexton's patterns, Petra, at the age of nineteen, produced FORM, a high-priced line of menswear that became the third best-selling menswear label at Harrods. Petra negotiated the Harrods contract herself with one of the store's buyers, rather than rely on her father's influence to short-circuit a deal with Harrods' owner. But after two years, FORM, with cashmere pullover sweaters priced in the hundreds of pounds, fell victim to the recession. Undaunted, Petra got busy designing and promoting a collection of womenswear, in a broader price range. Apart from designing, she serves as an ambassador for the Meningitis Trust; as a teenager her life had been threatened by the illness.

Both Tamara and Petra, presently twenty-seven and twenty-two, are exceptionally beautiful, like their mother, and they've done occasional modelling, so it was predictable that their lives – as progeny of the rich and famous – would become tabloid fodder. But rather than shrink from the camera's gaze, they have explored the potential for a partnership, Tamara with her television presenting and Petra with glitzy catwalk shows (most notably in New York), and there has also been Channel 4's *A Wife for William* in which Tamara was a contestant. Together they participated in a pilot for a reality TV show and there's 'Tamara's World' (the title says it all), which is perhaps reason enough for the press to link these talented young women with their American counterparts, the Hilton sisters, Paris and Nicky. But Tamara and Petra are not particularly fond of parties and alcohol. They are, however, keen on shoes, handbags and acres of clothes.

The break-up of their parents' marriage in 2009 brought a change to their lives that they are still coming to terms with, but they remain close to both Bernie and Slavica. With Slavica, however, they have the special relationship reserved for mothers and daughters. Slavica was always a hands-on mother, somewhat in the Italian mode or folklore. She is renowned for never having had a dishwasher, preferring to do the housework herself – dishes, making beds, cooking up a feast – and she made certain her daughters became familiar with the use of a dishcloth and running a household, though nowadays both young women employ housekeepers and other staff. Tamara and Petra take pride in Slavica's homeland, Croatia, and are able to speak the language. Petra has even designed fashions for the Croation company Siscica. What's more, they always make time for their maternal grandparents, who provide a welcome kind of simplicity not so easily available in London – particularly for Formula 1 heiresses caught in the perpetual fireworks of flashing cameras. Tamara was badly bruised at a young age when her boyfriend delivered a tell-all story to one of the tabloid newspapers. She got over her wariness of men and has since enjoyed happier relationships, although she distrusts reporters who have twisted her words – and Petra's – more than once.

In April 2011 Petra became engaged to wealthy businessman James Stunt. Bernie organised an eye-wateringly lavish party to celebrate the occasion in advance of the couple's August wedding in Rome. While tabloid journalists were speculating on the cost of the engagement party and wedding, Petra was acquiring – with Bernie's help – a hundred-roomed Los Angeles home priced at $150 million, reputedly the most expensive home for sale in the United States; she also owns a listed Georgian mansion in Chelsea worth £66 million, which out-prices Tamara's house, in Kensington Palace Gardens, valued at £45 million. Do the sisters worry that an inheritance of perhaps a billion pounds each might bring the genuineness of their relationships into question? Right now, Bernie's daughters are far more absorbed in modifying their acquisitions. Perhaps they've inherited their father's early talent for fixing-up and selling on at a profit. If so, they are well on the way to adding to their fortunes.

Bernie's restaurant venture with Tamara, the 'Swag and Tails', is only a soupçon in his property portfolio, which has continual additions in England and abroad, including office blocks, Asian shopping centres and the odd golf course. At one time the jewel in the crown was a twelve-bedroom mansion in London's Kensington Palace Gardens, in the same neighbourhood as Kensington Palace, the former home of Princess Diana, and the London home of the Sultan of Brunei. Said to be 'fifty-five times bigger than the average home', the house was complete with Turkish baths, a ballroom, an oak-panelled picture gallery, hair salon, a swimming pool (in the basement) surrounded by jewel-embedded marble columns, and – very useful to Bernie – a garage for twenty cars. More than 9,000 square feet of marble was utilised in the house, much of it taken from the quarry used for construction of the Taj Mahal. Bernie paid £50 million for it through a Liechtenstein-based trust in 2001, and in 2004 sold it to his friend and the richest man in Britain, steel magnate Lakshmi Mittal, for £70 million – making it, then, the highest priced domestic real estate transaction in the world. Slavica had not liked the house and preferred to stay in Chelsea, where Bernie bought a building near their home for a mere £25 million. It was formerly the home of Chelsea College, housing the college's department of pharmacology and a student hall of residence; Bernie planned to turn it into luxury flats.

In September 2007 he acquired a property of a different type altogether – Queens Park Rangers Football Club. QPR had struggled since relegation from the Premier League in 1996, taking on a debt of £13 million. Along with co-owners Flavio Briatore and, later, Lakshmi Mittal, Bernie agreed to pay off the debt and offered 1p in cash for each QPR share (62.3 per cent of the total shares, worth about £1 million). They also gave assurances to commit more money by, among other things, investing in the first-team squad, its academy and scouting system. They further agreed to loan the club £5 million towards buying new players. When the takeover was agreed, Bruno Michael – promoter of the GP2 and, more recently, GP3 motor racing series – joined the club's board along with Briatore. What is interesting is that, until the QPR takeover, it was widely believed Bernie – a Chelsea supporter – was about to become the proud owner of Arsenal Football

Club. True-blue Bernie style. And his style was positively flaunted in April 2011 when Queens Park Rangers returned to the Premier League after an absence of fifteen years. Prior to the promotion Bernie had acquired the majority of Flavio Briatore's stake.

Perhaps the most surprising aspect of Bernie's tale of humble Suffolk boy turned financial genius is that he has come to this point in life without developing an overly padded ego. If he is required to describe his occupation on formal documents, he'll write 'company director'; ask him what he does and he'll say 'used car dealer'. Yet this is a used car dealer who commands respect from world leaders, people like Nelson Mandela, the former South African President who in 1995 wrote to the then Prime Minister, John Major, in support of a nomination for a knighthood for Bernie. In his letter President Mandela wrote: 'Through motorsport, Mr Ecclestone has been well known to the people of South Africa for many years, and is indeed very worthy of this nomination for his lifetime achievements. His love for Britain and the promotion of the skills of her people are well known throughout the world, and his devotion to the promotion of British manufacturing in the face of great competition from other countries is much admired. Rarely do you find a man who has devoted his life to the promotion of a competitive sport, which is now shared by 100 million [then more like 350 million] people in over 132 countries.' Bernie, likewise, admires Mandela and over the years they have become good friends.

There were also letters supporting the nomination from figures such as Silvio Berlusconi, Italian business mogul and latterly controversial Prime Minister, and Bob Hawke, then Prime Minister of Australia.

Perhaps more interesting was the letter from Brazil's Minister of Sport, Edson Arantes do Nascimento, better known as 'Pelé', who wrote: 'Just as I and some of my countrymen have tried to focus attention on our great country and its friendly, talented people, so Mr Ecclestone has helped his country achieve pre-eminence in motor racing and its highly competitive technology upon which much of the progress in the development of modern road vehicles is based. It is widely known that he alone is responsible for keeping the political centre of motorsport firmly in Britain despite fierce competition from other countries.'

It was Max Mosley who had made the nomination, stating that Bernie had 'created 50,000 new jobs in Britain, over the past thirty years, by insisting all manufacturing to do with Formula 1 was carried out in Britain.' Bernie has not yet received a knighthood. Two prominent members of the Formula 1 community who have received knighthoods – Stirling Moss and Frank Williams – believe this honour must be extended to Bernie. 'Of course he should be knighted,' says Stirling. 'He's done so much for the sport and, what's more, he makes it happen on time. I don't agree with everything he does, but there's no doubt he should be knighted.' Most people who know Bernie are outraged that he isn't yet a recipient, although he himself doesn't actually care one way or the other. Meanwhile, other countries have been more generous. He has received honours from all over the globe. Most recently, the Emir of Bahrain conferred upon Bernie the 'Bahrain Medal of the First Degree', usually reserved for heads of state; the medal was bestowed by the now discredited King Shaikh Hamad bin Isa Al-Khalifa.

In 1997, as part of a tribute honouring Bernie's 'fifty years of service to the motorsport industry', Frank Williams, who has known Bernie for nearly forty years, said the following: 'Bernie, I watched your arrival in Formula 1 all those years ago. I watched your learning of it, I watched your mastery of it. And now, I can sit here and applaud your vision for it. Because what you did for Formula 1 and for all of us who have participated in it, and for all the fans has truly been remarkable. Many of us have profited from it and I hope we all show our gratefulness to you in some way or other. I would just like to say to you, from me, that I am astonished how you continue to do the brilliant deals. I have practised and tried myself, but never ever got near what you have achieved. I do wish you truly, from the bottom on my heart, many, many years of successful business as long as you let me continue to ride in your bandwagon.'

There were also tributes from Jurgen Schrempp, then Chairman of Daimler-Benz, and from Luca di Montezemolo, Chairman of Ferrari and President of Fiat, along with the 1964 Formula 1 World Champion John Surtees. Outside the motor racing community, Bernie was honoured with tributes from opera star Placido Domingo, the then Argentine President Carlos Saul Menem, actor Sylvester Stallone, Prince Albert of Monaco, Juan Antonio Samaranch, then President of the International Olympic Committee, and Jeff Kennett, then Premier of Victoria, Australia. Bernie's friend, Australian businessman Ron Walker, was responsible for putting the event together.

Bernie, of course, brushed off all the praise with humour: 'What an evil lot of people we have... Can't trust anybody... Everything's wrong. And I don't know how I could have been in motor racing for fifty years. My last birthday was in October; I was fifty. When you get to my age – fifty – you start thinking like an old vintage car. You start wondering if all the things are still going to work properly. And you know sometimes with old vintage car guys, they go out testing, but aren't allowed to do unofficial testing these days, or anything.' Then he thanked everyone who had contributed to the evening. Bernie showed not a trace of nerves, he actually appeared relaxed. After years of success, criticism yes, but also genuine praise for genuine achievement, the excruciatingly shy and private man, who often conceals his shyness with bravado, had stopped running away from attention. In 1997, at the age of sixty-seven, he was developing confidence.

The tributes may also have caused Bernie to think about his future in Formula 1: 'When people start saying nice things about you, it usually means they want you to go.' The quintet of manufacturers who then owned teams or had invested vast sums of money in them – DaimlerChrysler (Mercedes), Renault, Ford (Jaguar), BMW, and Fiat (Ferrari) – continued to worry Bernie. In the 1997 tribute Ferrari's Luca di Montezemolo had praised Bernie for making Formula

1 'the most important sporting event in the world'; in 2003 he called him 'greedy'. On 13 September 2004 in an article in *The Times,* di Montezemolo was more specific: 'Such an expensive sport cannot survive if we do not increase revenues and it is a mistake that the sport is now seventy-five per cent owned by the banks. A certain era is finished and we have to look at something new which is totally acceptable to the players who, at the moment, get only forty-seven per cent of the money from the television rights, and nothing from the tickets, advertising and other sources of income. It is not possible any more. We said these things three years ago but unfortunately somebody has not understood.'

The 'somebody' was dismissive. 'Yeah, he keeps having the same conversation. Ten or fifteen years, it's the same conversation. He came to Monza, does an act – very good, should get an Oscar, he should make a CD and play it every Monza. I've known him a long time, he's a very good friend so we always have a bit of a debate with each other, but we don't mean it.' Friend or foe, Ferrari and its president, like the other manufacturers, were determined to have a bigger portion of the commercial feast – estimated to be worth more than a billion dollars annually. As the first step in establishing a series to usurp Formula 1, the manufacturers set up Grand Prix World Championship Holdings BV (GPWC) in the Netherlands. The rival championship was to begin operating in 2008 following the expiry of the Concorde Agreement at the end of 2007. If Bernie would not change the arrangement for the dispersal of Formula 1's commercial revenue – giving them a larger share – the manufacturers would proceed with their plans, although they were no longer concerned about the control of companies interested in promoting pay-TV.

During 2002, EM.TV and Kirch Media had collapsed, and their seventy-five per cent stake in SLEC Holdings Limited was picked up by Speed Investments Limited, the investment vehicle for three banks: the ill-fated Lehman Brothers, JP Morgan and Munich-based Bayerische Landesbank; Kirch had pledged their shares against loans from the banks. Bernie continued to retain a twenty-five per cent stake through his

Jersey-based trust, Bambino Holdings Limited. The banks however had their own issues to settle regarding the control of the Ecclestone empire.

Although they owned the majority of the shares in SLEC, they did not have voting control of Formula One Holdings – which managed the day-to-day operations of the sport and the commercial relationship with the teams. The banks declared their intention to float SLEC in the 'short to medium term', and firming-up their control was seen as a preparatory measure so that the necessary level of transparency could be readily forthcoming. Writs were flying. Again, Bernie played it down. 'That's only about jurisdiction, about where the jurisdiction should be. It's not a problem.' Bernie's relationship with the banks was 'all right'. But not so the teams, who for the most part, like di Montezemolo, objected to 'outsiders' holding a majority stake; the car manufacturers, the Ferrari Chairman told *The Sunday Times*, were 'not prepared to fund the banks, they prefer to have it in their own pockets. Without us, in 2008, the banks will own 100 per cent of nothing.' So Bernie put together a plan to buy back fifty per cent of the shares on the condition that the Concorde Agreement would be extended until 2015. This was rejected. In addition, the FIA had attempted to impose new technical regulations without the required notice or the agreement of the teams. The team principals, disgusted, then considered ignoring the existing Concorde Agreement and explored the idea of starting the GPWC series as early as 2005. Now Bernie was getting nettled, and concerned. He had reason to be – not all his ventures were whirlwind successes.

By the end of 2002, Bernie's digital television company – begun with such optimism in 1997 – had closed down. He had invested more than $70 million in his pay-per-view service, but the returns were nothing like what was necessary to sustain the company. Formula 1 enthusiasts, instead of taking up the in-depth digital coverage produced by 'Bakersville', had tended to stick with channels in which they already had subscriptions or 'free' terrestrial coverage. Two hundred staff based at Biggin Hill had to be laid off, which Bernie found particularly difficult, so he continued to pay them until they had secured other jobs; none of his former digital TV employees suffered financially. During the 2003 Grand Prix season, Bernie hoped to offer the impressive, clear images provided by his digital service – gratis – to the terrestrial channels, but he failed to acquire the hosting rights from local television companies.

The move may have boosted television-viewing figures, which had begun to slide; the blame rested upon the predictability of Michael Schumacher's Ferrari victories. But the global viewing numbers for 2003 were more robust, averaging thirty-nine million per race or roughly 624 million for the season. In 2004 and 2005 the numbers slumped to 565 million, but improved again in 2006 – despite a World Cup – to 580 million, rising to some 600 million in 2007 and 2008, according to *Formula Money*. The 2006 viewing figures were boosted, in part, by the championship-deciding Brazilian Grand Prix, which was viewed by a record total audience of 154 million. The race was won by Brazilian driver Felipe Massa and the championship by Fernando Alonso – and this was the spellbinding final race of what was then thought to be the end of Michael Schumacher's Formula 1 career. The television audience for the season received 10,600 hours of dedicated Formula 1 programming in some 185 countries. With the success of these figures, accompanied by award-winning coverage, it was astonishing that ITV withdrew from their contract, worth £43 million per year, to take up Champions League football. Bernie assuaged his disappointment by handing the deal to the BBC for £250 million over five years from 2009, picking up an extra £30 million or so per year while he was at it. After a twelve-year absence, Formula 1 had returned to its BBC roots and fans could again watch the sport free from adverts and free in general – apart from their TV licences. ITV's decision came back to haunt them with the continued, nail-biting success of Lewis Hamilton, who finally secured the title in 2008 – boosting the figures yet again. And in October 2009 the BBC enjoyed a peak audience of nine million viewers who tuned in to watch Jenson Button clinch the World Championship in Brazil. Added to the BBC's race and practice coverage is a star-studded Formula 1 cast with veteran commentator Martin Brundle along with David Coulthard and former team owner Eddie Jordan – and, at the touch of the red button, viewers can indulge in practice commentary and an hour-long post-race fan forum. ITV didn't lose out altogether: they signed a deal with Bernie for the online rights to the 2008 Formula 1 season at a cost of £3 million, and the deal has since been renewed. And while the fans are surfing the web they can pick up Formula 1 video games, DVDs, clothing – with all or a portion of the proceeds going, variously, to the Formula One Group of companies.

But back to the TV viewing figures. Apart from British viewers' delight in Button's success, the year 2009 saw a 13% slump in the overall audience, which translates to a disturbing loss of 80 million viewers. Formula One Management's official figure for the year was 520 million. This time the blame rested on races staged during the night (Singapore) and towards twilight (Australia and Abu Dhabi), when many viewers were accustomed to watching other programmes. There was moderate improvement – 527 viewers – in 2010, thanks to a more exciting season. But will the predictable presence of a German on the podium – Vettel this time – cause viewers again to switch off? Bernie likes to look on the bright side: 'For the first time ever, High Definition television coverage is on offer to all broadcasters,' he announced, 'with several, including the United Kingdom's BBC, having already accepted the improved quality for their 2011 outputs.' The BBC, incidentally, is unlikely to renew its F1 contract after 2014, according to rumours. Meanwhile, Formula 1 receives an estimated £290 million annually from its global broadcast rights.

The principal problem with the lacklustre years between 2003 and 2005 was entertainment – the sport's life-blood. It was missing. The blame was due to the technological changes in the cars, which were restricting overtaking along with the riveting shoulder-to-shoulder/wheel-to-wheel dramas. Then there was the clinical exercise of single-lap qualifying and the uneven quality of production, along with competition – or at least better entertainment – from other motorsports such as NASCAR and A1GP. Races covered by Bernie's production company – those in Australia, Malaysia, Bahrain, Canada, USA, Turkey and China – generally provided excellent viewing. Formula One Management's in-house television production company (made up of a few remaining crew from the pay-per-view digital venture) won the FIA's Television Trophy for coverage of the 2006 Chinese Grand Prix: 'The race was one of the most thrilling of the season, featuring superb driving, on-track passing, and an exciting finish', according to an FIA statement. Not so some of the races covered by local television stations with local directors – with local interests.

This was a problem that more than distressed Bernie: 'entertainment' and 'value' are written in bold letters across his heart. Which is why he came up with a new format for Saturday qualifying, then arguably more exciting than the actual race. It involved, still does, two hard-fought elimination rounds followed by a pole position shoot-out. And it is why, for the opening race of the 2007 season, the Australian Grand Prix, the circuit was snaked with additional fibre-optic cables, and there were more cameras and camera angles – it was a visual feast. Then, the following April in Bahrain, 'Bakersville' rose from the ashes in the form of a building housing the television equipment with 'F1 Communications' – the new name of Bernie's TV organisation – emblazoned across its exterior. All broadcasters take what is known as the 'World Feed'. In 2007 F1 Communications, under the auspices of Formula One Management, took over production for nearly all of the 2007 races, providing better coordination between in-car cameras and the director. During the 2009 season, the World Feed was produced by FOM for all races other than the Monaco Grand Prix, which was produced by Télé Monte Carlo. Furthermore, Bernie, along with financial support from the teams, invested heavily in the High Definition equipment. With that under way, he then aimed (somewhat unsuccessfully) at further enticing Formula 1's homeland audiences by holding night races in

Australia and Asia – under Las Vegas-strength floodlighting – to correspond with comfortable European time slots. This he achieved in Singapore, and other Asian races followed suit. Australia liked its daytime race, so a compromise was reached; the race ran in the late afternoon, which was meant to suit viewers in Europe. With regard to measures that would allow for more action-packed sequences during the race, Bernie had various suggestions, irrigating the circuit with water being among the more interesting, but he'll have to be patient – it's up to the FIA's rule-making process. Now, while Vettel and Red Bull command the lead in points, there's still considerable competition among the lower tiers jostling to depose them, and entertainment – on Sunday as well as Saturday – has returned to the sport. Bernie's whole ethos had demanded it.

Back in the autumn of 2004, the dwindling television audience was only one part of a much broader concern – the distribution of the commercial revenue – that so chafed the manufacturers. They decided against starting their series in 2005, but remained resolute in their determination to obtain a greater share of the commercial revenue, and all along they had wanted more authority in the running of Formula 1. If the manufacturers pulled out – and there would be more car-makers joining GPWC – then future earnings in Formula 1 would evaporate – which is why the banks wanted to take control of the F1 companies. Bernie knew that he had to find a solution. What he, the three banks and the GPWC eventually came up with was 'a memorandum of understanding', in which the teams would gradually acquire a fifty per cent stake in SLEC; the GPWC would be allowed to have three directors on the board, although Bernie would remain in overall command for three years; the Concorde Agreement was to be extended; and SLEC could eventually be floated on the Stock Exchange. 'To discharge an unfulfilled obligation,' SLEC was to immediately give $150 million to Ferrari, Williams and McLaren. The definitive agreement was to be signed by mid-2004. But instead, says McLaren's Ron Dennis, 'Bernie torpedoed the deal, it was not in his interest.'

Had Bernie complied he might have prevented a legal process that sought to loosen his control of Formula 1.

With the shares in SLEC going to 'outsiders' – as the team bosses saw it – there developed an attitude that their contributions to Formula 1 – and their individual achievements – had not been properly appreciated or acknowledged. Like Bernie, these people are about challenging what is possible every single day. Formula 1 has never been about punching a clock and doing what is adequate. The sport belongs to those who work beyond normal physical and mental thresholds, and thus in the world of Formula 1 there are – seemingly – miracles in human achievement, technological achievement and in the way of financial rewards. Formula 1 is also about living with disaster – death, financial ruin – and overcoming it. If everything were lost tomorrow Formula 1 people would waste not one split second before grinding their way back. In the end they may not make it, like Arrows and many others, but their efforts would have been heroic.

Take McLaren boss, Ron Dennis, for example. While still a teenager, in the early Sixties, he began his career in motor racing as a mechanic for Cooper before moving on to Brabham; by 1968 he was chief mechanic to Jack Brabham himself. Ron clearly remembers the 'phenomenally hard work. Six or seven people looked after the cars and one of those individuals would be responsible for engines going back to the engine shop, and we would be responsible for manufacturing the cars and maintaining every aspect of the cars and the gearboxes and everything. I mean it was a horrendous job and not only that, we had no limitations to practice, so we could go to some circuits and practice probably six hours and then at the end of the day you would have to put the cars back in the transporters – a lot of which were sort of converted horse boxes – and drive them to the local garage that the team manager had previously arranged space in. Then it was unload the cars, work through the night and load them up again. After that we would go and have some sort of sink/basin shower.

'You rarely got home. It was great if you had enough time

to stop on the way to a circuit to have a night's sleep. The highlight of the year was going to Watkins Glen where you actually had a facility. I mean it was just a sort of large modern shed and all the teams were in there. But it had a hard floor and it had lights and heating and you wouldn't have to put the cars anywhere. You would just trundle them down to the pits or drive them down to the pits, which is what mechanics did in those days, you were driving the cars all over the place. After a Grand Prix you would load the cars up again and bring them home. It was intensive work, a little bit like being on an oil rig, you were working all the time. When you did get home it was like the sailor on a galleon who's getting off, he's got money in his pockets and all he's looking for is a girl and wine. I remember when I had a day off – a whole day – by eleven o'clock I'd go and have a haircut, and then I'd go to the coffee bar to meet with my friends. The next day, I'd go back to work.' The pay was such that Ron could afford 'trendy' cars: 'I had my Lotus Cortinas and Mini Coopers'. By the age of twenty 'I had an E-type Jaguar. It was unheard of for a twenty-year-old, so I used to get stopped all the time.'

It was while driving one of his 'trendy' cars that Ron had a serious accident. Exhausted from the usual succession of long days, he was driving from Crystal Palace to the Brabham factory to pick up some parts needed to repair one of the cars. Coming out of London he stopped at a traffic light and promptly fell asleep. The light changed, but Ron's car remained stationary. Someone tooted his horn, and Ron – though still asleep – responded by driving, at speed, straight across the road and into a lamppost. He was thrown through the windscreen, and suffered 'a lot of lacerations and damage to my eyes'; one of his pupils still resembles a burst star. A lengthy stay in hospital was followed by a lengthier convalescence. 'I wasn't allowed to do anything physical for three months because of the pressure it put on my eye. So we hired another mechanic and I took over managing the team, and really that was it, from that moment on I was managing.'

In 1983, I had lunch with Ron, maybe it was only coffee – I was buying. While I was looking over his crumpled, cotton suit worn with a knitted waistcoat in a rather interesting, ethnic pattern of mauve and fern green, he told me that he had just sunk everything that he had, and everything that he could borrow from banks, friends, relatives and anyone else who would loan him money, into buying a fifty per cent equity stake in the McLaren racing team. Then he calmly admitted that if it didn't work out he would probably have to commit suicide. Succeed or die is a common Formula 1 scenario, but the players are a rare few. Today Ron counts his well-deserved wealth in the hundreds of millions, and he has taken a great team and made it one of the greatest ever in Formula 1; a string of champions have raced under the McLaren banner. Gordon Murray has worked for Ron after leaving Brabham; only the best in their fields, including at least one Nobel prize winner, are employed by Ron Dennis.

McLaren's new main headquarters – designed by Sir Norman Foster and measured in acreage – also houses a few mega-business sidelines, including the new MP4 12C road car, and is implausibly high-tech; Disney World's Epcot Center has nothing to compare with Ron's taste in office design, nor does James Bond. Yet it is somehow fitting, big enough – almost – to represent what it had cost in bravery. Ron's own office is situated towards the centre of the building and is suspended – literally hovering in mid-air – so that he can look, in one fabulous gaze, upon all that he has created, with the help of 'only the best'.

During the years 2007 to 2009 Ron's bravery, along with that of the team, was severely and repeatedly tested, and, again, survival was on the line. Between March and July 2007, Nigel Stepney, Ferrari's disgruntled chief mechanic, renewed a friendship with Michael Coughlan, McLaren's chief designer, which involved texts and phone calls passed between them, culminating in 780 pages of documents detailing every aspect of the 2007 Ferrari's design. Trudy Coughlan, Michael's wife, took the sheaf of papers to a Surrey printer, asking him to copy the material on to two CDs. She couldn't have known that the middle-aged man who served her was an avid Formula 1 fan, nor that he would have the tenacity to Google her surname and discover the link to McLaren, followed by a second Google to Ferrari's Stefano Domenicali, the company's sporting director. Initially, no evidence could be found to show that the information on Ferrari's technology had been handed on to other McLaren employees, but then the corrosive rivalry between McLaren's drivers, Fernando Alonso and Lewis Hamilton, caused Alonso to reveal to Ron Dennis that he 'had something on his email system that is from one of the engineers' – incriminating Ferrari details. Ron immediately contacted the FIA, and during a second investigation more damning emails and text messages were discovered. 'Spy-gate', as it came to be known, became one of the biggest scandals in Formula 1's sixty-year history, and ultimately resulted in a historic ruling against McLaren by the FIA's World Council, costing the team the 2007 Constructors' Championship and a $100 million fine. There was, happily, a silver lining to this cloud: the $100 million was used to set up the Motor Sport Safety and Development Fund of the FIA Foundation, to be used for research, driver development and education. At the end of the 2007 season Ron apologised to the FIA; he and Max Mosley had had many a bitter dispute and for the sake of the team the wise course was humility. Ron also guaranteed that none of Ferrari's intellectual property would appear on the 2008 McLaren – which somehow made Lewis Hamilton's World Championship title in 2008 all the brighter. The McLaren boys really know how to make a comeback: they know how to swallow hard and look beyond mounting disappointment, which, in September 2008, included the controversial removal of their victory at Spa.

Ron was now able to step back, take a breath and devote his attention to problems closer to home, and to the development of other projects in the McLaren Group. In 2009, he handed the reins of team principal to Martin Whitmarsh, McLaren's chief operating officer, though he has continued to turn up in the pit lane at many Formula 1 races. Whitmarsh, with nineteen years of experience at McLaren, was soon paddling fiercely against the shockwaves of the Lewis Hamilton-supported deception in Australia that threatened, again, to bring down the mighty McLaren team. This time it was called 'Lie-gate', and sent McLaren back to the FIA's World Council for another hearing. The subtext was thought to be Max having a go at Ron, for Formula 1, after all, has long been about getting an advantage over the other team, making words such as 'lie' and 'cheat' seem out of context. Anyway, McLaren survived. Throw the whole book at them, add in a few financial woes and heartbreak, but they'll still come back – and back again. There was never any question about that.

Take Frank Williams as another example of the Formula 1 breed. After the accident in France that had left him quadriplegic he lingered around the hospital only long enough to be able to thank the doctors and nurses who had saved his life, if not his body. But he still had a brain, and what a brain: absolute clarity of mind, a creative but precise intellect, an entertaining speaker and a linguist to boot. Best of all, Frank possesses an indomitable will. Before the accident Frank was the team owner who stood out as a fitness freak. He was the one who was always jogging – all around the track, through the paddock and as far as his legs would carry him – jog, jog, jog, not an ounce of surplus flesh, correct nutrition, absolute discipline, that was Frank. It still is. But his exercise routine has become more extensive. Instead of jogging he takes bouts of standing, in a frame, several times a day in order to maintain his cardiovascular status. He exercises his upper limbs, in thirty-minute sessions, throughout each day; and at every opportunity he moves the wheels of his wheelchair with a pushing, shrugging motion of his arms. When he isn't exercising, he is working, flat out, as competitive as ever, and he still maintains a strict diet and carries no fat. Like Ron Dennis, Frank's world is full of gleaming technology spread across acres of land, and he can even boast a 'Frank Williams' roundabout at the entrance to his compound.

Frank has come a long way since the days when he was 'soup kitchen' poor, as described by a fellow racing driver. He raced in Formula 3 in 1964 and recalls 'a very erratic season', as were 1965 and 1966. 'At the end of 1967 Piers

Courage persuaded me to buy a car for him for the 1968 Formula 2 season, that's when I started motor racing as an entrant proper if you like, semi-professionally'. The pinch came in 1972, when Frank 'borrowed some money from Bernie and he took an engine as security. I did the same again two years later.' But then Frank's repayment became overdue, so Bernie 'sent three heavies with a Ford Transit van – a blue one – to make sure he got the engine', as per their previous arrangement, and that seemed to square it. In 1975 the Williams name appeared on the roster of Formula 1 constructors and since then Frank Williams and his team have joined the sport's holy firmament – Ferrari, Lotus, McLaren, Tyrrell, Brabham and Williams. The vanguard of top performance racing.

The greatest concentration of human ability, in all its aspects, exists within the Formula 1 arena; that is what it's about. The expertise of the designers, engineers, chassis craftsmen, aerodynamicists, physicists, mathematicians, meteorologists and mechanics is enormous. The Technical Working Group for Formula 1, at its meetings to decide the interpretation of the sporting regulations, gathers together, at one forum, a tremendous force of intelligence, innovation and competitive cunning. Over the years this has involved men like Patrick Head, Ross Brawn, Pat Symonds, John Barnard and Harvey Postlethwaite – all hugely talented and able to argue their patch with the profundity, and guile, of the foremost barristers. Of course they are well-paid, but their drive and competitiveness comes from within and is not the result of a dollar poultice. The mechanics, gofers, chefs and staff in the hospitality units are as dedicated and single-minded as the big chiefs. Their enthusiasm for the sport and its people is beyond a religion. To have only three or four hours' sleep during a race weekend does not faze them and, in particular, the job of the mechanics, refuellers and wheel-changers is not without danger during pit stops. In one year seven mechanics were burnt – fortunately not seriously – in the pit lane, five of them in the Benetton pit at Hockenhem; in 1984, four mechanics were injured at Imola; and in 2002 a

Ferrari mechanic had his leg broken after the race at Suzuka when heavy equipment fell on him. But the rewards for them are great, they worship their drivers, enjoy the excitement of the work and the joy of performing at their best. And they party with the same intensity. At a race at Suzuka, Saturday practice was cancelled because of an approaching typhoon, so Friday night became the nominated party night, and the circuit's pub, the beloved 'Log Cabin', closed at 5.45am.

The chiefs, of course, enjoy the lifestyle of chauffeured cars, helicopters, private jets and luxury yachts, and their playtime is much more sophisticated than that of the troops and it's more expensive. But the intensity of nineteen to twenty races with the testing and other preparatory days, the four days of the race event and the travel between races leaves little time for play during the season.

Preparation for the drivers is a physical ordeal to achieve maximum cardiovascular fitness and the muscle power to withstand the g-forces of cornering, acceleration and deceleration. The head, neck and helmet in a 4g corner weighs – during the period of exposure – 56lb instead of 14lb; most drivers regularly exercise their neck muscles using weights. Running, particularly in hot climates, was the recipe for Ayrton Senna's cardiovascular workout: eight kilometres the first day, sixteen the second, twenty-four the third, and the fourth day – rest. Nutrition is controlled by a team of nutrition experts, muscular fitness by a team of physiotherapists and mental approach by sport psychologists to produce men at their absolute prime. Just recall Michael Schumacher after a race, leaping from the cockpit – 'hi ho fans' – as if he'd been enjoying a Sunday stroll in the park; his overalls didn't even get creased. But not for a moment should we forget the courage it takes to drive in rain at 160mph, unable to see beyond the nosecone of the car.

And then there are the legions of journalists who trudge along swallowing up the dust of this cavalcade, and with it produce insights conveyed as eloquently as anything that has ever been written.

The whole circus with its attendant journalists,

photographers, television crew, hospitality crew, teams, sponsors and guests numbers about 5,000 people; a population large enough for a Group General Practice to tend to their health. Some of the teams have their own sports medicine doctors while the FIA provides two or three travelling doctors – depending on the location and individual race. Their primary task is to look after the drivers and teams, but with a population of 5,000, every type of illness or accident can occur. In one weekend, at Suzuka, the medical centre saw malaria, epilepsy, acute appendicitis and gall bladder colic. The standard of diagnostic equipment is such that in the gall bladder case the patient was in a London Hospital on the Monday morning, scans in hand. The Professor of Surgery wasn't sure that he had heard correctly when he was told that they had been produced – the day before – 'at the Suzuka Formula 1 circuit'.

The point is, they're all great, the Formula 1 breed; and it's worth repeating, the greatest concentration of human ability exists – OK, probably exists – within the Formula 1 arena. Did Bernie make them unique? No, they are self-selecting, they were born to be great, but in most cases – like Bernie – nobody told them about their innate greatness so they had to will themselves – against all odds, against all doubt – to the heights, more than once, every day, they keep on pushing. When Mercedes McLaren driver Kimi Räikkönen won the race at Spa in August 2004, Bernie was the first person to ring up Ron Dennis and congratulate him. It had been a long time since a McLaren driver had won a Grand Prix, and Bernie understood what the effort had involved.

Beyond the emotional, intellectual and physical commitment, Formula 1 is about financial sacrifice. New teams were required, from 2000 to 2007, to put up a bond (paid back over the course of the season) of around $48 million for the privilege of joining this exclusive club, having scraped together a budget of somewhere between $60 and $400 million (roughly the spread between the Spyker and McLaren expenditure). In 2008, the Japanese-owned Super Aguri team had to call it quits, and Spyker was bought by Orange India, which later became

Force India. By 2010, as a result of the need to reduce costs, the bond requirement was dispensed with and – in a complete change of heart – new teams were given a $10 million signing bonus. Lotus was able to return to the circuit (now backed by Malaysian investors) on a budget of around $89 million, while Virgin Racing was in business and ready to race on a budget of some $60 million. Of course, the world's economic woes still took a heavy toll on the sport, and notions of 'too big to fail' were dispelled at the track when manufacturer owners Honda and Toyota disappeared, as did BMW – apart from their name. Likewise sponsorship from banks dwindled. Only four teams – Ferrari, Force India, Red Bull Racing and Toro Rosso – managed to retain the same ownership structure in 2010. Most of Brawn GP, winner of both the Drivers' and Constructors' titles in 2009, was sold to Daimler AG, parent company of Mercedes-Benz. At the same time Mercedes began to withdraw its fifteen-year investment in McLaren, though it will continue to supply the engines. Today the majority of Formula 1 teams are independent of car manufacturers, allowing Cosworth – once so vital to the success of Bernie's Brabham, Colin Chapman's Lotus and others – to return to supply engines for cars. Even so, the new USF1 team, for which there was so much hope, failed to attract enough investment to make it to the grid, and there were others in the same situation. It is all part of the ebb and flow of the sport that in the end strengthens Formula 1 and those who have learned how to live, courageously, through the endless tossing of the dice.

Because of their continuous, uphill financial battles along with all the other reasons the teams – and their manufacturers – want to feel appreciated; and it is why they object to 'outsiders' – who haven't paid any visceral dues – from owning a controlling interest in the sport. Bernie's contribution to Formula 1 and its teams is that he buffed them up and packaged them up, made the show – by a variety of means – professional, both functionally and visually, giving it a value that would attract sponsors like moths to candlelight. And as part of this struggle, he helped make Formula 1 safer. Did that help the teams? Massively.

Formula 1 is also about competitive performance,

traditionally measured in technology, trackside decisions, the skills of drivers and pit crew. A secondary level of competition existed between the great manufacturers and their respective team principals such as McLaren/Ron Dennis, Ferrari/Jean Todt and BMW Sauber/Mario Theissen on the one hand and the smaller teams such as Spyker, Toro Rosso, Super Aguri and, for a time, Red Bull Racing on the other. Between the two poles have been Honda, Toyota, Williams and Renault; some have been for Bernie and others against him. Former Renault boss Flavio Briatore (and Bernie's frequent partner), a straightforward individual, has his own view on Bernie and the teams, and on Formula 1: 'Bernie helps everybody,' says Flavio. 'If a team has a cash problem, Bernie solves it [he once gave the Minardi team $4 million, for example]. He finds a deal for them, sometimes it's his own money. If a team has a problem with the FIA, Bernie is the one who finds a solution or a compromise. If a driver has a problem – personally, financially or with a team – he goes to see Bernie. Bernie's door is always open for the drivers. If anybody has a problem, it is Bernie's advice that they want. He has done a fantastic job for Formula 1, bringing it to be the sport at the highest level. Before Bernie, Formula 1 was an amateur sport for a bunch of petrolheads, and that includes the team owners, who today must thank Bernie for being as well off as they are! And Bernie has done it with a lot of cleverness and an iron fist, because that's the way Formula 1 needs to be managed, you need a very strong leader who takes decisions alone and also takes full responsibility for them. Bernie has done that and that is his strength… For me Bernie has been one of the most significant influences in my life, at both the professional and personal level. His outlook on things, his way to do business, has always been guidance to me. I owe a lot to Bernie and I turn to him for his opinion. There is no one else like him. When Bernie goes it will be chaos if they try to run it with a committee. Formula 1 needs a dictator, and the problem is – there isn't another one around.'

All the same, there are many who will be – and are – straining to squeeze into Bernie's shoes. Formula 1 is also about conquest.

CHAPTER 17

SILVERSTONE

Call Silverstone by another name and it would be 'controversy', or to put it more strongly, also 'truncheon', 'stick', 'tomahawk' or any other implement for beating against the heads of reasonable men.

Once upon a time we cherished this former World War II bomber airfield turned racing circuit, where the first British Grand Prix was held in 1948. Two years later, the British Grand Prix launched the Formula 1 World Championship at Silverstone with Giuseppe Farina's Alfa Romeo taking the chequered flag. Bernie drove his metallic-blue Cooper 500 in a support race that day; a year later he drove in the Formula 3 race, and José Froilán González gave Ferrari their first Grand Prix victory, with the legendary Juan Manuel Fangio second. In 1958 it was Britain's turn to shine when Peter Collins and Mike Hawthorn came first and second, albeit in Ferraris, but thereafter it was pure British Racing Green – Roy Salvadori, driving a Cooper-Climax, took third place just ahead of Stuart Lewis-Evans in a Vanwall.

When Bernie wasn't racing at Silverstone, in those early days, he was soaking up the atmosphere, and he was learning; events at the ex-RAF airfield were at the bedrock of his career in motorsport, in Formula 1. But then so were his experiences at Brands Hatch where, pre-1950, he had raced on two wheels, counter-clockwise, before it was surfaced with tarmac; and it was at Brands Hatch, in September 1951, that he had one of his more spectacular four-wheeled shunts. But thirty-five years later a choice had to be made. Only one circuit would be allowed to stage the British Grand Prix –

and nostalgia didn't enter into it. A maelstrom of criticism followed, and avarice, and bitterness, with Silverstone at its core. Many would blame Bernie. But it would be as well to blame a misalignment of the stars; the simple answer does not apply. Silverstone? Think of quicksilver.

The Royal Automobile Club's Motor Sports Association (MSA) – the national sporting authority – had been responsible, since 1964, for organising the British Grand Prix, which rotated between Brands Hatch in Kent and Silverstone in Northamptonshire. Since 1950 the RAC had owned the rights and trademarks for the race, the minimal profits of which were eventually ploughed back into British motorsport. The MSA was of the opinion that alternating the circuits was in the best interests of British motorsport, and appreciated by the fans.

But by 1985 Bernie had come to the conclusion that the rising costs inherent in staging a Grand Prix – upgrading circuits, media facilities, medical facilities, start money, and so on – meant that one venue per country was the best way forward. 'It seemed to be the right thing to do, to get as many countries as possible for the World Championship,' says Bernie. 'It wasn't so important to get the countries that are commercially important for the teams as it would be today.' Also, a franchise fee of around $3 million could be collected from circuit owners guaranteed a race each year; and it could be argued that this assurance created a more tangible asset, encouraging further investment in circuit improvements. The MSA thought differently, however, and what's more FISA President Jean-Marie Balestre had written to RAC chairman Jeffrey Rose giving his support for continuing with both British circuits on a rotation basis – subject to the agreement of the World Council.

Before the World Council met in Paris to nod through the President's recommendation, Rose met with Balestre and Bernie. Jean-Marie said very little during their discussion, while Bernie made it quite clear that, according to Jeffrey Rose, 'there would be no alternation'. Then, in the chamber where the Council held their meeting, Balestre, who had been expected to favour the RAC's position, unexpectedly withdrew his support with the limp explanation that he could only speak as a representative of the Fédération Française du Sport Automobile. The World Council therefore voted against what had satisfactorily existed in Britain for more than a decade, and it was later announced that, as of January 1986, the policy would be strictly 'one country, one circuit'. This ignored the fact that two Grand Prix races were then held in Italy (at Monza and Imola) and Germany (at Hockenheim and the Nürburgring), although their second races were respectively disguised as the San Marino Grand Prix and the European Grand Prix.

During the spring of 1986 Bernie signalled his intent to buy Brands Hatch with John Foulston, founder of a computer-leasing company and an amateur racing driver. The proposed acquisition had been initiated by John Webb and his wife Angela, who had received approval in principle from owners British American Tobacco (BAT) to inaugurate a management buy-out. John Webb had joined Brands Hatch in 1954 as a press officer and went on to play a pivotal role in the sale of the circuit to Grovewood Securities in 1961, which led to his appointment as a director of its board. Thereafter he had negotiated with the RAC, resulting in Brands alternating with Silverstone in staging the Grand Prix. In 1972 Grovewood Securities was taken over by Eagle Star Holdings, which was in turn acquired by BAT in the early Eighties. John Webb was also managing director of Motor Circuit Developments Ltd (MCD), which ran Brands. Angela Webb became a director of MCD in 1976 and, in the early Eighties, its deputy managing director.

The proposal that the couple put to Bernie and Foulston, and which they 'both accepted in principle', was an offer of $5 million for Brands Hatch (together with Mallory Park, Snetterton and Oulton Park), which would host the British Grand Prix well into the future. However, David Wickens, owner of British Car Auctions, soon made a higher bid. Wickens wanted to construct offices at the circuit and his offer was contingent upon obtaining planning permission; he had no interest in getting involved in motor racing.

Bernie now toyed with the idea of leasing back the circuit from British Car Auctions. By then, however, the circuit had become hot property. Wickens' bid was successfully out-trumped by others and eventually by an offer of $8 million from John Foulston, who had decided to go it alone. Bernie, so the story goes, had agreed to go fifty/fifty on the increased figure, but only if Foulston loaned him the money, interest-free; Foulston wasn't feeling generous. Then three days later – after the $8 million offer had been accepted – Bernie, as President of FOCA, signed a contract awarding the Grand Prix to Silverstone for the next five years. The contract was also signed by Jean-Marie Balestre on behalf of FISA and by Jimmy Brown, representing the British Racing Drivers' Club, which had bought the freehold to the circuit from the Ministry of Defence in 1971. Brands Hatch hosted its last Grand Prix on 13 July 1986, and it was won by a British driver, Nigel Mansell, in a British car, Williams – a last hurrah.

Meanwhile, up near Nottingham, millionaire builder Tom Wheatcroft was pouring money into Donington Park in the hope of staging the return of the British Grand Prix. The last Grand Prix held at the Leicestershire circuit was in 1938. Tom had built a museum in the circuit's grounds to house his collection of single-seater racing cars, and he would soon acquire – in 1987 – the right to hold the British round of the motorcycle World Championship. But before that, it was his heart's desire to stage the British Grand Prix. Unfortunately, Tom was unaware of both the new one-race-per-country rule and the fact that the RAC had lost control over the right to choose the venue. But the biggest blow was Bernie's five-year contract with Silverstone. When Tom found out about this he was livid and reportedly threatened to sue the RAC, but eventually he changed his mind.

Bernie, apparently to appease Tom, backed his application to the FISA to host a European Grand Prix, which – after another race was dropped from the calendar – was held on 11 April 1993, and never again. It was a wet, blustery weekend. Only the hardy few ventured outdoors to the grandstands. 'It cost me a million,' said Tom. 'Bernie cost me a million,' he added, laughing. 'I really like ole Bernie… nothing to say against him, ahrrr-ahrrr-ahrrr' [Long John Silver-like]. His eyes twinkled and a big, affectionate grin spread across his apple-red face. Others claim that Tom had actually lost £3 million.

Back at Brands Hatch, the situation got even more complicated and tense when forty-year-old John Foulston was killed while driving his 1970 McLaren Indianapolis car. His colleague, John Tompkins, was appointed chairman of what, in 1986, became Brands Hatch Leisure plc (instead of Motor Circuit Developments), with the executive management remaining unchanged. It had been decided, before Foulston's death, that the circuit group should go public. The Brands Hatch circuit had already been expanded and a hotel added – built by Brands Hatch Hotels Ltd, with Angela Webb as managing director.

In 1988 Foulston's widow, Mary, replaced Tompkins as chairman. She 'enjoyed an excellent relationship' with the Webbs, who had a twenty per cent interest in the company. Mary Foulston deferred the plan to go public until she had settled down in her new role. Then, in 1989, to gain business experience, Nicola Foulston, then only twenty-one, joined her mother and the Webbs as commercial director. Nicola, however, didn't need any lessons in running a business and she was a natural entrepreneur of outstanding ability and exceptional determination. Within a few months of her involvement at Brands Hatch Leisure, John and Angela Webb, with 'fifty-four years of joint service in building up Brands Hatch from a one-mile mini circuit to a 2.62-mile international venue', elected to resign from day-to-day operations, although they were retained as consultants until their contracts expired in 1992. In the meantime, they decided to exercise their option – previously agreed with Mary Foulston – to have their shares bought 'for a pre-specified amount'. The hotel was sold during their tenure, says John, 'for an enormous profit', and the money they received for their shares was 'many times $500,000'.

Nicola became the new Chief Executive, and then set about obtaining complete control of the company by buying her mother's stake. But even before this process had been completed, Nicola had begun adding additional amenities to Brands Hatch, building up the company, doubling turnover – preliminaries to what had been her father's intent: a flotation of the circuit group on the Stock Exchange. But then, it seemed, all of her well-thought-out efforts were part of a much broader plan, for nine years after her father's death Nicola Foulston was in a position to acquire Silverstone.

Nicola was clever, but Silverstone's owners, the British Racing Drivers' Club with its 850 suspicious, sometimes argumentative members, were more than a match for her. What she was about to engage upon was not so much a negotiation as a game of chess – on a roller-coaster. Initially she favoured appealing to individual members by offering the BRDC around $50 million, which would give each member roughly $60,000. But such a move risked breaking the listing rules of the Stock Exchange and the Financial Services Act which governed a private listed company's offer of shares to members of the public who form a cooperative, as was the case with the BRDC. Her interest alerted other bidders with higher offers, so Nicola was eventually forced to raise her bid to $75 million in a simple takeover. Meanwhile, the BRDC hired their own advisers and a game of angling ensued, but she was ultimately refused by an overriding vote of the BRDC members. Despite the windfalls, they did not want to have anything to do with her. No matter how Nicola played it, their door was firmly closed. Unless she used Bernie to wrench it open again.

Bernie and Nicola had never met, but when she walked into his office and began relaying the tale of her acquisition struggles, they became old pals. 'Nicola knew what she wanted,' recalls Bernie, laughing. 'She strove for it. I had no problem with Nicola, she was a good fighter, fought her corner, she was straight and did what she said she would do. She was all right.'

Having listened to her story, Bernie, a member of the BRDC, reacted with astonishment. Nobody had told him the BRDC wanted to sell Silverstone. He was supposed to be informed of such changes; it was written into their Grand Prix franchise – now extended to 2002 – otherwise he could cancel the contract. They settled down to negotiate, and a little while later Nicola left the Princes Gate office with an option proposal: if she managed to acquire Silverstone, the Grand Prix would remain at Silverstone, but if she failed, the Grand Prix would go to Brands Hatch. The terms for staging the Grand Prix were reported to be $10 million for ten years, plus five per cent annual compound interest. Silverstone was only paying $5 million.

Lord Hesketh, then President of the BRDC – which was making little headway on the Silverstone sale – now decided that Nicola Foulston was worth dealing with after all. In January 1999 he offered her a merger with a sixty/forty split, the BRDC taking the sixty per cent portion. But Nicola Foulston was not about to entertain any agreement reducing her control; and Bernie, suspecting that news of his discussions with Nicola had leaked, probably enjoyed disappointing Lord Hesketh. At one of the BRDC's official dinners at Silverstone, held on the Saturday night before the race, Lord Hesketh gave a speech in which he had complained of the circuit 'being overtaken by people in navy-blue blazers and grey flannels' – referring to the FIA officials, some of whom wished to walk out of the dinner but were restrained by their wives. Hesketh then went on to state that he objected to 'motor racing being run by a second-hand car salesman'. In any other circumstances Bernie would have laughed – after all he refers to himself as a used car dealer. It was Lord Hesketh's disparaging tone that was offensive.

There was another snub at the BRDC's annual general meeting, attended by Bernie. The club was suffering considerable disruption over a financial arrangement undertaken by its then chairman, Arrows boss Tom Walkinshaw, the result being that they were short of funds. Bernie, speaking to the assembly, offered to give the club £3 million or even £4 million. From somewhere in the room a voice said: 'We don't want your money you dirty little sod.' Not everyone heard it, but Bernie did, and he immediately walked out. 'I don't know what the BRDC is any more,' he said. 'It used to be a British racing drivers' club [emphasising the word 'drivers'], the racing drivers formed the club. And now I think for a couple of hundred quid or something you get about a couple of thousand pounds worth of benefit. I don't think you even need to drive an ordinary car. It's not what it was.' Not that his annoyance with the BRDC President – or anyone else – would have influenced Nicola Foulston. She kept right on wooing the BRDC members, or trying to, in the hope of reaching an agreement on her terms. But it was not to be. They could not come together with the majority agreement required to do business with her. All of Nicola's offers to acquire Silverstone met with failure. So, if she couldn't walk through the front door on a red carpet she would go around to the side entrance; she decided to finalise her agreement with Bernie.

But before pen was put to paper, the BRDC chairman, Tommy Sopwith, went to see Bernie to discuss details of a new contract for the running of the Grand Prix at Silverstone from 2002. Bernie says that he offered Sopwith 'the same sort of terms as the other European races. They didn't like that. Actually, I didn't realise that we had one circuit where the fee was lower, and I said: "OK, we'll accept that" – which was the lowest fee. They said: "This is how much we're prepared to pay and nothing else." So I said: "OK, I don't have a problem with that, it isn't enough money for us, that's all." They've got something to sell, we've got something to sell.' But not to each other. Bernie would not reveal the amount of the fee. 'I can't disclose that,' he said. 'Well, I could, but I don't want to.'

So with the BRDC now out of the picture, Bernie signed a contract, on 14 May 1999, with Nicola Foulston. From July 2002 the British Grand Prix was to be staged at Brands Hatch – for five years, with an option on an additional five years. Nicola was now faced with the gigantic task of upgrading the circuit to meet Formula 1's high-tech standards; the cost was estimated to be $60 million. There was also the sticky problem of obtaining the planning permission required to make the wholesale changes – media centre, heliport, new grandstands, new pit garages – that the venture would entail. Nicola felt that the time was nigh to cash in and retire, for she then entered into formal negotiations with the sports marketing group, Octagon, a branch of the Interpublic Group based in New York. Of course Octagon needed assurance that planning permission would be granted. Foulston had hired planning consultants and a formal application for outline planning permission was submitted to the local district authority in September 1999. Next, she had to prevent Bernie from exercising his right to cancel the contract in the event of changes – such as in the ownership of Brands Hatch. Foulston maintained that she had every intention of staying involved. Therefore, it wasn't so much a change at the helm as a necessary injection of money so that the improvements could be carried out. Bernie had no objections. Indeed, he would now be doing business with a substantial multinational organisation, one that would have no difficulty in fulfilling the financial terms of his contract. By the end of 1999, Interpublic/Octagon reportedly paid $192 million for Brands Hatch Leisure. Nicola Foulston stayed on for another month before walking away to Switzerland, with a profit of many tens of millions. At the age of thirty-three she could afford to spend the rest of her days in luxurious comfort.

So now it became Octagon's turn to woo the BRDC. While waiting for planning permission to come through, Rob Bain, who had replaced Foulston, decided to play it safe by engaging in talks with the BRDC to keep the British Grand Prix at Silverstone. It was a wise move because the then Secretary of State, John Prescott, called for a public enquiry, which was subsequently scheduled for 9 January 2001. It was unlikely that a decision would be reached before May – too late for builders to complete the work necessary to hold the Grand Prix the following year. And Octagon still had to pay Bernie his reputed $10 million – with or without the race – although he may have considered moving the commencement date to 2003. Octagon's Rob Bain knew his hands were tied, and decided to deal with the BRDC while maintaining a confident attitude concerning the ultimate success of their planning application; and by looking elsewhere. Bain pursued talks to hold the Grand Prix at Donington Park and there was some initial interest. But whatever enthusiasm existed, it ultimately came to nothing. The BRDC had Octagon in a vulnerable position, and they were ready to turn on the pressure – by suggesting that perhaps they didn't want to hold the Grand Prix after all! The whole business was becoming a nonsense.

In October 2000 Bernie held a meeting in his office in Knightsbridge to look for a solution. The BRDC's newest chairman, former racing driver Martin Brundle, was at the meeting, accompanied by McLaren boss Ron Dennis. A superb business strategist, Ron had been drafted in to assist the BRDC in their negotiations. Across the table sat Octagon chairman Sir Frank Lowe and Les Delano, the company's deputy chairman. Octagon had two objectives: to lease Silverstone for 2002 and to put together an arrangement whereby they could run the circuit on a long-term basis. Ron Dennis constructed a deal in which Octagon received a fifteen-year lease on Silverstone – minus the BRDC clubhouse – in exchange for an annual rent of $7 million. Ron also agreed to contribute $35 million, spread over the first five years of the rental period, to help fund the essential upgrading of the circuit, including public roads. The estimate for this work was $100 million. Bernie says that the plan conceived by Ron Dennis was 'to build the Taj Mahal at Silverstone – which would have been good. I mean he's proved he can do it because his factory is a fantastic factory. So if they had let him alone he would have probably done that. *If* the money was there. But then he saw that if the situation changed, everything changed. Then the money wasn't there. We made a contribution to it, IPG [Interpublic Group], the Octagon people, and the BRDC took a bit less rent and they put that money into doing things. But it all got squandered away; it really wasn't used properly. So we never had anything good in the end. I mean they spent a fortune to build a car park that you could use to put tanks on. It really was what you would expect from the BRDC. It was a very amateurish way of going about things.'

However, the plan, at its conception, presented yet another window of opportunity for Bernie. Octagon, having agreed to a fifteen-year lease on Silverstone, naturally wanted a fifteen-year Grand Prix franchise to go with it. Bernie was all compliance, and he knew that Octagon had to justify such a massive investment. He offered to extend the British Grand Prix contract with a five-year option, but his fee would now be $11 million, instead of the existing $10 million of the earlier Foulston deal, and there would now be an annual compound interest payment of – reportedly – ten per cent, instead of five.

Bernie, like the BRDC, also offered $7 million per year for five years towards the redevelopment of the circuit and access roads; the development funds were organised in a separate contract called the 'Master Plan'. Then, as an extra measure of goodwill, Bernie suggested that the deal should be brought forward to 2001 instead of waiting until his contract with the BRDC expired in 2002. However, both Ron and Bernie wanted their contracts guaranteed by Octagon's parent company, Interpublic. The suggestion gave Sir Frank Lowe cold feet and he asked Bernie, privately, for advice. Now, there are two versions of what constituted Bernie's advice. In *Business F1*, published in May 2003, it is reported that when Lowe asked Bernie if what he was about to enter into was a good deal, Bernie answered in the affirmative, according to Lowe. Bernie says the opposite. 'I told him it was crazy, he shouldn't do it.' When asked if he could explain the discrepancy, Bernie added: 'Something's wrong with Frank these days, he's moved to Switzerland, probably lost his memory. No, Frank was quite happy to go ahead. I remember he came to see me in the afternoon and said: "At eight o'clock tonight I'll know whether the deal's done." I said: "Well, you better start praying – now – that it isn't." And then he called me to say that it was done. Unlucky.'

Either way, on 1 December 2000 the deal was indeed 'done', but with one alteration. Bernie agreed to reduce his franchise fee to $10 million per year, but the annual compound interest would still be increased to ten per cent. The BRDC received its $7 million in rent per year; and the BRDC, Bernie and Octagon agreed to pay $7 million each, annually, into the Master Plan fund for the redevelopment of the circuit.

Now Octagon's problems really began. As part of the process of rationalising staff, sixty employees were made redundant. This attracted the attention of the British Office of Fair Trading who launched an investigation into the takeover by Octagon. Work – well under way – at the circuit came to a standstill. Added to this was the outbreak in February of foot and mouth disease, which held up construction on roads to the circuit for a further fourteen months. When the Grand Prix was held in July 2001, motorsport enthusiasts were forced to inch their way through solid congestion. The fans had already had their patience tried when, the previous year, the FIA had switched the British Grand Prix from its usual July slot to the Easter weekend, in April, when British weather is notoriously foul. Those staunch enough to turn out had to slosh along in knee-deep mud, which made the wind and rain barely noticeable, except perhaps for the unfortunates who had to stand by watching their cars being towed from pools of sludge – the designated car parks. The cynics thought that Bernie had manoeuvred the change of date in order to injure the BRDC, which ended up with a £3 million loss, including some £520,000 charged by the police, for the club still held the rights to promote the race – in that they owned the circuit. Yet, 'the BRDC don't own any rights,' Bernie points out. 'They own a circuit which was given to them, and that's what they own, for sure, one hundred per cent, but they don't own any rights to anything.' Actually, the BRDC had raised the money to buy the circuit, including some 800 acres from the Ministry of Defence. Bernie/FOM took over the circuit during the month of the Grand Prix. As for the schedule change, according to the FIA it had been necessary to avoid conflicting with Wimbledon.

It's important to point out that in championships such as Wimbledon, a portion of the profit is ploughed back into the sport. British motorsport, on the other hand, receives little or nothing in direct profit from staging the Grand Prix – a situation many find disturbing. To quote one member of the BRDC: 'FOM do bugger-all for the sport.' There is, however, an important knock-on effect, which benefits the overall industry. Anyway, back in 2001 there was much to make up for – whatever the reason – and it was disappointing. Rebukes were slung in every direction, with the choicest ending up in the broadsheets and motor racing journals. The FIA called on Octagon to atone for the inadequacy of the circuit's infrastructure. Max said it was like going 'up a farm lane to the Olympics', thus the FIA had no choice but to make the financially debilitating decision to limit circuit attendance in 2002 to 60,000.

There was a glimmer of hope when British Trade Secretary Stephen Byers announced on 6 September that the Octagon/Silverstone transaction would be allowed to proceed, and the Government then energised its programme to improve roads leading to the circuit. This had come about after the new BRDC president, Sir Jackie Stewart, met with some seventy-five Members of Parliament – from all three main parties – to raise government funding to support the Silverstone development, the British Grand Prix and the UK's motorsport industry. Sir Jackie had also organised £17.1 million of BRDC/Octagon money for the development of an expanded four-lane dual carriageway, car parks and spectator amenities. Meanwhile, the FIA was demanding a $5 million bond to guarantee that the work would be completed for the 2002 Grand Prix; and then they announced that the race was only provisional. As a result, many bookings were cancelled – although the race had actually been secured a year earlier. Following a series of meetings with the then Chancellor Gordon Brown and Prime Minister Tony Blair, Sir Jackie secured £8 million in government funds to finish the essential Silverstone village bypass in time for the Grand Prix weekend. It was clear to the Prime Minister that the presence of the international media at the circuit would bring the eyes of the world to his doorstep. Had the bypass remained unfinished, Silverstone's reputation would have sunk further into the mire. Mr Blair's insistence – at the critical hour – had reinvigorated building activity.

On the day of the race low cloud prevented helicopters – including Bernie's – from landing at the circuit. Bernie was forced to arrive by car. His driver, it seems, found the signs to entrances around the circuit confusing, and got lost. Then, upon finding the appropriate gate, the guard posted to check tickets and official credentials had never heard of a Mr Bernie Ecclestone. Bernie thought it was all a shambles and said so – in no uncertain terms – to the press. Rob Bain, who had worked hard as one of the leaders of the Silverstone project, also responded in the press. Then the FIA/FOM had their say by removing Bain's pass to the race, the race that he himself had helped to organise. Rob Bain resigned.

Inevitably, the 2002 British Grand Prix lost money, and just as inevitably Interpublic had had enough. They changed the name of their subsidiary from Octagon Motorsports to Brands Hatch Circuits Limited and put it up for sale. By 2004 Interpublic had sold all its circuits – Brands Hatch, Snetterton, Oulton Park and Cadwell Park – and its operations at Silverstone had become Silverstone Motorsports Limited. In April, Interpublic and its subsidiary Silverstone Motorsports agreed to pay Bernie's FOA $93 million to be released from their obligations to promote the British Grand Prix, effective after the race in July 2004. Interpublic was still bound to pay the BRDC for leasing their circuit. Bernie, who once more had control of the British Grand Prix, made it clear that he did not wish to be a promoter of the race at Silverstone, which left the members of the BRDC to wonder about the future of the Silverstone circuit as well as the future of the British Grand Prix.

Then, just before the July race, Bernie added to their discomfort by giving his permission for a spectacular Formula 1 demonstration in central London. It was thrilling. All the stars of Formula 1 were there, sashaying their screaming, high-tech machines down Regent Street with 500,000 spectators packed into every possible neck-craning position to cheer them on. London's mayor Ken Livingstone was ready to 'bust a gut' to make the capital the British Grand Prix venue of the future. It was, says Bernie, a 'great idea...

I mean if you had it at Hyde Park, if you like (although Battersea Park would be my place to put it), then it would work. It would work there and it would improve the park like we improved the park at Melbourne. Ken [Livingstone] was all excited about the street race. But I think as he looked into it he'd have realised it's not easy. He was an enthusiast and wanted to get it done.' He just needed to overcome the logistics of holding an actual race, which are such that it is unlikely that a full-blown grand prix will ever be staged on London's streets.

Even so, the BRDC must have felt that it had just received another bludgeoning. Formula 1 celebrity Martin Brundle was at the F1 London event. Martin made his name in racing before becoming a respected commentator for ITV and, later, the BBC. He is also a columnist for the *Daily Express* and, until fairly recently, was chairman of the BRDC. In his newspaper column Martin accused Bernie of having a 'vendetta' against the BRDC. Martin had become frustrated by all the twists and turns in the Silverstone saga, but he is really rather fond of Bernie. They first met at Chessington back in the Eighties when Bernie was moving out of Brabham having sold the team to Joachim Luthi from Switzerland. 'All Bernie seemed to have was a desk, a safe and a shredder,' says Martin. Later when they spoke about Silverstone and other issues, Bernie 'would always ring me back, he's never ever not rung me back… I haven't ever put a second call into Bernie. If he doesn't ring you back that day, you know it will be the next day because he's been out somewhere, and he always seems to know what you want to talk to him about, and all the details. I don't know how he keeps all the balls up in the air. It's just extraordinary, and then to sort of apparently win all the battles that he does – mentally, commercially, politically. I've worked out how he does it, he works on the divide and conquer philosophy, and I've seen it so many times. I heard it first at Brabham, how Bernie loves to set two people against each other and see who comes out on top – not physically but mentally. I'm pretty sure he operated on the "if they're all fighting each other, they're not fighting me" belief. What

I've found with him is that you have to listen very carefully to what he says because the devil is in the detail. While he won't always tell you 100 per cent the way it is, he'll give you a pretty good clue if you stop and take the trouble to listen, and take the trouble to think about it afterwards, which I didn't always do.'

Another flashpoint was the 'Master Plan Deed', which had been created with the help of Ron Dennis. Included in the plan was the need for Bernie to 'sign off' on particular phases of the work. 'It was the perfect platform for Bernie to destabilise it from time to time, as and when it suited him,' adds Martin. 'I was disappointed with one or two things that he did. He had a vision of what he wanted, and it was difficult to get it together with all the numbers. He seemed to agree, and then he seemed to disagree. But it was a totally unsatisfactory contract and, quite rightly, Bernie played havoc with it... Over the three-year period I was chairman of the British Racing Drivers' Club it caused me a lot of sleepless nights, and it cost me well over £1 million in lost revenue from things I could no longer do because I was giving up two, three, four days a week. Although one million would never buy you what I learned from Bernie, the lawyers, the accountants, Ron... all the things I learned through that process of how big business operates. A million quid wouldn't buy you that.'

In the September/October 2004 issue of the BRDC's *Bulletin*, Sir Jackie Stewart, in his 'President's Statement', resolutely pointed out to members that the BRDC's executive structure – president, chairman and board – 'believe that the Grand Prix will not be held or kept at Silverstone at "any" price. If it is economically unjustifiable, we will have to let it go. Finding a promoter for what is very likely to be a loss-making venture is not an easy task! However, I can assure you that we are working hard to try and ensure the best possible solution to hopefully retain the Grand Prix, and by doing so, ensuring that the British motorsports industry is retained in this country, as well as ensuring that our club is economically sound and being structured for long-term stability.' Sir Jackie, astute businessman that he is, realised it was necessary to separate the club membership from the business side of the BRDC, with the latter being run by the greatly respected Neil England; and it was from this platform that future negotiations took place. Nevertheless, while Bernie maintained his hard-line stance with the BRDC, instability continued to overshadow the British Grand Prix.

On 30 September 2004 – after Jackie's 'statement' had been published – Bernie announced that the British Grand Prix was off the calendar for 2005; the BRDC had been unable to reach his terms. But two weeks later, during the meeting of the World Council on 13 October, the provisional Grand Prix calendar for 2005 was circulated and Silverstone was back on it with a date for 3 July – should a final contract be agreed with Bernie. The BRDC's chief executive told *Autosport* that he was 'cautiously optimistic', and no doubt exhausted from all the convolutions that had brought them to what was still a gossamer thread. Between 30 September and 13 October salvation had temporarily appeared on the scene in the form of Brand Synergy, a consortium with Nigel Mansell on its board. The removal of the British Grand Prix had concentrated minds – wonderfully. It's a tried and true Bernie technique for flushing out bidders.

The proposal of Nigel's group was to lease Silverstone land from the BRDC for the development of a hotel, leisure facilities and new pits, and the anticipated revenue would allow them to promote the Grand Prix. The BRDC had a better idea and turned to the then Sports Minister, Richard Caborn, for assistance. Jackie Stewart, who had continuously urged the Government to fund the improvement of roads to the circuit, also beat the drum for Government assistance in upgrading circuit facilities. With Government backing – mostly verbal as it turned out – through the East Midlands Development Agency, half of the Silverstone 800-acre estate was to be leased or purchased, releasing some £150 million to upgrade the track, paddock and pits, 'as well as attracting hotels and an innovations complex to turn the circuit into a world centre for motor racing', as reported in *The Times*. Bernie would have liked that – the innovative, world-class part of it – bringing to mind his Paul Ricard circuit in France. Richard Caborn, who had assisted in the negotiations with Bernie, added: 'I hope we will get a two-year deal which will allow us to sit down and plan to realise the full potential of the Silverstone estate. I would very much welcome its inclusion on the Formula 1 calendar as it would be a major step in the right direction.' Bernie said he 'would be delighted' to continue to have the race at Silverstone. So would the seven British-based teams; so would everyone with jobs in motorsport; so would the British fans; and so would Max Mosley, who wished to retain a core of traditional races.

The 2005 calendar was finally fixed on 9 December, and the question as to whether or not Silverstone would be on it went right down to the wire. As things stood there were nineteen races tentatively scheduled. France and San Marino, along with Britain, were the Grands Prix that had big question marks hanging over them. And there was one more point: the provisional date allocated for the British race was 3 July, the very date scheduled for the Wimbledon men's singles final. But then, all of that was suddenly settled with France taking the 3 July date and Silverstone moved to 10 July. So it became official. The three question marks had at last signed contracts with Bernie, which meant there were nineteen races on the Formula 1 calendar for the first time ever. When Bernie started taking control of FOCA in 1971 there were only eleven races, eight of them in Europe. By 2005 it had become a global nineteen, and it was nineteen again in 2006. In 2007 there were only seventeen races – San Marino was off, as was Hockenheim, now run on alternate years with the Nürburgring. However, Bernie, whatever his preference, was actively dealing his way to a Formula 1 World Championship calendar of twenty races or more. In the Seventies the series produced revenue of only a few hundred thousand; today it is over $1 billion.

But, of course, back in 2004 before our great tradition, the British Grand Prix, could be granted any kind of a future, there were still more twists and turns to be endured. The race reinstated on 13 October, as previously mentioned, was axed again on 20 October and by 10 November it had – again – been revived. The latest rescue mission had been put together by Bernie and the teams, with the exception of Ferrari, and consisted of a £20 million proposal to restore both the British Grand Prix and the race in France; Bernie's contribution was reputedly £10 million. Then, for Ferrari to come on board, it only remained for the FIA to agree to a nineteen-race calendar; and for the BRDC to agree to the new proposal. The pressure had been almost unbearable. There had, however, been a slight degree of optimism owing to the fact that the manufacturers supporting the teams enjoyed hefty car sales in Britain; at Silverstone they liked displaying their logos and showing off their wares. They were pushing hard for a deal. A remaining factor against the race was cost. The cost to stage the British Grand Prix had not changed: it was still $13.5 million. The annual compound interest brought the cost of the race to $27 million after ten years. Against this background was the fact that governments in Asia and the Middle East – indeed most race-hosting countries – seemingly had no qualms about subsidising not only the construction of breathtakingly modern facilities, but also payments of fees to Bernie's company well beyond what the BRDC – with or without the recent financial contributions – could afford; at least in the next few years.

Which brings us to one more problem. Time. The BRDC had wanted a short-term contract, just in case the manufacturers actually went through with their threat of a separate series. For the same reason Bernie wanted to tie them into a contract that would cease some years after the expiry of the Concorde Agreement, at the end of 2007, when the GPWC championship series would theoretically commence. In the end he managed to extend the Silverstone time base by five years, agreeing a contract that expired after the race in 2009 – well after the existing Concorde Agreement, or so he expected, but still too close for the comfort of British race fans. By the end of 2005 it was also too close for the comfort of the BRDC, still seeking support from its members, from the Government and other sources for the development of the circuit and the surrounding acreage which, with regard to the circuit, must meet with Bernie's approval – and on it went.

So on to 2006, when a plan involving a lucrative fifty-year lease to develop the circuit and its facilities in conjunction with property developer, St Modwen, was tabled but later – after a heated dispute – rejected by the BRDC. Then in 2007 the BRDC considered yet another proposal – actually this time it was a purchase offer, talked about but never forthcoming – from a property company called Sceptre Developments. Meanwhile, Sir Jackie Stewart resigned as President of the BRDC and was replaced by Damon Hill, the son of Graham Hill and also a Formula 1 World Champion; the move was followed by other comings and goings on the board. Somewhere in the middle of all this shuffling Bernie had suggested that the British Grand Prix alternate with the French Grand Prix to allow the BRDC more time to carry out the necessary work at the track. This too was soundly rejected. Sadly, the race at Magny Cours in France was off the calendar for 2008 and – lacking government funding – hasn't returned. On a brighter note, an updated Master Plan, formulated by Spencer Canning, Development Director of Silverstone Estates, together with a property advisory committee of the BRDC, was being submitted, in stages, for planning permission. It includes concepts for new pit and paddock facilities – essential for the BRDC to keep the British Grand Prix – and new grandstands. To attract companies from the wider motorsport industry, the plan also includes a technology park, a manufacturer test centre, a Porsche Driver Training Facility and a Silverstone Study Centre, along with hotel and conference facilities. As before, finance for the project was to be raised by selling off around thirty acres of the site's 800 acres, and from outside sources.

By the spring of 2007 a palpable sense of vigour began emanating from the regions of the BRDC, stimulated by the Master Plan and the looming Grand Prix deadline, but also by our new hero, Lewis Hamilton. With Jenson Button, David Coulthard and Anthony Davidson there were, then, four

British drivers on the grid, and British ticket sales responded accordingly. That said, British Formula 1 fans will always be there, in spirit if not in person – their loyalty adds a luminous quality to the sport in the UK that is unmatched in other countries. Which is not to say that the vivacity of Formula 1 fans at the other circuits is not outstanding, it is all of that and more, it's just that in Britain there's a brotherhood/ sisterhood that exudes that extra 'something'. This is why, in 2008 and 2009, Bernie's announcements that, firstly, the British Grand Prix was moving to Donington Park from 2010 and, secondly, if Donington failed to be completed on time the British Grand Prix would no longer exist, came as axe blows to the heart.

In some ways the Grand Prix weekend of 2008 couldn't have been better, apart from the rain. Lewis Hamilton put in a scintillating drive to victory, and there was a general sense of festivity wrapped up in the sixty-year celebrations of the British Grand Prix at Silverstone. Bernie's announcement cast a pallor of doom over it all, but at the post-race entertainment, with Battle of Britain grit, there were plenty of smiles and bonhomie. Also, the BRDC members were well-rehearsed at smiling in the face of adversity, and if that smile was a tad cynical they were entitled to that – they knew that plans for Donington would struggle through the Ecclestone scrutineering process, not to mention the downturn in the economy and seismic rift between the teams, Bernie and Max.

Anyway, Bernie's discussions with the BRDC had finally reached deadlock. Without financial support from the Government – and there wouldn't be any, apart from improving roads to the circuit – the numbers were simply not viable. It is interesting that Bernie's attitude to government funding underwent a complete U-turn: having been staunchly against it, his voice eventually became one of the loudest in encouraging the government to chip in. Either way, the money wasn't forthcoming and the BRDC had to not so much withdraw as relax their interest. But then Bernie's old friend Tom Wheatcroft turned up to introduce him to Simon Gillett, who had big plans for the redevelopment of Donington Park and the promise of around £100 million to see it through. Why not move the British Grand Prix sixty miles north? At least it guaranteed that the race would be saved for Britain. Bernie liked the look of the Tilke-designed drawings for circuit revisions and the money seemed appropriate for getting the project up and running. He agreed. And twenty-three years of twists and turns brought us back to Donington. Now it only remained for the circuit to be built – within a scant two-year schedule. This was not unlike the prospect faced by Nicola Foulston and Interpublic.

So it is – perhaps – not surprising that in the early months of 2009 the Donington project was nearing collapse. The leaseholder of the site, Donington Ventures Leisure Limited (of which Simon Gillett was chief executive), was being pursued in court by Tom Wheatcroft and his son – owners of the land – for unpaid rent of nearly £2.5 million. Furthermore, the local planners, North West Leicestershire District Council, required Tom Wheatcroft's signature on one more document before they could grant final approval of the development. In the circumstances, Tom was unlikely to comply. Bernie had his own worries, personal and otherwise, and lashed out at the Government's 'disgraceful' behaviour in not stepping in to support the British Grand Prix, adding the warning that Britain would lose its race if Donington failed. Silverstone maintained a 'wait and see' attitude, while focusing on the increasingly popular MotoGP motorcycle racing, returning to Silverstone – from Donington – in 2010 after an absence of twenty-four years. And they were quietly getting on with the Master Plan. But then, in June, Simon Gillett surprised everyone by letting it be known that Bernie had extended his agreement from ten to seventeen years. It seemed that in spite of his earlier threat, Bernie would also allow the British Grand Prix to skip a year, returning in 2011. Donington had been rescued. Or had it? A few weeks later Bernie stated that if Donington could not complete the circuit in accordance with their agreement then 'for sure we will come back to Silverstone'. You can always trust the fans at Silverstone to express an opinion on shenanigans affecting their race, and this they did during the 2009 Grand Prix weekend: 'Silverstone we love you, Donington dream on' read one banner draped on the pits straight in prime view of the television cameras. It was a magical couple of days, with everyone cheering on the Brawn team and Lewis Hamilton, even though it was Sebastian Vettel who was the winner. Vettel made up for it at the post-race musical bash: 'I regret that I'm not an Englishman today,' he grinned. The crowd, imbued with a blend of British pride and Silverstone homage, immediately clasped him to their collective soft heart – after all his team's headquarters were just a few miles down the road. It was that kind of moment, day, weekend.

Back in the real world, Simon Gillett got busy launching a fund-raising debenture scheme to shore up the finances for his Donington project. But the timing – the introduction of this venture in 2008 – was all against him, a combination of tight money, due to the global recession, made tighter by inter-sport politics. In mid-November 2009, Donington Ventures Leisure Limited, with debts of £66.7 million, went into administration. It had been hoped that Tom Wheatcroft might step in and take over the project, but he had been struggling with an illness that claimed his life just before DVLL collapsed. It was time for the BRDC to renegotiate with Bernie. They probably knew all along that it would come to this. And Bernie probably enjoyed reopening negotiations in his temporary headquarters at the jaw-droppingly lavish Yas Marina circuit in Abu Dhabi. You want to build a circuit, how about one like this? Yet, Bernie was ready to deal. The business board of the BRDC successfully completed the negotiations along with BRDC President Damon Hill and former racing driver Jackie Oliver, who sat on both the membership and business boards. And in December 2009 Damon was able to announce that the British Grand Prix would remain at Silverstone for another seventeen years. And the cost? Around £310 million over the course of the contract, with an initial starting fee approaching £12 million. But instead of ten per cent annual compound interest, which Bernie had earlier insisted upon, the interest would now be five per cent. Moreover, a seventeen-year contract – in place of the skimpy five-year extension – meant that the job of obtaining investment would be that much easier; also, should Silverstone be unable to pay, they could pull out after ten years. The BRDC's managing director, Richard Phillips, called it 'peace in our time'. Lewis Hamilton and Jenson Button could now stand – securely – on the shoulders of a long line of heroes, not just those sitting behind the wheel but in every aspect of British motorsport. The point being – we need a British Grand Prix. We need a shrine-like circuit built on a foundation of scrapped Anderson shelters and discarded ships' boilers – the components for manufacturing dreams. When you *have to*. And, yes, it has taken an extra dollop of kit-car attitude to get here.

Bernie announced that he was very pleased Silverstone was retaining the British Grand Prix, that he had 'personally always wanted to see this happen', even though he had just taken what some say was a £60 million loss on the transaction. He had been under pressure from CVC's Donald Mackenzie and Lord Mandelson, then Secretary of State for Business, who had urged him to finalise negotiations in order to ensure the future of the British Grand Prix. As motorsport contributes £4 billion to the UK economy and an estimated 65,000 jobs, it was Mandelson's duty to apply the weight of his position to the negotiations, although he wouldn't be spending taxpayers' money. The Secretary of State for Business didn't mention what taxpayers are spending on the Olympics – a one-time event. No, Bernie didn't feel any pressure from Mandelson; it ran much deeper than that, and was as complex as the man himself. 'I never think about the past,' he says. But consider the pride of his racing car collection – a car that he is holding on to. This is the Ferrari driven by José Froilán González to win the British Grand Prix at Silverstone in 1951, giving Scuderia Ferrari their first Grand Prix victory. That same day at Silverstone Bernie drove his Cooper 500 in the Formula 3 support race. Also remember that he drove his Cooper 500 in the support race held the previous year, on the day of the first-ever World Championship race – the British Grand Prix. Held at Silverstone. Without that background Bernie may not have been in a position to negotiate the present seventeen-year contract.

Would he continue to be Formula 1's supreme negotiator? The question had been torturing him for five years. Back in 2004, just as he was signing the five-year extension to the Silverstone contract, another care-worn saga was reaching boiling point. The manufacturers and teams had been endlessly capturing headlines, flaunting their threat of a breakaway series. By 2009 that threat was becoming a reality, casting into doubt the staging of a Formula 1 World Championship Grand Prix anywhere. It is not overstating the seriousness of the situation to say that Bernie's life – for that is what Formula 1 means to him – was hanging in the balance.

CHAPTER 18

THE HOUDINI FACTOR

'Is this the day that we thought we would never see, the end of Ecclestone?' asked veteran motor racing journalist Alan Henry, on 22 November 2004, the day that proceedings against Bernie began in a British High Court. Bernie had wanted the case to be heard in Switzerland, but a Swiss court would serve 'no purpose but to increase the delay and expense', said Lord Justice Robert Carnwath, who described the row as a dispute 'concerning the control and the future of Formula 1 racing'.

The actual parties involved were Speed Investments Limited, representing Lehman Brothers, JP Morgan and Bayerische Landesbank (BLB) – owners of seventy-five per cent of the shares in SLEC Holdings Limited with its collection of companies, against Bambino Holdings, the minority shareholder with twenty-five per cent; whose beneficiaries were the Ecclestone family. The banks disputed the appointment – unilaterally, without a vote – of two of Bernie's friends, the Swiss lawyer Luc Argand and his wife Emmanuele Argand-Rey, to the board of Formula One Holdings (FOH), which controls the companies that, in turn, manage almost everything involved in the commercial side of Formula 1, including television contracts.

Bernie had known Luc Argand since the Sixties. They met, as mentioned earlier, through Jochen Rindt and Argand had, after the racing driver's death, helped to set up the Rindt Trust for the benefit of Jochen's daughter. Thus having, over a period of decades, developed confidence in Argand, he was a logical choice for the FOH board. Bernie, his legal advisor and the Argands occupied four of the board's seven seats. The banks wanted more voting power and with it more influence in decisions regarding the running of Formula 1. Although this had not been their initial objective, they had been forced into this position with the collapse of Kirch, the German media company to whom they had granted loans for the acquisition of the SLEC shares. Then the banks had to worry about the GPWC's ubiquitous rival series, which daily reduced the value of their shares as the end of the Concorde Agreement – and the start of the new series in 2008 – approached.

The banks began to panic. 'These people [the banks] didn't get their shares out of choice, they got them as security,' Bernie told reporters. 'They got the house and they don't want the house. Now they want to cash in the house and that's what they're trying to do.' But before cashing in 'the house' the banks needed to restore its value, which meant eliminating a breakaway series. So they wanted to be in a position to negotiate directly with the manufacturers. To do that, they needed more decision-making power. The manufacturers, for their part, watched the proceedings 'with great interest'.

As things stood, in 2004, it appears Formula 1 generated between $800 million and $1 billion in revenue, of which the teams received forty-seven per cent of the broadcast revenue plus an additional sum of around $30–$35 million from a prize fund that, added together, represented some twenty-three per cent of the total revenue. The balance of the money, after the deduction of costs, was used to pay back the Eurobond. The manufacturers and most of the teams thought they could do better. If the banks put together a deal with the manufacturers, Bernie may have been be sidelined. On the other hand, why should the manufacturers and teams bother to negotiate for an increase when, by holding out for their own championship series, they could divvy up the majority of the commercial pie. In which case the banks might have sued Bernie for the loss in value of their shares. Bernie was in a tight corner. 'I'm always putting out fires,' is a Bernie mantra. He now had to smother an inferno.

On 6 December, the court ruled against Bambino. Bernie's grip on Formula 1 was loosened, with the inevitable consequence – or so it seemed – that the sport's commercial operations would now be managed by a committee. Appointed by bankers.

Former BBC commentator Murray Walker has his own views on the overall running of Formula 1. His first BBC commentary of the Grand Prix was broadcast on radio on that momentous day at Silverstone in 1950. Since then he has seen the total transformation that Bernie has brought to the sport, and applauds it: 'Formula 1 has been gigantically successful – worldwide, like no other sport – because of Bernie and his powers of vision and his powers of leadership.' But Murray now fears for Formula 1's future should Bernie decide – or be forced – to abandon it: 'I view the post-Ecclestone era with alarm and concern. Bernie has succeeded because he is a razor-sharp dictator, and he emerged from a collection of equals – team owners – as the only one who could see that this thing, Formula 1, had gigantic commercial possibilities which depended on it being controlled as a single unit with one bloke in charge, doing the negotiations, the promotion and all the rest of it. Of those owners, he was the only one who was willing to take on the responsibility – which he willingly did to his great benefit – and good luck to him. Now, the next person or the next collection of persons will be appointed, because nobody is showing any inclination to do what Bernie did. That was to say: "Of you lot, I'm gonna run it." There isn't anybody. So the expectation is that it will be run by some sort of consortium, or a board of appointees, and we all know what happens when boards run something, because boards are a collection of people and people differ, people have arguments, people fall out. I'm not saying that with the strength of what Bernie has created, a board of the right people couldn't do the job. But I would view it with some apprehension.'

During the autumn of 2004 Bernie shared Murray's apprehension, but his fears concerned not so much the composition of the FOH board as the unsettling involvement of the manufacturers: 'I'm more concerned with them actually stopping than starting something else [the breakaway series], which has been demonstrated – manufacturers coming in and out.' In addition to a certain amount of research and development, manufacturers use motorsport as a marketing platform. If a manufacturer-supported team doesn't do well or the management at board level changes, then policy changes, and they pull out. For example, Ford withdrew their money from Jaguar Racing and put the team up for sale. Fortunately it was purchased by the Austrian drinks company, Red Bull, and headed back to the grid. But the danger remained. 'We don't need to do a deal with manufacturers, we need to do a deal with teams, a commercial arrangement with the teams, that's what we need to do,' Bernie added. He was also concerned about two other problems threatening the future of Formula 1: rivalry between the teams, which prevented them from achieving solidarity at critical moments; and Max's unwillingness to be cooperative. 'Unless we get our act together, I mean the teams get their act together, it's a bit dismal in my opinion. These guys can't agree with each other to do anything. They don't have any real, long-term visions. We've got Max who thinks he's doing the right thing and, in my opinion (Max knows this, I think), interfering in things which maybe the FIA shouldn't interfere with. If the manufacturers want to spend money they should let them spend it. You can't tell people what they can spend. I mean what I've said to Max is that the regulations should be such that it's not a necessity to spend fortunes to be competitive. That's all.'

Bernie was referring to changes in the regulations demanded by Max and the FIA. These included engine capacity and aerodynamics – 'Williams would have gone out of business without them,' said Max, recalling a comment by Patrick Head, the team's co-founder and Director of Engineering. The disputed changes also include customer cars but more on that later. Did Bernie think the cars should be simplified like they were in the Eighties?

'Well, I think the engines should be.'

'And the aerodynamics?'

'Yeah, yeah, but you can't stop people, you can't un-invent aerodynamics. I like the modern Formula 1 car, and I can't see any point in reducing power.'

Speaking of changes: 'What do you think will happen when you go?'

'When I go?'

'Yes.'

'I have no intention of doing that.'

'Theoretically then, what do you think would happen, would it fall apart?'

'I don't know. It would be run in a different way, perhaps. You'll suddenly find twenty or thirty people, each will want to run a bit, and do a bit. I don't know. I really don't know. I hope it doesn't. I've given a lot of my life to it, so the last thing I want it to do is fall apart. It needs a strong person, somebody that people will listen to and respect. People respect anyone who makes decisions – that are good. But I have no intention of leaving.' Understandably, Bernie feels the need to continue to manage a sport that he has given his life to, nurturing it – hourly – and enfolding Formula 1 with his concept of perfection, so the emotion runs that much deeper. It is inconceivable that he would ever be able to walk away.

However, the banks had been given more decision-making power in that, following the Court's decision, they now had five members on the FOH board instead of two, so Bernie had no choice but to find a way to manage what was, for a man of his independence, awkward – if not irritating in the extreme. For their part, the banks had two paths to pursue: a bail-out, should any reasonable offer be presented; and leaning harder on Bernie to find a compromise that would satisfy the teams. Of course they could now go behind his back and enter into direct negotiations. But where would they find someone with Bernie's contacts and the worldwide respect that he commands? It would be foolhardy to antagonise him. Even so, Bernie knew that he needed to create a little more wriggle-room. He began by actively going through the motions of seeking an agreement with the teams and

GPWC. There had been the Memorandum of Understanding agreed the previous December, but in the end the terms were changed and the deal collapsed.

For his next move, in October 2004, he agreed a deal with nine of the then ten teams which, it was reported, had involved paying them a total of around $500 million in prize money – per year for three years – starting in 2008. It is believed to have been $378 million in 2007, according to F1 financial experts Christian Sylt and Caroline Reid. Such an agreement, when finalised – with all the teams – would have increased the value of SLEC's shares. Ferrari, however, remained outstanding, which is not surprising at any time, but just then it fuelled suspicions that Ferrari were after their own deal with Bernie. It was one disappointment too many for the manufacturers and team principals, with the seemingly endless hours of talk and deal-making falling flat; their patience had been played out. They declared that they would have nothing more to do with any negotiation – whatsoever – involving Mr Ecclestone. They then added ballast to their plans for a separate series by entering into discussions for circuit contracts, and by appointing experts to promote the series – including International Sports and Entertainment AG, a successful and well-respected marketing agency.

Bernie was beginning to look (some said) and act (some said) like a doomed man. And, of course, he was feeling bruised. It wasn't his fault that Kirch had folded and the banks became saddled with SLEC Holdings and its group of companies – something they had never desired and would happily dispense with if they could only find a buyer not terrified of Bernie. It would have been so much simpler, and less bitter, if the manufacturers could have agreed to acquire for themselves the 100-year deal for the FIA's commercial rights. An amount of between $350 and $400 million probably would have clinched it – a bargain when you consider what they would have received for their investment. Instead, everyone was getting wounded. Most of all Formula 1.

That said, Bernie – regardless of hurt feelings – actually enjoys having his back against the wall. It makes him feel alive. Warmed-up with anxiety he rubs more shine on to the blade of his talents: sizing up the odds, checking the angles, the psychological element, the opportunities for *using other people's money*, the *loss-leader*, the *fast offer while others are distracted or quickly reckoning*, the *quick turnaround*, the *chop or partial exchange*, the *walking away from a deal, forever, only to be coaxed back to the table*, the *clean slate*, the *I will not be beaten no matter what* techniques; all of these come into play. Let the banks have their day in court. Let the teams walk away. What, in the final analysis, had they won? The day. Only. Maybe – that's the zest.

The snag was Bernie's love for Formula 1. It really is his life. So he would either save it or die trying. Call this the *Houdini Factor*, the most important deal of all. Max understood, and he had faith in Bernie's ability to wriggle out of most bindings. Even on that gloomy first day of the court proceedings, in November 2004, Max had said that 'Bernie was at the back of the queue, going thorough the revolving door, and he'll come out in front with everything in his hands, and cleaner than when he went in.' What did the court ruling mean to Bernie? 'Nothing at all,' he said. Besides, it seemed that sports run by dictators tend to be more successful. Both Max and Bernie could have taken comfort in an article published on 11 December 2004 in the *Financial Times*. It was written by the newspaper's chief business commentator who argued that 'Fans want teams to compete on a level playing field. Some mechanism is needed', such as a dictator, 'to preserve the balance of power among competitors. A dictator may do a better job of marketing his game and selling rights to broadcasters and advertisers.' He then went on to cite a study by McKinsey, the management consultancy, contrasting the financial returns of golf and tennis: 'The US Professional Golfers' Association gains $500 million a year from television and licensing, but the fragmented governing bodies of tennis do much worse in garnering revenues.' In F1, perhaps, the three banks, the manufacturers and team principals would do well to appreciate their benevolent dictator(s).

Max also understood Ferrari, and the old 'fulcrum' was

now primed with an 'under-the-table' kind of deal and ready to sway – again – in Bernie's direction. The nine teams had been right to be suspicious. In January 2005 Ferrari signed the Concorde Agreement, or rather its extension from 2008 to 2012, and they did a separate commercial deal with Bernie for reportedly $100 million paid out over four years. Without Ferrari, there could not be a plausible breakaway series, and that was that. Or it should have been, except the other teams were so enraged by Ferrari's actions that it only strengthened their resolve; and as if to underscore the point the GPWC, with Honda and Toyota joining their ranks, then changed its name to the Grand Prix Manufacturers' Association (GPMA).

The following July, the rift with the teams widened further as a result of the unsatisfactory handling of the Indianapolis race and by what were seen as Max's reprisals – the threatened banning of the seven teams using Michelin tyres. Max remains unequivocal: 'No other course was possible given the sporting rules, the FIA circuit rules and the American legal system.' Punishment was delayed until September and, in the end, resolved by Michelin taking the blame. Bernie's concerted efforts to solve the crisis at Indianapolis had, for a time, improved his relationship with the teams. But the breach with Max over Indianapolis, coupled with his seemingly unilateral rule-making with regard to aerodynamics and engines – everyone would be required to use a V8 engine – had cemented the schism. So there could not be a renewal of the Concorde Agreement which laid down not only the commercial regulations of Formula 1, Bernie's territory, but also the sporting regulations, the FIA's territory. Both sides would have to be satisfied to obtain the signatures of the team principals, and the security of the sport's future. At this point Bernie could only improve the odds by playing chess with money, and by implementing the *Houdini Factor* with absolute precision.

If he had been playing for time, waiting for the right buyer for the banks' shares, he had also been put putting together a new set of financial-cum-management plans, so that he could act, without hesitation, to burrow his way to freedom and even greater wealth. That moment arrived in the autumn of 2005 via two precipitating agents: Formula One Administration (FOA), SLEC's commercial rights-holding subsidiary, and CVC Capital Partners, a globally respected private equity group. As the result of vastly increased revenue flowing into FOA, the debt on the $1.4 billion bond that had been taken out in 1999 – and secured on future commercial revenue – was about to be paid off early; it wasn't actually due to end until November 2009. So FOA's ability to release more value through a new loan arrangement along with future prospects made its parent company, SLEC, an attractive acquisition for CVC. Probably aware of what was about to happen, Bernie's response was characteristic. In a statement issued by Formula One Management, dated 30 August 2005, he insisted the SLEC shares were 'not for sale', thereby increasing their value. Then he appeared to have turned around and encouraged CVC to start buying them. Just one year after the doomsayers had been cogitating his demise, Bernie was hopping aboard the crest of a wave, the biggest deal of his life – so far.

In November 2005, CVC announced that it would be purchasing shares held by SLEC. During the course of the following year it acquired – through a company formed for the purpose – shares held by the three banks along with a portion of the shares held by the Ecclestone family trust, Bambino Holdings. Bernie had become familiar with CVC through his long-standing association with DORNA, the rights-owner of the motorcycle championship series, MotoGP. CVC had reportedly acquired a seventy-five per cent stake in DORNA in 1998, which it sold – for a huge profit – in 2006. CVC was then in a position to proceed with the acquisition of its majority stake in SLEC. The deal was put together by Donald Mackenzie, managing partner of CVC's London office, assisted by Nick Clarry, CVC's UK managing director. In recent years Donald Mackenzie had become a familiar figure around the paddock, which was no hardship for the Scot as Formula 1 had long been something of an obsession.

However, during 2006 the most pressing matter for Donald

Mackenzie and CVC was to proceed with their financial strategy for Formula 1. To do that they needed Bernie's help in obtaining concrete support from the teams. Bernie rolled up his sleeves. A month after CVC began buying up SLEC shares, the Williams team – for an estimated $30 million – signed the 2008–2012 Concorde Agreement. They were soon joined by four other teams: Super Aguri, Toro Rosso, Red Bull and Spyker MF1. Bernie also put a proposal to the Grand Prix manufacturers DaimlerChrysler, Renault, Honda, Toyota and BMW, which involved moving back what was thought to be the fixed date – 2008 – by two years. He proposed that, starting in 2006, the teams would receive fifty per cent of the commercial revenue – after expenses but before tax. The manufacturers had wanted sixty per cent but it was, as usual, impossible for Bernie to avoid playing the hard negotiator. As a condition he asked that the five car manufacturers become signatories to the Concorde Agreement – for the first time in the sport's history. Bernie now appeared to have reversed his earlier position of not needing 'to do a deal with the manufacturers, we need to do a deal with the teams, a commercial arrangement with the teams'. But the fact was the manufacturers had by then become integral to Formula 1 and it seemed appropriate for them to formalise their involvement. The manufacturers, however, baulked at the idea and would not sign. Had they done so, giving the document additional commercial clout, Bernie/CVC would have given the teams the desired sixty per cent, according to an interview with Max and Bernie conducted by Michael Schmidt (*Auto Motor und Sport*).

So Bernie, with CVC beside him, tried again. The good news was the buoyancy of Formula 1's commercial revenue coupled with the fact that the manufacturers actually welcomed CVC – they were active investors unlike those interlopers, the banks, inheritors of unwanted shares. With Renault Sport chairman Alain Dassas leading the way, the commercial revenue distribution for the future was finally agreed, in May 2006, in a Memorandum of Understanding between the Grand Prix Manufacturers' Association, Bernie and CVC. The teams would receive fifty per cent of the underlying profits, as previously decided, but the offer was now enriched with revenue from Paddy McNally's Formula 1 hospitality company, Allsport, and from Allsopp, Parker & Marsh (APM), which received revenue from trackside signage, race-title sponsorship and timings sponsorship. CVC had also acquired both of these companies. In addition, it appeared the teams were to receive substantial millions in back fees for the 2006 season – to be received upon signing the Concorde Agreement – as well as an increase in the 2007 revenue when it became available. In answer to the manufacturers' cries for more involvement in key decisions, they were given board positions. After so many excruciating battles, it was a great achievement, and a great relief to all concerned.

With the Memorandum of Understanding in place, the first part of the financing could now proceed. It is in the nature of private equity companies to be aggressive in adding debt, and CVC was no exception. Call that phase one. During phases two, three and four they concentrate their energies on adding value – by improving the assets – before selling at a higher price. In Formula 1's case the improved assets would include more circuits, more television in a range of time slots, and perhaps a flotation, among other things. These would – according to past performance – bring a tidal wave of new money to overflow the coffers of CVC's investors, the teams and Bernie.

The whole basket of Formula 1's commercial companies had become known as the Formula One Group (F1 Group), which, is ultimately owned by Jersey-based Delta Topco; SLEC, which had been the ultimate holding company of the F1 Group, was superseded as more companies or branches – some fifteen since CVC's involvement – were added to the F1 Group tree. The Formula 1 World Championship series is supported by a forest of such trees. That which comprises the F1 Group is merely the tallest – and most fecund. Along with CVC, the two reinvesting banks, Bambino and others was a further individual investor, Bernie Ecclestone, with a reported 5.3 per cent stake, thus his involvement was monetary, corporeal and spiritual – as always. For his money and manoeuvring he had obtained freedom. Gone was the litigious voice of the banks. Their control – though presenting an invigorating challenge – had made him uneasy. Nor had he enjoyed filtering his activities through Bambino's board, regardless of the family link. Now he was a direct investor in the F1 Group and with it came a greater measure of flexibility, of room to live in and, of course, profit – along with an exhilarating amount of risk.

It was reported that the Ecclestone family wealth had remained consistent at an estimated $4.1 billion. That's not bad going for 'Titch', 'the Whippet', son of a Suffolk fisherman. It's as if a voice in Bernie's head had kept upping the odds against him, so he had to outperform all expectations, perhaps from birth. Of course the $4.1 billion may be a conservative estimate. Bernie's not telling. What he will do is continue with the same old tally system, keeping score with money, in ever-increasing amounts.

Bernie's emancipation, however, came with a few strings, if not a whole new set of bindings. It would now be Bernie and Donald Mackenzie at the helm of the Formula 1 group of companies, a coupling that, at first glance, recalls the old Max and Bernie double act, at least for cunning with flair. Bernie always chooses interesting playmates. The then forty-nine-year-old Mackenzie qualified as a Chartered Accountant and holds an LLB from the University of Dundee. With those in hand he proceeded to build a reputation as a tough negotiator. In 1988 he became a co-founder of CVC Capital Partners, taking a ten per cent stake in the company. He was instrumental in the transaction of headline-making acquisitions that included William Hill, Halfords, Debenhams and the Automobile Association. Prior to joining CVC he had worked for 3i Group PLC, then one of the largest, publicly traded venture capital and private equity firms in the world, but he left out of frustration after they had repeatedly ignored his investment advice. Donald Mackenzie's advice was worth listening to. His stake in CVC was reputedly worth $115 million. One team principal described Mackenzie as 'a straight shooter'. Bernie liked him too, but added the codicil: 'In business there are no friends.'

So, with Formula 1's commercial companies restructured and the commercial relationship with the teams defined in the Memorandum of Understanding, it only remained for all the signatures of all concerned parties to be put to that outstanding bit of paper – need I say it again – the Concorde Agreement. The sporting side of the document was yet to be hammered out, which put the burden on Max to cooperate with the manufacturers, and Bernie to apply pressure – if he could. But it would not be the familiar united force of Max and Bernie against all comers. CVC and their wider interests had to be considered.

Bernie was now the chief executive of Formula 1, earning a salary that would impress even the most powerful top executive in the world of global finance. And he would have to be accountable. In any other circumstance Bernie would have suffocated under the constraints of this arrangement, but his ultimate boss always has been and always would be Formula 1 – the race, the show, his duty to raise standards and keep score with money – so, effectively, there was no change. Of course he would never be a tight-lipped, slipper-footed, furtive-glancing, automaton-in-a-suit kind of director. Bernie was Bernie. Take him or leave him, he didn't care because he was far too busy concentrating on the sport. And just then, the sport sorely needed his attention.

During the summer and autumn of 2006 Max Mosley, also a former flag-bearer for the independent teams, began devoting his attention to the manufacturers' needs. Following meetings in Nice and Munich – attended by the press – a transcript appeared on the FIA website announcing an agreement between the FIA/Max and Professor Burkhard Göschel, a former BMW board member and chairman of the Grand Prix Manufacturers' Association. The agreement – verbal – concerned 'objectives' from which the technical rules could be formulated. As with the Memorandum of Understanding, the manufacturers now obtained direct involvement in the decision-making process, which in this instance gave them a stronger voice in the formulation of the sporting rules. Other agreements dealt with cost-cuts; technologies that could ultimately be used by road cars; green technologies such as fuel recovery; and ways – such as overtaking – to achieve better entertainment. As for the independent teams, Max gave the assurance that they 'are still very much represented by us [FIA] because we have always been defenders of the independent teams and we are in full agreement with the manufacturers that we need the independent teams and we must arrange the rules so that they can stay in. With this principle, that the manufacturers will make these new technologies available to the independent teams very economically, then their interests are taken care of. At the same time the independent teams don't have to spend fortunes on wind tunnels. So we will take them even more into account.' With the manufacturers' signatures and their direct involvement neatly spelled out, the Concorde Agreement could now be finalised. The press responded with plaudits galore, and rightly so. It seemed that five years of rancour had come to an end and new headlines could now be written. Formula 1 had a secure future to look forward to. Except. There is always an 'except'.

This time it was called 'customer cars', and it came to a climax at Melbourne during the first grand prix of the 2007 season. There is a fresh sense of optimism at the start of every Formula 1 season, even if, like Bernie, you've been turning up for sixty years. There is always a feeling that this season will be better than the last; the car will be faster, the engine will out-perform all others, as will the driver; it's a better chance. Like falling in love all over again, or gambling: 'This time I'll be lucky'. A sense of family unity – initially – infuses all the handshakes, hugs and smiles; and there is open admiration, or not, for the cars' new livery, new sponsors, the new uniforms, new banners, newly appointed hospitality units. It's all part of the furniture of what is for many – like Bernie – home. But in Melbourne, while the atmosphere in the paddock was not exactly chilling, there was the awkward perception that a couple of gate-crashers had just barged into a distinctly private affair. The miscreants were Toro Rosso and Super Aguri, the possessors of customer cars. According to the sporting rules that were in effect until the end of the 2007 season, each team must race in a chassis of its own manufacture or one commissioned to its own design. From 2008, under the proposed new Concorde Agreement, teams could – if they wished – buy customer cars from another team. The purpose of the rule change was to open up competition by allowing teams to compete at less cost but on equal terms. Prodrive, for example, had plans (never realised) to enter the 2008 season with an economical $100 million budget, having saved many millions on design and testing. This is what Max was referring to when, among other technologies, he said from 2008 'the independent teams [won't] have to spend money on wind tunnels'. Instead, new teams would be able to purchase complete up-to-date cars from an established team.

But in 2006 Scuderia Toro Rosso had seemingly jumped the gun by running a Red Bull RB01 redesignated as an STR01. The FIA's position was that some parts of the car were built by a company that was not a racing team and, therefore, legitimate. In 2007 Toro Rosso again joined the grid at Melbourne in a Red Bull car and Super Aguri – apparently – entered in the 2006 Honda, which was soon edging up to the tails of its parent. The Spyker and Williams teams, among others, were outraged; such chassis sharing was 'blatantly illegal', and raised the question of 'what constitutes a constructor?' And what about the intellectual property? According to the first part of Section 3 of the existing Concorde Agreement: 'A constructor is a person... who owns the intellectual property rights to the rolling chassis it currently races, and does not incorporate in such chassis any part designed or manufactured by any other constructor of F1 racing cars.' That seemed clear enough, at least in spirit, and on that basis it was being demanded that Toro Rosso and Super Aguri be excluded from future races. Honda team principal Nick Fry decided that in 2008 the team would be holding on to its intellectual property. But the Honda solution didn't solve the problem for 2007; it was escalating.

Bernie proposed various compromises, including a pooling of the constructors' money. A few details remained outstanding but a hoped-for resolution was about to be agreed.

Meanwhile, the teams had much to contemplate, as did Max. In October 2007 Max, then aged sixty-seven, had only two years remaining in his term as President of the FIA, and he had – for a long time – let it be known that he would not be seeking re-election. He looked forward to a more leisurely lifestyle away from the full-time demands of his office, and he wanted to be free to devote time to general road safety and environmental concerns. Yet there remained much to be done in Formula 1 and other FIA championships, 'tidying-up' as Max called it, so that he could leave with the satisfaction of knowing he had achieved all or most of his goals. Without a signed Concorde Agreement in place – which also concerned the sporting rules of Formula 1 and was thus binding upon the FIA – Max had greater flexibility to push through his concepts: the cost-cuts, the development of green technologies that would be road-car relevant, and opening up the grid to smaller, independent teams. Overall, Max was concerned with the sport's sustainability.

As has been said, in 2008 it became permissible for a team to purchase both chassis and engine from another team – the complete customer car. Prodrive were negotiating an engine/ chassis package with McLaren. Max welcomed other teams to do likewise, seeing it as an opportunity to return the sport to its entrepreneurial, 'let's all go racing' days of the Sixties and Seventies, and a good way for a new team to get into Formula 1 and gradually build their design organisation to develop their car's uniqueness. In function it was not unlike a top team hiring a designer from another team – knowledge inevitably travels with the person. Yet the teams continued to raise objections to chassis-sharing, aerodynamics and so on. There is always an element of confrontation between the regulator and competitors – in Formula 1 it's simply more visible.

After arduous discussions back and forth, the politics and sporting rules of Formula 1 solidified into a kind of flat triangular configuration. The three points were: the teams; Bernie representing the commercial sector; and Max representing the FIA, with broader concerns extending not only to the teams and sporting rules but also encompassing the promoters and rights holders. Previously, it had been more polarised, with Bernie and Max at one end, connected by a telephone, and the teams at the other. The teams staunchly maintained their insistence upon having a stronger voice in deciding the sporting rules, including veto rights, which could be incorporated in the new Concorde Agreement – if the FIA would only sign up to it. That said, they had often been invited to the FIA's table to offer their input but apparently failed to turn up. Formula 1, with its high stakes and high profile, made it inevitable that the teams would have their own agendas. The same held true for CVC/FOM. For Max, the terms being proposed would reduce his power to govern – to this he could never agree. And, as always, the teams wanted a greater share of the commercial revenue. The three sides were locked in a stalemate. The opportunity to break the stalemate occurred in a basement flat of a Chelsea apartment building in the spring of 2008.

On Sunday 30 March 2008, an exposé of Max's sexual activities, conducted in private – or so he thought – among consenting adults, became the *News of the World*'s front-page story. The exposé continued on the inside pages of the tabloid newspaper, complete with blurry stills, secretly filmed by one of the women involved in the affair – who had been paid by the *News of the World*. A cut-down version of the five-hour video of these activities was available for the world to see on the newspaper's website. It received over three million hits. On the Monday, newspapers – seemingly in every country around the globe – were carrying the story with accompanying images. The following Sunday, the *News of the World* published further extracts, and offered to deliver DVD copies of the footage to members of the FIA Senate, and make further copies available to the national motoring clubs. Some of the manufacturers became concerned that the scandal would tarnish the sport's image, making sponsors reluctant to be associated with Formula 1, and it was thought the embarrassment it had caused would impinge upon Max's role as President.

Bahrain's crown prince suggested Max should not attend the upcoming World Championship race in his country, fearing the focus would shift from the circuit to the FIA president; and a few of the FIA's member clubs demanded that Max step down. Instead, he squared his shoulders, faced his critics and handled the press with aplomb. Max's initial concern, apart from the pain brought upon his family, was the allegation by the *News of the World* that his activities had involved 'Nazi-style' role-playing. This he could not tolerate – nor could anyone else. 'All my life, I have had hanging over me my antecedents, my parents, and the last thing I want to do in some sexual context is be reminded of it,' he later stated from the witness stand during court proceedings. The allegation caused the Israeli Automobile Touring Club to withdraw an invitation to Max to visit their country, and there was criticism from organisations such as the Holocaust Educational Trust. The former Formula 1 champion, Jody Scheckter – along with other revered racing drivers – called for Max's resignation. Stirling Moss couldn't see how Max could continue as President, although he approved of what he had achieved and hoped that he would be able to finish his term. Bernie apparently didn't feel Max had done anything wrong – it was all 'a bit of a joke' – but he was coming under pressure to distance himself from the friendship that had existed for forty years. 'Max should do what he thinks is right,' he is reported to have said. In a later BBC interview he was more circumspect: 'a lot of companies have Jewish people on their boards', the inference being that such companies might be feeling uncomfortable and withdraw support from Formula 1.

Yet Max was anything but racist, having energetically encouraged RaceFree, an anti-racist campaign, following scenes of abuse against the black driver Lewis Hamilton during testing at Barcelona. Some found the unprecedented 'Spy-gate' fine against McLaren – a measure to preserve the integrity of the sport – at odds with Max's behaviour. Others argued that Max's sexual activities were meant to be private and did not set out to damage anyone, even though the result was just the opposite. The team principals met to discuss Max's future: was this their chance to depose him? Which may have been interesting to ponder but impossible in reality as the teams do not have the documented power to get rid of an FIA President. And they were, as usual, unable to agree. What was certain, however, is that the affair had drawn attention to the rift between the teams, Bernie and Max. Bernie, representing the commercial rights holder, CVC, began to align himself with the teams.

On 16 May, Max wrote to the presidents of the FIA member clubs explaining that he had (a few weeks earlier) asked the Senate to call an Extraordinary General Assembly to be held on 3 June to decide if he would see out his term and remain in office until October 2009. Furthermore, there were important negotiations under way concerning 'the 100-year commercial agreement between the FIA and the Formula One Commercial Rights Holder (CRH)' – Bernie and CVC. Among other things, the CRH had 'now asked for control over the Formula One regulations and the right to sell the business to anyone – in effect to take over Formula One completely'.

Max did not believe the FIA should agree. A company had been formed in 2002 with two share issues: one of them gave the FIA power over who bought the commercial rights and the appointment of chief executives. But Max's concern went well beyond this, he felt that should the FIA agree they would be abandoning the 'core elements of the FIA's patrimony', such as their 'ability to protect the traditional Grands Prix'. This was significant in view of the fact that the majority of Formula 1 championship races were now held outside Europe. Moreover, to concede to the CRH proposal would make the FIA 'weaker financially', and would 'risk the viability of the FIA as the regulatory authority of international motorsport and lose a valuable communication platform for the wider interests of the organisation'. The CRH also wanted 'a new Concorde Agreement... because of its influence over the teams (which comes mainly from its ability to offer favours in and around the paddock) the CRH sees a Concorde Agreement as another way to exercise control over the sport'. Again, Max did not believe the FIA should agree. 'The sport and the commercial interests should be kept separate. The teams and the CRH should be consulted and listened to at all stages, but it must be the FIA, not the CRH or the teams, which decides the regulations. My refusal to concede on this has led to a difficult situation and compounds the problem with the CRH over the 100-Year Agreement. In my view, we should only sign a new Concorde Agreement if it reinforces the authority of the FIA and deals properly with the major financial crisis, which appears imminent in Formula One. Costs have gone out of control, income is insufficient and major manufacturers are in difficulty with their core businesses. Only with fair and realistic financial arrangements will we avoid losing more teams.'

He went on to discuss other matters but returned to the business of Formula 1, adding a sinister suggestion. 'During my period as FIA President the economics of Formula One have changed beyond all recognition. We are now dealing with a sport involving billions of dollars and interests that would like nothing better than to remove the FIA from the Championship entirely. I have been determined to fight for the rights and role of the FIA in Formula One and it is possible for this reason that the media have been encouraged by those who have an interest in undermining my Presidency. I believe, therefore, that whatever the Extraordinary General Assembly decides, it should not reward those who have deliberately set out to destabilise the FIA at such a crucial time in its history.'

Needless to say, Max's letter was dynamite and, as it was accessible to anyone with a computer, extracts appeared in motor racing journals and in the press. Bernie hit back. 'I sincerely hope that it [Max's letter] isn't a declaration of war,' he told a reporter for *The Times*, because 'then we'll have to defend ourselves.' He rejected Max's claim that Formula 1 faced an imminent financial crisis: such a suggestion threatened the commercial value of the sport. Bernie also pointed out that CVC would be replying to Max's letter –

which they did. Donald Mackenzie made it clear that they had no intention of selling up: CVC were in the sport for the long term. Meanwhile, Bernie joined the chorus calling for Max's resignation – to no avail. During the Extraordinary General Assembly on 3 June, Max received a resounding vote of confidence. This may have given him the encouragement, if he needed it, to woo the teams to his side of the table by asking the CRH to give the teams ninety-two per cent of the total promotional revenue and sixty-seven per cent of the revenue from TV earnings. Hold on, wasn't that going beyond the bounds of the FIA's remit, the division of the sporting side of Formula 1 from the commercial side as set out by the European Commission? CVC were probably doing a quick refresher course on the legalities, because to buy the commercial rights to Formula 1 they had taken out a series of loans amounting to $2.5 billion repayable by 2014, according to *bloomberg.com*. The good news was 'CVC had paid off $84 million of its Formula One loans in 2007'. Even so, the arrangement being proposed by Max would likely make servicing the debt difficult. Having dropped this latest bombshell Max turned his attention to removing the Nazi slur from his personal reputation.

In July, he brought a legal action against the *News of the World*, primarily on the grounds of invasion of privacy. The court ruled in his favour and, more importantly, the judge indicated there was no substantiating evidence of a Nazi element to his sexual activities as reported in the newspaper – which he subsequently sued for libel; and he pursued similar proceedings against the German newspaper, *Bild*. Max was well and truly back. He even managed to patch up his friendship with Bernie. 'I think that Bernie was under tremendous pressure from one or two people, so he reacted to that,' he told *Autosport*'s Jonathan Noble. 'We've had frank discussions about the whole thing and I think it's now really behind us.' Max still believed that he had been set up. As early as January, Bernie had warned him to be careful, naming someone 'not unconnected' with Formula 1; and he had received a second warning from another quarter that he was being watched. Accordingly, Max had taken precautions. He knew and trusted all but one of the women he was involved with sexually – the lady with the needle-sized camera.

With regard to CVC, he was working with Bernie to sort out a redrafting of the 100-year lease of the commercial rights and the Concorde Agreement. And until that ever-elusive bit of paper was signed, Max was free to get on with his plans for transforming Formula 1. It was up to the ten teams to react to Max's proposals by coming up with ideas for their implementation. When that was agreed the FIA would enforce it. Max was able to wield power because of the rule-making structure introduced in 2006, as laid out in Appendix 5 of the sporting regulations. Signing up to the 2008 championship had committed the teams to that mechanism. What the teams – along with Bernie – were seeking was a reversion to the old Concorde Agreement, which had existed with its various extensions since 1981. Under that agreement the teams were integral to the rule-making process through the FIA's Formula One Commission, upon which Bernie and Max sat, along with representatives of the teams, sponsors and promoters. They worked together to write the rules, which were then passed by the World Motor Sport Council ('World Council') and ultimately the General Assembly. A rules package existed for 2009 but, in making technological changes, time and expense are vital considerations. As the 2010 season fast approached, and the following seasons were being planned, there was growing pressure: the circuit owners and promoters, sponsors, manufacturer owners, CVC and the teams were all getting edgy. Yet Max remained adamant that he would only affix his signature to a document that upheld the FIA's governance of the sport at a level he considered appropriate.

The familiar themes that bound the teams together – the desire for a larger portion of the commercial pie and the need for more power in making the rules – now included a more recent concern, the omnipresent gloom of recession. The exit of Honda from Formula 1 had been chilling. Fortunately, the team was taken over by Ross Brawn, with great success, but the general unease remained. Tobacco sponsors had been replaced by high-tech companies and banks, but now many of the latter were pulling out, most notably Credit Suisse, the Royal Bank of Scotland and ING. Added to this was the knock-on effect of the slump in car sales. Obtaining sponsorship – always a struggle – was suddenly that much harder for the teams and circuits as corporations thought twice about conspicuous consumption and, indeed, a sport oiled with mega millions. Perhaps Max had seen the recession coming. In any event the spending on Formula 1 had to reach a ceiling sooner or later. Didn't it? A lot of people were thinking about the answers. Most of all, the teams, who could now take a more considered look at customer cars and cost-cuts, and start to work out a compromise – over time. Compromise being the operative word, for they would not be dictated to.

In mid-2008 the teams braided together their mutual ties and formed the Formula One Teams Association (FOTA). By March 2009 they felt bold enough to hold a press conference to flaunt their newly found solidarity and therefore bargaining power. Ferrari president Luca di Montezemolo opened with an address: 'This is an unprecedented moment in Formula 1 history... for the first time the teams are unified and steadfast with a clear, collective vision. Thanks to this unity, the teams have already managed to make a significant reduction to their costs for 2009. And, while we will continue to compete vigorously on track, we all share one common goal: to work together to improve Formula One by ensuring its stability, sustainability, substance and show for the benefit of our most important stakeholder, namely the consumer. It is with this mindset that we now intend to work hard, with our partners at the FIA and FOM, our shared goal being to optimise the future of Formula 1.'

He went on to introduce the representatives of the FOTA Working Groups: technical, commercial and sporting. They would halve the 2008 cost of running a team by 2010 through restrictions on items such as aerodynamic spending, the use of wind tunnels, software use, engine expense, staff numbers and so on. With regard to environmental considerations, engines would increase mileage by 100 per cent; kinetic energy recovery systems could become standard, and race lengths could be dropped to 155 miles or one hour forty minutes instead of the maximum two hours. FOTA, like Max, could introduce revolutionary changes. And there were more items on the shopping list.

They wanted a new points-scoring scheme, proposing that the 10–8–6–5–4–3–2–1 system be changed to 12–9–7–5–4–3–2–1. There would be a point awarded to the team achieving the quickest pit stop, plus other point-scoring opportunities. Bernie had suggested awarding medals and/or the championship to the driver who won the most races. Neither suggestion was favourably received.

FOTA also wanted more on-screen data, jazzed-up television interviews and, generally, a better show. This meant more overtaking – which Max favoured – as some of the recent races had been painfully processional. It was hoped that the introduction of driver-adjustable front wing flaps would help overtaking, but then, with the new technical changes, there would be more distance between the cars, and more distance between the front and back of the grid. Mr Showbusiness-Ecclestone knew better than anyone that his Formula 1 extravaganza was getting a tad dull. He would have been the first to encourage Michael Schumacher's return in 2010, alongside a glittering cast headed by superstar champions Lewis Hamilton, Jenson Button and Fernando Alonso. But in 2009 Bernie, like everyone else, was keeping an eagle eye on the purse-strings. Well… how about a comeback in America? Would he take his travelling show there? The FOTA members wanted to know. They would like to have three races in North America, a country not known for lavish spending, particularly on hefty price-tag items such as FOM's fees, which averaged $2.8 million in 2009 according to F1 industry report *Formula Money*. For the first time in the history of the World Championship, North America was off the Formula 1 calendar. FOTA wanted to participate in North American races, even if they had to pick up some of the costs. They were serious. Bernie was working on it and in the US he eventually managed to do a deal that involved the creation of a new, purpose-built Formula 1 circuit: the race near Austin, Texas, was scheduled to be in business in 2012. Canada was back in 2010, and Bernie would really, 'absolutely', like to have a championship race in the 'Big Apple', New York City. But would the financially and physically stretched teams be willing to add yet another race or two or three to the calendar – or sacrifice another one of the classic races? We'll have to wait and see. Meanwhile, FOTA would 'work together' with FOM/Bernie for a greater share of the commercial revenue. And, finally, at the FOTA conference Luca di Montezemolo stated: 'All the teams and car manufacturers are prepared to commit to enter in the new Concorde Agreement until the end of 2012.' Bernie didn't object to the teams becoming unified if it brought them closer to signing the aforementioned document, just as long as they understood he was the boss. Max had other views. The FIA, *ie* Max, was the big chief running Formula 1 – which he was about to make clear.

Twelve days after FOTA's inaugural press conference, the FIA's World Council passed a £30 million (later £40 million) total cost cap to be introduced in 2010. It was optional. However, the cost-capped cars would be allowed greater technical freedoms, and the FIA had 'the right to adjust elements of these freedoms to ensure that the cost-capped cars have neither an advantage nor disadvantage when compared with cars running to the existing rules.' FIA accountants would be appointed to examine the books of the cost-capped teams and fines would be imposed on over-spenders. The FIA's decision effectively created a two-tier championship. One recalls the introduction of Renault's turbocharged V6 engine in 1980 that had jolted the nerves of Brabham's Gordon Murray – along with the rest of the paddock. The mix of turbo and non-turbo engines had been awkward to say the least. Yet the sport survived. Actually, it thrived. But in 2009 such a move might confuse sponsors – and also the fans who cheered to glory the optimum levels of expertise and performance of their favourite teams as well as their favourite drivers. These high-performance levels were reflected in the public's choice of road cars.

If the new rules favoured the smaller teams, the big-money teams might respond by leaving the sport. Di Montezemolo, so statesmanlike at the press conference, now changed his tone: 'FOTA would like to express its disappointment and concern at the fact that these decisions have been taken in a unilateral manner.' It was a call to arms. Although Max had been discussing cost-cutting measures for some time, it was the finality of the decision that was so striking. It was also the start of a whole new chapter in the history of Formula 1. This time, it was entitled the 'FOTA/FIA War'. The crisis would swiftly escalate – and it would become vicious.

Ferrari fired the first shot by announcing it would be willing to leave Formula 1 over the FIA's decision, which they followed up by filing an injunction with a French court in Paris, in a move to stop the regulations from being implemented. Years earlier Ferrari had been given the power to veto technical changes but, as they had failed to exercise their veto during the recent decision-making round, the courts ruled against them. The possibility of an FIA Formula 1 Championship series without Ferrari was potentially bad for FOM's businesses, and it was certainly bad for Formula 1. Bernie tried to broker a compromise but even his considerable efforts failed. During the weekend of the Monaco Grand Prix the ten FOTA teams met and unanimously decided to withdraw by the end of the 2009 season – unless, among other conditions, the cost cap was removed. Ferrari, however, was contractually obliged to race in future FIA championships through to 2012, as was Williams. But, unlike Ferrari, Williams decided to lodge an entry – unconditionally – for the 2010 season. Ferrari took the position that their contract was invalid on the grounds that the FIA had failed to recognise their right to veto. Force India would follow Williams' lead by entering as a budget-capped team. Both teams were suspended from FOTA. The FIA, meanwhile, turned up the pressure by publishing the entry list, which included definite entries for Toro Rosso, Red Bull and Ferrari, along with three new teams: Campos Grand Prix, Manor Grand Prix and USF1. Toro Rosso and Red Bull were included because they had legal agreements with FOM, obliging them to compete through 2012. The FIA then gave Brawn, McLaren-Mercedes, Renault, BMW Sauber and Toyota one week to remove the conditions attached to their entries. The FIA had several other teams waiting in the wings should the FOTA teams not take up their slots. To be fair, Max had tried to compromise, offering them self-assessment of the cost-cap or whatever they wished to call it, and broader agreement on expenditure. He was even willing to sign the Concorde Agreement but, apparently, the vexing governance question remained unresolved and the FOTA teams would not back down.

On 18 June the FOTA members – Ferrari, Toro Rosso, Red Bull, McLaren, Renault, Toyota, Brawn and BMW Sauber – met at Renault's factory in Enstone and, following a four-hour meeting that finished around midnight, they agreed to break away from the FIA and start their own series. They even went so far as to sign a $50 million bond payable to the others by any member breaking ranks. After that they needed a little liquid courage. Flavio Briatore, with – it was said – tears welling up in his eyes, started popping the champagne corks. They had held fast. Who said the teams could never agree on anything, that at the final hour they would fail to make a united stand? Echoes of Benjamin Franklin and Bernie during the FISA/FOCA War come to mind: 'Gentlemen, we will hang together or most assuredly we will hang separately', or words to that effect. Lawyers for both sides were grinning at the prospect of untold wealth.

The FIA announced that it would be taking legal action, suing for billions 'without delay'. Max later added that the dispute could not be easily resolved and might drag on into the following year. Bernie, who had more legal experience than most, knew that hauling the FIA/FOTA arguments through the courts could bury Formula 1, never mind the individuals involved. All the same, he was jumping aboard the lawsuit bandwagon. Of course legal actions have long been a favourite pastime in Formula 1. But this felt different, more menacing. Max believed the cost-cap dispute was a smoke screen covering up the real purpose of the teams – to depose him and snatch the commercial takings. 'The teams want the sporting power and they want the money – and I am not going to let them grab the power or the money. Bernie knows this is an attempt to grab his business,' he told *The Times* reporter Kevin Eason. It may have been that the sex scandal of the previous year had left Max short on backbench political support and the teams were pressing an advantage in a sideways attempt to get rid of him. But if that were true the FOTA members were doing a convincing job of carrying off the bluff. If you compare the FOTA breakaway series with the FIA series as it then stood, FOTA had most of the superstar cars and drivers – Lewis Hamilton, Jenson Button, Fernando Alonso among them. Let us then look at the circuits. The traditional circuits, falling by the wayside, would be delighted to do deals to attract FOTA's string of big names, and there were plenty of other circuits (without expensive FOM contracts) scattered around the globe – including Indianapolis in America – that would suit FOTA's high-performance cars. FOTA representatives were actively lining these up.

Television? Again, the breakaway teams had an attractive package: never underestimate the power of the prancing horse. It was being suggested Sky would be a prime mover in the TV coverage and would be using High Definition. The current TV rights holders, those who had signed contracts with Bernie, might have been able to withdraw from their contracts on the basis that the show they had signed up to had altered out of all recognition – it wasn't the same product. Similarly, sponsors could feel slighted if the teams they were sponsoring didn't appear in the more appealing version of the sport; likewise the circuits' sponsors and corporate hospitality might be affected. Everyone was examining the fine print on his or her contract. But Bernie, the daredevil, the ultimate risk-taker with nerves of steel and an indestructible will, wasn't losing any sleep. It amounted to 'basically, nothing' he said to the media. He could comfort himself with the knowledge that the teams, although they were said to have support from the manufacturer owners, were not yet in a position to promise a long-term future for the breakaway series. Also there was their habitual disunity, although that appeared to be past history.

The F1 split of 2009 was compared with the division between America's CART and IRL in 1996, with the popular teams and drivers joining the new championship. But was either series, or indeed both combined, ever really on a par with the financial powerhouse, the globally impacting series that Formula 1 had become? It was thought that Bernie/FOM/CVC might part company with the FIA and join the rebel teams. Which would mean ignoring their agreement with the FIA to produce twenty cars on the grid and kissing goodbye to the 100-year commercial rights deal and all it entailed. Alternatively if they didn't join the teams they might sue the FIA and vice versa. Did Max say the dispute could drag on into the following year? Try eternity. Sleep or no sleep, something, or someone, had to give. Bernie determined that, whatever it took, the sport would have a future. For him – personally, spiritually, professionally – there was no alternative. Here, again, was the most important deal of all, the *Houdini Factor*. Come what may.

On the morning of 24 June 2009, at the FIA's headquarters in Paris – at Place de la Concorde – a meeting of the World Council was about to take place. Max, to everyone's surprise, told the assembled members he had some business that demanded his attention; it wouldn't take long. He then handed over the chairing of the meeting to the FIA Vice-President, Nick Craw, and left the room accompanied by Bernie and Luca di Montezemolo. While the members of the Council listened to reports from chairmen of the various working committees, they waited for Max's return. And waited. After lunch they reassembled. Max arrived and took his usual place. Bernie took his usual place, directly opposite Max, and di Montezemolo sat down beside him. Max had an announcement to make. He would resign as of October when his term of office was over. For Formula 1 it was suddenly tomorrow. It was said the emotion in the room was stifling, the kind that walls up words into frozen frames along with the countenances. Di Montezemolo looked at his hands. Bernie was a study in despair. And Max? Rigid but controlled as always. In a cruelly short period of time Max had suffered the deaths of his mother, his older brother and his son, the anguish of the globally publicised sex scandal, and now, after sixteen years in office, he had seemingly been amputated from influence in Formula 1 – a sport he had always loved, and always would. That said, he spent the whole of July negotiating the Concorde Agreement and continued to work on F1 matters into October. The future? He would go on trying to save lives, but now his focus would extend beyond the circuit to arguing for the rights of individuals to retain their privacy and to avoid destruction by the media – unless it was truly in the public's interest.

He took his case to the European Court of Human Rights where he challenged UK privacy laws, which allow publication without giving the targeted subject prior notice and therefore a chance to seek an interim injunction to prevent publication. In May 2011 the court ruled against him, declaring: 'The European Convention on Human Rights does not require media to give prior notice of intended publications to those who feature in them.' Among other issues contributing to the ruling, it was pointed out that freedom of expression might be breached, adding: the notion of 'private life' was well understood by the press and its reporters...' In that vain, the scandal absorbing the global media two months later must have brought a smile to Max's lips; the *News of the World* – in existence since 1843 – was closed as a result of its reporters engaging in phone tapping and computer hacking. There were also allegations of police bribery. The *News of the World* was published by News International, a subsidiary of News Corp – founded by media mogul Rupert Murdoch, the company's Chairman and CEO. As the allegations escalated, Murdoch and his son, James, Chairman and CEO for Europe and Asia, were called to testify before a Parliamentary Committee investigating the illegal hacking. It seems it was not only the phones of celebrities and politicians that were being hacked, but also those of private citizens: the victims of the '9/11' terrorist attacks, the '7/7' bombings in London, families of soldiers killed overseas, lawyers and the victims of crime – some of them children. The hacking allegations may involve other News Corp papers in Britain and beyond; law enforcement authorities in America are conducting their own investigations. In the meantime, Max has reportedly set up a fund to provide financial support, if required, for civil cases being brought by the victims of the journalist hackers. And he'll be appealing the decision of the European Court of Human Rights: 'We're going to give it our best shot.'

In June 2009 Bernie was quick to take advantage of Max's lame duck position – as outgoing President of the FIA – by demanding that his own version of the Concorde Agreement be signed 'within twenty-four hours' of the World Council meeting. But Max wasn't all that weak, he and the FIA lawyers ignored him. Would Bernie's negotiation strength improve with the arrival of the new regime? One thing was certain: come October, the Formula 1 scene, for Bernie, would suddenly get lonelier. In fact, for the man who moved in frenzied crowds with microphones and recorders shoved under his nose, blinking away the cameras' flashes, rushing, rushing, always rushing – lonely was a word that covered most of 2009. His marriage to Slavica ended in March on the grounds of 'unreasonable behaviour'. After twenty-four years Slavica had finally understood that Bernie *is* Formula 1, so she sought a divorce from the sport. If she could have had Bernie without motor racing they would probably still be married. Forget the height difference, forget the age difference or the lure of money, Bernie is genuinely lovable. But he's a package deal. Slavica would have no difficulty in attracting candidates to share her £36.5 million jet and *circa* $1 billion bank account. That was the problem she had settled for, but she would have her freedom. And, no, there wasn't a third party involved on either side, the divorce had been 'amicable', as Bernie told the legion of reporters who had asked. The problem for Bernie was Slavica – he still adored her. He had begged her to come back to him but she refused. He was heartbroken.

Another friendly face in the paddock – someone with whom he had begun to share his troubles – had also been axed from Formula 1: Flavio Briatore. Three months after Max's dramatic announcement, Briatore stepped down from his post as Renault's team principal, along with the executive director of engineering Pat Symonds, for their alleged involvement in race-fixing. This particular scandal became etched with the moniker 'Crashgate'. It began when Renault driver Nelson Piquet Jr crashed into a concrete wall during the 2008 Singapore Grand Prix. The young Brazilian put it down to driver error, a simple mistake, that was all. But then, following his acrimonious departure from the team in August 2009, Piquet Jr had a little more to say about the Singapore accident: he had been asked to deliberately crash his car (with the resulting deployment of the safety car) so that his team-mate Fernando Alonso could win the race – or so it was reported. The FIA launched an investigation, which led to Flavio Briatore being charged with bringing Formula 1 into disrepute. At a hearing of the World Council he was found guilty and banned from FIA-sanctioned events – indefinitely.

Briatore was not permitted to attend FIA events, even as a spectator. Furthermore, the FIA would not renew any superlicence granted to drivers he managed. Flavio had managed the racing careers of Fernando Alonso, Mark Webber, Jarno Trulli, Heikki Kovalainen and Nelson Piquet Jr. The decision meant he was effectively banned from managing any driver with hopes of competing in an FIA-sanctioned race. Pat Symonds received a five-year ban. Renault was allowed to continue racing but was put on probation for two years, until the end of 2011. Should the team commit a similar offence during that period they would be permanently banned. Flavio had resigned from Renault, he said, 'to save the team… It was my duty.' But he was reported to have been 'devastated' by the FIA's ruling, and sued the FIA in a French court. On 5 January 2010 the Tribunal de Grande Instance overturned the FIA's decision. The FIA immediately announced that it would appeal but, the following April, settled out of court after Briatore and

Symonds recognised their individual responsibility for the deliberate crash, expressing their regrets and apologies. That was the end of it, at least for Flavio Briatore, who had no intention of returning to Formula 1. Two months earlier, he had also stepped down from his post as chairman of Queens Park Rangers.

As always with disappointment, Bernie – already overworked – pushed himself that much harder and the strain was becoming evident. Unfortunately, his loneliness became twisted into outright alienation over a series of ill-considered slips, the jarring comments he was prone to make when his mind is engaged elsewhere. Let's see, where to begin… racism 'is a bit of a joke' or Hitler was a leader who was 'able to get things done'? How do you defend the indefensible? The more Bernie tried to explain to members of the press, the worse it got. He is emphatically NOT a racist or a Hitler supporter. Unusually, for Bernie, he seemed unable to put that into a simple declarative sentence. However, he was a Lewis Hamilton supporter: 'Lewis has achieved an awful lot,' he told Ed Gorman of *The Times*, 'and it would be bloody difficult for any of us to be the same as him… I get upset with people who say he is an arrogant bastard.' Next question?

After the FIA's ruling against Briatore, Bernie publicly expressed his opinion that the punishment was excessive. 'A year's ban is enough,' he said, and he had advised his friend to appeal. It was considered one loose remark too many for Delta Topco board member Sir Martin Sorrell. 'First we had Hitler did good,' he told the *Daily Mail*, 'now we have cheating is acceptable. Where will it end? His latest comments are yet another example, I'm afraid, of Bernie being totally out of touch with reality.' Perhaps Sir Martin felt Bernie had become reconnected with reality when it was subsequently reported that Formula 1's commercial revenue rose to a record £680 million. And the Concorde Agreement was signed.

Following Max's agreement to step aside, the World Council published the following press release. 'All currently competing teams have committed to the FIA Formula One World Championship. There will be no alternative series or championship and the rules for 2010 onwards will be the 2009 regulations as well as further regulations agreed prior to 29 April 2009. As part of this agreement the teams will, within two years, reduce the costs of competing in the championship to the level of the early 1990s. The manufacturer teams have agreed to assist the new entries for 2010 by providing technical assistance. The manufacturer teams have further agreed to the permanent and continuing role of the FIA as the sport's governing body. They have also committed to the commercial arrangements for the FIA Formula One World Championship until 2012 and have agreed to renegotiate and extend this contract before the end of that period. All teams will adhere to an upgraded version of the governance provisions of the 1998 Concorde Agreement.'

It seems Max was also in touch with reality. He had achieved most of his goals: cost cuts, new teams on the grid, and a future for the sport under the FIA umbrella. His occasional threats to continue after 2009 may have been a ploy to urge everyone back to the table. Who knows? But that's what happened – with plenty of help from Bernie. When Max left, he indicated that the teams probably wouldn't like the next president any better than they had liked him – the next president being former Ferrari team principal Jean Todt. Whether or not the teams – or Bernie – are happy with Todt still remains to be seen. 'It's early days,' says Bernie. 'The problem for Todt is he's taken on a task that's bigger than he had anticipated. He'll be popular with the teams only as long as he's doing what they want him to do. But he's not up to negotiating the Concorde Agreement. Nobody is.'

Yes, it's Concorde negotiating season again, time for the three sides of the triangle to start snarling. But this time around there's a new twist enlivening the festivities: the possibility of Bernie going to jail for paying a bribe.

In order to understand what led to this predicament, we must look back to the beginning of this chapter, to the case in November 2004 of Speed Investments versus Bambino Holdings. At the time, Speed Investments represented three banks: Bayerische Landesbank, JP Morgan and Lehman Brothers who collectively owned a seventy-five per cent stake in SLEC, then the ultimate holding company of the Formula One Group of companies. Of the three banks the stake belonging to Bayerische Landesbank – 47.2 per cent – was the largest. The remaining twenty-five per cent belonged to Bambino Holdings, the Ecclestone family trust. In spite of its minority stake, Bambino had the power – resulting from a 2002 restructuring of its company boards – to run Formula 1. Against this background, the Formula 1 manufacturer teams had formed their own collective group, then called the GPWC, threatening a breakaway series set to commence in 2008 at the end of the existing Concorde Agreement. The banks feared the alternative championship – combined with the modest level of power allotted to their seventy-five per cent interest – would render their Formula 1 shares worthless, which is why they were asking the Court for more control. The following month the Court ruled in favour of the banks, empowering them – commensurate with their F1 shareholding – to participate in decisions on the running of the sport.

Enter Dr Gerhard Gribkowsky, who became Chairman of SLEC. He also sat on the boards of at least three other Formula 1 companies: Formula One Holdings, Formula One Administration and Formula One Management. Gribkowsky had risen through the ranks from branch manager at Bayerische Landesbank to become its chief risk officer and a member of the board between 2003 and 2008. But, although he could wield considerable control on behalf of his bank, he realised that removing Bernie would further destabilise the sport. Besides, while the Court had been deliberating, Bernie got busy improving his relationship with the teams by offering them a total of £260 million over three years in exchange for a unanimous renewal of the Concorde Agreement. Dr Gribkowsky took the prudent course of announcing that the banks had no intention of removing Bernie from the operational helm, and Bernie, for his part, appeared to enjoy introducing the

German banker around the paddock as his 'boss'. With that straight, Gribkowsky and Bernie engineered the sale of Bayerische Landesbank's shares to CVC in 2005; CVC also bought a portion of the shares belonging to Bambino Holdings. Gribkowsky then became a board member of Alpha Prema, the investment vehicle through which CVC had acquired its initial stake in SLEC. He later joined the board of Delta Topco, formed after CVC had bought up still more Formula 1 shares in 2006, concluding their majority stake. Delta Topco replaced SLEC as the ultimate holding company of the Formula One Group of companies. Bernie became the company's CEO.

Now flash forward to 2011. On 5 January the hefty, fifty-three-year-old Gerhard Gribkowsky was arrested on accusations that he had deposited money from overseas sources into a company in Austria – where taxes are levied at 25% as opposed to Germany's 40% where he is resident. It was further alleged that he had undervalued the SLEC shares belonging to the state-owned Bayerische Landesbank (by now renamed Bayern LB) when they were sold to CVC. 'The stake was sold without being properly evaluated,' insisted Barbara Stockinger, spokeswoman for the State Prosecutor's Office in Munich where four teams of investigators – and the German media – were looking into the tens of millions 'in payments disguised via two consultancy agreements' that had found their way to Austria. Bayerische Landesbank had received a €10 billion government bailout following losses on US sub-prime mortgages, according to *Bloomberg Businessweek*, so the bank and the State may have had more than one reason for being unhappy with Gerhard Gribkowsky. The prosecutors were also investigating testimony linking Bernie's name to the money deposited in Austria. Had the banker received a kickback or bribe for selling the bank's shares for less than market value? Gribkowsky had earlier claimed his millions had been inherited from his family and that connecting his wealth to Bernie was 'pure speculation'. Nevertheless, the former banker remained in custody in Stadelheim Prison, where Adolf Hitler had once been detained. Gribkowsky applied for bail but it was refused on the grounds he might flee the country. CVC immediately distanced itself from the case: They had 'no knowledge of, nor any involvement in, any payment to Mr Gribkowsky or anyone connected with him in relation to CVC's acquisition of Formula One.' Two weeks later it was the F1 Group's turn to issue a statement, explaining that Gribkowsky had received only $50,000 per year since 2006 as a non-executive director of Formula 1 and, for the record: 'The Formula One group and Mr Ecclestone have no knowledge of, nor any involvement in, any other payment to Dr Gribkowsky nor anyone connected with him.' CVC's next move was to launch their own investigation by asking their accountancy firm Ernst & Young and their lawyers Freshfields Bruckhaus Deringer, the second largest law firm in the world, to carry out the work. Their findings cleared Bernie, whose job as CEO of Formula 1 remained – for the time being – secure.

By April the case was being billed as one of the biggest corruption scandals in Germany's history. At the same time, Munich prosecutors had begun to explore the possibility that the Gribkowsky payments were part of a deal to keep Bernie at the top of Formula 1. Yet when the banks' shares were sold to CVC it was reportedly documented that 'Bernie Ecclestone is to retain operating control to continue growing the business' – evident for everyone to see or dispute when the sale had been agreed. Even so, Bernie engaged a team of German lawyers before heading to Munich to answer the Senior State Prosecutor's mounting questions. He also issued another statement: he would 'continue to give the State Prosecution Office [his] full co-operation in whatever capacity it may ask', and he was confident that when the full facts had been established, he would 'be exonerated of blame for any wrongdoing'. Three months later Gerhard Gribkowsky was formally charged with tax evasion, breach of trust and with having been in receipt of corrupt payments. It appeared the Prosecutor's Office still held to the allegation that the banker had been paid for undervaluing Bayern LB's stake in

SLEC. *Formula Money* editors Christian Sylt and Caroline Reid point out that CVC was understood to have paid $828 million for Bayern LB's shares in Formula 1 compared to offers of $472 million from Hutchison Whampoa and $708 million from private equity firm Clearbrook Capital. The sale to CVC was concluded in 2006; the bank's annual report for that year shows that it received a valuation yield of $433 million, the sale having 'decisively contributed to the positive result'. In addition, the accountancy firm Deloitte reportedly carried out an independent assessment and concluded that CVC had paid a fair price.

The charge that Gribkowsky had received corrupt payments was connected to $45 million from a person the prosecutors named as 'Bernard E' and a company owned by Bambino Holdings. Mauritius-based First Bridge Holding (now defunct) paid Gribkowsky's company GG Consulting – set up on the very day CVC bought the bank's stake – an initial sum of $4 million followed by $1.6 million over a period of ten months starting in August 2006. A second company, Lewington Invest, based in the British Virgin Islands, was reportedly due to pay $25 million in five instalments from August to October 2007, the combined amounts from the two companies totalling $45 million. Bayern LB claimed to be unaware of these payments. The prosecutors also contend that to compensate for these payments Bernie himself received $41.4 million, paid by Gribkowsky on behalf of the bank, and that an additional $25 million was paid to Bambino. 'These payments would not have been asked for were it not for the bribes to be paid to the accused,' said the prosecutors, adding that Bayern LB had 'incurred damages of almost $66.5 million through the conduct of the accused'. Bernie was outraged. He had never been party to a bribery; the money paid to him had been a commission of five per cent, less than any bank would have received for a deal of that magnitude. Furthermore, he had to give Bayerische Landesbank an indemnity 'for an awful lot of money' to insure that the accounts were in good order.

In an article published in *The Telegraph* on 21 July, Bernie admitted to Christian and Caroline that he had indeed paid Gribkowsky. But it wasn't a bribe, it was a 'loan' to help the banker start a new business. The loan – only $23 million according to Bernie – was paid following the German's false allegations that he was involved in the running of Bambino, accompanied by a 'threat' to inform the Inland Revenue. Back during the court hearing in 2004, the lawyers for Bambino Holdings had been careful to stress Bernie's 'separateness' from the Ecclestone family trust, the reason being that the tax authorities were about to conclude a long process that would reduce the tax impact on Bernie's family following his death. This had involved, in 1996, the transfer of his Formula 1 shares to Bambino, and according to strict Inland Revenue rules he could not have a role in the running of the trust. If Gribkowsky carried out his intention the tax authorities would have been obliged to investigate, which may have taken years. Having undergone an operation on his heart, these were years Bernie couldn't count on. 'He was shaking me down and I didn't want to take a risk. Nothing was wrong with the trust. Nothing at all.' The demand for the loan came with two stipulations: Gribkowsky 'wanted to be paid so it didn't look like it came from me and didn't look like it had come from England.' Bernie then discussed the banker's threat with his lawyers and the decision was made to pay up. Looking at it from this angle, Bernie wasn't the villain in the piece, he was the victim! So why, having previously denied making payments to Gribkowsky, make a public admission at this stage? Because the Prosecutor had instructed him not to talk about the case. That changed when the State Prosecutor's Office put out a press release specifying his involvement. 'If they can talk why can't I?' He had 'nothing to hide'. Then he had some fun. 'Actually, I might ask to get my money back.' Most recently, four lawyers connected to Bernie and Flavio Briatore have interested the Munich prosecutors. Bernie sums up the case by adding: 'Gribkowsky was a bully. He was trying to do the best he could for himself.'

'Are you worried about testifying when the case comes to trial?'

'No. At the time, I was lucky enough to have the money to do what needed to be done. That's all. We'll have to see what happens.'

In the meantime, Bernie is burrowing away, creating more wriggle-room and employing the *Houdini Factor* for all it's worth. Which doesn't prevent him from indulging in a moment of personal stocktaking. At the German Grand Prix, with reporters huddled around him, he mused: 'So many things in life are hindsight. So many things we all wish we hadn't have done...' If Gribkowsky is found guilty he could receive up to ten years in prison, while Bernie, at the time of writing, has yet to be formally charged. Is it likely he'll be joining Gribkowsky in a German jail? I wouldn't bet on it. 'What could anyone do, give me life?' said Bernie, laughing, as he approaches his eighty-first birthday.

Another octogenarian, Rupert Murdoch, added his own piquancy to the Concorde negotiating season when his company News Corp (News Corporation) released a statement saying they were ever-so-tentatively considering the acquisition of Formula 1. Actually, the potential bid came from a consortium which included Exor and followed on months of speculation concerning the sale of the sport. Other bidders in the frame were telecommunications billionaire Carlos Slim, the richest man in the world and sponsor of the Sauber team, and at least one Middle Eastern investment firm. CVC were polite. They recognised 'the quality of Exor and News Corporation as potential investors, but any investment in Formula 1 will require CVC's agreement and will need to demonstrate that it is in the interest of the sport and its stakeholders, taken as a whole.' New Corp's alignment with Exor was significant in that the latter is a 30.45% shareholder in Fiat, which in turn owns Ferrari, whose team wields extraordinary political clout. The other teams and Bernie were all attention. Some interpreted the possible takeover as a ruse to further enhance Ferrari's bargaining power in the Concorde negotiations. Ferrari president Luca di Montezemolo has continued to express his frustration with both the commercial and sporting structure of Formula 1. But if the move was meant to add financial muscle to the Prancing Horse, there would be no 'under-the-table' dealing. The current Concorde Agreement contains a clause preventing the commercial rights holder from 'conferring on any Team any material preferential right, benefit or privilege', nor can Bernie/CVC 'discriminate against any other Team or subject it to more onerous material obligations than any other Team.' Should Ferrari be offered another $100 million bonus, the other eleven teams would have to receive the same.

Meanwhile, another scenario was being debated. It concerned News Corp's genuine plans to acquire 61% of broadcaster BSkyB; they already owned 39%. Bernie, among others, thought News Corp's flirtation with Formula 1 may have been part of a strategy to secure investors for the total acquisition of British Sky Broadcasting (BSkyB). After all, Formula 1 enjoys the largest TV audience of any sporting series. That said, their BSkyB bid was withdrawn after pressure from both the Labour and Conservative parties in light of the on-going investigations into the *News of the World* phone hacking scandal. Or, as one reporter expressed it, News Corp's take-over bid 'just got kicked into the long grass'. It is interesting that two months before the hacking story broke, Max Mosley said: 'People are recognising that the Murdoch empire has far too much power. They have huge influence over Parliament. Huge influence over the police. It has got to stop, and I am by no means the only one who thinks that.' As has been mentioned earlier, the FIA must approve any new owner of Formula 1. Max has a seat on the FIA Senate, while Bernie, who has never held fond feelings for Rupert Murdoch, maintains an influential position on the FIA's World Council. Bernie had also expressed a very practical reason for not wanting to sell to the News Corp media organisation: it would hamstring his negotiating power with other broadcasters. The fact that another media group, Kirch, had once owned Formula 1 (though it later ended up in the hands of its creditor banks) seemed to have escaped his notice. But he was fully aware the acquisition of Formula 1 by a News Corp-led consortium would probably violate EU competition law. News Corp had been prevented from buying Manchester United football club because of Sky Sports' dominance in broadcasting the sport. CVC, remember, was required to sell its interest in Dorna, the rights owner of the motorcycle championship series, MotoGP, before purchasing a major stake in Formula 1. But should that not be enough to block the sale of F1 to the Murdoch consortium, Bernie could fall back on a clause in the existing Concorde Agreement, which specifies the sport cannot be shown 'only' on Pay-TV. Yet, by the end of July, Bernie turned around and signed a contract to screen all of the 2012–18 Formula 1 races on Sky Sports – operated by BSkyB – which is indeed a Pay-TV company. Among Bernie's countless talents is a well-honed skill for spotting loopholes. It seems rumours of the BBC pulling out of Formula 1 were *partly* correct – they will still screen ten of the twenty races live, which deftly obliterates the competition dominance and 'only' restrictions. In addition to broadcasting half the races the BBC will show extended highlights, a full seventy-five minutes to be exact. The deal will save them about £16 million per year. Sky is expected to provide enhanced coverage of all the action including practice sessions and qualifying. In addition, it has plans to improve viewing on mobile phones and the internet – reaching out to a younger audience, which will please the teams. The teams will also receive an extra $1.6 million or so, while their sponsors have been promised higher viewing figures. Everyone is happy except the fans who cannot afford Sky. 'We couldn't do much,' says Bernie, 'because the BBC wouldn't renew their contract. Now, Sky will do more.'

With regard to the News Corp/Exor bid for Formula 1, an offer has not been forthcoming. The loss of *News of the World*, the second-largest selling paper in the English language, may have inhibited them. In the meantime, CVC maintains that Formula 1 is not – 'currently' – for sale. When the commercial rights holder does start to entertain bids,

Bernie reckons 'six or seven billion dollars' would be a fair price. CVC has been bumping up the value of Formula 1 by reducing its debt, while Bernie has been improving revenue in the form of new circuits and broadcasting contracts among other measures that make the sport ripe for selling. Does Bernie regret selling Formula 1 to its various owners, three different times?

'I didn't sell it. I gave it to my wife.'

'All right. If you could go back to that moment, would you have held onto it?'

'Definitely. I would have held onto it.'

'Would you like to buy it back?'

'If the opportunity arises... We'll see.'

Standing in the way of CVC's opportunity to part with its stake in Formula 1 is the renewal of the Concorde Agreement. It's hard to sell a product that will come to an end on 31 December 2012. The Agreement guarantees the signatory teams will turn up and race in the FIA Formula One World Championship series. Bernie likes to think it's just about their portion of the sport's income. He'd be happy to dispense with the document, providing the teams pay a massive fee to race on the circuits he's contracted, shown by broadcasters with whom he has deals – the longer the better. During the present round of Concorde negotiations the teams continue to hum their mantra for more money, and calls for another breakaway series are becoming innocuous by their omnipresence. But there are numerous design and engine changes to be debated or rejected, arguments for reinvestment in the sport, in its marketing, and there remains the identity issue: what actually constitutes a Formula 1 car in a field that allows for mixed levels of competition? Moreover, the teams, the FIA, Bernie/CVC must ponder an ever-changing financial reality. Which means it will be a hard grind before signatures can be affixed to the new/renewed Agreement.

Another problem preventing the sale of Formula 1 is the uncertainty surrounding the future of the sport without its mop-headed dictator – should he decide not to re-acquire it. Formula 1 without Bernie Ecclestone is an untested commodity. Who else could keep his or her – or their – fingertips on every aspect of the sport down to the minutiae? Who else could negotiate until the opposition is lifeless? Who else could put so much heart into it? CVC would be foolish to get rid of Bernie. He would like to remain CEO 'as long as I'm in a position where I can do some good. I do a very good job for the teams.' Even so, there are those – and plenty of them – who would gladly see the end of his reign, of his vision attached to an iron grip that has recreated Formula 1, shaping it into a colossus of money. But the deposers will have to be patient. Bernie has nothing if not staying power. Despite Munich prosecutors. Despite threats, shake-downs and physical brutality.

On 24 November 2010, just days after he had approved the publication of this book as it happens, Bernie was beaten unconscious outside his London office. The incident took place at 10.30pm, just as he and his girlfriend Fabiana Flosi were returning from dinner. The muggers, four of them, were lying in wait for the couple. Bernie was kicked and beaten before his assailants removed his watch. Fabiana's earrings were snatched from her earlobes, but it was the violence meted out to Bernie that left her badly shaken. Fortunately, he quickly recovered consciousness, the police were called and he was taken to a nearby hospital where a laceration to his face was stitched-up. How the thugs knew when he would be returning to his Knightsbridge headquarters is not clear, nor do we understand why it took four men to grab an eighty-year-old's watch. Bernie always knows when the odds are stacked against him. Had the gang simply asked for the watch he would have handed it over. The muggers have not been apprehended. The day after the incident Bernie had a photo taken of his face, using a mobile phone. He then sent the untouched image to Swiss watchmaker Hublot, suggesting they use it in an advertisement. The day after that, Bernie was back at his desk, working as if nothing out of the ordinary had happened. The Hublot advertisement appeared in the *Financial Times* and the *International Herald Tribune*. The product being advertised was an 'F1 King Power' watch, and next to a large picture of the watch was a larger picture of Bernie's torn face, his eyes – one of them bruised black – conveying an unshakeable will. A caption read: 'See what people will do for a Hublot.' And if the gang had been sent to deliver a message, Bernie had an unwritten message of his own – sent around the world. It was simply this: 'I'm still here.'

Bernie's Beatle-bob has turned greyish-white, his spectacles are more conservative, his face is divided with deep furrows. In a sombre mood, his face is as cold as the effigies chiselled into Mount Rushmore, and as hard. Then, in an instant, his eyes sparkle – dense with treasure like a schoolboy's pockets – and he is once more the mischievous Dartford lad, unchanged. So he will continue to hold a telephone to each ear while carrying on a third conversation. He will continue to travel the world over, all of the time, never suffering jet lag. He will continue to juggle hundreds of balls in the air, effortlessly passing from a chat with China's Premier to demanding why so-and-so wants another pit pass, to making a mega-offer on one more irresistible piece of property, to seeing that an ailing mechanic is flown to the best hospital for treatment, to handling a domestic crisis, to swapping vintage cars, to advising a racing driver on a contract, to approving the design of a new circuit, to obtaining half-a-dozen opinions from his lawyers, to negotiating a television deal, to returning phone calls, to 'putting out fires'… to–to–to. And he will continue to court controversy like it was the biggest romance of his life.

Bob Lobell, a long-serving member of the Formula 1 community, sums up the history of the man who has been his friend for more than forty years: 'Bernie himself created and directed the Bernard Charles Ecclestone life story, and pretty much he played the major role, produced and wrote it the way it is – no compromises. How many people can say that? Agreed?'

Agreed. Except that I would not put anything to do with Bernie in the past tense. He is still playing 'the major role', and it is still a command performance.

ACKNOWLEDGEMENTS

My foremost thanks to Bernie for three decades of friendship and conversation that have contributed to this book; and my gratitude – always – to my husband Sid who has been my partner in this work as in everything, and to my family for their unstinting support. To my dear friend Vanessa Harwood Scully for her support from day one, and to Lynne Sharpe who has tirelessly transcribed interviews and chased after facts at all hours seven days per week; Ros Osinski for her kind assistance. I am also indebted to Nigel Roebuck for inspiration, encouragement and his no-less-than heroic contribution; Quentin Spurring for his suggestions and for kindly editing the chapters covering the Brabham years; Tom Rubython for his generous advice, suggestions, and for enlightening me on the immediate details following Ayrton Senna's fatal accident; Duncan Smith for his helpful criticisms and suggestions; Christian Sylt for his help in editing the chapters concerning the financial aspects of Bernie's life, along with Caroline Reid's edit of parts of Chapter 18; Herbie Blash for patiently reading through the manuscript and offering moral support along with advice and suggestions; Alan Young for his help in sorting out Bernie's properties; Roy Salvadori for his great help and advice; John Surtees for his considerable input and suggestions; John Coombs for his generous help and advice; David Ward for his kind contribution; also the late Peter Warr and Bob Dance for their suggestions and corrections; Gordon Murray for his contribution and suggestions on the Brabham years; and Ron Smith for his generous assistance on the Cooper

500 era; Sir Stirling Moss, whose dinner conversations have certainly contributed to this book; Sir Jackie Stewart for his kindness in reading through the Silverstone chapter; and a special thank you to Ron Dennis, whose conversation over the years has found its way into this work, and for his patience in sitting through a very long interview; and to Sir Frank Williams for his time and assistance; Les Lilly for a delightful – and informative – day on Warren Street along with Archie Malin, Laurie MacGuire and Ted Farrow; and to Tuana Tan for her gracious contribution. My most grateful thanks also to: Eddie Baker; Sir Jack Brabham; Flavio Briatore; Tony Brooks; Ian Brown; Martin Brundle; Fred Compton; the late Jabby Crombac; Dr David Cranston; the late Neil Eason Gibson; Carmelo Ezpeleta; Laurence Flury; Frank Foster; the late Frank Gardner; David Gillet; Roy Golding; John Hogan; Niki Lauda; Margaret Leckie; Bob Lobell; Yvon Lyon; Paddy McNally; Deborah Marks; Burdy Martin; the late Teddy Mayer; Ray Morris; Tony Morris; Stella Murray; Max Mosley; Ian Holmes; Thomas O'Keefe; Mike Osborne; Tim Parnell; James Penrose; Dominic Piedade; Marco Piccinini; David Richards; Nina Rindt; Jeffrey Rose; Bob Rowe; Colin Seeley; Marc Surer; Ron Tauranac; Hermann Tilke; the late Marian Tingey; Bob Tyrrell; Christian Vogt; Murray Walker; Ron Walker; John Watson; Angela Webb; John Webb; the late Tom Wheatcroft; Penny Whitaker; Ray Whitehand; the late Brian Whitehouse; Charlie Whiting; George Wicken; Richard Woods; Alan Woollard; Peter Wright; John Young, all of whom have made important contributions, and to the countless others, too many to name (and those who don't wish to be named) who, over the years, have provided anecdotes and information about this remarkable man.

I must also acknowledge my gratitude for the never-to-be-forgotten friendships of Dean Delamont, James Hunt, Ayrton Senna, Ken Tyrrell and Innes Ireland, all of whom contributed to my motor racing education.

BIBLIOGRAPHY

Reference works and periodicals I have consulted during the writing of this book include:

Autosport, published weekly
  (Haymarket Specialist Motoring Publicatons Ltd);
Behind the Scenes of Motor Racing by Ken Gregory
  (MacGibbon & Kee, 1960);
Bernie's Game by Terry Lovell (Metro Publishing Ltd, 2003);
Beyond the Limit by Professor Sid Watkins
  (Macmillan, 2001);
Brabham, Story of a Racing Team by Phil Drackett
  (Arthur Barker, 1985);
Brabham Ralt Honda, The Ron Tauranac Story
  by Mike Lawrence (Motor Racing Publications Ltd, 1999);
British Racing Hero by Derek Allsop (Magna Books, 1990);
Business F1, published monthly (Business F1 Magazine Ltd);
Chasing the Title by Nigel Roebuck (Haynes, 1999);
Colin Chapman by Jabby Crombac
  (Patrick Stephens Ltd, 1986);
Cooper by Mike Lawrence (Sutton Publishing Ltd, 1999);
Emerson Fittipaldi by Gordon Kirby
  (Hazleton Publishing, 1990);
Enzo Ferrari by Richard Williams (Random House, 2001)
F1 Racing, published monthly
  (Haymarket Specialist Motoring Publicatons Ltd);
Formula Money 2009/2010 by Christian Sylt and Caroline Reid
  (CNC – Communications and Network Consulting);
Formula One by Derek Allsop (Headline Book Publishing, 1998);

Government and Labour Party documents made available
through the Freedom of Information Act;

Grand Prix People by Gerald Donaldson
(Motor Racing Publications Ltd, 1990);

Grand Prix 10 by Louis T. Stanley (W.H. Allen, 1969);

Grand Prix Who's Who by Steve Small
(Guinness Publishing, 1994);

Hit 'Em Hard by Wensley Clarkson (Harper Collins, 2002);

Jochen Rindt by Alan Henry (Hazleton Publishing, 1990);

Ken Tyrrell by Maurice Hamilton (Collins Willow, 2002);

Life at the Limit by Professor Sid Watkins (Macmillan, 1996);

Marlboro Grand Prix Guide edited by Jacques Deschenaux
(Charles Stewart and Co);

Murray Walker: Unless I'm Very Much Mistaken by Murray Walker
(Collins Willow, 2002);

The Paddock, published monthly, May 2007 issue
(Grand Prix Media Ltd);

The Piranha Club by Timothy Collings (Virgin Books, 2001);

The Powerbrokers by Alan Henry
(Motorbooks International, 2003);

Roy Salvadori by Roy Salvadori and Anthony Pritchard
(Patrick Stephens Ltd, 1985);

Senna by Tom Rubython (Business F1 Publications, 2004);

Servants of the People by Andrew Rawnsley
(Hamish Hamilton Ltd, 2000);

Silverstone 50 Golden Years edited by Ray Hutton
(Motor Racing Publications Ltd, 1998);

To Draw a Long Line by C.E. Johnny Johnson
(Bookmarque Publishing, 1989);

To Hell and Back by Niki Lauda and Herbert Volker
(Stanley Paul, 1986);

Vanwall: The Story of Tony Vandervell and His Cars
by Denis Jenkinson and Cyril Posthumus
(Patrick Stephens Ltd, 1975).

INDEX

Figures in italics refer to illustrations